ISBN 978-1-332-51281-2
PIBN 10241014

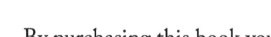

English
Français
Deutsche
Italiano
Español
Português

www.forgottenbooks.com

Mythology Photography **Fiction**
Fishing Christianity **Art** Cooking
Essays Buddhism Freemasonry
Medicine **Biology** Music **Ancient**
Egypt Evolution Carpentry Physics
Dance Geology **Mathematics** Fitness
Shakespeare **Folklore** Yoga Marketing
Confidence Immortality Biographies
Poetry **Psychology** Witchcraft
Electronics Chemistry History **Law**
Accounting **Philosophy** Anthropology
Alchemy Drama Quantum Mechanics
Atheism Sexual Health **Ancient History**
Entrepreneurship Languages Sport
Paleontology Needlework Islam
Metaphysics Investment Archaeology
Parenting Statistics Criminology
Motivational

A HISTORY

OF THE

PURITAN MOVEMENT IN WALES

CYNYRCHION EISTEDDFOD GENEDLAETHOL CASTELL-NEDD, 1918
O dan Olygiaeth E. Vincent Evans (Vinsent)

A HISTORY

OF THE

PURITAN MOVEMENT

IN WALES

FROM THE INSTITUTION OF THE CHURCH AT
LLANFACHES IN 1639

TO THE

EXPIRY OF THE PROPAGATION ACT IN 1653

BY

THOMAS RICHARDS, M.A.,

THE SECONDARY SCHOOL, MAESTEG

PUBLISHED BY THE NATIONAL EISTEDDFOD ASSOCIATION,
64, CHANCERY LANE, LONDON
1920

PRINTED (FOR THE ASSOCIATION) BY
WESTERN MAIL LIMITED, CARDIFF

CONTENTS

EDITORIAL NOTE

At the National Eisteddfod of 1918, held at Neath, the Eisteddfod Association offered a prize of Fifty Pounds for the best work of original research, in Welsh or English, on any subject connected with Wales, in regard to its history, language, or literature. Several works were submitted to the adjudication of Dr. John Edward Lloyd, M.A., author of the "History of Wales," and the Essay now published was awarded the prize, and was declared to be worthy of publication. The extraordinary difficulties from which the country is suffering renders the production of new books all but impossible. In this instance, however, the substantial sum handed over to the Association for Eisteddfodic purposes, by the Committee of the Neath Eisteddfod, supplemented by a generous donation from the Proprietors of the *Western Mail*, coupled with the emphatic recommendation of Dr. Lloyd, has induced the Association to incur the present heavy expense of producing the "History of the Puritan Movement in Wales from 1639 to 1653." To all those who have assisted them in the enterprise, including the Neath Eisteddfod Committee and their Secretary, Mr. Philip Thomas, the Proprietors of the *Western Mail*, Dr. John Edward Lloyd, and particularly the author, Mr. Thomas Richards, who took infinite trouble in seeing his work through the press, and in securing minute accuracy for all his statements, the Committee of the National Eisteddfod Association desire to tender their most grateful thanks. They commend the volume to the serious perusal of all those who value work of real research in the hidden paths of Welsh life and Welsh history.

E. VINCENT EVANS,

Honorary Secretary of the National Eisteddfod Association.

St. David's Day, 1920,

INTRODUCTION

By Dr. John Edward Lloyd, M.A.

The period of the Puritan Revolution is one which makes a strong appeal to the modern Welshman, for he discerns in it the roots of the movement which has resulted in making Wales so largely Nonconformist. Puritanism, indeed, reached the country before Wales was fully ready to receive it, and it did not for some time gather into its fold the entire Welsh people. But its influence was felt, nevertheless ; its ideas found a lodgment in the heart of a community naturally religious, and no dispassionate observer will doubt that, for a full understanding of the revival of the eighteenth century, it is necessary to go back to the seventeenth. Special interest, therefore, attaches to the story unfolded in the following pages, in which the impact of Puritanism upon Wales is for the first time described from contemporary official records. The ground has often been covered by writers who used the available printed sources, but Mr. Richards is the first who has examined and collated the MS. evidence and then presented the results in such a form as to furnish a sound basis for further discussion. To all minds the material thus set forth may not suggest precisely the same conclusions, but no controversy can be conducted with any advantage save upon a foundation of ascertained facts, and this the present work, in my opinion, fully and handsomely supplies. It is no mere ephemeral essay, hastily put together for the purposes of competition, but represents the scholarly toil, extending over many years, of a writer who has made the subject peculiarly his own. I have never made an award with more confidence than when I adjudged to "Ambrose Mostyn," out of eleven competitors, the National Eisteddfod Association's prize, offered at Neath in 1918, for the best work of original research. The student of the period is now placed in a position to form his own estimate of the merits of this work.

JOHN EDWARD LLOYD.

AUTHOR'S FOREWORD

The Propagation Act had for its primary cause the deficiencies of an ecclesiastical order which had failed to appreciate the inner spirit of the Protestant Reformation ; it was made possible by the growth of Puritan sentiment both in Wales and England and by the triumph of the Puritan armies in the Civil War ; the chief propagators were men who, through a forced sojourn in England, had come into contact with the fertile thought of a new liberty ; and the Act itself was the final concession to Wales from a Parliament that had gradually come to recognise its unique condition and its especial claims.

To view the Act from a proper perspective requires some consideration of these diverse factors. And as the Act was the most advanced development of a many-sided cause, its history, both in its long-shadowed coming and in its chequered career, not only tells of the rise and growth of Puritan feeling in Wales, but also of the moral fervour and the material interest that were inextricably interwoven in it.

LIST OF CONTRACTIONS

Add. MS. = One of the Additional MSS. in the British Museum Collection.

Bodl. = One of the MSS. numbered 322 to 328 in the Bodleian Library at Oxford.

Lamb. = One of the MSS. in the Lambeth Palace Library,

Lib. Inst. = ' Liber Institutionum ' at the Record Office.

Walk. = One of the MSS. in the " J. Walker " Collection at the Bodleian Library. These MSS. came into the possession of Dr. John Walker when compiling his " Sufferings " in the reign of Queen Anne.

A HISTORY

OF THE

PURITAN MOVEMENT IN WALES.

I.

THE OLD ORDER.

—Penry's suggestions in 1587 for reform of the spiritual con-

CORRIGENDA.

Page 3, line 31	..	Dr. Hill was not vicar of the Llanrhaiadr mentioned in the text, but of Llanrhaiadr yng Nghinmeirch (see p. 116).
Page 8, line 6	..	Delete stop after " circa."
Page 233, n. 7	..	(Porskin) to be placed after n. 6.

these fell into the hands of Court favourites and the favourites of these. The tithes of the " late Abbey of Strata Florida " fell into the hands of the Vaughans of Trawscoed,[3] the living of Chirk, an appropriation of Valle Crucis, lay at the disposal of Sir Edward Wotton.[4] Dr. Ellis Price (" y Doctor Coch ") had in 1559 obtained the sinecure rectory of Llangwm upon the allegation that it belonged to the Abbey of Cymmer, and Queen Elizabeth granted him the lands that had formerly belonged to the Knights Hospitallers of Ysbytty Ifan, and in addition he got possession of the sinecures of Llandrillo

[1] A Treatise Containing . . . . an Humble Supplication in the behalfe of the Countrey of Wales (1587).
[2] An Exhortation to the Gouvernours . . . . (1588).
[3] State Papers. Dom. Interreg., F1, f. 315.
[4] Thomas : Hist. of the Diocese of St. Asaph, p. 498.

AUTHOR'S FOREWORD

The Propagation Act had for its primary cause the deficiencies of an ecclesiastical order which had failed to appreciate the inner spirit of the Protestant Reformation; it was made possible by the growth of Puritan sentiment both in Wales and England and by the triumph of the Puritan armies in the Civil War; the chief propagators were men who, through a forced sojourn in England, had come into contact with the fertile thought of a new liberty; and the Act itself was the final concession to Wales

LIST OF CONTRACTIONS

Add. MS.	=	One of the Additional MSS. in the British Museum Collection.
Bodl.	=	One of the MSS. numbered 322 to 328 in the Bodleian Library at Oxford.
Lamb.	=	One of the MSS. in the Lambeth Palace Library,
Lib. Inst.	=	'Liber Institutionum' at the Record Office.
Walk.	=	One of the MSS. in the "J. Walker" Collection at the Bodleian Library. These MSS. came into the possession of Dr. John Walker when compiling his "Sufferings" in the reign of Queen Anne.

A HISTORY

OF THE

PURITAN MOVEMENT IN WALES.

I.

THE OLD ORDER.

Penry's suggestions in 1587 for reform of the spiritual condition of Wales were to a great extent adopted after a lapse
of sixty years[1]; his terrible indictment of the existing state
of things fell upon deaf ears.[2] The evils he described were
the inevitable concomitants of a time of transition, when
the minds of bishop and queen were more intent upon compromises of doctrine and readjustments of ritual than upon
setting up a " preaching ministry." Pre-Reformation times
had handed over a veritable ' damnosa hereditas,' and the
development of a political Reformation left its material
impress upon the Church. Confusion became worse con-
founded. The revenues of many rich benefices had been
appropriated by the monasteries, and, on their dissolution,
these fell into the hands of Court favourites and the favourites
of these. The tithes of the " late Abbey of Strata Florida "
fell into the hands of the Vaughans of Trawscoed,[3] the living
of Chirk, an appropriation of Valle Crucis, lay at the disposal
of Sir Edward Wotton.[4] Dr. Ellis Price (" y Doctor Coch ")
had in 1559 obtained the sinecure rectory of Llangwm upon
the allegation that it belonged to the Abbey of Cymmer,
and Queen Elizabeth granted him the lands that had formerly
belonged to the Knights Hospitallers of Ysbytty Ifan, and
in addition he got possession of the sinecures of Llandrillo

---

1 A Treatise Containing . . . . an Humble Supplication in the behalfe of
the Countrey of Wales (1587).
2 An Exhortation to the Gouvernours . . . . (1588).
3 State Papers. Dom. Interreg., F1, f. 315.
4 Thomas : Hist. of the Diocese of St. Asaph, p. 498.

B

and Llanuwchllyn.[1] The tithe-sheaf belonging to the dissolved monastery of Llantarnam in the parishes of Mynyddislwyn and Bedwellty in Monmouthshire were bought by
the family of Llansore.[2] Apart from these, *lay impropriators*
in various ways had possessed themselves of the profits of
Church livings. To take the case of Pembrokeshire only,
the Survey Commissioners of October, 1650, found twenty-
four livings 'in the donation of the late king,' eight in the
hands of Sir James Phillips of Cardigan, three in Sir John
Stepney's of Prendergast, and five in Maurice Canon's.
One, that of St. Ismaell's, belonged to the town of Tewkes-
bury, while Marloes and Castlemartin were enjoyed by Mons.
Melchior de Sabran, the French agent, in right of his wife
Mary, the only daughter of Sir Arthur Lake.[3] Indeed, the
principle of impropriation had become so interwoven with
the ecclesiastical order that some time before 1650 even
Parliament itself, on account of the disaffection of their
Royalist owners, had conferred three livings in this county
upon 'Colonel Horton's brigade' in a corporate capacity.[4]
Tithes, also, had been alienated without scruple. For
example, those of Llanycefn (worth £28), of Newcastle in
Kemeys (worth £20), and of Clarbeston (worth £21), were
all in the hands of the Sir John Stepney aforesaid[5]; Valentine
Proger, a papist, held the impropriate tithes of Grosmont
in Monmouthshire[6]; and on 14th November, 1638, the
tithes of Llandinam were leased to Sir Edward Lloyd of
Berthlwyd by Dr. Thomas Bayly for twenty-one years
at £120 a year.[7] In a number of cases in south-eastern
Wales, livings were in the hands of 'papists': Baynham
Vaughan, of the county of Gloucester, held the impropriate
rectory of Clyro in Radnor,[8] and Lord Charles Somerset the
impropriate rectory of the town of Monmouth.[9] Many
livings, and those not the poorest, belonged to English

---

1 St. Asaph : Landmarks in the Hist. of the Welsh Church, p. 105.
2 Cal. Comm. Comp., IV, p. 2816.
    3 Lamb. 915 *passim* for Pembrokeshire livings.   de Sabran was 'resident envoy'
London from 29 April, 1644, to 7 July, 1646. (App. I, 37th Report of Deputy
Keeper of Public Records [No. 3, p. 190] ; also House of Lords MSS. Comm. Report.
App. I, p. 112).
    4 Lamb. 915, ff. 114, 175. Livings=Martletwy, Slebech, and 'Mainweare'
(MS. illegible).
    5 Cal. Comm. Comp., Vol. II, p. 1036.
    6 Bodl. 326 f.206.
    7 Cal. Comm. Comp., III, p. 1725.
    8 Bodl. 323, f. 250 ; Cal. Comm. Comp., III, p. 2360.
    9 Bodl. 323, f. 200 ; S. P. Dom. Interreg., F1, f. 128.

dioceses and cognate interests. The rectory of Llanbeblig (value £104 14s. 0d.) was in the hands of the Bishop of Chester[1]; Towyn in Merioneth, with its average yearly tithes of £57, belonged to the Bishop of Coventry and Lichfield[2]; Knighton in Radnor to the Dean and Chapter of Hereford[3]; and £80 rent was reserved out of the rectory of Gresford to the Dean and Chapter of Winchester.[4] Again, the profits of the rectory of Aberdaron was annexed to the College of St. John's in Cambridge,[5] and that of Manorbier in Pembrokeshire to ' Christ Church Colledge ' in the same University.[6] The living of Churchstoke in Montgomeryshire was an impropriation in the hands of the Warden of the Hospital of Clun in Salop,[7] and the parsonage rent of Old Radnor was paid to " the Colledge of Worcester."[8]

A natural corollary of these dispositions was the diminution of episcopal and capitular revenues in · Wales, and out of this grew the practice of the bishops holding livings " in commendam," plausibly described in a letter of the Archbishop of Canterbury to his clergy as " the reward of their former deserts, and for the countenancing of their degrees."[9] The rectory of Amlwch for many years was held by the Bishop of Bangor " as an addition to the Bishoprick, being a small Bishoprick,"[10] and the living of Lamphey was held in commendam by the Bishops of St. David's with the result that " it was long destitute of a minister."[11] The rectory of Abergele was similarly held by the Bishops of St. Asaph,[12] so that the sinecure thereof counted but little in the pluralities of Dr. Gabriel Parry ; the same Bishop had also the sinecure of Llanrhaiadr-ym-Mochnant in commendam,[13] and it was fortunate that the vicar, Dr. William Hill, held also the prebend of Llanfair Dyffryn Clwyd.[14] Another practice was the leasing by the

1 Lamb. 904, f. 142.
2 Ibid., f. 124.
3 S. P. Dom. Interreg., F3, f. 275.
4 Bodl. 323, f. 73.
5 Bodl. 325, f. 11.
6 Lamb. 915, f. 144.
7 Exch. Misc., slips 114, 119. Returns of First Fruits, 1657-8.
8 Exch. Papers, 251 (County Committees' Orders and Correspondence). Guide to the Public Records ((Scargill-Bird), p. 357.
9 Wilkins, Concilia, p. 414. (April, 1605).
10 Lamb. 902, ff. 54-55 ; Exch. Returns (First Fruits). Anglesey, 1652.
11 Lamb. 905, f. 6.
12 Bodl. 326, f. 72.
13 Addit. MS., 15671, fol. 68.
14 Thomas : St. Asaph, p. 420.

Bishops and by members of the Chapters of the " premises " of livings which were theirs as of right. *E.g.*, the Bishop of St. David's had leased the rectory of Llangyfelach to William Thomas of Swansea for an annual reserved rent of £34 6s. 8d.[1]; similarly, the Canons of St. David's had leased the rectory of St. Twinnells in Pembrokeshire to Sir Hugh Owen of Orielton.[2]   The Bishop of Llandaff had leased the rectory of Bassaleg (of the yearly revenue of £200) to the Catholic Earl of Worcester.[3]   Archdeacon Price (" Edmwnd Prys ") had by indenture of the 20th of August, 1622, demised the glebelands of the rectory of Llandudno to Sir John Wynn of Gwydyr for £100 " had in hand," and a yearly sum of £18 to be paid in two equal portions, to be held by the lessee and his three sons during the life of the longest liver of them.[4]   The premises of the prebend of Llanfair D.C. had been demised since 14th January, 1553, by Griffith Wynn, a former prebendary, unto John Wynn ap Meredith and Morris Wynn of the county of Carnarvon for 99 years at the yearly rent of £26 13s. 4d.[5]   The assigning of rich livings to the support of the bishops and the higher Cathedral clergy was a time-honoured practice witnessing the evolution of the mediæval theories of maintenance, but the practice of beneficial leasing was part of a policy of adaptation, which strove to make some amends for the mortmain of a lay Reformation and the acquisitions of clergy and colleges from over the Border.   When the See of St. David's lost the gift and patronage of thirteen churches by one transaction,[6] its Bishop had perforce to become an expert man of business.

But the gains of greedy laymen and the compensations of bishops and deans accentuated other evils.   The lower clergy suffered grievously.   The lessee of the prebend of Meliden, demised by the Treasurer of St. Asaph, only granted £10 out of the yearly rent for the curate-in-charge,[7] and a similar sum was granted by the Wynns of Gwydyr to the curate of Llandudno.   The farmer of the impropriate

1 Lamb. 905, f. 1.
2 Lamb. 915, f. 135.
3 Cal. Comm. Comp., Vol. III, p. 1711.
4 Lamb. 902, ff. 60–61.
5 Lamb. 902, f. 65.
6 St. Asaph : Landmarks in the History of the Welsh Church, pp. 103–104.
7 Thomas : Hist. of the Diocese of St. Asaph, p. 296 (" *in Bishop Lloyd's time* "— reverting to the conditions before the Propagation Act).

rectory of Lledrod under the Collegiate Church of Brecon left *no* maintenance for the incumbent.[1] The stipends granted the vicars of the ten churches in the Hundred of Dewsland annexed to the Chapter of St. David's varied from £2 a year at Llanwnda to £10 13s. 4d. at Llanrhian.[2] The vicar of Llanfair in Dyffryn Clwyd had to be satisfied with the fourth part of the tithes of the said parish, and had to live in " a little house out of repair with a little garden."[3] The vicar of Aberdaron, with its two churches and 1,000 communicants, only received " a tenth parte of the tithes,"[4] and in 1647 the whole profits of the sinecure rectory of Pennant in Montgomeryshire were granted to the officiating vicar to afford him a decent maintenance.[5] The evidence is uniform for the whole of Wales. That of the Bodl. MS. 323 supplies a fair average. The maintenance of the minister of the parish Church of Merthyr Cynog in Breconshire was only ' 20^{tie} markes per annum,' he who ' officiated ' at the Chapel of Llanfihangel Nantbran ' 20^{tie} nobles per annum,' at the Chapel of Llandilo £6, at the Chapel of Dyffryn Honddu £4.[6] The ' clerk ' of Llanbadarnfawr in Cardiganshire, with ' 4,000 soules ' to superintend, lay at " the will of the Impropriatour "[7] ; the vicarage of Llanarth was worth only £10 per annum[8] ; and the curate of Llanstephan in Carmarthenshire was only allowed £8.[9] On a higher scale comes the vicar of Machynlleth (£23),[10] the vicar of Monmouth (£23 6s. 8d.),[11] of St. Ismaells in Pembrokeshire (not above £25),[12] of Clyro in Radnor, a parish of " 200 families," £40.[13] The incumbent of Hanmer received only £40 a year " in the best times,"[14] and the vicarage of 'Gresford " was once worth £90 a year," but is " now much impaired."[15] It is true that neither of the above fits the extreme case of

1 S. P. Dom. Interreg., F1, f. 293.
2 Lamb. 915, ff. 119–132.
3 Lamb. 902, f. 66.
4 Bodl. 325, fol. 53b.
5 Bodl. 324, fol. 189b.
6 Bodl. 323, fols. 5, 5b ; also S. P. Dom. Interreg, F1, ff. 353-354.
              ,,   ibid.   F2, f. 550.
7 Bodl. 323, fol. 48b. ; also S. P. Dom. Interreg., F1, f. 62.
8 Bodl. 323, fol. 49 ;   ,,   ibid.   ,,   f. 257.
9 ,, Ibid. f. 53 ;   ,,   ibid.   ,,   f. 33.
10 ,, Ibid. f. 195.
11 ,, Ibid. f. 200 ;   ,,   ibid.   ,,   f. 128.
12 ,, Ibid. f. 240.
13 ,, Ibid. f. 250 ;   ,,   ibid.   ,,   f. 273.
14 ,, Ibid. f. 110 ;   ,,   ibid.   ,,   f. 182.
15 ,, Ibid. f. 73 [1646].

the curates referred to by the Archbishop of Canterbury in
his letter of April, 1605, " who are content to serve for ten
groats a year and a canvas doublet."[1] But only comparatively illiterate clergy would be satisfied with such meagre
maintenance. On a payment of only £7 a year for the
incumbent of St. Peter's at Carmarthen, the inhabitants of
the town found that "no good or able man will perform
the duty."[2]

  Some of the best men, such as Richard Owen, "the
loyalist vicar of Eltham,"[3] and Richard Lloyd of Llangristiolus,[4] were drawn to the richer livings of the English
dioceses ; the others were only content to stay in Wales
when granted two or more livings at one and the same time.
Birth and episcopal influence favoured some ; rectories
without cure of souls fitted naturally into the system ; Wales
became a land of pluralists and non-residents. *E.g.,* Matthew
Herbert was rector both of Llangattock in Brecon and of
Cefnllys in Radnor, with total profits of £400 a year.[5]
Dr. Gabriel Parry was sinecure rector of Abergele,[6] rector
of Llansantffraid in Montgomery,[7] and also rector of Llanfwrog[6] in Denbighshire. At Abergele "he commonly
resided."[6] William Langford was vicar of Welshpool,[8]
rector of Llanerfyl,[9] and sinecure rector of Llanfor in
Merioneth.[10] Dr. Hugh Lloyd, the future Bishop of Llandaff,
in addition to one of the Archdeaconries of St. David's,
enjoyed the livings of St. Nicholas and St. Andrew's in
Glamorgan, valued at £200 a year.[11] And John Bayly, son
of Lewis, Bishop of Bangor, drew his revenue from ten preferments between 1617 and 1631.[12] Nor did it follow that
the fortunate pluralists made their homes in Wales at all.
Hugh Lloyd, the sinecure rector of Denbigh, was rector of

1 Wilkins, Concilia., p. 414.
2 Cal. Comm. Comp., Vol. III, p. 1826.
      An Anti-propagation writer of 1654 admits of the old order of things
      that "there were Scandalous Livings too in these Countries as well as Scan-
      dalous Ministers, and those produced these." (Gemitus Ecclesiæ, p. 4).
3 Gweithiau Morgan Llwyd, II, xii. (Introd.),
4 D. N. B., Vol. XXXIII, p. 431.
5 House of Lords MSS., Comm. Report. Appendix I, p. 96.
6 Addit. MS., 15671, fol. 135.
7 Lib. Inst. Assaphe, fol. 163 ; Exch. Misc., slip 119. (First Fruits, 1657–8).
8 Lib. Inst. Assaphe, fol. 166.
9 Lib. Inst. Assaphe, fol. 165.
10 Lib. Inst. Assaphe, fol. 179.
11 Walker : Sufferings, Part II, 16.
12 Registrum Collegii Exoniensis, pp. 95–96. (Oxford Hist. Soc. Publications.
Vol. XXVII, ed. C. W. Boase).

Fordham in the county of Cambridge[1] ; Dr. Griffith Williams, rector of Llanfihangel Ysceifiog in Anglesey, was Bishop of Ossory in Ireland, " where he resideth."[2] Nor were the sinecures in many cases reserved for Welshmen. Dr. Peter du Moulin, who spent " most of his time on the Continent,"[3] was sinecure rector of Llanarmon[4] ; a certain Jeremiah Holt, rector of Stoneham Ashpole in Suffolk, was possessed of that of Llangeler in Carmarthenshire[5] ; and Isaac Singleton, one of the Canons of St. Paul's, became in 1619 Archdeacon of Brecon,[6] next year sinecure rector of Bleddfa in Radnor, and prebendary of the Collegiate Church of Abergwili in 1624, all in addition to important preferments he held in the diocese of Carlisle.[7]

In addition to the aforesaid pluralists, the " Book of Institutions " provides strong evidence of the presence of men of English blood among the general clergy. Naturally, many incumbents with English surnames are found in south Pembrokeshire, along the coast of Glamorgan, and on the English border. English was much spoken even at that period in Monmouth and Radnor.[8] But in Welsh Cardigan- shire we find John Hanley at Aberporth,[9] Thomas Bright at Llanilar,[10] and William Freeman at Llangeitho[11] ; in Car- marthenshire John Blenkowe at Abergwili,[12] and William Nicholson, afterwards Bishop of Gloucester, at Llandilo-fawr[13]; in North Pembroke, Edward Provand at Cilgerran[14] ; in South Pembrokeshire, among a large admixture of English names, there is one cleric, the rector of Angle, of the name of John Ganwy de la Champnolle.[15] Coming to North Wales, we have Maurice Robins at Llanbeblig,[16] John Payne at

---

1 Cal. State Papers, Dom. Interreg., 1654, p. 329.
2 Bodl. 324 fol. 247.
      In 1660 Williams describes himself as Dean of Bangor and lawfully seized of the parish of Gyffin in that Deanery ; that " he had been ejected and thrust out from the exercise of his Ministeriall duty there " ! (House of Lords MSS. Lords Petitions W.)
3 Walker, Sufferings. Part II, p. 7.
4 Lib. Inst. Assaphe, fol. 156. Walker candidly admits he was unaware either of the *name* or *situation* of this sinecure rectory. (Suff. Part II, p. 7, second column).
5 Addit. MS. 15670, fol. 203a.
6 Lib. Inst. Meneuen, fol. 45.
7 Nightingale : Ejected of 1662 in Cumberland and Westmoreland, p. 649.
8 Penry : Treatise . . . . [1587], p. 51.
9 Lib. Inst. Meneuen, fol. 19, instituted 1640.
10 ,, ,,   Ibid. ,, 31,   ,,   1639.
11 ,, ,,   Ibid. ,, 33,   ,,   1640.
12 ,, ,,   Ibid. ,, 73.   ,,   1637.
13 ,, ,,   Ibid. ,, 71,   ,,   1626.
14 ,, ,,   Ibid. ,, 35,   ,,   1621.
15 ,, ,,   Ibid. ,, 2,   ,,   1638.
16 Lib. Inst. Bangor, fol. 2,   ,,   1614.

Llaneigrad,[1] Robert Marshe at Eglwysael,[2] John Luston at Llandrillo-yn-Rhos,[3] Roger Hampton at Llanddoget,[4] Thomas Atkinson at Bettws Gwerfyl Goch[5], and as vicar of Northop comes Archibald Sparks, a B.D. of the University of Aberdeen.[6] These names are taken as representative. In the diocese of Bangor (circa. 1640) there are eight clergymen with pronounced English surnames, nineteen in St. Asaph, forty-two in Llandaff, and fifty-five in St. David's.[7] That these clergy had English surnames is not conclusive evidence that they could not preach in Welsh ; that a large proportion of them could not, and of the professedly Welsh clergy as well, is substantiated by the reference of Parliament in November, 1646, to " the scarcity of preaching ministers in the Welsh tongue," more especially in South Wales,[8] and by the exclamation of Walter Cradock in a sermon preached before the House of Commons in July of the same year that there were not in the " thirteene counties thirteene conseientious ministers who preached profitably in the Welch Language twice every Lord's Day."[9] The expedients adopted by Thomas Clopton to retain the rectory of Castell Caereinion at the end of the seventeenth century were no doubt paralleled by the Englishmen who held livings in Welsh Wales up to 1650.[10] The classical training of the Universities and the Canons of 1604 produced the boast of the orthodox churchmen at the Newchapel disputation in 1652 that their champion surpassed all his opponents in his " gift of praying in True Latine."[11] And so far had the Anglo-Latin spirit permeated that it is an actual grievance with a conservative Welsh peasant that the new preachers of Propagation times were " eternally thundering out in the ancient British tongue."[12]

The complex system of pluralities, the institutions of

1 Lib. Inst. Bangor fol.   9, instituted 1631.
2   ,,   ,,   Ibid.   ,, 10,   ,,   1617.
3   ,,   ,,   Assaphe ,, 148,   ,,   1635.
4   ,,   ,,   Ibid.   ,, 153,   ,,   1628.
5   ,,   ,,   Ibid.   ,, 181,   ,,   1626.
6   ,,   ,,   Ibid.   ,, 141,   ,,   1639 ; Thomas ; St. Asaph, p. 249.
7 Lib. Inst. passim.
8 L. J., Vol. VIII, p. 569.
9 The Saints' Fulnesse of Joy, p. 34.   [*Marginal Note.*—" God grant there be more. I know not so many."]
10 Thomas : Hist. of the Diocese of St. Asaph, pp. 119-120.
11 Animadversions on an Imperfect Relation in the Perfect Diurnall, No. 138, Aug. 2, 1652, p. [13].
12 Phillipps MSS. 12453 (Cymdeithas Llên Cymru—" Hen Gerddi Gwleidyddol," p. 28).

Englishmen, slender maintenance, and the consequent inferior type of lower clergy, led to the fearful picture of spiritual apathy presented in the report of the visitation of Dr. Lewis Bayly, Bishop of Bangor, in July, 1623. There was a serious lack of preaching the Word,—no sermons for a whole year at Penmon, Dolwyddelen, Llangwyllog, and Llanwnog, one only at Llanfihangel-y-traethau, only two at Llanfwrog, Llandecwyn, and Llanfair-pwil-gwyngyll, and only three at Llanddeusant and Caerhun,—desecration of churches at Llanllechid and Dwygyfylchi, clergy brawling and quarrelling with the parishioners at Llanddeusant, and general dereliction of the ordinary pastoral duties of a cure of souls, such as the christening of children, visiting the sick, and even burying the dead. The curate of Llanddeusant and the vicar of Aberdaron frequented ale-houses.[1] Then from Powys writes the author of " Carwr y Cymry " (1630), with his quotation of Nehemiah xiii. 29 and I Samuel ii,. 17,[2] that there were " forty or sixty churches without a sermon on Sundays,"[3] which finds corroboration in the opening words of the Guilsfield Petition of 1652, which declare that an unpreaching vicar had kept the parishioners " in penury of the Word for full sixty years."[4] Sir William Meredith of Stansty, in his will dated July 6th, 1603, says that " a learned and godly minister . . . , . hath not bin within my memorie in anie of the parishes within Bromfield and Yale."[5] Again and again Rees Prichard refers to the " loitering parsons " who fail to reprove the sins of their countrymen[6] ; John Lewis, the Glasgrug Puritan of Cardigan-shire, writes in a marginal note, unconsciously echoing the Bayly report, that " there was not in many places a sermon once a year "[7] ; a certain S. R., accompanying the army of General Mytton at the capture of " Carnarven " on June 4th, 1646, puts it that " the Country Towns here abouts have been quite without all manner of preaching almost."[8]

---

1 Rees : Prot. Noncon., pp. 8-10 [quoting Archæologia Cambrensis, Third Series Vol. IX, p. 283].
2 " Rhag-ymadrodd at Eglwyswyr Cymru," p. 17.
3 Ibid., p. 13.
4 Thomas : Hist. of the Diocese of St. Asaph, p. 734.
5 Gweithiau Morgan Llwyd : Vol. II, Introd. xxii.
6 Gweithiau—" Canwyll y Cymry " (Rice Rees)—I, p. 14, verse 20 ; CX, p. 183, verse 8.
7 The Parliament explained to Wales (1646), Part III, p. 26.
8 The Taking of Carnarven (Civil War Tract, N.L.W.), p. 5.

Vavasor Powell, quoting the terms of the Puritan petition
to Parliament in 1641, states that "there were not, upon
strict enquiry, so many conscientious and constant preachers
as there were of Counties in Wales."[1]   Christopher Love
did not hear a sremon at Cardiff until he was fourteen years
of age.[2]   The remark in the Preface to the "Directory"
of January, 1645, about "a time of such scarcity of faithful
pastors," mainly applied to England, could with added
force be extended to Wales.[3]   Penry's "dumbe ministers"[4]
have their successors in the "blind overseers" of Oliver
Thomas[5] and the "silent priests" of Morgan Llwyd.[6]
That many of the clergy were unable to preach, and some
guilty of drunkenness and gross immorality, is well substantiated by the Walker MSS. at the Bodleian Library;
three were ejected in Cardiganshire under the Propagation
Act for themselves keeping ale-houses.[7]   The church visible
had become a herd of goats, and the parish church was like
a country pound put under lock and key.[8]   A somewhat
different note is struck by Robert Lloyd, vicar of Chirk, in
dedicating his translation of Dent's "Plain Pathway" to
Bishop Owen of St. Asaph in 1630, saying that many of the
lower clergy were "careful watchers of the flocks,"[9] but in
the next page describes vividly the decadent social life of
the period with its taverns, its lewd games, its wandering
minstrels singing their ballads on Sundays and destroying
the higher life of "holy days."[10]   A loyal Churchman, like
Sir Marmaduke Lloyd of Maesyfelin, had to admit that
"the light of the gospell had growne dimme" in Wales.[11]
Vicar Prichard points the moral of crowded ale-houses and
empty churches on the day of God,[12] and Oliver Thomas
regrets the entire absence of interest in religious topics.[13]
There would be no objection to the "Book of Sports" in

1 Bird in the Cage Chirping . [and a] . Brief Narrative of the former Propagation, p. 2.
2 Speech at his Death, p. 127.
3 Reliquiæ Liturgicæ, Vol. III, p. 14.
4 An Exhortation .   .   .   . (1588), p. 23.
5 Car-wr y Cymru : Y Rhag-ymadrodd at Eglwys-wyr Cymru, p. 3.
6 Gwaedd Ynghymru. Gweithiau I., p. 129.
7 Walker MS., e. 7, fol. 213.
8 Llwyd. Cerddi a Chaniadau xlv, verse 3. (Gweithiau I, p. 86.).
9 Llwybr Hyffordd yn cyfarwyddo yr anghyfarwydd i'r nefoedd. :" Yr Epistol,"
p. [4].
10 Llwybr Hyffordd. "At y Darllennidd," p. [5].
11 Lloyd Records and Pedigrees (Lucy E. Lloyd Theakston and John Davies), p. 28.
12 Canwyll y Cymry (Rice Rees), cvii, p. 178.
13 Car-wr y Cymru, p. 31.

the overwhelming majority of Welsh parishes. Even after the dissemination of the Middleton Bible of 1630, the translator of Perkins's " Foundation of the Christian Religion " in 1649 roundly avers that " among twenty families there can scarce one Welsh Bible be found "[1]; " not one in five hundred families " says Vavasor Powell in 1646.[2] The sordid atmosphere of Llanymddyfri,[3] the sin and ignorance and the scorn of saints prevalent in Merioneth,[4] English satires at the expense of the " Welsh-mans Postures,"[5] the virtual exclusion of the lower classes from the newly-founded grammar-schools against the intentions of the founders,[6] and the narrow and restricted character of University studies as directed by Royal authority[7]—some illustrate, and some explain, the moral decadence and intellectual torpor which overspread Wales during the early Stuart period, and which the native clergy, caught in the toils of a materialistic system, could do but little to alleviate.

Such conditions made Wales the happy hunting-ground of the obscurantist and the reactionary. Mediæval ideas about divination lived peaceably side by side with persistent survivals of the ancient religion. Llwyd makes the Eagle in a series of questions to suggest that prosperous times issue from the movements of the planets, that our ancestors had seen well to keep off the evil hour by making the sign of the cross on their foreheads, and that the sorcerers were guardians of many secret mysteries.[8] Robert Holland, vicar of Llanddowror, had deliberately written a book to unmask the art of " men of magic."[9] Rees Prichard has to enter an emphatic protest against praying for the dead,[10] the belief in conjurers,[11] and the whole doctrine of purgatory,[12] though he himself in his exposition of the Catechism con-

1 Sail Crefydd Gristnogawl . . . E.R. " To the Reader," p. [2].
2 Scripture's Concord. Preface [quoted in " The Bible in Wales," p. 30].
3 Cauwyll y Cymry (Rice Rees), cxlii, pp. 228-230.
4 Letter of Col. John Jones to Morgan Llwyd, Oct. 9, 1651. Gweithiau II,
pp. 287-290.
5 Civil War Tract (N.L.W.), Feb. 10, 1643. Catalogue, p. 9.
6 J. R. Phillips : Civil War in Wales and the Marches, I, p. 24.
7 Wilkins : Concilia, p. 459.
8 Llyfr y Tri-Aderyn. Gweithiau, Vol. I, p. 235.
9 Y Ffydd Ddiffuant (Charles Edwards), 1677, p. 205 ; Hanes y Bedyddwyr
(Joshua Thomas), 1778, p. 29 footnote (quoting from Morris Williams' " Cofrestr,"
loaned by Richard Morris).
10 Mr. Rees Prichard, Gynt Ficcar Llan-ddyfri . . . 1657, Ed. by Stephen
Hughes, pp. 145-148 (N.L.W.) ; Gweithiau (Rice Rees), cxxxvii, 223-225.
11 Gweithiau (Rice Rees), cci, 288-290.
12 „ „ „ clvii, 251-252.

cerning the inner meaning of the Lord's Supper verges dangerously near the eucharistic theory.[1] Dr. George Griffith of Llanymynech had to admit the force of Vavasor Powell's sarcasm in referring to "the singing of Psalms before a dead corps buried that very morning the dispute was" at Newchapel.[2] John Lewis refers to the "swarm of blinde, superstitious ceremonies that are among us, passing under the name of old harmless customs; their frequent calling upon saints in their prayers and blessings; their peregrinations to wells and chappels."[3] Cradock deemed the London method of observing Christmas day only worthy of the "mountains of Wales."[4] "Gylynied mab Mair" is the culminating epithet of a Royalist wench in describing her lover's Roundhead enemies.[5] And it is doubtful if Llwyd, in referring to the days of his youth, spoke for the majority of his countrymen when he said that he partook of the consecrated bread, but did *not* see the body of Christ,[6] or when he objects to the "deceptive splendour" of the Latin Mass.[7] Laud's insistence on the full ritualistic details of the Anglican settlement of Elizabeth was readily agreed to by a people bound by tradition to oppose the severe simplicity of the Calvinistic Reformation; and the grand organs at Wrexham,[8] the Jesse window at Llanrhaiadr,[9] the Prayer Book at Hawarden,[10] the cope, two crosses, and "other relics of Rome" found at St. David's[11] were abominations only to the English sailors of Capt. Moulton and to the English soldiery who in the main composed the armies of Brereton, Mytton, and Middleton.

The 'via media' was a complete success in Wales, and the highest embodiment of its ideals, the Third Prayer Book, was the sacred palladium of the immigrant clerk and the unpreaching pastor. "The Service Book was a great hindrance to the preaching of the Word, and in some cases

1 Gweithiau (Rice Rees], xc (properly xci), p. 155 (verse 4 from bottom of page sec, col.).
2 Animadversions on an Imperfect Relation . . . (N.L.W.), p. 19.
3 The Parliament explained to Wales (1646), Part III, p. 26.
4 Divine Drops Distilled. Exps. & Obsns. on Jeremiah VI, 1, 2, p. 238.
5 Phillipps MSS. 12453, p. 12 ["Hiraith merch am ei chariad a ymladde o blaid y Brenin"].
6 Llyfr y Tri Aderyn. Gweithiau I, p. 258.
7 Gwaedd Ynghymru. Gweithiau I, p. 129.
8 J R. Phillips : Hist. of the Civil War, Vol. II, Doc. XXXVI, p. 114.
9 St. Asaph : Landmarks in the Hist. of the Welsh Church, p. 120.
10 J. R. Phillips : Hist. of the Civil War, Vol. II, Doc. XXXVI, p. 114.
11 Ibid., Vol. I, p. 274.

it tended to the justling of it out as unnecessary . . . . it was no better than the idol of ignorant and superstitious people . . . . [merely] lip-labour, tending to careless-ness of saving knowledge and true piety."[1] John Lewis, again, brings his testimony that a murmurer against the Prayer Book was " presently [dubbed] a Puritan, while unworthy and scandalous men who would make no bones of the same should passe for orthodox ministers, and have livings heaped upon them."[2] Llwyd describes such services as merely mechanical religion, and advises the Eagle that it is high time to bury it.[3] Besides the indirect impediments to actual preaching inherent in literal observance of the liturgy,[4] the annoying growth of Puritan sentiment in England drove the kings and their ecclesiastical advisers to adopt further restrictions. First came the attack on the ' lecture ' system. This was an arrangement inspired by the Puritan laity to provide preaching by establishing unordained men to ' teach, preach, and catechise,' princi-pally in the market-towns.[5] The scheme was in vogue from about 1620 to 1636, and feofees were chosen to purchase church property to provide adequate salaries for them. As early as 1622 King James refers to them as " a new body severed from the ancient clergy of England, as being neither parsons, vicars, or curates,"[6] and in the same year they were restricted from preaching except upon some part of the Catechism, or some text taken out of the Creed, the Ten Commandments, or the Lord's Prayer. The lecturers to be licensed by the Court of Faculties only upon the recom-mendation of the bishop of the diocese, the ' fiat ' of the archbishop, together with confirmation by the Great Seal.[7] Later, in 1633, they were confined to catechise only in the afternoon and to read divine service according to the liturgy.[8] The method and range of sermons for the generality of

1 Reliquiæ Liturgicæ, Vol. III. Preface, p. 15. [" The Directory."]
2 The Parliament Explained to Wales. Part III, p. 30.
3 Llyfr y Tri Aderyn. Gweithiau I, p. 254.
4 Llyfr Gweddi Cyffredin a Gwenidogaeth y Sacramentay. . . .1630 and 1634 Edition (bound up with the 3rd Edition of the Bible of 1630), vide Rhagymadrodd—last page.
5 *E.''' Brecon*—" The Colledge of Brecon, where formerly there was a Lecture once a fortnight " (True and Perfect Relation, p. 31). The reference here, no doubt, is to the ' Collegiate Church ' of Brecon.
6 Wilkins : Concilia, p. 465.
7 Wilkins : Concilia, ibid.
8 Wilkins : Concilia, p. 480 [King's instruction . . . . to William, Lord Archbishop of Canterbury].

beneficed clergy had been circumscribed even earlier. In the King's direction to the Universities in 1616 no man was to be suffered to maintain dogmatically any point of doctrine not allowed by the Church of England[1]; the King's only important instruction to the divines sent by him to the Synod of Dort (1618) was to advise those churches [on the Continent] that the " ministers do not deliver in pulpit those things for ordinary doctrines which are the highest points of schools, and not fit for vulgar capacity "[2]; and his letter to the Archbishop in 1622 contains a derogatory reference to " divers young students who read late writers and ungrounded divines." The same letter contains a direction that no preacher whatsoever [with the exception of some specified higher clergy] were to take as text anything not comprehended in the Articles of 1562, or in some of the authorised Homilies, or to expound in ' any popular auditory ' the deep points of predestination, election, reprobation, or of the universality, efficacy, resistibility, or irresistibility of God's grace . . . . but leave these themes to be handled by learned men.[3] These were instructions not observed by Oliver Thomas, when he refers his " Cymro " to Romans xv. 4 and goes on to say that God allows, even commands, not his ministers only, but the members of his church in general, to discover his whole counsel ;[4] nor by Rees Prichard in his prayer for election,[5] his attack on the Arminian tenets,[6] and his defence of original sin[7] and freedom of will transcended by God's grace[8]; nor by John Cragge,[9] vicar of Llantilio Pertholy in Monmouthshire, who, if his 1653 sermon on Psalm iv. 6 was typical of his earlier efforts, must have dumbfounded his hearers with his wealth of syllogism and elaborate sub-division.[10] But these were exceptions. Ignorance from below and restrictions from above acted and reacted on the mental content of the clergy, and Wales became a land of " wretched

---

I Wilkins : Concilia, p. 459.   Direction VIII.
2 Wilkins : Concilia, p. 460.   Instruction IV.
3 Wilkins : Concilia, p. 465.   Direction III.   [" Concerning Preachers."]
4 Car-wr y Cymru, pp. 61-62.
5 Canwyll y Cymry (Rice Rees), XCVIII, pp. 161-162.
6   ,,   ,,   ,,   ,,   CXCII, pp. 283-284.
7   ,,   ,,   ,,   ,,   CLXXXI, p. 234.
8   ,,   ,,   ,,   ,,   CLXXXII, p. 275.
9 Lib. Inst. Llandaff, fol. 110 [instituted 10 Oct., 1636].
   10 Light of God's Countenance . . . Sermon preached June 5th, 1653.
(Civil War Tract, N.L.W. Catalogue, p. 64).

sermons,"[1] light, empty sermons,"[2] and the petition presented
to Parliament by the " thirteene shires " goes so far as to
say that " Cobblers and Doctors of Divinity be equall competitors " in theological learning.[3] This rash statement
is quite in keeping with other unbalanced remarks in this
petition of " many hundred thousands " ; a more serious
fact is the part played by Wales in the fortunes of the
Westminster Assembly of Divines which met on the first
of July, 1643. Of the divines nominated[4] by the knights
and burgesses of Wales to be members of this body only
one (Edward Ellis of Guilsfield[5]) was a Welsh clergyman
holding a living in the Principality. Two were Welshmen
who had stayed in England, one as " chaplain to the Lord
of Peterborough,"[6] and the other as rector of Sonning in
Berkshire[7] ; two were Englishmen who had made their
home in Wales, Dr. Christopher Pashley[5] of Hawarden and
William Nicholson of Llandilofawr[5] ; the other " approved
divines " point to the fact that Wales was a mere geographical
convenience for including in the Assembly distinguished
London clergy and learned Doctors of the Universities.[8]
For example, Dr. Temple of Battersea was nominated for
Brecon, and Henry Tozer, " Senior Fellow of Exeter College
in Oxford," for Glamorganshire.[9] Nicholson was later left
out,[10] and Matthew Newcomen of Dedham substituted, and
in the final approved list the name of Richard Lloyd is
absent.[11] The records of the Assembly hardly contain a
reference to either Ellis, or Bulkeley, or Pashley, and months
before the Confession of Faith was presented to the Houses
of Parliament as a complete instrument,[12] the first had to
appear before the Committee for Compounding as a delin--

1 John Lewis : The Parliament explained to Wales (1646), Part III, p. 30.
2 Morgan Llwyd : Gweithiau. Vol. I, Gwaedd Ynghymru, p. 130.
3 To the Honourable Court The House of Commons . . . . Directed to
the House the 12th of February, 1641 (N.L.W.), p. 4.
4 Commons Journals, Vol. II, 524 (order for nominations, 20th April, 1642).
    ,,   ,,   ,,   540 (approval of Welsh nominations, 25th April,
1642).
5 C. J. II, 540.
6 Richard Bulkeley, B.D. (for Anglesey) : " Burlye," B. Museum, 108, B. 40.
7 Richard Lloyd, D.D. (for Denbigh) ; D.N.B., Vol. XXXIII, p. 431.
8 The imminence of the Civil War, and the undoubted loyalty of the great majority
of the M.P.'s for Wales in the early Long Parliament, may have conduced to make
these nominations a matter of " management." There is no proof of this, however,
either in the Journals of Parliament or the political diaries of the time.
9 C. J. Vol. II, 541.
10 C. J. Vol. II, 916.
11 W. M. Hetherington : Hist. of the Westminster Assembly of Divines, pp.
109-110.
12 Mitchell and Struthers : Minutes of the West. Assembly, p. 309.

quent,[1] and the last is presenting a petition for his " fifths "
as a sequestered clergyman.[2] Thus by an unfortunate com-
bination of circumstances Wales, except that Christopher
Love sat by co-optation as one of the London representatives,
had practically no share in shaping the most comprehensive
standard of faith formulated by Protestant Christendom.
She had to suffer virtual disfranchisement on account of
the comparatively low standard of her theological scholar-
ship.   And though Rowland Vaughan of Caergai, writing
in 1658, sets up Doctors Prideaux, Brough, and Jasper
Maine as the acknowledged expositors of the Word of God
" in the previous generation,"[3] few indeed could possibly
be disposed or mentally equipped to assimilate their learned
volumes.   It is true that the " Bruised Reed " of Richard
Sibbes[4] strengthened Vavasor Powell in his early wrestling
with spiritual difficulties,[5] and that the works of John Preston
and William Perkins are freely quoted in the marginal notes
of Walter Cradock and William Erbery.[6]   But they were
other men, and the protagonists of a new order.

The supreme authorities in Church and State were not
uncognisant of the evils which grew up in the shadow of the
Anglican ideal, and projected many important reforms,
and suggested even more.   The XXXIVth Canon of 1604
laid down a not inconsiderable minimum of learning on the
part of the clergy about to be ordained, and specified conditions as to age, University study and the testimony of
grave ministers[7] ; the Xth Canon of 1640 impressed upon
all the clergy to observe a ' pious, regular, and inoffensive
demeanour,' and to avoid all excess and disorder, thus
repeating and emphasising the LXXIVth and LXXVth
of the Canons of 1602.[8]   The Archbishop's letter of 1605
to his clergy refers to the King's dissatisfaction with those
that hold two or more ecclesiastical preferments, and his

---

1 Montgomeryshire Collections (1883), pp. 386-388.
2 Addit. MS. 15670, 173a.
3 Prifannau Crefydd Gristnogawl   . . .   O Waith Iago Usher, Escob Armagh.
" At y Darllennydd " p. [2].
4 Published 1630.   D.N.B., Vol. LII, p. 183.
5 Life and Death of Mr. Vavasor Powell (1671)—Powell's *own* Account of Conversion and Ministry prefixed, p. 3.
6 Vide also *Henry Nicholls* : The Shield Single against the Sword Doubled,
pp. 32, 50, 76 (Brit. Mus. Thomason Tract.).
7 Wilkins : Concilia, p. 386.   " Certae conditiones in ordinandis requisitae."
8 Nalson : An Impartial Collection of the Great Affairs of State (1682).   Vol. I,
p. 558.

command that the names of such, of their benefices ' with
cure or without cure,' and the distance of miles between
them, should be laid before him. Those who provided their
cures with poorly-paid insufficient curates were to be
admonished by their Bishop, have their dispensations called
in question, and in case of disobedience, summoned before
the High Commission Court. And King and Primate agree
that " some course be taken for such as have all the best
ecclesiastical livings in the land, named impropriations "[1];
in July, 1632, King Charles addresses a letter to the Archbishop concerning the necessity of recovering for the Crown
the patronage of livings.which had fallen into other hands.[2]
In 1633 the Archbishop issues the King's instructions for
all bishops to be in residence in one of their episcopal houses,
and not upon lands they had purchased or upon their ' com-
mendams '[3]; that no bishop, especially when nominated to
another bishopric, was to grant out extensive leases of church
property ; and that no bishop was to put out of his ' commendam ' any benefices or other preferments to friends
or relations.[4] The practice of some bishops to change their
leases from terms of years (21) to lives (3), brings from Charles
in 1634 a strong recommendation that the exact reverse be
adopted,[5] and follows this up with a sharp reprimand to
Roger Mainwaring, Bishop of St. David's, who had leased
the rectories of Kerry in Montgomery and Glascwm in
Radnor for a term of years, but had allowed ' concurrencies
in trust ' to lie with the leases, to the effect that on the
' expiration ' of these arrangements, any further leases were
to determine at death or preferment.[6] A similar rebuke
was necessary to the Treasurer of St. Asaph, who on 2nd
November, 1639, granted the prebend of Meliden on a lease
for *lives* to William Mostyn, and the Surveyors of Bishops'
Lands under the Act of October, 1646, report, evidently
with regret, that his survivor is only " 46 years of age."[7]
On the other hand, Sir Edward Lloyd obtained a lease of
the tithes of Llandinam from Dr. Thomas Bayly for twenty-

1 Wilkins : Concilia. pp. 413-414.   April, 1605.
2 Ibid., p. 478, 17th July, 1632.
3 Ibid., pp. 480-481.
4 Ibid., p. 481.
5 Ibid., p. 493.
6 Wilkins : Concilia, p. 535.   9th July, 1637.
7 Lamb, 902, fol. 28.   Report of 7th Sept., 1649.

one years, with the proviso that the latter " so long lived."[1]

There were signs of progress in other directions. Dr. William Morgan of St. Asaph had arranged in the chapter of 8th March, 1601, that forty-four sermons should be preached annually by the members thereof,[2] and this scheme was developed by Bishop Owen to include a series of Welsh sermons to be preached in the parish church of St. Asaph on the first Sunday in each month by such members of the Chapter as derived a portion of their income from the tithes of the parish.[3] It was ' understood ' that everything read or sung in the Church services should be in Welsh,[4] and in the Nineteenth Session of the Convocation of 1640 a petition was presented from the Diocese of St. Asaph for " the correction and amendment of a false impression of the Liturgy in Welsh," and desiring " the form of prayer read at the King's Coronation to be translated into the British language and used there."[5] It was Bishop Hanmer, Owen's predecessor at St. Asaph, who had given Robert Lloyd of Chirk a copy of Dent's " Plain Pathway " to be translated into Welsh,[6] and it was another Bishop, Dr. Lewis Bayly of Bangor, who had composed one of the most widely-read devotional books of the age, which was translated in 1630 by Rowland Vaughan of Caergai. Laud exerted his influence for the appointing of Welsh-speaking bishops ; such were John Owen of St. Asaph, Morgan Owen of Llandaff, and William Roberts of Bangor.[7] Then there was the supreme gift of the Welsh Bible. In 1567 William Salesbury and his coadjutors had issued the New Testament in the native tongue, in 1588 appeared the complete translation of the Bible, and the revised edition by Doctor Parry and Doctor Davies in 1620. These were solely for use in the churches. In 1630 an edition of the Welsh Bible for the use of the people was published through the generosity of Sir Thomas Middleton and Rowland Heylin. Various versions of the Psalms appeared from that contained in

1 Cal. Comm. Comp., Vol. III, 1725.
2 Thomas : Hist. of the Diocese of St. Asaph, p. 201.
3 Ibid., p. 202. First sermon on 6th March, 1630-1.
4 Llyfr Gweddi Cyffredin a Gwenidogaeth y Sacramentay (1630), Rhagymadrodd.
5 Nalson : An Impartial Collection. Vol. I, 370. [May 22, 1640].
6 Llwybr Hyffordd. " Yr Epistol," p. [1].
7 St. Asaph : Landmarks in the Hist. of the Welsh Church, pp. 110-111.

the Prayer Book of 1567 to the "Salmau Cân" of Edmwnd Prys in 1621.[1] The Book of Homilies was also translated into Welsh. And a goodly number of Welsh books—grammars, dictionaries, translations—had been issued culminating in the literary activity of the years 1630-1632, working "for the instruction of our preachers and the spiritual edification of all."[2] One can hardly associate the authors of "Carwr y Cymry," "Llwybr Hyffordd," and "Llyfr y Resolusion" with a warm welcome to the "Book of Sports" of 1633 ; Dr. Field, Bishop of St. David's up to 1635, is reputed to have been singularly lenient in exacting obedience to it ; and his successor, Dr. Roger Mainwaring, the author of the notorious sermon on Apostolic Obedience, appears in a new light as a friend of Vicar Prichard and executor of his will in conjunction with Morgan Owen of Llandaff.[3] Apart, also, from the schemes adopted by the two Bishops of St. Asaph, there are other indications of the desire for more efficient "preaching of the Word." Sir William Meredith of Stansty by will left "£30 for the wages of a Preacher at Wrexham for one yeare," wishing for such good effect that "the people of that Parish" would never live without such,[4] and Sir John Hanmer in 1624 bequeathed the corn tithes of Bettisfield to a learned and painful preacher who should preach twice every Sabbath day in the parish church.[5] Thomas Prichard, Archdeacon of Llandaff, had demised the premises of Bishton in the deanery of Netherwent to William Prichard of Llanmorthin, and the latter or his assigns were bound by covenant to find and maintain a "sufficient preaching minister" in the said Church.[6] A similar covenant appeared in a lease of the rectory of Llanhenog in the same county of Monmouth granted on the last day of June, 1637, by the Chapter of Llandaff to Giles Morgan of Pencrug.[7]

And with all its worldly distractions the Welsh Church

1 The Bible in Wales (Ballinger), pp. 16-29, and "Bibliography."

2 Charles Edwards : "Y Ffydd Ddiffuant," 1677, p. 206 ; Bible in Wales, p. 28 ; Hanes y Bedyddwyr (Joshua Thomas), 1778, p. 29 ; Rees Prichard . . . Ficcar Llan-ddyfri, Rhagymadrodd, p. [17], ed. Stephen Hughes, 1657.

3 Canwyll y Cymry (Rice Rees). "Hanes ei Fywyd," p. 317. [Will dated 2nd December, 1644].

4 Gweithiau Morgan Llwyd, II, Introd. xxi-xxii (July 6, 1603)

5 Thomas : Hist. of the Diocese of St. Asaph, p. 823.

6 Lamb, 913, folios 768-769.

7 Lamb, 913, folios 770-771.

of the first half of the seventeenth century had some noteworthy members. There was William Salesbury of Bachymbyd, the Royalist governor of Denbigh Castle during
the greater part of the Civil War, who heads his answer to
Middleton's summons to surrender ' in nomine Iesu ' and
punctuates his note no less than five times with " God "
and God's help "[1] ; the Sir Lewis Mansell of Margam who,
despairing of worldly succour in times of affliction, appeals
for advice to Rees Prichard[2] ; the generous Vaughans of
Llwydarth in Montgomery, to whom Richard Jones of Llanfaircaereinion pays such a warm tribute[3] ; and Judge David
Jenkins of Hensol in Glamorgan, who was ready to walk to
the scaffold with the Bible under one arm and Magna Charta
under the other.[4]   And there were some, indeed, who per-
ceived the danger of driving the politico-religious pretensions
of the Church to their logical extremes : men like Dr. Griffith
Williams, Bishop of Ossory, who regretted the tenor of the
Canons of 1640 much in the tone of Clarendon[5] ; Rees
Prichard, who sparingly denounced the evils of the sinecure
system[6] ; Dr. Gabriel Goodman, Bishop of Gloucester, who
was suspended ' ab officio et beneficio ' for his dramatic
protest in 1640[7] ; and William Thomas of Aber, Member of
Parliament for the borough of Carnarvon, who, in his speech
to the House of Commons (May, 1641), delivered a long
diatribe against the Bishops sitting in Parliament, and
indulged in a ' short ' review of their action " from 1116 to
1641."[8]

But laudable intentions and worthy personalities could
not save a cause saddled with the dead weight of materialism,
and it is difficult to believe with a recent writer[9] that the
Anglican Church in Wales would have worked out its own
salvation had it not been for the cataclysm of the Civil War.
To an institution cherishing so many of the scholastic ideals

<hr>

1 Phillips : Civil War, II, Doc. XXIX, p. 95-96.
2 Canwyll y Cymry (Rice Rees), cxxi, p. 200.
3 Testûn Testament Newydd. " At yr enwog urddasol Edward Vaughan o
Lwydiart, Esq.," Dedication, pp. [1-3].
4 Phillips : Civil War, Vol, I, p. 254 [quoting from Kingdom's Weekly Intelli-
gencer, No. 77], gives a much different view of Judge Jenkins—" in times of peace he
lived like a heat'Peh, and swore like a devil."
5 The Discovery of Mysteries   .   .   .   By Gr. Williams L. Bishop of Ossory.
[cp. Clarendon, Hist. of Great Rebellion, I, 209], p. 40, N.L.W.).
6 Canwyll y Cymry, 1657 Edition, pp. 2, 6, and especially 7.
7 Nalson : Impartial Collection, Vol. I, pp. 369-370, 372.
8 A Speech of William Thomas, Esquire, in Parliament.   .   .   .   (N.L.W.).
9 J. C. Morrice : Wales in the Seventeenth Century, pp. 8-10.

of the Middle Ages and wedded by its political antecedents and associations to the possibility of setting secular limits to a̅ great intellectual uprising, some iconoclastic touch was• necessary : this was applied when the sinecure rectory of Llangwm in Denbigh was sequestered from Dr. Griffith, he ' being no minister but a doctor of the Civill Lawe,'[1] when the violent contemner of clergy, Richard Parry of Llanfallteg, became a minister under the Propagation Act at £50 a year,[2] when a member of the Assembly of Divines could not become vicar of Abergele without ' relinquishing his other ecclesiastical promotions and proposing residency there,'[3] and when a forceful itinerant in Breconshire confessed ' he never read the Primmer in English.'[4] Yet, amidst all this mutation of values which accompanied the fall of the old order, the ejected rector of Llandyfaelog in Brecknock always received his proper degree of ' Doctour,'[5] the defender of the hierarchy at Newchapel was allowed in 1650 to keep his living of Llanymynech,[6] and the greatest names among the Puritans of the Commonwealth never receded from the principle of a doctrine ' owned by the State '[7] and a ' public profession of these nations.'[8] At the Restoration it was evidently possible to set the Anglican Church on a new basis by a wise scheme of comprehension. But, bred under the shadow of the High Commission Court, embittered by the disasters of the interregnum, the old order were not morally equipped to achieve this consummation ; instead, George Morley, the new Bishop of Winchester and once the sinecure rector of Pennant in Montgomery, contributed not a little to make the Savoy Conference with the Presbyterians futile,[9] and the new Bishop of St. Asaph assisted in drawing up the Act of Uniformity.[10]

---

1 Rawl. M.S., c. 261. [26]. Strictly speaking, the statement of the Clerk to the N.W. Commissioners given in the MS. is not correct. Griffith was a Ll.D., not a D.C.L.; inst. 4th Aug., 1635 (Lib. Inst. Assaphe, p. 151) ; Thomas : Hist. of Dioc. of St. Asaph, p. 556.
2 J. R. Phillips : Hist. of Civil War, Vol. I, pp. 64-65 ; Walk, c. 13, f. 19 (Carmarthenshire Accounts).
3 Lamb. 997, lib. ii, f. 101.
4 Walker : Sufferings, Pt. II, p. 409.
5 Walk., c. 13, f. 60 (Brecon Accounts).
6 Rawl. c. 261 [18].
7 Proposals of Dr. Owen's Committee re Propagation of the Gospel (general), No. 12 (C. J. vii, 258).
8 ' Instrument of Government ' ; Clause XXXV, quoted in Shaw : Hist. of the Church, II, p. 85.
9 Lodge : Political History of England, Vol. VIII, p. 65 ; inst. to Pennant, 6th April, 1644 (Lib. Inst. Assaphe, p. 164).
10 Morrice : Wales in the Seventeenth Century, p. 63.

NOTE.—NATURE OF THE EVIDENCE.

The conclusions arrived at in this Chapter mainly depend on :—

(a) The testimony of contemporary writers, both Anglican and Puritan.

(b) The names furnished by the 'Liber Institutionum' (infra, Chap. VIII, xiii).

(c) The evidence supplied before and by the Plundered Ministers' Committee (p. 54).

(d) The facts reported by the Surveyors of Church Lands (1646-1650) (infra, Chap. VIII, viii).

(e) The 'state of the livings' as found in Anglesey and Pembroke by the Parochial Commissioners of 1650 (infra, Chap. VIII, vii).

II.

THE PURITAN MOVEMENT IN ENGLAND—ITS REACTION UPON WALES.

With the failure of the Hampton Court Conference, men Puritanically inclined had to adopt new methods. Some, inclined more to questions of doctrine and ritual than to matters of Church government, became involved in the Sabbatarian controversy, in the struggle against Arminianism, and in resisting the innovations of Laud ; others, accepting with important qualifications the theories which Browne retracted and for which Barrowe, Greenwood, and Penry had suffered, began to publish pamphlets embodying their opinions. Henry Jacob in his "Humble Supplication" (1605) makes the Church to have Pastors, Elders, and Deacons, advises those 'who enter this way' to take the oaths of Allegiance and Supremacy and "to keep brotherly communion with the rest of our English churches as they are now established," and to pay all dues, ecclesiastical and civil.[1] In his "Principles and Foundations of the Christian Religion" (1605) he defines a " true Visible or Ministeriall Church " as one " having power within its selfe immediately from God to administer all Religious meanes of faith to the members thereof," and further asserts that such a true Church is to be "gathered by a free mutuall covenant joyning and covenanting to live as members of a holy Society."[2] The main contention of William Bradshaw in his "English Pvritanisme Containeing The Main opinions of . . . . those that are called Puritanes " (1605) is that " Churches or Congregations communicating . . . together in divine worship are in all Ecclesiasticall matters equall," and that " yf any wholl Church or Congregation shall erre in any matters of faith or religion, noe other Churches or Spirituall Church officers have power to censure, punish, or controul

1 Burrage : The Early English Dissenters, Chap. XII, p. 286.
2 Ibid., pp. 286-287.

the same," which function he leaves to the " Civill Magistrat."[3] Bradshaw exalts the " Magistrat " to be chief arbiter in all ecclesiastical matters ; he was to preserve the national character of the Church and to prevent the actual establishment of separation. Jacob became minister of the English Church at Middleburg at the end of 1605, John Robinson and the Scrooby Church migrated to Holland in 1607-8, and John Smyth and the Gainsborough Church in the latter year or even earlier, where the latter adopted the ideas of the Dutch Mennonites regarding the subjects and mode of baptism. Two of his followers, Thomas Helwys and John Murton, disagreed with Smyth over the proper persons to administer the rite, and returned to England in 1612 to found the first *General* Baptist Church, holding that baptism and not a Church-covenant was the true ' form ' of a church. By 1626 there were five such congregations in England. Henry Jacob had returned to England in 1616 to found the first *Independent* Puritan Church on the precepts laid down by him and Bradshaw in the pamphlets of 1605. His church covenanted together " to walk in all God's ways as he had revealed or should make known to them."[2] In 1616 also appeared his "Confession and Protestation " published for " the clearing of Certaine Christians from the slaunder of Schisme and Noveltie, and also of Separation and undutifullnes to the Magistrate."[3] This pamphlet contains some new points : Teachers are included among the Church officers ; imposition of hands (' if it is meete ') ; one pastor to have precedence ; the officers to have no power except what the congregation gives to them. And though the members refused to be " ordinary and constant " attendants of any " Church visible politicall," yet " members of them occasionally we refuse not to be, seeing in them many true visible christians, with whom we cannot deny publike communion absolutely."[4] In 1622 Jacob left for Virginia and never returned, and John Lathorp became his successor in 1624. He left for New England in 1634, and in 1637 *Henry Jessey* became pastor, who in 1639 was sent to Wales

---

1 Ibid., p. 288.
2 Burrage : The Early English Dissenters, p. 314, Vol. I.
      Ibid., p. 214, Vol. II. Document XVIII.
3 Ibid., p. 315, Vol. I.
4 Ibid., p. 317, Vol. I.

by the congregation " for the assisting of old Mr. Wroth,
Mr. Craddock, and others in gathering and constituting the
Church at Llanyvaches, in Monmouthshire."¹ Before this,
another Indpendent Church had been founded in Deadman-
place by John Hubbard,² and the Church founded by Jacob
had suffered two ' separations.' Those who went out in
September, 1633, disliked conformity of any kind and
appointed as pastor John Spilsbury ; those who left in the
spring of 1638 were convinced that baptism, without as yet
a belief in immersion, should be administered to professed
believers only. They also joined John Spilsbury's congregation, and gradually, through their correspondence with
the Dutch Anabaptists, they came to believe that ' dipping '
was the only gospel form of the ordinance, and became
known as *Particular* Baptists.³ Meanwhile, most of the
" Five Dissenting Brethren " by a forced residence in Holland
were acquiring that store of learning and experience of
controversy which stood them in such good stead in the
debates of the Assembly, and large numbers of the Puritan
clergy were arguing themselves into a Presbyterian system
of church-government as the only refuge from an episcopal
system which, notwithstanding the sincere protests of Laud,
seemed to be making straight for Rome.

Such were the main manifestations of English Puritanism
when Jessey made his journey to Llanfaches, and the forces
behind them were at work along the entire Welsh border.
The pages of the Broadmead Records reflect the slow but
sure advance of Puritan sentiment in Bristol under Yeamans
of St. Philip's and Hazzard of St. Nicholas⁴ ; Gloucester
was even now preparing for the Cavalier epithet of " godly
city "⁵ ; and the land between Severn and Usk, with its
reminiscences of the loose jurisdiction of the Lords Marchers
and of the comparative freedom that resulted from the
conflicting authority that obtains in all Borderlands, was
of old the delectable mountains of religious exiles and
spiritual independence, facts sufficient, according to the

---

1 Life and Death of Mr. Henry Jessey (1671), pp. 9-10.
2 Dale : Hist. of Eng. Congregationalism, chap. XII, p. 361.
3 The account of these " separations " in the main follows that given by Burrage :
Early Eng. Dissenters, Vol. I, pp. 319-335.
4 Pp. 6-8 (ed. Haycroft).
5 J. R. Phillips : Hist. of the Civil War in Wales, Vol. I, p. 147.

Baptist historian, to account for the definite appearance of that sect at Olchon in 1633.[1] Further north, in Herefordshire, was Bishop's Castle, the home of Walter Stephens, and the Castle of Brampton Bryan, with its Puritan knight and his Puritan chaplains, Thomas Pierson and Stanley Gower. The lecture system had been particularly successful in Cheshire,[2] and within Wales itself, in the Wrexham district, the bequest of Sir William Meredith seemed to have had its effect. Here Arise Evans heard in 1629 a sermon by Oliver Thomas,[3] and here, most probably, Morgan Llwyd was converted by Walter Cradock.[3] Very slowly, with this probable exception, Wales began to respond to the Puritan appeal from across the Border. It is true that there is an imposing theory, based on the Iolo MSS., of the existence in Glamorgan of a band of Puritans, even of Separatists, during the sixteenth century.[4] Sure historical evidence begins with the year 1634.[5] In January of this year the. Bishop of St. David's reports the suspension of a lecturer, for his " Inconformity," and in the following year he had to dismiss the same (" one Roberts ")[5]; and one or two others, " that had with their giddiness offered to distemper the people," were likewise driven out of the diocese. The same year (1635) the Bishop of Llandaff found that William Erbery, vicar of St. Mary's at Cardiff,[7] and Walter Cradock, his curate, " a bold ignorant young fellow," had been disobedient to His Majesty's injunctions, and had " preached very dangerously and schismatically to the people." Erbery was admonished, and Cradock suspended. William Wroth,[8] vicar of Llanfaches, is also reported as " leading away many simple people." Articles were " carefully " preferred against both Wroth and Erbery in the High Commission Court in

---

1 Joshua Thomas: Hanes y Bedyddwyr (1778), pp. 66-68 ; Pontypridd edition (1885), pp. 125-135.
2 Urwick : Historical Sketches of the County Palatine of Chester, Introd. XI . Gregory Norris : Friends' Historical Soc., Supplement No. 6, p. 2.
3 Gweithiau Morgan Llwyd : Vol. II, Introd. xxii-xxiii. [John Jones, Maesygarnedd, married the daughter of John Edwards, one of the executors of Sir Wm. Meredith's will.]
4 " Hen Bendefigion Glyn Nedd " (Taliesin ab Iolo) ; Wilkins : History of Merthyr chap. VIII, pp. 82-92 ; Malkin : South Wales, Vol. I, pp. 297-8 ; J. Spinther James : Hanes y Bedyddwyr, Vol. II, 48-68.
5 Extracts from Laud's annual account to the King of the State of his Province—Lambeth MSS., Vol. 943. [Quoted in Rees : Prot. Noncon., pp. 35-37. 1634-1640.]
6 " Griffith Roberts of Llandecwyn "—J. H. Davies, Introd. xiii. to Gweithiau Morgan Llwyd. II.
7 Lib. Inst., Llandaff, fol. 12. Instituted 7th August, 1633.
8 Lib. Inst. Llandaff, fol. 125. Instituted 17th July, 1617.

1636.[1] " Three or four " were released by the Bishop of St. David's upon hope given of their obedience to the Church. In 1636 the same Bishop reports Marmaduke Matthews, vicar of Penmain, for " preaching against the keeping of all holy-days," and in 1638 finds that " some had been meddling with things forbidden."[2] The same year saw the resignation of Erbery and the ejection of Wroth. The Bishop of St. Asaph in 1634 is " not anywhere troubled with Inconformity,"[3] but in 1640 " a conventicle of mean persons is laid hold on," most probably in the Wrexham district, and hardly important enough to be included in the " spiritual Goliaths " who were blaspheming the " children of Israel."[4]

The outstanding personalities of this nascent Puritanism of Wales were all associated with the eastern border, some born very close to it, others in places not far distant. Walter Cradock was of Trefela near Usk,[5] William Erbery was the son of a merchant of Roath,[6] and William Wroth was descended from an old Monmouthshire family[7]; these were soon reinforced by Henry Walter of Piercefield, near Newport,[8] and by Richard Symonds of Abergavenny.[9] Vavasor Powell was born at Knucklas in Radnor,[10] and Morgan Llwyd, from Cynfal in Ardudwy, is inevitably associated with Wrexham. And the march of events tended to bring the ' new ' men of South and North together ; then, after the lapse of a few years, to bring the greater number of them into contact with the governing principles of Jacobite Puritanism in England. After his ejection from Cardiff, Cradock became curate to Robert Lloyd at Wrexham, where he drew large crowds to hear him, even at six o'clock in the morning, but so offended the maltsters of the town and the vested interests of the old order, that after less than a year's stay, he had perforce to take refuge at the Puritan stronghold of Brampton Bryan.[11] Here Morgan Llwyd

1 William Erbery : Testimony, p. 313 (C.F.L. copy).
2 Vide supra, p. 14.
3 Thomas : Hist. of the Diocese of St. Asaph, p. 98.
4 Robert Lloyd : Llwybr Hyffordd. " Yr Epistol," p. [4].
5 Rees : Prot. Noncon., sec. ed., p. 46.
6 Brasenose College Register, Vol. I, p. 139. [Ox. Hist. Soc. Pub., Vol. LV].
7 Rees : Prot. Nonconformity, Sec. ed., p. 37.
8 Diary of Walter Powell of Llantilio Crossenny (ed. J. A.   a n), p. 41, n. 1.
9 Foster : Alumni Oxonienses (1500-1714), Vol. IV, p. 145Br d ey
10 Life and Death of Mr. Vavasor Powell, p. 106. [S°m° remarkable passages . . .]
11 A. N. Palmer : Hist. of the Parish Church of Wrexham, pp. 72-74 [traditions of Cradock's stay at Wrexham quoted from Edmund Jones' Life of Evan Williams (1750)].

eventually joined him.[1] Powell also, after his conversion by Cradock,[2] seems to have been a welcome visitor.[3] Thence in 1639 proceeded Cradock, and probably Llwyd,[4] to the historic meeting at Llanfaches in November of that year, whereto the other Puritans who laboured in Monmouthshire had congregated.[5] This was the climax of the veteran Wroth's powerful ministry. His direct forceful preaching and his sympathetic intimacy with the daily life of his hearers[6] made himself 'the apostle of Wales,'[7] his Church 'the Antioch in that gentile country,'[8] and the rallying-point for the saints of the neighbouring English counties.[9] Llanfaches had become the recognised centre of the spiritual energy described by Erbery in a classic passage[9] and by Llwyd in one of the earliest of his Songs.[10] Powell at this period confined his activities to his native county, amidst much annoyance and persecution from his relations and the High Sheriff[11]; finally, a writ was served upon him for using extreme words in reference to the King.[12]

But though Powell admits he battered down a 'meeting-house door' and paid scant respect to the Book of Common Prayer,[13] and though Wroth after his ejection " separated from ye worship of the World and gathered his people into Gospell-order of Church-government,"[14] there is no evidence that they had irretrievably broken with the Church of England. The new church at Llanfaches was organised on the " New England pattern,"[15] an ideal of church polity shadowed forth in the later writings of John Robinson and in the controversial works of John Cotton, the most distinguished divine in the colony of Massachusetts Bay. Robinson, it is true, published in 1610 a " Ivstification of

1 Gweithiau Morgan Llwyd, Vol. II, Introd. xxiii.
2 Life and Death of Vavasor Powell, pp. 4, 106; Strena Vavasoriensis, p. 2.
3 Ibid., p. 9.
4 Gweithiau II, Introd. xxv.
5 Erbery : Testimony, pp. 162-163.
6 Walter Cradock : Saints Fulnesse of Joy, p. 12.
7 Ibid., p. 12 (marginal reference).
8 Life and Death of Mr. Henry Jessey (1671), pp. 9-10.
9 Erbery : Apocrypha, pp. 8-9.
10 Gweithiau, Vol. I, Song I., vv. 5, 7, 8, 9, p. 4. [This is a matter of inference from the account given by Mr. J. H. Davies in Vol. II, Introd. xxiv-xxv.]
11 Life and Death of Mr. Vavasor Powell (own account of " Conversion and Ministry " prefixed), pp. 10-11.
12 Memorials of Old North Wales, p. 223 [Article by J. H. Davies on " The Origin of Nonconformity in North Wales "].
13 Life, p. 11.
14 The Broadmead Records (ed. Haycroft), p. 6.
15 Erbery : Apocrypha, p. 8.

Separation " from the Church of England, but by 1618 he is receiving members of the Church of England into his congregation, and the year before his death issued a treatise in which he emphasises the points of agreement between himself and the Mother Church.[1] When the Pilgrims landed at Plymouth in 1620 they did not establish a new congregation, but until Robinson's death in 1625 remained a branch of the parent church at Leyden ; afterwards for some time they seem to have become more strictly separatist ; at a later stage still they became more and more under the influence of the larger colony at Boston, composed of men with a less chequered religious development, and therefore unlikely to follow the extreme path of separation from the Church of England. The writings of John Cotton, John Higginson, and Governor Bradford are conclusive as to the attitude of the larger colony. They breathe a dutiful respect to the Church of England ; they are separated "from the world, not from the saints " ; " they were forced to make a local secession, not a separation." The seceders came to hold restricted views on toleration, and among their own churches went far on the way to Presbyterianism, but in their attitude towards actual separation they are at one with Henry Jacob, John Lathorp, and Henry Jessey. Visits of the New England divines to London brought a clearer knowledge and a closer understanding.[2] " The Independent Churches were born of Mr. Cotton and others in New England . . . . not only their Church-Covenant, but that forme of Ministry and Magistracy made up in one Church-State."[3] This is quite in keeping with Jacob's oath of allegiance, Bradshaw's exalted power of the " magistrate,' and with the wide latitude allowed the civil power in the " Apologeticall Narration " of the Five Dissenting Brethren.[4] Hence it was not only possible, but probable, that the Welsh Puritans organised in the ' New England way ' might have remained in ' gathered ' churches as collateral members of the Church of England, or at least in a Church of England

1 Burrage : The Early English Dissenters, pp. 290-293.
2 Burrage : The Early English Dissenters. Vol. I, Chapter XIV. " The Churches of New England until about 1641." [Authority for the main conclusions on this page.]
3 Erbery : Testimony, p. 327. [C.F.L. copy.]
4 Dale : Hist. of English Congregationalism, p. 283.

adjusted to the Presbyterian·model, with a new theory of 'jus divinum' in church-government, and with somewhat rigid views on the spread of sects. But all these possibilities were ruthlessly swept aside by the Laudian canons of 1640. Canon I sanctioned the Divine Right of Kings in the most express terms[1] ; Canon VI committed the whole kingdom to the Episcopal system by the 'et cætera' oath[2] ; Canon VII justified all the new ceremonies enjoined by Laud[3] ; Canon XVII enjoined all preachers "twice every year to preach for Conformity[4] ;" and Canon V compelled all to repair to their parish churches, to receive Holy Communion there, and put the "despisers and depravers" of the Book of Common Prayer under heavy penalties.[5] The impossibility of compromise and the vicissitudes of the war brought the men who gathered at Llanfaches to take refuge within the 'lines of communication,' where they witnessed the Parliament achieving the downfall of the hierarchy, and the Army 'purging' the Parliament because it attempted to mark out boundaries for the advance of religious liberty. The Puritan Revolution had no room for the "New England pattern," and a 'way' that had wrought the expulsion of Roger Williams from Salem was made impossible in Wales of the Propagation.

1 John Nalson : An Impartial Collection of the Great Affairs of State, Vol. I pp. 545-547.
2 Ibid., p. 554,
3 Ibid., p. 555.
4 Ibid., p. 560.
5 Ibid., p. 553.

III.

THE CIVIL WAR—REVOLUTION BY COMMITTEES.

The marriage of Henry VII doubly assured the loyalty of Wales to the English Crown ; the Act of Union and the Court of Great Sessions brought its people into contact with English law ; the fortunes of its landed gentry had been firmly founded at the expense of the Tudor Reformation ; the story of Elizabethan triumphs contains the names of many Welsh sailors and soldiers. The Stuarts entered into this heritage of loyalty. The important families, with a few notable exceptions, declared for the King at the beginning of the Civil War, and, notwithstanding the occasional defection of ' trimmers ' and the resentment felt towards the attitude of Royalist commanders of the Gerard school, did not relax their devotion up to the conclusion of the Anglesey articles in 1648. The speech of Sir Hugh Vaughan before Prince Charles at Raglan in 1642,[1] the distribution of soldiers' clothing among the tenantry of the Merioneth squire of Rhiwlas,[2] the inability of Rowland Vaughan of Caergai to rise above the hoary prejudices of his order,[3] and the invincible confidence of Sir John Owen of Clenennau at the battle of Llandegai,[4] are typical aspects of the spirit which animated the Cavaliers of Wales. And when the day of Roundhead reckoning came, their names are freely scattered over the Calendars of the Committee for Compounding.

The clergy, on their side, almost to a man, remained true to the Laudian canons of 1640. They would be delighted to read in their churches the proclamation of the King at Wellington declaring his loyalty to the law and his fidelity to the Protestant religion,[5] and the petition of the clergy of

1 Phillips : CivilpWar in Wales, Vol. II, Doc. VI, pp. 26-27.
2 Ibid., Vol. I, . 343.
3 Pregeth yn erbyn Schism . . . Cyfleith, R.V. Dedication to Evan Vaughan.
4 Narrative Together with Letters Presented by Captaine Taylor To the Honourable House of Commons Concerning the late Successe . . . in Carnarvanshire, pp. 5-7. (N.L.W.).
5 Phillips : Civil War in Wales, Vol. I, p. 109. Sept. 19, 1642.

North Wales (together with the gentry) disclosed their " perplexity and grief " at the mere rumour of a so-called reformation.[1] The means of Rees Prichard were freely spent " for the entertayning of the King's partie,"[2] and Rice Rudd, the Archdeacon of Carmarthen, had, as early as April 19th, 1643, been the subject of a discussion in Parliament on account of his delinquency.[3] There still exists in the vestry of Llansilin church a framed letter from Sir John Watts, the Royalist governor of Chirk Castle, to the vicar, Richard Jervis[4]; and in 1646 articles were exhibited against the vicar of Guilsfield for ' privately sending monies ' to the garrisons of Shrawardine and Chirk.[5] Jacob Wood of Llandevally in Brecon contented himself with praying for " the King's success in publick "[6]; Robert Morgan of Llanddyfnan with " high-swelling words and bitter language " helped to draw up the Anglesey declaration of July, 1648[7]; and about the same time William Nicholson of Llandilofawr " was doing much hurt in persuading the people for the King."[8] Two vicars in Breconshire and two rectors in Monmouthshire went so far as to take up arms for the King.[9] Many of the clergy fled to the Royalist castles for safety ; others joined the Royalist armies as chaplains. Capt. Byrch with a touch of rhetoric says that " *all* the honest and religious clergy of Wales were fled to Conway and other safe places "[10] before the landing of the Irish contingent at Mostyn in November, 1643. There were ' malignant ' clergy in Carnarvon Castle when it surrendered to Mytton in June, 1646,[11] and very probably there were some clergymen from Wales among the " ministers who had to march out without swords " at the surrender of Chester in February of the same year.[12]

1 The Humble Petition of the Gentry, *Clergie* of . . . the Sixe Shires of North Wales To the Honourable the Honourable (sic) the Knights . . in Parliament assembled. Presented this present March the 5th [1643]. (N.L.W.).
2 Canwyll y C mry (Rice Rees), p. 314. [Full text of letter to Dr. Olyver Lloyd, Advocat. (reypetition to Commissioners of Array.)]
3 Phillips : Civil War, Vol. I, pp. 164-165.
4 Thomas : Hist. of the Diocese of St. Asaph, Vol. VII, p. 22 (1912 Ed.).
5 Royalist Composition Papers, Vol. XXIV, p. 119 (First series).
6 Bodl. Walker MS., e. 7, fol. 213b.
7 Phillips : Civil War in Wales, Vol. II, Doc. CXVII, pp. 399-400.
8 Cal. Comm. Comp., Vol. III, pp. 1824-1826.
9 Bodl. Walker M.S. e. 7, fol. 213b and fol. 215 ; " A Particular Charge . . . in the name of his Excellency Sir Thomas Fairfax, and the Army under his command." (1647), makes a general accusation against the Welsh clergy of " leading their parishioners in arms . . . against the Parliament." But the tract is highly partisan in tone. (N.L.W.).
10 Phillips · Civil War, Vol. II, Doc. XXXVI, p. 114.
11 The Taking of Carnarven . . . [Title page.] N.L.W. Signed : S. R.
12 Phillips : Civil War in Wales, Vol. II, Doc. LXXXVIII, p. 294.

Robert Frampton, rector of Bryngwyn, is included among the list of prisoners at Raglan,[1] and " Dr. Lloyd and severall other malignant ministers " fell into the hands of Horton at the battle of St. Fagans (May, 1648)[2]. Archbishop Williams committed almost all the sins of a ' delinquent ' by leaving his province of York, aiding the Commissioners of Array in North Wales, fortifying Conway Castle at his own expense, and entering into protracted negotiations with Ormonde.[3] And the fifty ejected clergy who petitioned the House of Lords in 1660 for seizing the revenues of their old livings declare without exception that their harsh treatment was due to their " affection and loyalty to His Majesty of blessed memory."[4] The loyalty of the clergy would not be lessened by the ordinance of Parliament against " pictures, crucifixes and altars,"[5] the suppression of the Common Prayer Book,[6] the desecration of churches by the exigencies of war, and occasionally, their own rough usage at the hands of the Puritan soldiers. *E.g.*, Philip Williams of Robeston in Pembrokeshire was " imprisoned at Land " and was " taken a prisoner on shipboard eight weeks the first time and three weeks the second time " by the Parliament ships which cruised in Milford Haven[7]; Edward Evans, the newly-admitted ' parson ' of Llanllwchaiarn in Montgomery could not " quietly yet repaire to read there the Articles of 1562 for fear of the enemies"[8]; the epitaph of John Hughes of Hirnant in the same county keeps in memory that he also was " surrounded by a fanatical mob and malevolently thrown into prison "[9]; and Archbishop Ussher was stripped of his books and papers when on his way to St. Donats in 1645.[10] Few indeed were the clergy in Wales who would imitate the Master of Jesus‧ and prove their affection to Parliament " by praying for them in the Welsh and English

1 A Letter from his Excellencies Quarters [containing account of the Surrender of Raglan, dated Aug. 21, 1646. List of *Prisoners*, pp. 4-6. (N.L.W.)]
2 Letter from Horton to the Earl of Manchester, p. 8 (really 6). Dated 8th May, 1648; but in a further latter sent from *Bridge-end* on the 13th, *no mention* of the Ministers is made. (N.L.W.).
3 D.N.B., Vol. lxi, p. 419.
4 House of Lords MSS., 1660, Petitions for restitution of livings.
5 C. J. III, 220. 28th Aug., 1643.
6 C. J. IV, 70. 5th March, 1644-1645; C.J. IV, 251. 23rd Aug., 1645. Ordinances for the " Directory."
7 Lamb. 1027. No. 49.
8 Thomas : Hist. of the Diocese of St. Asaph, pp. 202-203.
9 Ibid., p. 739, note 2.
10 D.N.B., Vol. lviii, p. 69.

D

languages."[1] It was quite as inevitable that during the first years of the war Wales was not a pleasant land for the Puritan ministers of the eastern border. Wroth had died before the war began, and Powell, finding life impossible in Radnor, reaches London in August, 1642.[2] Most of the members of the church at Llanfaches fled to Bristol.[3] Erbery claims the honour of being the " first plundered minister in Wales."[4] Llwyd in a song " sung in 1643 " refers to the " desolation of the Welsh Saincts." Some were in hiding, others in prison ; to him all was steeped in darkness ; the vain and arrogant boasts of the disaffected filled the hearts of the leaderless Puritans with dismay.[5] Until the capture of Montgomery and Red Castle in 1644 " honest and godly men in those districts were utterly undone."[6] On June 19th, 1647, the Committee of Monmouth report to the Speaker that " our godly ministers are threatened with destruction."[7] Poyer, the quondam captain of the " godly garrison " of Pembroke town, is charged in 1648 with beating two orthodox ministers so that one of them was sick of his ' brusies ' for about ' halfe a yeare.'[8] The attitude of the clergy was undoubtedly very much that of John Clegg, rector of Llangibby, who sent the soldiers in pursuit of " godly people,"[9] and of Thomas Cecil, rector of Llanbedr Patrisho, who was charged with firing beacons to raise the country against Sir William Waller.[10]

The uncompromising Royalism of the great majority of the clergy and the plight of persecuted Puritans who had fled from the enemy's quarters became a matter of serious concern to the Parliament. Significant steps had been taken before the war broke out. The Long Parliament met in November, 1640, and on the 6th of that month they appointed a Grand Committee of Religion,[11] and this Committee subsequently appointed a Sub-Committee " to consider and

1 Calendar of the Committee for the Advance of Money, Vol. II, pp. 1066-1067.
2 Life of Vavasor Powell—own account of " Conversion and Ministry " prefixed, p. 11.
3 The Broadmead Records (ed. Haycroft), p. 25.
4 Testimony, p. 313.
5 Gweithiau, Vol. I, Song I, Stanzas 1, 3, 4, 9, 15.
6 Phillips : Civil War in Wales, Vol. II, Doc. LXV, pp. 219-221.
7 Ibid., Vol. II, Doc. XCIXB, pp. 341-2.
8 A Declaration of Divers Gentlemen of Wales concerning Collonell Poyer, p. 5. April 19, 1648] (N.L.W.).
9 Bodl. Walker MS. e. 7, folio 214.
10 Old Wales (ed. W. R. Williams), Vol. I, No. 3, p. 70 (1905).
11 Commons Journals, Vol. II, 21.

inquire the true Grounds and Causes of the great scarcity
of preaching ministers through the whole kingdom, to consider of some way of removing Scandalous ministers and
putting others in their Places " ; further, " that all the
Knights and Burgesses of every county [were] to inform
the House concerning the State and Condition of their
Counties concerning Preaching Ministers." Sir Robert
Harley of Brampton Bryan[1] was a member of this Committee, and (according to the wording) all the Knights and
Burgesses of *Wales* were included.[2] Cradock and others
were authorised to preach in Wales[3] ; there was some
unspecified obstruction[4] ; and the petition for redress to
the Parliament was referred to the above Committee, now
known as the *" Committee for Scandalous Ministers."* The
parties complained of were summoned to appear before it.[5]
One result of the Committee's investigations led to an order
of the Commons that it should be lawful for the parishioners
of any parish in the kingdom of England and dominion of
Wales " to set up a lecture, and to maintain an orthodox
minister at their own charge, to preach every Lord's Day
where there is no preaching, and to preach one day in every
week when there is no weekly lecture."[6] There is one record
referring to Wales : Ambrose Mostyn was on 19th April,
1642, appointed Lecturer at Pennard in Glamorgan.[7]
Attention was next given to the " plundered ministers "
who had fled to London at the outbreak of the war.[8] On
the 27th of December, 1642, the Commons ordered a
collection to be made in all the parishes in and about London
for their relief,[9] and four days later it appointed a Committee " to consider the fittest way for the relief of such
good and well-affected ministers as had been plundered."[10]
This was the origin of the important *" Committee for Plundered
Ministers."*[11] At first its duties were restricted to the work

1 Supra, p. 26.
2 C. J. II, 54, 12th Dec., 1640 (" Die Sabbati ").
3 C. J. II, 189. [Words describing the petition of Cradock.]
4 It is just possible that Jenkin Richards of Blaenau Gwent was referring to this
opposition of 1641 in gloating over the ' immersing ' and ' injuring ' done to Cradock
in Glamorgan. (Llanover MS. C 4, f. 281, vv. 7, 8).
5 C. J. II, 189. 26th June, 1641. No further reference to the matter in the
records.
6 C. J. II, 281-283. 8th Sept., 1641.
7 C. J. II, 551.
8 Supra, p. 34.
9 C. J. II, 899.
10 C. J. II, 909.
11 " The Committee for Plundering Ministers " (Walker : Sufferings. I, p. 73).

of relief, but it gradually gathered to itself the powers once exercised by the Committee for Scandalous Ministers, and very soon the area of its activities embraced the whole country. The procedure adopted was as follows. The *Committees of Parliament* for the various counties had to examine witnesses against scandalous or delinquent ministers, and forward the proofs to the C.P.M.[1] To them also fell the duty to forward petitions from parishes for the appointment of a ' preaching minister,' as in the case of Ystrad and Dihewid in Cardiganshire[2] ; to acquaint the Committee of livings void by death, as in the case of Llansantffraid in Denbighshire[3] and Pwllycrochan in Pembrokeshire,[4] of the particular patron of the living sequestered, of the number of communicants in the parishes concerned, and also, though the records are silent on the point, of the names of suitable candidates to minister in the sequestered livings. These had to be ' referred ' to the Assembly of Divines for examination.[5] When their approbation was forthcoming to the effect that the suggested nominee was ' godly and orthodox ' and ' painful ' in his preaching, the C.P.M. decide that he is ' to officiate the said cure ' and ' preach diligentlie ' to the parishioners, adding that all who obstruct his entry do so at their peril and have to answer for such conduct before the Committee.[6] Then the whole case was submitted for the approval of Parliament ; but very soon this does not become a matter even of form, and the Committee enjoyed almost complete autonomy of jurisdiction. Armed with his certificate or order, signed by the Chairman (usually Harbottle Grimston) the approved minister proceeded " to the country," deposited a copy of the order with the Committee of the County,[7] entered upon his cure, and the ' sequestrators of the premises ' are to pay to him the specified profits " at such times and seasons of the year as they become due and payable."[8] After all taxes and due charges were deducted, he was to allow the " fifth " part of the revenues of the

---

1 C. J. III, 231. 6th Sept., 1643. C.P.M.=" Committee for Plundered Ministers."
2 Bodl. MS. 325. fol. 46.
3 Addit. MS. 15671, f. 50a.
4 Bodl. MS. 324, fol. 27b.
5 C. J, III, 270 : Lords Journals V, 138.
6 E.g. Order re Bangor Monachorum, Addit. MS. 15670, fol. 133.
7 E.g., Certificate of ' preaching minister ' of *Swansea* (Lamb. 905, fol. 1).
8 Based on oft-quoted order of Commons, May 2, 1646. Bodl. MS. 323, *opening pages*—" General Orders."

sequestered living to the wife and children (if any) of the previous incumbent, according to the rate laid down by the supplementary ordinance for sequestrations in 1643.[1] The C.P.M. had no funded income of its own. In the case of a living being sequestered on account of the incumbent leaving his cure to follow the King, or of indirectly assisting the King's interest, or of saying anything against the Parliamentary cause, or by the working of the ordinance against plurality of benefice,[2] or by process of the various ordinances of sequestration[3] (where the clergy were subject to the regulations against delinquents in general), or by being guilty of scandal in his private life, the Committee had simply the duty of seeing that its Puritan nominee got the revenues of the ejected Royalist clerk. *E.g.*, the vicarage of Llanfair Dyffryn Clwyd stands " sequestered from Dr. David Lloyd to the use of Richard Edwards,"[4] the rectory of Bangor-on-Dee from Henry Bridgeman to Robert Fogg,[5] the donative of Llanrhaiadr-ym-Mochnant, " lately belonging to the Bishop of Bangor " to Evan Roberts[6] ; similarly the rectory of Llanfihangel Ysceifiog to William Lloyd, sequestered from Dr. Griffith Williams for plurality.[7] Again, on February 14th, 1645-6, the House of Commons had passed an order that the interest and estates in all advowsons and rights of patronage to any churches belonging to lay delinquents should, upon their composition, be reserved to the disposal of Parliament, and that the Committee at Goldsmith's Hall were to except the same[8] ; later, the disposal of these impropriate interests was to be the subject of an understanding between the C.G.H. and the C.P.M.[9] ; and that the latter were fully alive to the danger of delinquents compounding for their *whole* estates notwithstanding the above order of the Commons is illustrated by their letter of the 12th August,

1 C. J. III, 169 ; L. J. VI, 133, 182, 17th August, 1643.
2 L. J. V, 558. 16th Jan., 1642-3.
3 Esp. Firth and Rait : Acts and Ordinances I, 106-116 ; 255-258.
4 Bodl. 324, fol 118.
5 Addit. MS. 15670, fol. 133.
6 Addit. MS. 15671, fol 68.
7 Bodl. 324, fol. 247.
8 C. J. V, 442.
9 C. J. V, 5.
   C.G.H. = Committee at Goldsmiths' Hall.
        = Lords and Commons' Committee (Central) for Sequestrations.
        = Called Committee for Compounding after ' compounding ' principles allowed

1646, to the allied Committee.[1] A typical result was that
the delinquent John Carey had to pay £40 a year out of his
impropriate rectory of Llanarth for increase of the minister's
maintenance there[2]; £40 out of his impropriate rectory
of Llanddewibrefi for increasing the maintenance of Rees
Meredith[3]; and £40 out of the impropriate rectories of
Llanboidy and Trelech for increasing the maintenance of
Lewis Davies of Mydrim.[4] Next, by the ordinance of
31st March, 1643, "for sequestration of several delinquents'
estates," all the possessions of bishops and capitular clergy
who were actively hostile to the Parliament were confiscated[5];
their private estates fell into the hands of the County Committees for Sequestrations, and their impropriate interests
were disposed of as seen fit by the C.G.H. and C.P.M. working
in conjunction. The earliest order of the C.P.M. relating
to Wales reports the sequestration of the impropriate rectory
of Mydrim from Archdeacon Rudd to supply £52 as maintenance for Richard Jewell at Tenby,[6] and on February 11th,
1645-6, £50 was ordered out of " the revenues of the Collegiate
Church of Brecknock, parcell of the possessions of the
Cathedrall Church of St. David's " for increasing the maintenance of the minister of Cardigan.[7] The profits of the
rectory of Amlwch (£60), " belonging to the late Bishop
of Bangor," were granted as an augmentation to the
incumbent of St. Mary's at Beaumaris.[8] The records contain
a considerable number of similar orders. Later, when the
revenues of the impropriate interests belonging to both
Bishops and Chapters throughout the country were taken
out of the jurisdiction of local and central Committees of
Sequestrations and vested in Treasurers appointed under
the Ordinances of 9th October, 1646,[9] and 30th April, 1649,[10]
the C.P.M. had only to issue orders to the aforesaid Treasurers
to pay the sums settled as salaries or augmentations to
approved ministers in pursuance of its previous instructions.

1 Bodl. MS. 323. *General* Orders prefixed.
2 Bodl. MS. 323, fol. 49 ; State Papers, Dom. Interreg. F1. 257 (Nov. 26th, 1646).
3 Bodl. MS. 325, fol. 46. Oct. 14th, 1647.
4 Bodl. MS. 326, fol. 46. May 28th, 1649.
5 Scobell : Ordinances, Vol. I, p. 97.
6 Bodl. 327, fol. 187 [order of July 10, 1650, *based* on previous order of 10th *May*,
1644 ; no record in MSS. of the latter specifically] ; Lamb. 979, fol. 315.
7 Bodl. 322, fol. 70.
8 Bodl. 325, fol. 1.
9 L. J. VIII. 513, 517 ; Ordinance in full—Scobell : Ordinances I, 99.
10 Scobell : Ordinances, Vol. II, 16

Bodl. MS. 327 contains a long series of such orders; either to the Treasurers of 'Bishops' Landes' as in the case of Lawhadden (fol. 185), or to those of 'Dean and Chapters Landes' as in the case of Llangoedmor (fol. 366). For some unascertained reason the Commons in April, 1650, delegated some of the Committee's most important duties to the Committee for the Reformation of the Universities.[1] Its power of appointment to sequestered livings still remained, and six weeks before the above date it had been constituted a court of appeal from the proceedings of the Commissioners appointed under the Act of Propagation in Wales.[2]

A fair proportion of the Committee's orders were increases of maintenance granted to vicars[3] settled in parish churches under the old order; not, however, before the Committee had assured itself of their 'abilities and deserts' by the evidence of responsible adherents of the Parliament,[4] and not before the Assembly had appointed a special Committee to deal with the cases of ministers who came out of 'enemies quarters.'[5] Such were Robert Sparks of Llanynys,[6] Archibald Sparkes of Northop,[7] Evan Ellis of Pennant,[8] William Prichard of Manorbier,[9] John Brigdale of Llannefydd,[10] David Roberts of Llandinam,[11] and Simon Swayne of Machynlleth.[12] Some of these had been instituted even after the official sequestration of the Bishops in 1643. The greater number, as a matter of course, were new men nominated by the Committee. Such, for example, were Robert Tounson at Narberth,[13] Edward Bold at Hawarden,[14] and

1 Scobell: Ordinances, Vol. II, 111-116.
2 p. 84. "Text of the Act."
3 There occur peculiar and isolated payments recorded in the Commonwealth Exchequer Paper 251—money paid out of the revenue of Royal Family lands to one or two vicars and *curates* of churches in Pembrokeshire. (No date). (Report of the Auditors of the Committee of the Revenue, according to the Ordinance of 21st Sept., 1643: Firth and Rait: Acts and Ordinances, Vol. I, pp. 299-303).
4 Bodl. 323. General Orders, 16th August, 1646. It was Richard Price, later a Commissioner under the Propagation Act, who procured an order in 1648 from the Committee to pay Mostyn and Powell £100 each for certain services (Examen et Purgamen, p. 12).
5 Mitchell and Struthers: Minutes of the Westminster Assembly, p. 334. (Session 802, March 3, 1646).
6 Lib. Inst. Bangor, fol. 4. Instituted 15th Dec., 1623.
7 ,, ,, Assaphe, ,, 141 ,, 4th July, 1639.
8 ,, ,, Ibid., ,, 163. ,, 5th June, 1644.
9 ,, ,, Meneuen ,, 5. ,, 28th May, 1631.
10 ,, ,, Assaphe, ,, 149. ,, 9th May, 1643.
11 ,, ,, Bangor, ,, 6. ,, 7th Jan., 1622.
12 ,, ,, Assaphe, ,, 173. ,, 20th Feb., 1644.
13 Bodl. 324, fol. 52b.
14 Addit. MS. 15670, fol. 162a—"referred to Assembly"; Thomas: Hist. of the Diocese of St. Asaph, p. 587—"buried at Hawarden, 5th Jan., 1655."

Charles Price at Glascwm in Radnor.[1]   In certain circumstances the Committee saw well to vary the order.   Evan
Roberts was to ' preach diligentlie ' not only to the ' 4,000
soules ' of Llanbadarnfawr but to the " adjacent places "
as well, for which he was to get £100 a year.[2]   Ambrose
Mostyn was not so fortunate ; for £50 " he was required
to preach and officiate as well in yᵉ parish church of Swansey
as in yᵉ parishes and places thereto adjacent."[3]   David
Walter for the same sum per annum was to " preach, catechise,
and instruct in severall Churches and Chapples within the
county of Glamorgan the severall parishioners and inhabitants within the severall Towens and parishes in the said
County."[4]   In *June*, 1644,[5] the Commons had appointed
a Committee to provide some ministers able to preach *in
Welsh* and send them to Sir Thomas Middleton during his
victorious career in the Severn Valley.   On June 7th, 1648,
the C.P.M. order £120 to be paid to Morgan Llwyd and
£100 each to Vavasor Powell and Ambrose Mostyn for their
services in the interim, referring to the great success their
ministry " have had and is like to have " and to the dis-
couragement they are " like to meete withall for want of
maintenance."   The order winds up, though obscurely
worded, to the effect that they were to enjoy the aforesaid
sums *per annum* ' for and during such times ' as they continued to preach diligently to the people of *North Wales.*[6]
Generally the Committee made generous provision for the
' approved ' ministers.   *E.g.*, John Brigdale's maintenance
at Llannefydd in 1649 amounted to £122 a year—£40 formerly
as vicar, £32 increase from the sequestered prebend of Llannefydd, and a further augmentation of £50 out of the tithes
and profits of the same not in lease[7] ; Dr. John Ellis of

---

1 Addit. MS. 15671, fol. 219 ; Lamb. 905, fol. 63.
2 Bodl. 323, fol. 49.
3 „   Ibid. „ 114.
4 „   Ibid. „ 114.
5 C. J. III, 565 : " July " ; the Journals and the Bodl. MS. 325, f. 68, are at
variance on the particular *month.*
  6 Bodl. MS. 325, fol. 68.   There is no evidence that either of the three proceeded
to North Wales in 1644, but Llwyd was evidently with the Parliamentary garrison
at *Montgomery* when it was relieved by Sir Thos. Myddelton on Sept. 18th, 1645.
(Gweithiau, Vol. I, xxvii, stanza 5, line 2, p. 57 ; Phillips : Civil War, Vol. I,
pp. 247-250.) Mr. J. H. Davies places the return of Llwyd from his exile in England
either in 1646 or 1647 (Gweithiau : Vol. II, Introd. xxx, xxxviii) ; Powell distinctly
states he spent four years and a half in and about London from 1642 (Life, p. 14) ;
and Mostyn was appointed to preach at *Swansea*, July 27th, 1646 (Bodl. 323, fol. 114).
These facts explain to a great extent the Committee's seeming niggardliness.
  7 Bodl. 326, fol. 72b.

Dolgelly £120, made up of £40, the reserved rent due from the rectory of Towyn to the Bishop of Coventry and Lichfield,[1] and £80 from the prebend of Vaenol[2]; and Robert Brabourne, vicar of Monmouth, £139 6s. 8d., viz., £23 6s. 8d. formerly as vicar,[3] £50 grant out of the impropriate rectory of Monmouth,[3] and a £66 "yearly exhibition from the Society of Haberdashers Hall for preaching a weekly lecture in the said Church."[4]

But, notwithstanding occasional vagaries in their virtue of generosity, the C.P.M. performed its duties with great thoroughness and efficiency. It brooked no evasion of the payment of fifths: Robert Tounson's quibble in the case of Narberth was sternly brushed aside,[5] and the Committee of the County of Denbigh were to see "the full cleere fifth parte" paid to the wife of Samuel Lloyd of Gresford.[6] No dereliction of duty was suffered in the case of the sequestrators of the various 'premises.' The Committee of the County of *Salop* were to examine whether Richard Price had carried out the orders of the Committee concerning the living of Hissington[7]; Howell Gwyn was enjoined to pay punctually the arrears of the augmentation granted to the ministers of Cardigan[8]; and after protracted inquiries Matthew Williams of Llangattock received his arrears of £75 from Thomas Lewis.[9] And the sequestrators of the prebend of Clydey were called to give a strict account of the moneys in their hands.[10] The molestation of Sir Richard Wynn, 'farmer of the Rectory and Prebend' of Llanfair D.C., was to cease, and those who had "seised on parte of the goods and personall estate" of Wynn had to restore them,[11] since in certain circumstances it was not the policy of the Committee to disturb existing interests; on the other hand, a certain Robert Lloyd who had thrust himself into

---

1 Lamb. 989, folios 190-191.
2 Bodl. 325, fol. 166. These grants to Ellis were in addition to the profits of the rectory of Dolgelly, which were *near* £100 per annum (Lamb. 904, f. 124).
3 Bodl. 323, fol. 200; State Papers, Dom. Interreg. F1, f. 128.
4 Bodl. 326, fol. 206. The Committee of the County had 'denyed' the £50 because of the 'exhibition' he enjoyed; the C.P.M. order the full payment.
5 Bodl. 324, fol. 208b.
6 Bodl. 324, fol. 72b.
7 Bodl. 326, fol. 210.
8 Bodl. 326, fols. 42, 252b; 325, fols. 46, 49.
9 Bodl. 326, fol. 18, 18b; 327, 12-13b, 62, 63; Bodl. 327, 63—actual acquittance under the hand of his aug Anne.
10 Bodl. 325, fol. 46b. hter
11 Bodl. 325, fols. 68b, 69

the rectory of Pwllycrochan was summoned to appear
before the Committee.[1] To act equitably in certain cases
the Committee did not hesitate to summon to its aid such
persons as possessed the most complete information concerning the same, or could carry out its orders most effectively.
E.g., the members of Parliament for the County of Radnor
had to take measures for ' gathering ' an augmentation for
the ' Chappelries ' of Llanhir and Rhayader[2]; the claims of
an ' alleadged ' minister at Haverfordwest were delegated
to the consideration of Major-General Harrison[3]; the
respective petitions of the inhabitants of Dihewid and Ystrad
in Cardiganshire were referred to the two ' next ' Justices
of the Peace " to examine the truth thereof "[4]; and on
account of the disaffection of Anglesey in 1648 the duty of
collecting the profits of the rectory of Amlwch for an
augmentation to Dr. Rowland Chedle of Beaumaris was
allotted to the Deputy-Governor of Beaumaris Castle and
the " garrison Captain of the Fort of Holyhead."[5] And as
the scope of the Committee's operations grew wider, it had
perforce to delegate some of its own inherent duties to local
interests. The petition of ' Mistris Lloyd ' of Gresford was
to be examined by the Committee of Denbigh[6]; the articles
exhibited against John Luton of Llandrillo-yn-Rhos were
referred to the same body[7]; and those against Matthew
Evans of Penegoes, Rees Price of Llanllwchaiarn, and
Dr. Coote of Montgomery were all referred to the Committee
of Parliament for Montgomeryshire.[8] But at best the Committee's work was often handicapped by insufficient, and
sometimes false, information. They complain of the late-
ness of the information concerning the death of Humphrey
Smart, the rector of Pwllycrochan in Pembrokeshire, which
led to the living being " neglected and unprovided for
eighteen months."[9] They display a lack of faith in the

1 Bodl. 324, fol. 103b. The Committee in such cases could apply the Act, passed
on Aug. 23, 1647, " for assuring their livings to the intruded Parliamentary clergy."
L. J. IX, 399-400 ; Scobell : Ordinances, I, 131.
2 Bodl. 325, fol. 202.
3 Bodl. 327, fol. 186b.
4 Bodl. 325, fols. 46, 46b.
5 Bodl. 325, fol. 1.
6 Bodl. 324, fol. 72b.
7 Bodl. 324, fol. 117. ' *Luston* ' in Lib. Inst., Assaphe, fol. 148.
8 Evans, Addit. MS. 15670, 45a ; Price, Addit. MS. 15671, 88 ; Coote, Addit. MS.
15671, 124. Dr. Coote died in 1647, or very shortly after—" died ten yeare ago "
(Exchequer First Fruits Report, *7th Feb.*, 1657-8—Montgomery).
9 Bodl. 324, fol. 30b.

Committee of Carmarthen, and ask ' Mr. Harbert and Coll. Jones ' to inform themselves concerning the petition of Lewis Davies of Mydrim[1]; and the Committee's stern order of 31st August, 1646,[2] in the matter of Lord Henry Percy's impropriate rectories in the Llanelly district had to be considerably toned down on September 11th because of ' consideration had of the right of the Earl of Northumberland ' in the same.[3] Comparatively unimportant were the discoveries of the Committee that Lord Charles Somerset was not a delinquent only, but a recusant in addition,[4] and that John Vaughan farmed the profits of Lledrod under the ' Colledge of Brecon ' and not under the Dean and Chapter of Hereford[5]; of greater consequence was the ignorance concerning the ancient disposal of the rectory of Aberdaron to the Master of St. John's College, Cambridge, for it led to the revocation of the Committee's grant of £40 to a certain John Jones.[6] In another direction, the provision of divine services in the language best understood of the people, the Committee, probably unconsciously, adopt Penry's suggestion in 1587.[7] Evan Roberts had to preach *both in English and Welsh* to the parishioners of Llanbadarn,[8] and the minister at Abergavenny received an augmentation of £50 per annum because he had *to preach to the Welsh at St. Mary's* as well as in English at St. John's.[9] They were equally alive with the feofees of the lecture system to the importance of having preaching ministers in market towns, as witness their augmentation of £50 to the minister of Grosmont.[10] They were aware, also, of the disadvantage of having aged and infirm clergy in large parishes : they make special provision for a coadjutor to Richard Pigott at Llanwrin in Montgomeryshire.[11] One problem, however, remained, which was to hamper the action of the C.P.M. throughout its whole career ; the *unexpired* leases of prebends and sinecure ' rectories guaranteed by due forms

1 Bodl. 326, fol. 46. [(Henry) Herbert of Coldbrook, and Col. (Philip) Jones.]
2 Bodl. 323, fol. 53.
3 Bodl. ibid., fol. 53b.
4 Bodl. 326, fol. 206.
5 Bodl. 325, fol. 47.
6 Bodl. 325, fol. 53.
7 Treatise, p. 51.
8 Bodl. 323, fol. 49.
9 Bodl. 325, fol. 168b.
10 Bodl. 326, fol. 206.
11 Bodl. 324, fol. 153. " 80 years of age.".

of law. The emoluments of John Brigdale at Llannefydd would be even greater if all the interests of that prebend were *out* of lease,[1] and the grant of the sinecure rectory of Pennant to Evan Ellis could only be efficacious at the ' expiracion ' of the existing arrangements.[2]

The efficiency of the Committee had its counterpart in the devotion of the Divines. Their approbation was not easily obtained. Such certificate was made essential to the proposed nominee on 9th October, 1643,[3] and on 4th October, 1644, an ordinance was passed appointing rules for the guidance of the Assembly in the examination of candidates.[5] They must bring a testimonial of having taken the Covenant, of diligency and proficiency in their studies, of their stay at the University, and what degree they have taken there, of their age (which had to be twenty-four at the very least), and especially of their life and conversation. The Committee of the Assembly appointed to ordain were to examine the candidate's skill in the ' Originall Tongues ' by asking him to read portions of the Hebrew and Greek Testaments, and render them into Latin ; his skill in Logic and Philosophy was also to be tested. They were to ascertain the authors in Divinity he had read, his knowledge in the ' cheife grounds ' of religion, his ability to defend the orthodox doctrine against all unsound and erroneous opinions,[5] his skill both in explaining the sense and meaning of such places of Scripture as shall be proposed unto him and in analysing ' cases of Conscience '; last of all, his knowledge of the ' Chrologie '[6] of Scripture and of Ecclesiastical History. The candidate was also ' in a competent time ' to frame a discourse in Latin upon ' such a commonplace, or controversie in Divinity ' as shall be assigned him and ' exhibit such Theses as expresse the summe thereof, and maintaine a Dispute upon them.' Persons formerly ordained in the Church of England were to bring a testimonial of their ordination and to be afterwards tested by actual preaching ; if necessary, they were subjected to examination according to the above rules. All recommendations made by the Assembly were to be recorded

1 Bodl. 326, fol. 72b.
2 Bodl. 324, fol. 189b.
3 C. J. III, 270.
4 Firth and Rait : Acts and Ordinances of the Interregrum, Vol. I, pp. 521 525.
5 " Especially those of the present age." Ibid., p. 523.
6 Chronology.

in a special Register.[1] Finally, all ministers in all benefices in England and Wales were to conduct the services in the manner specified in the ordinance passed 5th March, 1645.[2] The rules laid down for the guidance of the Assembly marks the advance of the Puritan revolution on the intellectual side in the hands of the moderates. The standard of learning postulated by the XXXIVth Canon of 1604 is considerably raised ; greater emphasis is laid upon knowledge of the Scriptures and theological learning generally ; approved ministers must be actually able to preach. The mediæval practice of disputations at the Universities has a spell too potent to be broken off, and the reference to ' erroneous opinions ' bespeaks a fear of complete toleration. Further, both Parliament and its advisory Divines were convinced that England could not be made Puritan in a day ; they attempt to dovetail into the new system all episcopally ordained clergy who are competent and well-affected.[3] Some were " excused from coming up " and many were approved upon their " former examination." The Assembly applied the rules very strictly. They find some candidates of ' great insufficiency,'[4] some are asked " to bring a better testimonial,"[5] some are respited for a further examination,[6] and in one case they have to ask the C.P.M. to consider of the appointment given him lately by the Assembly, they since having heard so ill of him.[7] William East, the Committee's nominee for the rectory of Begelly in Pembrokeshire, was found " not competently qualified for the undertaking of a pastorall charge,"[8] and John Henley, referred to the Assembly by the C.P.M., is found unfit to officiate the cure of Diserth in Radnor on account of his inability to preach in *Welsh*, with the further result that the Assembly are asked to judge between the claims of John Perrott and John Phillips as to which is the fittest to take his place.[9] One ground for

---

1 This invaluable ' Register ' appears to have perished.
2 C. J. IV, 70 ; ' on March 4, 1644-5, the Assembly appointed a Committee " to think of fit men to be employed in the translating of the Directory into Welsh "— however, there is no further reference to the subject in the Minutes. (Session 391. Mitchell and Struthers : Minutes . . . p. 67).
3 For necessity of approved testimony, vide supra, p. 39 ; also Minutes, pp. 339, 499.
4 Minutes, p. 183.
5 Ibid., p. 317.
6 Ibid., p. 332.
7 Minutes, p. 911.
8 Addit. MS. 15670, 32a ; Minutes, Sess. 839, p. 363.
9 Addit. MS. 15671, fol. 89.

granting a certificate to Vavasor Powell was his " having the Language of his own Countrey of Wales."[1] And there is evidence that a special Committee was appointed by the Assembly " to consider of the ministers for Wales."[2] But notwithstanding all its Committees, anomalies existed which the commotions of the times made inevitable. Cradock, Walter, and Symonds, in pursuance of the ordinance of July, 1646,[3] proceeded to Wales *without* a certificate, which evoked a strong protest from the Assembly.[4] The Lords, however, refused to take any action.[5] Charles Price had officiated at Glascwm for, seven months before his case was referred to the Assembly,[6] and Robert Tounson supplied the vacancy at Pwllycrochan between the death of the old rector and the appointment of William Young without any sanction from the Divines.[7] Further, the gradual undermining of the power of a moderate Parliament after the conclusion of the Second Civil War in 1648 affected also the authority of the Assembly. It was sufficient that the ministers appointed to Abergavenny, Chepstow, Grosmont, Mynyddislwyn, and Newport that they should receive the approval of the Committee of Parliament for the county.[8]

Reference has already been made to the examination of delinquent clergy by the Committees of Parliament for the various counties, and the duties assigned to the same by the C.P.M. in its later stages. There were also two ordinances of Parliament passed to enable the Parliamentary Committees generally in all the counties to sequester the livings of scandalous ministers *and put religious and learned men in their places.*[9] These powers were included in the Ordinance of 5th February, 1643-4,[10] and that of February, 1644-5[11], by which Sir Thomas Middleton was to exercise plenary powers in the six counties of North Wales ; also in the Ordinance of 10th June, 1644, for the ' associating '

---

1 Life, p. 16. Christopher Love endorsed the certificate (among others), Sept. 11, 1646 ; Animadversions re Newchapel Conference, p. 22.
2 Minutes, Session 918, Sept. 17, 1647, p. 479.
3 Vide infra, p. 61.
4 Minutes, Session 689, p. 267.
5 Minutes, Session 690, pp. 268, 301.
6 Bodl. 325, fol. 202 ; Addit. MS. 15671, fol. 204.
7 Addit. MS. 15669, 167a ; Bodl. 324, fol. 30b.
8 Bodl. 325, fols. 168, 168b ; 326, fol. 206—1648-1649.
9 C. J. Vol. III, 153, 3rd July, 1643 ; C.J., Vol. III, 231, 6th Sept., 1643.
10 Firth and Rait : Acts and Ordinances of the Interregrum, Vol. I, 378-381.
11 An Additionall Ordinance of the Lords and Commons in Parliament . . .
Printed Feb. 21, 1644-5. (N.L.W.).

of the counties of Cardigan, Carmarthen, and Pembroke.[1] As a resultant of these general and particular ordinances we find Morgan ap Morgan, 'a curate,' placed at Meliden' by the Committee of Flint[2] ; the prebend of Meifod was ' passed ' by the Committee of Denbigh from Richard Evans into the hands of ' one Hugh Jones '[3]; while the " Committee of that Association " ordered and disposed the profits of the impropriate rectory of Lamphey to " one Mr. Mountfort, an honest able minister that came out of Ireland."[4] The *actual sequestration* of delinquents and pluralists seems to have been the duty of the County Committees, but the right of appointing to the vacant cures was gradually absorbed by the C.P.M. The latter felt it necessary in some cases to reverse the order of the County bodies.[5] On the other hand, the " setting, letting, and gathering " of the profits of the sequestered livings fell to the lot of the County Com- mittees *for Sequestrations*, according to the rules laid down by the Central Committee for Sequestrations and its successor, the Committee for Compounding.[6] It was their duty to appoint the sequestrators for each individual living. That these Committees held the aforesaid profits in their posses- sion is further illustrated by the letter of John Hughes from Carmarthen[7] and the answer of the new *Commissioners* for Sequestrations to John Peck and Thomas Crachley in August, 1654.[8] On December 23rd, 1648, the Committee for Sequestrations " sitting at Denbigh " granted John Holland the tithes and profits of the sinecure of Bettws for an augmentation to his living of St. George's,[9] and in 1647 the same Committee had allowed to William Jones of Denbigh the tithes and profits of the sinecure rectory amounting to £100 a year.[10] Both these orders trespassed upon the recognised functions of the C.P.M. ; indeed, the

1 Firth and Rait : Acts and Ordinances, Vol. I, pp. 443-447 ; An Ordinance of the Lords and Commons. . . . 8th Junii, 1644. (N.L.W.).
2 Lamb. 902, fol. 28. (No *date* of order given).
3 Lamb. 1027. Report of Constables of 1662 re Richard Evans of Llanasaph.
4 Lamb 905, fol. 6.
5 E.g., in the case of Lamphey ; in May, 1649, they grant the profits of the rectory to Thomas Feild, Minister of Lawhadden. (Bodl. 326, fol. 252.)
6 Except in the cases of rectories, tithes, etc., belonging to the *Bishops* and Chapters, which after 1646 (Bishops) and 1649 (Deans and Chapters) fell into the hands of *Special Treasurers*, supra, pp. 38-39.
7 Cal. Comm. Comp., Vol. I, pp. 391-2. " General Proceedings."
8 Ibid., Vol. I, p. 697. Do. (explaining that the profits of Seqd. livings on the expiry of the Act of Propagation reverted to the old bodies).
9 Lamb. 902, fols. 9-10.
16 Cal. State Papers, 1654, p. 329.

latter body 'stormed very much' in consequence of
analogous action by the Committee for Cornwall.[1] But it
was inevitable on account of the continued disaffection
of Wales towards the Parliament, the approximately similar
duties assigned in some cases to the Committees, and the
plethora of orders and ordinances issuing from the supreme
authority, that there should be some serious conflict of
jurisdiction. The advent of the Surveyors of Bishops' and
·Chapters' Lands added to the confusion. They think that
the disposition of the profits of Lamphey to Mountfort
was 'ultra vires,' and their allusion to "those that have
power to dispose thereof" seems to refer to the Trustees
for Sale of Bishops' Lands. They adjudge the profits at
£9 10s. 0d. higher than the Associating Committee had ;
but on account of "the dryness of this present autumn"
and the fact that Mountfort had already gathered "the
most part of the tithes," they let the old arrangement stand
for 'this present year.'[2] The C.P.M. not only dispossess
Mountfort, but place the value of the profits at £18, the
old reserved rent to the Bishop of St. David's.'[3] The Surveyors maintain the same critical tone towards the C.P.M.'s
dispositions at Carew,[4] Llangyfelach,[5] and Glascwm,[6] and
with some justification point out the over-generous treatment of Dr. John Ellis of Dolgelly.[7] Again, we read of
the C.P.M. ordering the Committee of Montgomery to hear
articles against Rees Price of Llanllwchaiarn,[8] newly
approved by the Divines[9] and appointed by order of the
Lords,[10] and of the Barons of the Exchequer quashing an
appeal·from Edmund Gamage of Llanharry,[11] also appointed
by the Lords in 1645.[12] Parliament, alive to the over-

---

1 Cal. Comm. Comp., Vol. I, 290. General Proceedings. [The Protector's
proclamation of July 3, 1655, which enumerated the various 'ejecting' authorities,
did *not* include the Committees for *Seqestrations.* Cal. State Papers, 1655, p. 224].
However, the Petitioners of 1652-3, who presumably were quite conversant with the
affairs of 1642-1650, distinctly state that 'great numbers of ministers were ejected
by the Committees of Sequestration in the respective counties in 1647, 1648, and
part of 1649.' (*True and Perfect Relation, pp.* 43-44).
  2 Lamb. 905, fol. 6. Report signed 23rd July, 1647.
  3 Bodl. 326, fol. 252. Order dated May 5, 1649.
  4 Lamb. 905, fol. 4.
  5 Ibid., fol. 1.
  6 Ibid., fol. 63.
  7 Lamb. 904, fol. 124.
  8 Addit. MS. 15671, fol. 88.
  9 Minutes, Session 837, p. 361. May 6, 1647.
  10 L. J. IX, 183.
  11 State Papers, Dom. Interr. B. 8, ff. 233-234.
  12 L. J. VIII, 142.

lapping of authority and its dangers, add a special clause in the Act of January 25th, 1649-50, that the aforesaid Act did "not take away the powers of the Committee for the sequestering scandalous and delinquent ministers."[1] The understanding, however, between the C.P.M. and the C.G.H. seems to have been complete, which led the latter body to make a contribution of its own to the dissolution of the old order. In addition to providing augmentations by way of composition in the cases of advowsons annexed to the estates of delinquents,[2] *it actually bought in impropriations*, again by composition, to be settled in the hands of named trustees for the use of the Church "for ever." This process led in some cases to the reversal of previous orders of the C.P.M. in making grants to ministers[3] out of impropriations reserved by Parliament's order of February, 1645-6.[4] In some cases the action of the C.G.H. was caused by petitions from the inhabitants attending parish churches affected by the composition.[5] The Committee adjudged the fine for the *whole* estate first, and then proceeded to remit from it (roughly) £100 for every £10 a year allowed to "the minister and his successors"[6]; then the whole transaction was to be formally ratified by Parliament. The records preserve the date of this formality, and of the deed of settlement drawn up by Edward Rich, the counsellor-at-law, who was also deputed to keep a 'Register' of it, and of the certificate issued by him from Lincoln's Inn to the delinquents in question. Sir Rice Rudd of Aberglasney in Carmarthen settled the rectory of Eglwys Newydd for the raising of £50 per annum for the minister of St. Peter's in the town of Carmarthen[7]; Morgan Owen of Glasallt the rectory of St. Ismaell's in the same county for raising £50 a year for the minister there[8]; Sir Thomas Hanmer the tithes of Bettisfield for raising £50 for the minister of Hanmer in Flintshire[9];

---

1 Cal. Comm. Comp., Vol. I, 167. "Act for managing the estates of papists and delinquents."
2 Supra, p. 37.
3 Esp. the order re Hanmer (Bodl. 323, fol. 110) and Llandilo Talybont (323,114)
4 Supra, pp. 37-38.
5 Cal. Comm. Comp., Vol. II, 1036; III, 1826.
6 E.g., Morgan Owen's fine, £508 15s. 0d.; allowed for settling £50 a year upon Minister, £500 0s. 0d. £8 15s. 0d. remaining before Sequestration discharged.
7 S.P. Dom. Interreg., G. 35, entries 26-27; Exch. 331. No. 26. Date of Deed, 7th Oct., 1648.
8 S.P. Dom. Interreg., G. 35, entries 28-29; Ibid., No. 28. Date of Deed, 10th June, 1648.
9 Ibid. entries 80-81; Ibid. No. 80. Date of Deed, 18th June, 1647.

E

William Thomas of Swansea the rectory of Llandilo Talybont for the minister there[1]; Sir John Aubrey of Llantrithyd settled the Manor of Gelligaer to raise £25 there[2]; and Sir John Stepney of Prendergast settled the tithes of the chapels of Lawhadden and Llanycefn in Pembrokeshire to raise £40 for the minister of Llanycefn,[3] the rectory of Newcastle-in-Kemeys to raise £27 per annum for the minister there,[4] and the rectory of Clarbeston to raise £30 a year for the minister there.[5] A similar arrangement with Sir Francis Fane, who held the large rectory of Merthyr Cynog in right of his wife, was not 'settled'[6]; the dispositions made by the C.P.M. on November 4th, 1646, were allowed to stand.[7] And in a category of its own stands the warrant[8] issued by the C.G.H. to their Treasurers on an order of the House of Commons (9th January, 1646-7) to pay £500 to Robert Fogg, the new incumbent of Bangor-on-Dee,[9] for his 'services and sufferings' out of the fine of Sir Roger Mostyn, 'late Governor of Flint Castle'.[10]

There was no evading these deliberate orders of Parliament. But an appeal lay from the sequestration orders of the various County Committees to the Barons of the Exchequer[11] according to the rules laid down by the original Act of July, 1643, and its supplementary ordinances. The Barons referred the petition of the appellant to the Committee of his county to certify the grounds and causes of the sequestration together with the proofs already taken, and what else they should think 'meete' touching the premises, to the said Barons within three weeks after notice thereof. They were also to give the petitioner the heads of the charge, examine the witnesses and proofs on both sides on oath; the parties on both sides were to cross-examine, and some

---

1 S. P. Dom. Interreg., G. 35, entry 83; Exch. 331. No. 83. Date of 'Deed, 24th April, 1647. (Algernon Sidney, one of trustees).
2 Ibid., entry 84-85; Ibid. No. 84. Date of Deed, 28th May, 1649.
3 Ibid., entry 168; Ibid., No. 168. Date of Deed, 24th July, 1649.
4 Ibid., entry 169; Ibid., No. 169.   Do.   do.
5 Ibid., entry 170; Ibid., No. 170.   Do.   do.
6 Shaw :. Hist. of the Eng. Church during the Civil War . . . Vol II, Appendix V, p. 484; Cal. Comm. Comp., Vol. II, pp. 1003-1004.
7 Bodl. 323, folios 5, 56; S.P. Dom. F1,353-4; F2,550.
8 Dated Jan. 14, 1646-7; Cal. Comm. Comp., I, 800 (" Warrants ").
9 Addit. MS. 15670, fol. 133, July 1, 1646. Chaplain to Major-Gen. Mytton, and one of the signatories of articles of Surrender of Ruthin Castle. (N.L.W. catalogue, p. 21).
10 Re Mostyn's fine, *vide* Cal. Comm. Comp., Vol. III, p. 1666.
11 John Wylde, Thos. Gate, and Henry Thorpe usually heard these appeals.

J.P. of the said county (who was not one of the Committee) or ' some other trusty and fit person ' to be approved of by the Committee was to be present on the petitioner's behalf. The ' state ' of the whole case was to be sealed up and forwarded to the Barons.[1] The latter further recommended to the Committees for the sake of more ' cleerenesse ' that two witnesses at least be examined to prove the delinquency, and these were to speak of their own knowledge and not from hearsay ; further, " if any of these be dead or remote, the same be clearly certified."[2] Katharine Bridgeman, wife of the ejected rector of Bangor in Flintshire, though allowed her ' fifths ' as the wife of a sequestered clerk by the C.P.M.,[3] is found petitioning the Barons for the full fifth of his temporal estate. The same is granted.[4] The appeal of Dr. Hugh Williams[5] against the sequestration from him of the tithes and profits of Llandinam does not succeed, for on December 6th, 1647, the C.P.M. are found disposing of the same.[6] ' Euball ' Lewis, rector of Newtown, met with better fortune[7] ; but Edward Ellis, vicar of Guilsfield, after successfully resisting the articles of 1646,[8] is sequestered again in 1649, and remained so throughout the Propagation period.[9] Dr. Gabriel Parry's efforts to retain the rectory of Llansantffraid in Montgomery were doomed to failure,[10] and so was Owen Lloyd's in the case of Llanengan in Carnarvonshire.[11] The appeals of Griffith Morris of Cemmes (Mont.)[12] and Edmund Gamage of Llanharry (Glam.),[13] and also that of Henry Vaughan of Panteg[14] in Monmouthshire, one of the preachers before the Court at Oxford,[15] were all dismissed. The appeals of seven Breconshire clergymen— Jacob Wood of Llandevally, Richard Williams of Llanthetty, Richard Habberley of Llyswen, John Griffith of

1 State Papers Domestic Interregrum, B. 8, folio 14.
2 Ibid., B. 8, folios 233-234.
3 Addit. MS. 15670, fol. 161. July 22, 1646.
4 S.P. Dom., B. 2, fol. 518. 23rd Sept., 1646.
5 Ibid., B. 2, fol. 442. 5th Aug., 1646.
6 Bodl. 325, fol. 164.
7 S.P. Dom. Interr., B. 3. fol. 328 (21st June, 1647) ; Exch. Misc. slip 119 (First Fruits, Montgomery, 1658).
8 Exch. Misc. (Mont.), slip 119 (1658).
9 Cal. Comm. Comp., Vol. IV, p. 3056.
10 S.P. Dom., B. 8, fol. 15 ; Exch. Misc. (Mont.), slip 119.
11 Ibid., B. 8, fol. 170 ; Exch. Misc. (Carn. 1652), slip not numbered ; Walker, Sufferings, Part II, p. 301.
12 S.P. Dom. Interreg., B. 8, fol. 8 ; Exch. Misc. (Mont.), slip 114.
13 Ibid., B. 8, fols. 233-234 ; Walker MS. e. 7, fol. 209.
14 S.P. Dom. Interr. B. 8, fol. 284 ; Walker MS. e.7 , fol. 215b.
15 Walker : Sufferings, Part II, p. 388.

Llanfihangel, Thomas Vaughan of Llansantffread, William Walters of Llangasty, and Griffith Hatley of Abereskir— seem to have been all successful, since they all survived to be ejected under the Propagation Act.[1] That of Thomas Powell of Cantref, he having adhered to the King in the wars, failed.[2] One case stands by itself, the appeal of John Williams, rector of Llanfyllin, to the "Committee of the Lords and Commons for Sequestrations"[3]; it was unsuccessful, since John Davies, who was referred to the Assembly by the C.P.M.,[4] officiated the cure in 1649 and 1650.[5]

The forementioned appeals afford but an uncertain clue to the activities of the "sequestrating saints."[6]. Thirty-five of the clergy were ejected "before the Act" in Glamorganshire alone.[7] Of these, Dr. Hugh Lloyd was sequestered for plurality and for 'refusing the Covenant,'[8] Thomas Morgan of Llandough for obstinacy,[9] Theodore Price, Erbery's successor at St. Mary's, Cardiff, for a particularly aggressive pluralism,[10] Nathaniel Gamage of Eglwysilan for lack of preaching,[11] Dr. Gordon of Porteynon for not taking the Engagement,[12] Francis Davies of Llangan for not reading the Directory,[13] and Thomas Bassett, a great pluralist, was "an Eyesore to the ruling powers because he was superior to them in the copiousness of his expressions and the strength of his arguments."[14] The zeal of this Committee was strongly commented upon by the Glamorgan men who broke out in revolt in the summer of 1647[15]; they charge its members with abusing their power, with having committed some of

1 S.P. Dom. Interreg., B. 8, fols. 293-294 ; Walker MS. *e.* 7, fol. 213b. With the names of Thomas Powell and Jacob Wood in the Brecknock appeal list occurs the name of ' Samuel Gwyn, Clerke.' No incumbent of that name is found in the ' Liber,' but the vicar of Llangorse was *Rowland* Gwyn. If, by some clerical mistake, both entries refer to the same man, Gwyn's appeal was unsuccessful, since he was ejected ' before the Act.' (Walk. *c.* 7, f. 214). It seems, however, that Walters was not " totally dispossest." (Walk. Suff. Pt. II., p. 423.)

2 S.P. Dom. Interreg., B. 8, folio 293 ; Walker MS. *e.* 7, fol. 213b.

3 C.G.H.; Addit. MS. 15671, fol. 168a.

4 Addit. MS. 15671, fol. 164a. Aug. 11, 1647.

5 Exch. Misc. (Mont.), slip 115, 1657.

6 A New Ballad of the Plague . . . the year 1647 (Wrexham) ; epithet of Daniel Lloyd, Treasurer of Denbigh Committee of Sequestrations.

7 Walker MS. *e.* 7, 208b-209.

8 Cal. Comm. Comp., Vol. V, p. 3211.

9 Walker MS. *c.* 4. fol. 68.

10 Walk. *e.* 7. ff. 208b-209 ; instituted 22nd July, 1638 (Lib. Inst. Llandaff, f. 12).

11 Walk. *c.* 4, f. 65b.

12 Ibid., f. 72

13 Ibid., f. 68.

14 Ibid., f. 65b

15 Phillips : Civil War in Wales, Vol. I, pp. 356-357 ; Vol. II, Doc. LXXXIX. pp. 298-300 .

the clergy, sequestered them, and forbidden tithes to be paid to the ablest and ' sufficientest ' divines in the county for " refusing to take such Oathes as were tendered to them " ; further, they say the Committee had not provided any others to take their places.[1] In Monmouth, eighteen clergymen had been ejected ' before the Act,' in Brecknock six, in Radnor six.[2] To these particulars given in the Walker MS. must be added, in their respective counties, Francis Price, the successor of Wroth as vicar of Llanfaches[3] ; Matthew Herbert, rector of Llangattock, sometime tutor of Henry Vaughan the Silurist,[4] who is alleged to have been " sequestered contrary even to the orders of the then Parliament, before any charge was exhibited against him "[5] ; and William Bevan, vicar of Glascwm in Radnor.[6] With the exception of John Dashfield, rector of Prendergast in Pembroke,[7] Dr. Evan Owen, rector of Narberth[8] in the same county, and that of Llandyssul in Cardiganshire,[9] none of the parish clergy either in these two counties or in Carmarthenshire seem to have been ejected before 1650.[10] Colonels Poyer and Rice Powell do not refer to the oppressions of any Committees in south-western Wales, but express their great determination to restore the Book of Common Prayer, ' the sole comfort of the people heere.'[11] And the ejections in North Wales were on a much more limited scale than those in the south-east. They are represented by the sequestrations which called for the C.P.M. settlements already referred to,[13] by those whose families were in receipt of fifths,[13] by the Exchequer appellants,[14] and, in addition, by William Griffith of Llanbedrog,[15] John Roane of Hanmer,[16] and Rowland Owen of Wrexham.[17]

1 The heads of the present Grcevances of the County of Glamorgan . . . . Gravamina VII and X, pp. 4-5 (1647). N.L.W.
2 Walk. *e.* 7, ff. 214, 214b, 215b.
3 Walker : Sufferings, Part II, p. 332.
4 Morrice : Wales in the Seventeenth Century, p. 297.
5 Lamb. 1027, f. 30 ; House of Lords MSS. Comm. Report, Appendix I, p. 96.
6 Addit. Mus. 15671, f. 219 (' William Evans ' ; William Bevan in Lib. Inst. Meneven, p. 59).
7 House of Lords Petitions. 1660. W.—' for these 15 years last past illegally ejected.'
8 Lamb. 1027, f. 35 ; Bodl. 324, ff. 23b, 52b.
9 Ibid. (' Llandissill ').
10 Walk. *e.* 7, ff. 212, 212b, 213.
11 The Declaration of Col. Poyer and Col. Powell (April 10, 1648), p. 5. N.L.W.
12 Supra, p. 37.
13 Supra, p. 41.
14 Supra, pp. 51-52.
15 Exchequer Return (Carn.), 1652. First Fruits.
16 Walker : Sufferings, Part II, p. 350.
17 Palmer : History of Older Nonconformity in Wrexham, p. 2.

APPENDIX.

ACTIVITIES OF PARLIAMENTARY COMMITTEES—
AUTHORITIES.

(A). *Committee for Plundered Ministers* : *Proceedings.*

(i) *Bodleian* MS. 322 ; (ff. 1–319) orders ranging from 26th July, 1645, to 22nd April, 1646 ; chronologically.

Bodleian MS. 323 ; (ff. 1–373) orders ranging from 4th November, 1646, to 17th November, 1646 ; by counties.

Bodleian MS. 324 ; (ff. 1–489) orders ranging from 21st November, 1646, to 21st April, 1647 ; chron.

Bodleian MS. 325 ; (ff. 1–314b) orders ranging from 21st April, 1648, to 20th March, 1649-1650 ; counties.

Bodleian MS. 326 ; (ff. 1–363) orders ranging from 12th October, 1649, to 7th November, 1649 ; counties.

Bodleian MS. 327 ; (ff. 1–632) orders ranging from 2nd February, 1650, to 14th August, 1650 ; counties.

Bodleian MS. 328 ; (ff. 1–485) orders ranging from 1650 to 1652 ; counties.

(ii) *British Museum* Addit. MS. 15669 ; (ff. 1–553) orders from 30th January, 1644-5 to 27th December, 1645 ; chron.

British Museum Addit. MS. 15670 ; (ff. 1–242a) orders from 6th January, 1645-6 to 18th September, 1646 ; chron.

British Museum Addit MS. 15671 ; (ff. 1–262b) orders from 7th May, 1647, to 19th October, 1647 ; chron.

(iii) *Record Office.*

 State Papers Dom. Interreg. F1 ; numbered 1–360, ranging from 3rd December, 1645, to 20th May, 1646 ; chron.

 State Papers Dom. Interreg. F2 ; numbered 439–774, ranging from 3rd December, 1643, to 8th April, 1653 ; chron.

That the above are only *surviving* records is illustrated by these typical facts :—(*a*) orders for payments to Richard Jewell at Tenby in 1649 and 1650 are based on a previous order of *10th May, 1644*, of which there is no record (327, f. 185 ; 327, f. 187) ; (*b*) a John Lusye was appointed to the living of Angle in Pembrokeshire (Lamb. 915, f. 138) by the C.P.M., but there is no such entry in the minutes ; (*c*) there is no corroboration also to the statement of Robert Frampton of Bryngwyn (Mon.) (Cal. Comm. Comp., III, 1710) that he was approved by the Committee, and admitted there 4th October, 1649 ; (*d*) there is no record of an appeal from the proceedings of the Commissioners for the Propagation in Wales, though such an appeal, and a successful one, is vouched for in the Mont. Exch. First Fruits Return, February, 1657.

(*B*) *Committee for Compounding.*

 (i) S. P. Dom. Interreg. G 22. Entries ranging from 6th October, 1652, to 4th September, 1655 ; payments made at the request of the C.P.M. ; little reference to Wales.

 (ii) S. P. Dom. Interreg. G. 35. " Book of all such Settlements for Augmentations of Ministers as have been made by appointment of Parliament handed over to the Trustees " appointed under Cromwell's ordinance of 2nd September, 1654 (Rich's Register).

 (iii) Commonwealth Exchequer Papers, Bundle 331, MS. 95. " An Inventory of several deeds and conveyances of impropriate rectories . . . . in the keeping of John Phelps . . . . to be delivered to the Remembrancer in the Exchequer on 1st March, 1660."

 (iv) British Museum $E\frac{464}{30}$; an official list of all such transactions (vide iii) up to 5th September, 1648. (Printed 22nd September, 1648.)

(v) Calendar of the Committee for Compounding, passim.

(vi) Lamb. MS. 970, ff. 11, 13, 139, 195.

(vii) House of Lords MSS. Comm. Report, Appendix I, p. 84.

(*C*) *County Parliamentary Committees and Local Committees for Sequestrations.*

No minutes or other records of these have survived, and their proceedings are reflected by—

(1) the correspondence contained in Cal. Comm. Comp., Vol. I.

(2) the orders and correspondence contained in the Commonwealth Exch. Papers, Bundle 251.

(3) references in the petitions contained in the House of Lords MSS.

(4) statements made in the Surveyors' Reports of 1647–1649.

(5) declarations of the constables in 1662.

(*D*) *Authorities of allied interest.*

(i) The Minutes of the Sessions of the Westminster Assembly of Divines (November, 1644—March, 1649), ed. A. F. Mitchell and J. Struthers. (1874.)

(ii) State Papers Dom. Interr. B1—B8. Appeals from Sequestrations. Order Books. (Vide pp. 50-51 for procedure.)

The results of these appeals are not recorded in any of the State Papers ; those have to be ascertained from the " Propagation " Documents (Chapter VIII).

(iii) Audit Office. Declared Accounts. Bundle 367, roll 3.

This roll contains an " Account of the Sales of Dean and Chapters' Lands," including payments made from the revenue arising therefrom to ministers in Wales in pursuance of the ordinances of 1646 and 1649 (pp. 38-39).

IV.

THE NOMINEES OF PARLIAMENT—EXTENT OF PURITAN SETTLEMENTS.

Throughout this period Parliament reserved to itself the right of nomination, more especially to a certain type of vacant livings. These appointments are all recorded in the Lords' Journals, but the entry in the case of the rectory of Llanbeulan in Anglesey shows that the concurrence of the. Commons was also necessary.[1] The action of the Lords was based on a sanction of the right of private patrons, when these were not delinquents or members of the deposed hierarchy ; and though the Lords' order to appoint a committee to draw up an ordinance requiring patrons to present their nominees to the Houses of Parliament went no further than the first reading,[2] and the two ordinances of the Commons to establish the right of private patrons did not pass the Committee stage,[3] the facts prove that in practice these principles were adopted. Eight of the Lords' orders are only efficacious when the ' clerk ' produces the presentation of the lawful patron of the living. The right of presentation to livings in the donation of the King gradually fell into the hands of the Commissioners of the Great Seal[4] as successors to the Lord Keeper, who had the right to appoint to such vacant benefices of below a certain value in the King's Books[5] ; this right was regulated by an order of both Houses.[6] Thirty-three out of the forty-two appointments in Vols. VIII, IX and X of the Journals are " granted under the Great Seal," but the wording of the orders seem to show that in each case they were to be sanctioned by the Upper House, who were somewhat jealous of the discretionary

1 L. J. X, 402.
2 L. J. VIII, 582, 590. Nov., 1646.
3 C. J. III, 302. Nov., 1643 ; IV, 203. July, 1645.
4 First Commissioners appointed 7th Nov., 1643.
5 Shaw : Hist. of the English Church under the Civil War, Vol II, p. 272.
6 L. J. IX, 573 ; C. J. V, 380. 13th Dec., 1647.

powers arrogated by the Commissioners. For the latter
are found transcending the customary authority of the
Lord Keeper by presenting to livings in the donation of the
King *above* the value (as in the case of Llanfyrnach in Pembrokeshire),[1] in the gift of the Prince of Wales (as in the case
of Dolgelly),[2] in the gift of the Bishop of St. David's (as in
the case of Llanegwad)[3], and in the gift of private individuals
(as in the case of Llanddowror)[4]. It is probable that suitable
candidates to fill the vacant livings were suggested either
by the Committees of the counties or by the members of
Parliament who attended at Westminster ; one " Mr. Owen "
was specially recommended for " a parsonage in Wales "
by the Earl of Pembroke to the approval of the Assembly[5] ;
all were ' referred ' to the latter body, and twenty are
expressly described as being Bachelors or Masters of Arts ;
in the earlier orders the nominees must take the Covenant ;
and all without exception had to be " instituted and
inducted " either by Sir Nathaniel Brent, Laud's old Vicar-
General, or by Doctors Aylett, Bennett, or Heath, Commissaries of the Faculties.[6] There was no ostracism of
approved members of the old order. John Gumbleden,
the new rector of Coyty[7] in Glamorgan had been for six
years rector of St. Juliet's[8] in the same county[9] ; Humphrey
Lloyd had been rector of Erbistock since 1626[10] before he
was appointed to the vicarage of Ruabon at the death of
his father[11] ; Thomas Foulkes had served nearly three years
at Llanarmon Dyffryn Ceiriog[12] before he was instituted at
Llanfechain in 1647[13] ; Lodowick Lewis had been for nearly
thirty years rector of Cosheston in Pembrokeshire[14] before
he was presented to the ' parsonage ' of Llandyssul in
Cardiganshire in 1646,[15] and his death made way for Edmund

1 Value, £36. Lamb. 915, fol. 157.
2 L. J. VIII, 568.
3 L. J. IX, 92.
4 L. J. X, 546.
5 Minutes, Session 654. June 8, 1646, p. 240. Probably Thomas Owen—once
Lecturer at St. Leonard, Shoreditch (C. J. II, 543) ; appointed by Lords to Llanfyrnach. L. J. IX, 544 (26th Nov., 1647).
6 For authority, vide L. J. V, 717 ; C. J. III, 87, 88 ; Landmarks in the History
of the Welsh Church (St. Asaph), Appendix G, p. 306, note.
7 L. J. VIII, 17.
8 " Scti Julit."
9 Lib. Inst., Llandaff, fol. 15.
10 Lib. Inst., Assaphe, fol. 155.
11 L. J. IX, 252.
12 Lib. Inst., Assaphe, fol. 160.
13 L. J. IX, 146.
14 Lib. Inst., Meneuen, fol. 8.
15 L. J. VIII, 555.

Vaughan in 1647[1]; Morgan Williams, presented by the Commissioners of the Great Seal to the rectory of Letterston in Pembrokeshire in 1646,[2] had already been instituted in December, 1628, to the rectory of Johnston[3] in the same county, also in the gift of the King[4]; and Evan Lloyd, already since April; 1615, vested with the rectory of Rhoscolyn[5] in Anglesey gets in addition the rectory of Llanbeulan with its four annexed chapels.[6] Three orders dated 7th July, 1648, show the Lords diverting previous arrangements of the C.P.M. Griffith Evans, referred to the Assembly for the cure of Ystrad in Cardiganshire,[7] is appointed by the Lords to the living of Llanrhystyd[8]; William Brigdale, referred to the Assembly for the 'Church' of Gyffin in Carnarvonshire,[9] is ordered by the Lords to be instituted to the rectory of Llanrwst in Denbighshire[10]; and " Reeves " Meredith, appointed by the C.P.M. to the living of Llanddewibrefi,[11] is promoted by the Lords to the vicarage of Lampeter[12]; and Dr. Rowland Chedle, rector of Llandegfan with its chapel of St. Mary's at Beaumaris,[13] is instituted in July, 1648, to the rectory of Llanfaethlu,[14] notwithstanding the Committee's grant to him on 29th June, 1647, of £60 from the rectory of Amlwch.[15] The C.P.M., on the other hand, are found exercising their discretion in varying some of the Lords' orders. Henry Pugh, the newly instituted rector of Llanystumdwy (20th July, 1647)[16] is in February, 1648, minister of Abergele,[17] and Robert Powell, appointed by the Lords in November, 1648, to the vicarage of Nantmel in Radnor,[18] is removed by the C.P.M. to the rectory of Merthyr Cynog in Breconshire.[19] Nor do some of the

1 L. J. IX, 401.
2 L. J. VIII, 635.
3 Lib. Inst., Meneuen, fol. 18.
4 Ibid.
5 Lib. Inst., Bangor, fol. 8.
6 L. J. X. 402.
7 Bodl. 324, fol. 235.
8 L. J. X, 368.
9 Addit. MS. 15671, fol. 222a.
10 L. J. X, 368.
11 Bodl. 325, fol. 46
12 L. J. X, 368. Surveyors of Bishops' Lands report him as ' Rees ap Meredith.' (30th Oct., 1649). Lamb. 905, fol. 49.
13 Lamb. 902, f. 38.
14 L. J. X, 383.
15 Bodl. 325. fol. 1.
16 L. J. IX, 341.
17 Bodl. 325, fol. 68.
18 L. J. X, 611.
19 Bodl. 326, 18b. Nov. 30, 1649. Surveyors report him at Nantmel (8th Nov 1649). Lamb. 905, f. 32.

nominees of the Lords appear to be of such distinctive Puritan stamp as those approved by the Committee. Within six weeks of his order from the Lords[1] articles are exhibited against Rees Price of Llanllwchaiarn in Montgomeryshire before the C.P.M.[2] ; and though the latter body nominated Edward Thelwall to fill the vacancy at Llanynys (Denbighshire) at the death of Robert Sparkes on June 12th, 1647,[3] four days later a certain Edward Vaughan is nominated by the Lords to the same cure.[4] There follow petitions and counter-petitions,[5] but on October 26th of the same year Thelwall is finally confirmed,[6] and is officiating the cure in 1650.[7] Three cases (Jenkin Lloyd of Llangoedmor,[8] William Young of Pwllycrochan,[9] and Thomas Griffith of Llangeler[10]) occur both in the records of the C.P.M. and the Journals of the Lords ; the former body grant an augmentation to Lloyd because of the insufficiency of his living,[11] and two several augmentations[12] to another Lords' nominee—Dr. John Ellis of Dolgelly—probably to reward the accession to the Puritan ranks of one of the most distinguished scholars of his time.[13] Lastly, the C.P.M. appointed to three livings void by death, but under the combined force of the recognition of satisfactory patrons and the acquired rights of the Commissioners of the Great Seal, such appointments became the special province of the Parliament. " Void by death " is the moving cause of twenty of the Lords' institutions.

In a category of their own stand the Parliament's orders dispatching *three itinerant ministers to South Wales.* On 15th August, 1645, it was ordered by the Commons that £300 per annum should be allowed out of the ' Lands ' of the Bishops, Deans and Chapters of Llandaff and St. David's, to Henry Walter, Walter Cradock, and Richard Symonds to be equally divided amongst them ' towards their main-

---

1 L. J. IX. 183. May 11, 1647 ; Minutes, p. 358, May 3, 1647. *Respited for a better testimonial;* p. 361, May 6. 1647. Certificate granted.
2 Addit. MS. 15671, fol. 88. June 26, 1647. Ejected before 1649. (Exch. Misc. Slip, 114).
3 Addit. MS. 15671, fol. 108.
4 L. J. IX, 268.
5 Addit. MS. 15671, f. 203. Sept. 11, 1647.
6 Ibid., f. 259.
7 Bodl. Rawlinson, *c.* 261, p. 19. [Cymdeithas Llên Cymru Reprint.]
8 Cp. Addit. MS. 15670, fol. 447 : L.J. IX, 108.
9 Bodl. 324, fol. 30b ; L. J. IX, 58.
10 Addit. MS. 15670, f. 203 ; L. J. X, 567.
11 Bodl. 325, fol. 46b.
12 Lamb. 989, fols. 190, 191 ; Bodl. 325, f. 166 ; L. J. VIII, 568.
13 D.N.B., Vol. XVII, p. 283.

tenance in the work of the Ministry in South Wales.'[1] But there was no definition of the particular 'work' they had to do ; South Wales was at this time in a turbulent condition[2] ; and the greater part of the revenues from Bishops' lands were hypothecated to pay the Scots for their services in the war.[3] A more explicit and workable order was introduced into the Commons on 22nd July, 1646,[4] and received its third reading in the Lords on 13th November, but not before the Lower House had on 28th October ordered, the ministers to proceed to Wales 'with all convenient speed,' forgetting the jurisdiction of the Divines of the Assembly.[5] They were to preach 'itinerantly' in the Welsh language, and their salaries were to issue out of the revenues of the Deans and Chapters of the two dioceses. A special committee was appointed to sequester such of the capitular interests as would produce £300 a year ; this sum was to be payable on 29th September and 25th March in two equal portions.[6] The Surveyors of the Dean and Chapter Lands under the ordinance of 30th April, 1649, account how £201 out of this sum was obtained : £120 from the twenty 'cursory prebends' of the parish of St. David's in Pembrokeshire,[7] £36 from the prebend of Mathry in the same county,[8'] £10 from the 'tything barn' of Canton in Glamorgan,[9] £20 from the rectory of Merthyr Mawr,[10] and £15 from the rectory of Pentyrch.[11] The remaining £99 had no doubt to be supplied by the various County Committees for Sequestrations, since Walter Cradock received his second moiety of £50 in September, 1649, from the Treasurers of the Dean and Chapter Lands,[12] to whom the

---

1 C. J. IV, 242.
2 King Charles himself spent a fortnight at Raglan, Sept. 7-21 ; Phillips : Civil War, Vol. I, p. 322.
3 L. J. VIII, 517 ; Scobell : Ordinances I, esp. pp. 111, 117.
4 C. J. IV, 622.
5 C. J. IV, 707 ; L. J. VIII, 463. Strong protest of the Divines against giving any approbation to the " itinerant " ministers " without conference first had with them." Also supra, p. 46.
6 L. J. VIII, 568-569.
7 Lamb. 905, fol. 61. Survey on 5th Oct., 1649.
8 Lamb. 905, fol. 62. Survey on 5th Oct., 1649
9 Lamb. 913, fol. 746. Survey on 28th Sept., 1649.
10 Lamb. 913, fol. 751. Survey on 27th Sept., 1649.
11 Lamb. 913, fol. 752. Survey on 27th Sept., 1649. The Surveyors incorrectly describe the last three orders as made by the " Committee for the *County of Glamorgan*, appointed for Welsh ministers " ; three of the eight members were from the county of *Monmouth* (L. J. VIII, 569).
12 Record Office. Audit Office, Declared Accounts, Bundle 367, Roll 3 ; C.P.M.'s order for payment (Bodl 327, fol. 273 ; wrongly numbered 263)

above Committees had to transfer their ecclesiastical
revenues in that year.[1]

These records of Parliament and its deputed Committees
are far from covering the whole extent of the Puritan settlements up to 1650. There are additional references in the
Minutes of the Assembly to men approved for ministerial
work in Wales, while the Lambeth MSS. prove that they
took up their duties ; the ' Book of Institutions ' contains
entries[2] of ministers inducted to livings after the downfall
of the official hierarchy in 1646, and who must have been
deemed satisfactory by the ruling powers ; the Surveyors
of Bishops', Dean and Chapter Lands respectively found
incumbents in legal possession of livings from which
delinquent clergy are known to have been ejected ; the
reports submitted to the Exchequer authorities during the
Commonwealth concerning the payment of first-fruits refers
to other appointments made under the Great Seal ; the
constables' reports to the Restoration Parliament in 1662
refer to further orders of the C.P.M. ; the circumstantial
account supplied to John Walker by Edward Mansell in
1709 points to the access of new blood in Glamorgan[3] ; and
the Commissioners appointed under the Act for " maintenance of preaching ministers "[4] to give information of
all parsonages and vicarages certify two cases in Pembrokeshire of ministers appointed by the C.P.M. for which there
is no official support in the surviving records of that body.[5]
The following list is a summary of this somewhat diverse
evidence. It contains the names of those—whether new
Puritan nominees or ' approved ' clergy of the old order—
who were engaged in ' preaching the Word ' more or less
efficiently on the eve of the Propagation Act.

1 Supra, pp. 38-39.
2 I.e., in addition to the entries corroborating the Lords' orders for institution
and induction, supra, pp. 58-60.
3 Vide letters of Mansell from Henllys—(a) Feb. ye last, 1708-9 (Walker c. 4,
fol. 63) ; (b) March 21st, 1709-1710 (Walker c. 4, fol. 63a).
4 Firth and Rait : Acts and Ordinances of the Interregrum, Vol. II, p. 147.
5 Further, occasionally there are ministers in possession of livings before 1650,
who figure in the Episcopal returns of 1665 (vide p. 70, case of Thomas Evans of
Llanbister).

NORTH WALES.

	MINISTER.	SPHERE OF LABOUR.	DATE OF ORDER, INSTITUTION, OR APPROVAL.	MS. REFERENCE OR OTHER AUTHORITY.
ANGLESEY	Francis Meyrick	Eglwysael	March 1, 1646-7	Minutes of Assembly, pp. 332-333 ; Lamb. 902, f. 53.
	Evan Lloyd	Llanbeulan and Rhoscolyn	July 20, 1648	L. J. x, 402.
	Rowland Chedle	Llandegfan and Llanfaethlu	July 13, 1648	L. J. x, 383.
	Evan Jones	Llanddyfrydog	Oct. 22, 1647	L. J. IX, 491.
	William Lloyd	Llanfihangel Ysceifiog	April 21, 1647	Bodl. 324, f. 347.
CARNARVON	Jeffrey Oldfield	Conway	Before July 4, 1649	Bodl. 326, f. 50.
	Morris Owen	Llanystumdwy	Oct. 19, 1647	Minutes of Assembly, p. 485 ; Exch. First Fruits Return, 1652.
DENBIGH.	Henry Pugh	Abergele	Feb. 5, 1647-8	Bodl. 325, f. 68 ; Lamb. 902, f. 8.
	William Jones	Denbigh	1647	Cal. St. Papers, 1654, p. 329.
	David Jones	Llansantffraid Glan Conwy	Feb. 23, 1646-7	Bodl. 324, f. 181 ; Lamb. 902, f. 12.
	Thos. George	Llandrillo-yn-Rhos	June 6, 1648	Lib. Inst. Assaphe, f. 148.
	Richard Edwards	Llanfair Dyffryn Clwyd	Jan. 16, 1646-7	Bodl. 324, f. 118.
	William Jones	Llanfwrog	1646	Add. MS. 15671, ff. 135, 258a.
	John Wynne	Llangwm	Nov. 20, 1648	L. J. X, 597.
	John Brigdale	Llannefydd	March 29, 1649	Bodl. 326, f. 72b.
	Evan Roberts	Llanrhaiadr-ym-Mochnant	May 29, 1647	Add. MS. 15671, f. 68.
	William Brigdale	Llanrwst	July 7, 1648	L. J. X, 368.
	Hugh Morris	Llansannan	Nov. 4, 1649	Lib. Inst. Assaphe, f. 150.
	Edward Thelwall	Llanynys	June 12, 1647	Add. MS. 15671, f. 108.
	John Lloyd	Marchwiel	June 1, 1648	Lib. Inst. Assaphe, f. 155.

NORTH WALES—*continued.*

	MINISTER.	SPHERE OF LABOUR.	DATE OF ORDER, INSTITUTION, OR APPROVAL.	MS. REFERENCE OR OTHER AUTHORITY.
DENBIGH (*con.*).	Humphrey Lloyd	Ruabon	June 10, 1647	L. J. IX, 252.
	John Holland	St. George's	Dec. 23, 1648	Lamb. 902, ff. 9–10.
	William Smith 1	Wrexham	1646	Lab. 1027 (Ilsa Report) ; St. Asaph : Landmarks, App. G., p. 306.
FLINT	Dr. Harding	Wrexham and District	Before July 6, 1649	Bodl. 326, ff. 73, 73b.
	Henry Morgan	Cilcen	Uncertain — MS. mutilated	Lib 1027 (Kilken Report).
	Robert Fogg	Bangor Monachorum	July 1, 1646	Add. MS. 15670, f. 133.
	Rice Williams	Diserth	May 28, 1647	Add. MS. 15671, f. 50a.
	Edward Bold 2	Hawarden	July 30, 1646	Add. MS. 15670, f. 162a.
	William Smith	Llanasa	1647	Lamb. 1027 (Llanasa Report) ; Lamb. 997, lib. ii, f. 83.
	Morgan ap Morgan	Meliden	In possession on 7 Sept., 1649	Lamb. 902, f. 28.
	Arch. Sparkes	Northop	Oct. 21, 1646	Bodl. 323, f. 110.
	Robert Edwards	Rhiwlyfnwyd	Feb. 27, 1648	Lamb. 902, f. 7.
	Evan Lloyd	Ysceifiog	Nv. 26, 1647	L. J. IX, 544.
MERIONETH	Edward Roberts ·	Cwen	June 10, 1648	L. J. X, 316.
	John Ellis	Dolgelly	Nv. 17, 1646	L. J. VIII, 568.
	Stephen Lewis	Gwyddelwern	Sept. 21, 1647	L. J. IX, 442.
	Richard Pearkes	Llillo	May 21, 1647	Addit. MS. 15671, fol. 27.
	Evan Evans	glyn	July 25, 1648	L. J. X, 395.
	Cadwaladr Wynne	Llanenddwyn and Llanddwywe	July 14, 1648	Lib. Inst. Bangor, fol. 7.
	Edward Wynne	Llanymawddwy	Nov. 27, 1649	Lib. Inst. Assaphe, fol. 177.

County	Minister	Place	Date	Reference
MONTGOMERY..	Edward E ans	Hissington	May 3, 1648	Bodl. 325, fol. 164.
	David Roberts	Kilm	Dec. 6, 1647	Bodl. 325, fol. 164.
	Roger Jones	Llanerfyl	ude 10, 1647	L. J. IX, 252.
	Thas Foulkes	Kelin	April 21, 1647	L. J. IX, 146.
	John Davies	Syllin	Aug. 11, 1647	Addit. MS. 15671, fol. 64a.
	John Vaughan	Llangedwyn	June 12, 1647	Addit. MS. 15671, fol. 65a.
	Edmund Hall	Llansantffraid	April 21, 1647	Bodl. 324, fol. 244.
	Humphrey Rowl nds	Llanwrin	D. 23, 1649	Bodl. 324, f. 153; Lib. Inst. Assaphe, 174.
	Simon Swayne	Machynlleth	D. 28, 1646	Bodl. 323, fol. 9a.
	Ralph Davies	Mcl	April 13, 1647	L. J. IX, 134.
	Evan Ellis	Pennant	March 17, 1646-1647.	Bodl. 324, fol. 189b.
	Hugh Pugh	Trefeglwys	1649	Exch. Misc., slp. 116. 1657.
	Morgan Llwyd	Itinerant Ministers for North Wales	July 20, 1644; reaffirmed on June 7, 1648	C. J. III, 565.
	Ambrose Myn			
	Vavasor Powell			Bodl. 325, ff. 68-68b.

SOUTH WALES.

County	Minister	Place	Date	Reference
BRECKNOCK ..	Matthew Williams	Llangattock	August, 1646	Bodl. 326, fol. 18.
	Robert Powell	Merthyr Cynog	Nov. 30, 1649	Bodl. 326, fol. 18b.
CARDIGAN ..	John Roberts	Aberporth	Dec. 11, 1648	L. J. IX, 571.
	Richard Owens	Cardigan and Verwick	Feb. 11, 1645-6	Bodl. 322, fol. 70.
	Morgan Evans	Cilie Aeron	March 3, 1646-7	L. J. IX, 56.
	Rees Meredith	Lampeter	July 7, 1648	L. J. X, 368.

1 The "Llanasa[fn] Report" to the petty constables of 1662 (dated 11th June in that year, and signed " Ric: Evans of Halkyn," the sequestered vicar) proves that Smith was once 'Vicar of Wrexam,' and afterwards of Llanasa. A collation of this MS. with Lamb. 902, f. 30 (which supplies the date of the sequestration of the Meifod prebend in Denbigh, another of the dispossessed vicar's interests) fixes the time of Smith's settlement at Llanasa in 1647.

2 He is designated ' Mr. Edward Boles of Harding ' in the ordinance of 23rd Aug., 1654. (Firth and Rait : Acts and Ordinances, Vol. II. p. 983).

F

SOUTH WALES—*continued.*

MINISTER.	SPHERE OF LABOUR.	DATE OF ORDER, INSTITUTION, OR APPROVAL.	MS. REFERENCE OR OTHER AUTHORITY.
CARDIGAN (*con.*)			
Evan Roberts	Llanbadarn	July 27, 1646	Bodl. 323, fol. 49.
Edmund Vaughan	Llandyssul	Aug. 23, 1647	L. J. IX, 401.
David Pierce	Llangranog and Llandisiliogogo	Dec. 7, 1646	Bodl. 327, fol. 36.
Griffith Evans	Llanrhystyd	July 7, 1648	L. J. X, 368.
Thos Evans	Lld	June 14, 1647	dAit. MS. 651, 8a.
Jenkin Lloyd	Llangoedmor	Sept. 22, 1646	Addit. MS. 650, f. 447. L. J. IX, 108.
Did Idyd	Penbryn	March 3, 1646-7	L. J. IX, 56.
David Davies	Tremaen	June 10, 1646	Bodl. 323, fol. 48.
eeRHughes	Troedyraur	Sept. 21, 1647	L. J. IX, 442.
William Idyd	Ystrad Meurig	Feb. 26, 1646-7	Bodl. 324, fol. 10.
CARMARTHEN			
Nicholas Owen	Cenarth	Aug. 22, 1648	L. J. X, 451.
William Jones	Llanegwad	March 20, 1646-7	L. J. IX, 92.
Daniel Jones	Llanddowror	Oct. 16, 1648	L. J. X, 546.
Hugh Edwards	Llangadog and Llanddeusant	June 30, 1648	L. J. IX, 353.
Thos Griffiths	Llangeler	Aug. 24, 1646	dAit. MS. 15670, f. 203a.
Lwis Davies	Mydrim	May 28, 1649	Bodl. 326, fol. 46.
GLAMORGAN			
Benjamin Flwer	Cardiff	"Upon a vacancy during ye civil wars"	Walk. c. 4, f. 67.
John Gumbleden	Coyty	Nov. 29, 1645	L. J. VIII, 17.
John Powell	Eglwysilen	In possession, 11 Aug., 1649	Lamb. 913, f. 755.

		Parish			
GLAMORGAN (con.) ..	David Davies	Gelligaer	..	'1 At the 4th or 5th yeare of the late C. Mrs",	Walk. c. 4, f. 65.
	—— Alsop	Penarth and Lavernock	..	Before 50, according to context.	Walk. c. 4, f. 69.
	Rees Davies	Pentyrch	..	In possession, 27 Sept., 1649	Lamb. 913, f. 752.
	Thos ?	St. Bride's Minor	..	Feb. 3, 1645-6	L. J. VIII, 142.
	Edmond Ellis	St. Fagans	..	On deprivation, before 1650, of old incumbent.	Wlk. c. 4, f. 67.
	Ambrose Myn 1 ..	Swansea and parishes adjacent.	..	July 27, 1646	Bodl. 323, f. 114.
	Timothy Woodroff 2	We		Oct. 6, 1647	L. J. IX, 471.
	? Walter	Itinerant Mster for the whole ug.	..	July 24, 1646	Bodl. 323, f. 114.
MONMOUTH 3 ..	George Wte	Llanfihangel Ystern Lдrn	..	Oct. 6, 1648	L. J. X, 531.
	1 ? Dauncer	Llanover	..	Dec. 24, 1647	Minutes, p. 497; Lamb. 913, fol. 774.
	George Quarrell	Llanfetherin	..	June 2, 1649	Lib. Inst. Llandaff, fol. 18.
	Moore Pye	Llanvapley	..	Dec. 13, 1649	Lib. Inst. Llandaff, f. 17.
	Richard Jones	St. Michael's juxta Rhymney	..	Aug. 21, 1648	Lib. Inst. Llandaff, f. 115.

1 How ... in the Swansea district is uncertain, for in 1648, he seems to be at work in North Wales (p. 65). It was about 1646-7 that ... must are organised the first 'gather'd church' at Swansea. (... of Mary Maurice in 1675—Broadmead Records, ed. Underhill. (Ba B, p. 514)

2 A *Timothy Woodroff* was ... rle by the Lords (Journals X, 88) ... rtor of Kingsland in Herefordshire on *14 Nov., 1648.* This ... wld ... uke ... rom for John French.

3 Probably *Robert Frampton, rector of Bryngwyn,* ought to be included here. He had been one of the prisoners taken at the surrender of Raglan ... p. 33), but asserts (Cal. Comm. Comp., Vol. III, p. 710) that he was approved by the C.P.M. and admitted ... Oct., 1649. This is ... ily proved by the ... ble in 1662—" the parsonage of Bryngwyn was not ... t ... at all ye right ... er enjoyed it all along." (Lamb. 1027, f. 9). In face of this, Walker's ... fees to him, as a " ... Rector," seem to ... ve no sure ... s, Part II, p. 244; also Wlk. MS. c. 7, ff. 25, 26b).

SOUTH WALES—*continued.*

	MINISTER.	SPHERE OF LABOUR.	DATE OF ORDER, INSTITUTION, OR APPROVAL.	MS. REFERENCE OR OTHER AUTHORITY.
MONMOUTH (*con.*).	Robert Brabourne	Monmouth	Aug. 5, 1646	Bodl. 323, f. 200 ; S. P. Dom. Fl, f.128.
	Henry Rees	Mynyddislwyn	Oct. 1, 1647	Bodl. 325, fol. 168.
	Henry Nills	Bedwas	Soon *after* depriva-tion of Bishop of Llandaff.	Walker c. 4, fol. 66.
PEMBROKE	John Lusye	Angle	" By order of the C.P.M."	Lamb. 915, fol. 138.
	Wm Jones	Burton	Jan. 28, 1648-1649	Lib. Inst, Meneven, fol. 17; Lamb. 915, fol. 100.
	Henry Wms	Carew	Dec. 18, 1646	Lamb. 905, fo. 3-4.
	Edward Provand	Cilgerran	May 1, 1648	Bodl. 325, fol. 196 ; Lamb. 915, fol. 147.
	David James	Cilrhedyn	April 16, 1646	Bodl. 327, fol. 185b.
	Henry Miles	Dinas	Oct. 7, 1647	L. L IX, 474.
	Rard Longstreet	Haverfordwest (St. Mary's)	July 5, 1647	Bodl. 327, fol. 186.
	Thas Field	Lawhadden	May 5, 1649	Bodl. 326, fol. 252.
	Thas Freeman	Llanddewi Efelfre	Feb. 26, 1646	Ms, p. 332 ; Lamb. 902, fol. 108.
	Thomas On	Llanfyrnach	Nov. 26, 1647	L. L IX, 44.
	Morgan Williams	Letterston	Dec. 27, 1646	L. L VIII, 635.
	Edward Mason 1	Mathry	In possession 5 Oct., 1649	Lambeth 905, f. 62.
	William Prichard	Manorbier	July 10, 1647	Bodl. 326, 252b.

			Preaching before Cromwell during siege of Pembroke, 1648	Palmer's Noncom. Memorial
PEMBROKE (con.).	Peregrine Phillips	Munkton	..	II, 629–630. Lamb. 915, fol. 140.
	Robert Tounson	?th	Nov. 13, 1646	Bodl. 324, fol. 30b.
	Jenkin Lewis	Puncheston	May 16, 1649	Bodl. 326, fol. 252.
	Wm Young	Pwllyerochan	Nov. 12, 1646	B dlo 324, fol. 30b ; L. J. IX, 58.
	Lewis Gwynn	St. Bride's	Aug. 24, 1648	L. J. X, 454.
	dAm Waller	St. Florence	Oct. 16, 1648	L. J. X, 546.
	Adam Hawkins 2	St. Ismaell's	July 8, 1646	Bodl. 323, fol. 240.
	Richard Jewell	e?by	May 10, 1644	Bodl. 327, fol. 185.
	Francis Coulton	Uzmaston	Jan. 14, 1646-7	Bodl. 327, fol. 187b.
	3	Wiston	Jan. 14, 1646-7	Bodl. 327, f. 185b.
RADNOR	John Phillips	Diserth	1647	Addit. MS. 15671, fol. 89.
	Charles Price	Glascwm	Sept. 21, 1647	Addit. MS. 15671, fol. 214.
	John Siddall	Knighton	Oct. 11, 1647	State Papers Dom. Interreg. F. 3, MS. 275, fol. 44.
	Richard J neso	Llandegley	In possession 8 Nov., 1649	Lamb. 905, fol. 22.
	John Reynolds	Llansantffraid in Elfel.	In possession 8 Nov., 1649	Lamb. 905, fol. 26.
	Robert Bidwell	Old Radnor	June 13, 1649	Bodl. 326, fol. 256.

1 In the House of Lords MSS. there is a petition (dated 31st July, 1660) of John Owen, sequestered 'divers yeares last past' from the vicarage Mathry. Mason was presumably his successor, and must have been more or less satisfactory to the pre-1650 authorities.

2 Mr. Adam 'Haughkins' is described in Walk. c. 12, f. 8b (1650) as having part of his salary (i.e., an augmentation), viz., £12 6s. 8d., granted him by the *Commissioners for Scandalous Ministers.* Strictly speaking, there was no body so-called ; there had been a *Committee for Scandalous Ministers* (p. 35 supra), and there were to be *Commissioners for the Ejection of Scandalous Ministers* under the Act of 1654 (Firth and Rait : Acts and Ord. II, 968-990).

3 His name is not found in the 'Liber,' nor is it given in the Bodl. MS., nor in the list of Shaw (II, 540). But the Pembroke parochial commissioners report him rejected before 2nd Oct., 1650, although on July 24, 1650, the C.P.M. are giving orders to the Treasurers of Dean and Chapter Lands to pay him arrears of £37 10s. 0d. (Bodl. MS. 327, f. 187).

SOUTH WALES—*continued.*

MINISTER.	SPHERE OF LABOUR.	DATE OF ORDER, INSTITUTION, OR APPROVAL.	MS. REFERENCE OR OTHER AUTHORITY.
RADNOR (*con.*).			
Thomas Evans	Llanbister	In possession 8 Nov., 1649. Ej ed from 'vicaradge' before 1665	Lamb. 905, f. 35. Cod. Ten., vol. 639, f. 337.
Henry ᴀer, ᴀer Cradock, Richard Symonds	} Itinerant Ministers for South Wales.	Nov. 13, 1646	L. J. VIII, 568-569.
[SALOP 1 Rowland ᴀtt	Oswestry	March 3, 1647	ᴅ. ᴀl Comp., Vol. IV, 2529.
ᴀer ᴀas	' of Oswestrey '	1647	Bodl. 4° D, 62 Th. (quoted by Shaw: Hist. of the English ᴀh, Vol. II, App. IIIb, p. 408.)]

1 Inserted here because Oswestry and some adjoining parishes were in the diocese of St. Asaph, had a large Welsh population (vide, "Two great Victories : On obtained by the Earl of Denbigh at Oswestry," p. 4, N.L.W.), and more especially because Nevett and Thomas ("Car-wr y Cymru") became approvers under the Act of Propagation [p. 85.].

Future events were to prove that the Puritanism of many in the foregoing list was highly artificial. Here and there pluralists still lingered on notwithstanding the ordinance of Parliament, and the great majority of Welsh livings remained in the possession of the episcopal clergy. They had the wit to conceal their love of the Common Prayer Book and the sense to conduct the services according to the Directory; the fear of ejection undoubtedly forced many to observe a higher standard of pastoral duty; and they profited by the continually multiplying duties of the comparatively small knot of men who were devoted to the service of the Parliament. And the interests of moderate men were not unsafe in the hands of a Parliament which feared the attitude of the Army and sought to make terms with the King.[1] The real feeling of the average clergyman about 1649 is typified in Matthew Evans of Penegoes, who, though he survived the inquisition of the Committee of Montgomery,[2] bitterly objected to his son John falling to nonconformity[3]; in Nathan Jones of Merthyr Tydfil, who came out scatheless from the 'cunning and power' of the C.P.M. to write an account of the pagan Puritans of East Glamorgan[4]; in the short-lived freedom of the appellants of Brecon[5]; and in the embarrassed fortunes of Charles Browne, the vicar of Llangunllo in Radnorshire.[6]

With all its limitations, the first Puritan revolution had gone far. It had diverted the revenues of sinecure livings to the maintenance of a preaching ministry; it had provided suitable spheres of labour to the Puritans of the Llanfaches school; it had acknowledged the claims of the Welsh language; and through it the Church had been completely disestablished and partially disendowed. The second

---

1 Last order of *Parliament* re Wales on 25th Nov., 1648; Pride's Purge, Dec. 6 1648.
   2 Committee ordered by C.P.M. to examine charges on March 21, 1645-6 (Addit. MS. 15670, 45a): Evans in possession 1649-1650 (Exch. Misc. Slip 115).
   3 Palmer's Nonconformist Memorial, Vol. II, p. 842; A. N. Palmer: Hist. of the Older Nonconformity of Wrexham, p. 45.
   4 Wilkins: History of Merthyr Tydfil, IX, p. 94 (" Twelfth Charge "); Walker MS. c. 4, folio 65. Whether Nathan Jones's appeal was to the C.P.M. or to the Barons of the Exchequer remains doubtful, as no record of his case occurs in the surviving reports of either body.
   5 Supra, pp. 51-52.
   6 Sequestered early in 1649; appealed to C.P.M.; Col. Philip Jones appointed to report on the case (Bodl. 326, f. 256, Aug. 17, 1649); found in possession by Surveyors on 8th Nov., 1649 (Lamb. 905, f. 28); within a few months finally ejected by C.P.G.W. (Walk. c. 13, . 65); appointed in 1651 schoolmaster at Llangunllo by the same body (Walk. c. 13, f. 68).

▲

Puritan revolution was to be organised by Commissioners nominated by the Rump, and by Approvers whose guiding spirits had heard new and strange ideas during their exile from Wales.

V.

THE PURITAN SOJOURN IN ENGLAND— COMING OF AUTONOMY.

The London to which the Welsh Puritans fled in 1642-1643 was the scene of actual and imminent changes. The canons of 1640 had been brushed aside by a resolution of Parliament,[1] and men sought in the proposals of Archbishop Ussher,[2] the recommendations of Archbishop Williams' committee,[3] the introduction of the Root-and-Branch Bill,[4] and in correspondence with the Scots and Reformed Churches abroad, for some satisfactory solution of the problems of Church government. In this atmosphere of implied toleration old sects felt the fervour of a new life, and the stored-up Puritanism of the last forty years burst forth into that wonderful confusion of theory and doctrine described by the Raven in-"Llyfr y Tri Aderyn."[5] The Independents moved away from the Jacobite ideal towards complete separation.[6] The seven churches of the Particular Baptists drew up their first Confession of Faith in 1644.[7] And alongside these grew up the Familists who said they were 'godified,' the Sabbatarians who wished to observe the old Sabbath of the Jews, the Anti-Sabbatarians who said that every day was a Sabbath to the Christian, the Seekers who prayed silently for the advent of new apostles, and the Ranters who fell into a vague pantheism and blurred the distinction between good and evil.[8] Religious exiles returned from Holland; divines passed and repassed from New England. The reading of the Bible received great impetus from the orders of the

---

1 C. J. II, 51, 52; L. J. IV, 273.
2 Shaw: Hist. of the English Church during the Civil War, Vol. I, p. 70 (also footnote 1).
3 Ibid., Vol. II, Appendix 1, pp. 287-294.
4 C. J. III, 57.
5 Llwyd, Gweithiau, Vol. I, p. 179.
6 Henry Burton's "Protestation Protested" (1641); Katharine Chidley's "Justification of the Independent Churches of Christ" (1641); Lord Brooke's "Discourse" (1641). Dale: Hist. of English Congregationalism, pp. 369-371.
7 McGlothlin: Baptist Confessions of Faith, pp. 174-189.
8 Braithwaite: The Beginnings of Quakerism, pp. 13-15; Jones: Studies in Mystical Religion, p. 469.

Directory,[1] and there was almost complete liberty of the press. This pervasive spirit of untrammelled freedom found its most virile exponents in the Army, since 1645[2] mainly commanded by officers who saw the direct hand of God in all their victories, and full of New Model privates who were daring enough to discuss the highest points in statecraft and Church polity.[3] Here Levellers and Agitators flourished ; hence was to issue the Heads of the Proposals, the Case of the Army, and the Agreement of the People with their emphasis on religious toleration.[4] Powell stayed in the Army for ' some space ' after his arrival in 1642[5] ; Cradock has left a glowing description of the defence of Bristol by Fiennes and of the ' spirituality, self-denial, and fidelity ' of the Parliamentary forces[6] ; Llwyd attended almost every battle and siege in the South of England during the first Civil War[7] ; and Erbery became chaplain in Skippon's regiment at 8/- a day.[8] Projects of social reforms[9] mooted in the Army debates found in the latter a warm defender,[10] and echoes of the same spirit are found in Powell's appeal on behalf of ' beggers' and ' poor prisoners,'[11] and in Llwyd's opposition to capital punishment in a case of mere theft.[12] Gradually as the war waned they all settled down in London and the neighbourhood. Cradock preached at All Hallows in Lombard Street,[13] Powell was at Dartford in Kent for two-and-a-half years,[14] Richard Symonds went further afield as lecturer to Andover,[15] and later was ' beneficed ' at Sandwich in Kent.[16] Erbery spent some time at the Isle of Ely before settling down in London.[17] The undoubted abilities of the Welsh Puritans as preachers soon brought

1 Reliquiæ Liturgicæ, Vol. III, pp. 23-25.
2 Self-denying Ordinance passed April 3, 1645.
3 Baxter : Life, Vol. I, i. 77 ; Simpkinson's Life of Harrison, pp. 40, 41.
4 Gooch : English Democratic Ideas in the Seventeenth Century, chapter IV, pp. 150-156.
5 Life : p. 14.
6 Divine Drops Distilled, pp. 111, 115-116.
7 Gweithiau, Vol. I, Hanes Rhyw Gymro, Song XXVII, pp. 57, 58, esp. stanzas 2, 3, 4, 5, 7, 8.
8 Love : A Cleare and Necessary Vindication, p. 36. (C.F.L).
9 Gooch : English Democratic Ideas, IV, passim.
10 Gweithiau Morgan Llwyd, Vol. II, Introd. xxxii.
11 Saving Faith, p. 93 (N.L.W.) ; also Epistle Dedicatory re ' widdows ' p. [1].
12 Gweithiau, Vol. I, Llyfr y Tri Aderyn. p. 264.
13 Title-page of " Divine Drops Distilled."
14 Life : p. 14 ; the 'Dartmouth' of " Examen et Purgamen Vavasoris " (p. 11) must be a misprint.
15 C. J. II, 432, 440, 735.
16 Edwards : Gangræna, III, pp. 241-2 (1646 edition).
17 D. N. B., Vol. XVII, p. 384.

them recognition from the highest quarters. Cradock delivered a sermon before the House of Commons at St. Margaret's, Westminster, on July 21st, 1646,[1] and Symonds two sermons before the same body, one on 30th September, 1646.[2] and another on 26th April, 1648,[3] while Powell preached before the Lord Mayor of London on 2nd December, 1649,[4] and before the Parliament on February 28th, 1650.[5] This oratorical discipline prepared them for disputations with the leading controversialists of the time. Erbery had in 1646 dared to face the mordant Francis Cheynell in a debate on the delegation of duties in the Christian Church to particular ministers,[6] and Vavasor Powell championed the cause of high Calvinism against the ' sneaking Socinianism ' of John Goodwin.[7] Nor could they remain long unaffected amidst the contagious spread of new ideas. Though sparingly at first, Powell was drawn to the Millenarian calculations of Henry Archer[8] ; Llwyd added to these the mystical notions of Jacob Bœhme, whose works were being translated into English by Ellistone and Sparrow, and published by Giles Calvert[9] ; Erbery fell under the influence of the Seekers and assimilated the teachings of John Saltmarsh and Roger Williams.[10] Cradock alone, Wroth's successor at Llanfaches, and the direct inheritor of his tradition of simplicity, had no sympathy with metaphysical opinions, ' chymeras,' or ' sublimate ' religion.[11] To men such as these, driven from their homes by persecution, obsessed by the inquiring spirit of the Army, and tinctured in most cases by the most advanced of the new ' heresies,' toleration became a ' fundamental.' Cradock resents the idea that the main part of religion is the setting up of ' government '[12]; to Powell ' matters of Discipline and Government ' are grouped under ' other Circumstantialls '[13]; to Llwyd there are ' many forms in our Gamaliels schoole '[14];

1 Saints' Fulnesse of Joy, title page
2 C. J. IV, 678.
3 C. J. V, 545.
4 God the Father Glorified, title page (N.L.W.) ; D.N.B.'s 10*th Dec.*, is a mistake
5 Saving Faith, title page ; D.N.B., Vol. XLVI, p. 250.
6 D.N.B., Vol. XVII, p. 384.
7 D.N.B., Vol. XLVI, 250, 31st Dec., 1649.
8 The Personall Reign of Christ upon Earth (1642). B. Mus. Thomason Tract.
9 W. Hobley : Article II on " Jacob Bœhme "—Traethodydd, May, 1900, p. 170.
10 Henry Nicholls : The Shield Single against the Sword Doubled, pp. 34, 37.
11 Divine Drops Distilled, pp, 225, 226.
12 Saving Faith. Dedication [2.].
13 Christ and Moses Excellency, p. 180.
14 Gweithiau : Vol. I, Song VIII, " 1648." The Spring, stanza 11, p. 25.

the preaching of Erbery's 'dangerous opinions' would only be possible under conditions of absolute toleration. The author of 'Gangræna' is filled with dismay that persons who decried confessions of faith and penal ordinances[1] and dubbed Presbytery 'a limb of Antichrist'[2] should go among such people as the Welsh. The imposition of a rigid Presbyterianism, consequent upon the Royalist victories of 1643 and the compact with the Scots, would be as thoroughly unwelcome to Cradock and his friends as to Selden and the Erastian lawyers of the Parliament. Before their return to Wales they would rejoice to find irresistible forces at work assuring the full triumph of the Puritan movement : such were manifested in the speech of Philip Nye before the Assembly against the proposed institution of a new hierarchy,[3] Cromwell's appeal to the Commons on behalf of 'tender consciences,'[4] Benjamin Rudyard's remark that he could find no guarantee for the new 'jus divinum' in the Sermon on the Mount,[5] and above all, the brilliant victories of the 'heretic' Army of the New Model. And their later itinerant labours would be considerably lightened by the news that the days of the Covenant were over,[6] and that an oath of loyalty to the Republic had taken its place.[7] Thus the intransigeance of the 'old priest' had saved Wales from the 'New England pattern,' and Pride's Purge had saved it from the shackles of the "new presbyter."

The preaching of men so equipped wrought a great transformation. The gospel ran over the mountains between Brecknock and Monmouth like fire in the thatch[8] ; a place of great 'untowardness' like Llangurig became the rallying-point of Puritans under the leadership of Powell and Roberts of Llanbadarn[9] ; and though Llwyd's 'learning was butt a

1 Part III (1646), p. 183. Quotation of Cradock's sermon at Thames Street.
2 Ibid., pp. 241, 242. Quotation of Symonds' sermon at Bath before Fairfax.
3 Dale : Hist. of English Congregationalism, Chapter VI, Note B. [Feb. 21, 1643-4].
4 Shaw: Hist. of the English Church during the Civil War, Vol. II, p. 36. [13th Sept., 1644].
5 One of the Commons' deputation before the Assembly [April 30, 1646]. (Minutes of the West. Assembly, pp. 448-460).
6 C. J. V, 604. 16th June, 1648 : Debate in the Commons whether those taking new commissions under the Parlt. should swear the 'solemn oath.' For : 54 ; against, 84.
7 "The Engagement." Passed third reading in Commons 3rd Jan., 1649-1650. (C. J. VI, 321, 326, 342) ; Firth and Rait : Acts and Ordinances of the Interregnum, Vol. II, pp. 325, 348.
8 Glad Tydings from Heaven to the Worst of Sinn-ners on Eearth (Cradock), p. 50.
9 John Lewis : The Parliament Explained to Wales (1646), p. 32.

zealous face '[1] he gathered together a strong band of ' sainets '
at Wrexham, whom " the countreys feard round about."[2]
In 1646 Powell published his " Scriptures' Concord," whose
Preface states that " in some parts where the Gospel came,
they far and near pressed to hear it night and day,"[3] and in
1647 Matthew Symonds ' from near the Golden Lion in
Aldergate Street ' printed the first Nonconformist Bible for
the people, the work of Powell and Cradock.[4]   In the same
year Oliver Thomas, the author of ' Car-wr y Cymru ' (1630)
issued from the Press an exhausting analysis of the various
types of Christians,[5] and in 1649 appeared a translation
into Welsh of Perkins's " Foundation of the Christian
Religion " by E. R. under the imprimatur of Edmund Calamy
the elder.[6]   The missionary zeal of the London churches
brought new men to the Border. Jeremiah Ives came to
Radnor from the Old Jewry[7] ; Thomas Lamb to the land
west of the Severn from Bel-Alley[8] ; the Church of All
Hallows sent as many as six preachers to Wales, notably
Thomas Barnes and Thomas Ewins, who became pastor of
the Church at Llanfaches.[9]   All these efforts however, were
greatly hindered by the spiritual inertia of the countryside,
the ' seduced ignorance ' of the people[10] and their subservience
to the gentry,[11] and the growing confidence of the unejected
episcopal clergy who construed the downfall of the Presbyterian system and the elimination of the Covenant as heralding
larger freedom.[12]   The year 1648—that of the second Civil
War—made this disaffection active throughout Wales.
Poyer and his followers involved almost all South Wales in
their treason ; Carnarvon responded to the call of Sir John

---

1 A New Ballad of the Plague . . . . p. 8, verse 22. (N.L.W.).
2 Gweithiau : Vol. I, p 88 ; stanza 3, Song xlvii.
3 The Bible in Wales, p. 30 ; Rees : Prot. Noncon., pp. 68, 69.
4 The Bible in Wales, pp. 29, 30 ; Bibliography, p. 10.
   5 Trysor i'r Cymru (ed. Stephen Hughes, 1677) containing " Drychau Ysbrydol "
of Oliver Thomas—" ddarfod printio . . . . Drychau . . . . agos deng
mhlynedd ar hugain a aethant beibio." Llythyr at y Darllennydd [2].
   6 Sail Crefydd Gristnogawl. Imprimatur, page 55. [Art. in ' Beirniad,' Vol. II,
No. 3, October, 1912, by T. Shankland, proves by analogy E.R. to be Roberts of
Llanbadarn, p. 180.]
   7 John Price : The Sun Outshining the Moon, p. 9 (Thomason Tract) ; Wynell
The Covenant Plea for Infants, Preface (Thomason Tract).
   8 Taylor : History of the General Baptists, pp. 100-101.
   9 Broadmead Records (ed. Haycroft), p. 31 ; Calamy : An Account of the
Ministers . . . . [1713], p. 473 (re Barnes).
   10 Phillips : Civil War in Wales, Vol. I, p. 414, Cromwell's opinion ; Vol. II,
Doc. CXIII, pp. 377, 378.
   11 Letters of Horton to Fairfax and the Speaker after the Battle of St. Fagan's
(N.L.W.).
   12 Cal. State Papers, 1649-1650, p. 199.

Owen ; Anglesey to the example of the Bulkeleys of Beaumaris. Vavasor Powell and Ambrose Mostyn had more or
less to give up their preaching for the "disarming of the
disaffected '[1]; the former followed the Parliamentary army
which pacified Anglesey in the summer of 1648.[2] The six
counties of North Wales were associated for mutual defence,[3]
and when the rebellion died out, a fine of £20,500 was imposed
upon South Wales[4] and £24,000 upon North Wales.[5] Even
then Bardsey Island became a vantage-ground for attack,[6]
and St. Tudwal's Road was frequented by Royalist frigates[7] ;
soldiers of the Parliament were detained prisoners at Presteign[8] ; and the Surveyors of Hereford Church lands had
to beat a hasty retreat from the highlands of the county of
Radnor.[9] Moreover, the orders of the C.P.M. in Wales
were subsidiary to their wider activities in England, and the
examining committee of the Assembly, to the great dissatisfaction of Cradock,[10] were very loth to grant their certificates to sectaries of doubtful academic learning. The
conditions seemed to suggest that the difficult problem of
Wales demanded *special* treatment, a policy unhesitatingly
adopted by the Parliament in other parts of the country.
As early as February, 1644, Lord Fairfax had been given
a free hand to place ' able and learned Divines ' in the
Northern parts,[11] and this was followed by an ordinance
making special provision for the maintenance of preaching
ministers in the five principal towns north of the Humber
in 1645[12]; arrangements similar were made for the city and
county of Hereford in 1646[13]; an Act was passed for the
better advancement of the Gospel and Learning in Ireland on
March 8th, 1649-50[14]; and six months before an Act for the
propagation of the Gospel in New England had been adopted
by the Commons.[15] And there was abundant evidence that

1 Phillips : Civil War : Vol. II, Doc. CXI, pp. 373-374.
2 Life, p. 17.
3 Firth and Rait : Acts and Ordinances, Vol I, pp. 1183-1184, 21st Aug., 1648
4 Ibid., Vol. II, pp. 14-15, 23rd Feb., 1648-9.
5 Ibid., Vol. II, pp. 207-212, 10th Aug., 1649.
6 Cal. St. Papers, 1649-1650, p. 4.
7 Ibid., p. 13.
8 Ibid., p. 54.
9 Lamb. 917, fols. 72, 100, 103.
10 Divine Drops Distilled, p. 205 ; Glad Tydings, p. 49.
11 Firth and Rait : Acts and Ordinances, Vol. I, pp. 391-392.
12 Firth and Rait : Acts and Ordinances, Vol. I, pp. 669-671.
13 Ibid., Vol. I, pp. 840-841.
14 Ibid., Vol. II, pp. 355-356.
15 Ibid., Vol. II, pp. 197-200, 27th July, 1649.

the supreme powers in England were not oblivious of the peculiar claims of Wales. The resolution to send *Welsh* ministers to Sir Thomas Middleton in 1644,[1] the order to explain the ' case ' of the Parliament to the people of South Wales after the battle of Naseby,[2] the proposal to enlist the services of a Welsh writer to do similar work for North Wales,[3] the accelerating order to the Committees of North Wales concerning scandalous ministers in 1646,[4] the appointment of itinerants for South Wales in the same year,[5] the suggestion of the Parliamentary correspondent from the investing army of Carnarvon Castle,[6] Cromwell's letter from Putney to Archbishop Williams,[7] the exception from the articles of composition arranged for North Wales of all clergymen ' sequestered or sequestrable,'[8] the solicitude for distinctive Welsh parishioners shown by the C.P.M.,[9] and the desire of the Assembly for a translation of the Directory[10] made up,—together with the reports presented by the Surveyors of Church lands,[11] the dispatches of the Parliamentary generals in 1648, and the persistent iteration of the spiritual needs of Wales by the now influential Welsh Puritans,[12]— a fructifying milieu for the grant of autonomy. July, 1649, saw the appointment to the South Wales command of Major-General Thomas Harrison,[13] one of the most efficient officers of the New Model Army, and one who believed that " God will worke on us soe farre that we are [to be] made able in wisedome and power to carry through thinges in a way extraordinarie, that the workes of men shall bee answerable to his workes."[14] Hugh Peters, a protagonist of Puritanism in Holland, New England, and the Mother Country, landed

1 Supra., p. 40.
2 C. J. IV, 242, 15th Aug., 1645.
3 Phillips : Civil War, Vol. I, p. 320 [quoting The Weekly Account, No. 34, Aug. 26, 1645]. (No evidence that this was actually carried out).
4 C. J. IV, 622, 22nd July, 1646.
5 Supra, p. 61.
6 The taking of Carnarven . . . . . p. 5 (N.L.W.). [Parliament (I doubt not) will take care to send a powerful Ministry so soone as North Wales is totally reduced.]
7 Phillips : Civil War, Vol. I, p. 378—" we shall endeavour to our utmost so to settle the affairs of North Wales as to the best of our understandings does most conduce to the public good thereof." 1st Sept., 1647.
8 Firth and Rait : Acts and Ordinances, Vol. II, p. 209.
9 Supra, p. 43.
10 Supra, p. 45 ; Reference (2).
11 Presented at varying dates from 1647 to 1650.
12 Powell's " Scriptures' Concord," Preface ; Cradock's Saving Faith, p. 34 ; Divine Drops, p. 10.
13 Simpkinson : Life of Harrison, p. 96.
14 Clarke Papers (Camden Society), Vol. I, pp. 282-283. Extract from speech at a meeting of Army officers [Jan. 6, 1649-1650], discussing the " Agreement of the People."

in Pembroke in October of the same year, and remained
there for some months organising supplies for Cromwell's
expedition into Ireland, and incidentally examining the
religious condition of south-western Wales.[1] There is
evidence that Vavasor Powell was in London from the early
days of December, 1649, to the end of February, 1650.[2]
The impressions of the pious soldier, the analysis of the
secular Puritan, aud the expert advice of the Welsh minister,
together with tbe co-operating influence of petitions from
North and South Wales respectively,[3] and the general
sympathy of the Commons, led to the introduction of the
Act of Propagation on 29th January, 1650,[4] and its final
adoption on February 22nd.[5] A week later a similar Act
was passed for the four northern counties of England.[6]

1 D. N. B., Vol. xlv, pp. 72, 73.   (C. H. Firth).
2 Sermon before Lord Mayor (2nd Dec., 1649) ; Sermon before Parliament (28th
Feb., 1650) ; D.N.B., Vol. xlvi, p. 250.
3 C. J. VI, 336, 20th Dec., 1649.
4 C. J. VI, 352.
5 C. J. VI, 369.
6 C. J. VI, 374.

VI.

THE TEXT OF THE PROPAGATION ACT.[1]

[Modernised spelling.]

AN ACT

FOR

THE BETTER PROPAGATION AND PREACHING OF THE GOSPEL

IN

WALES

AND REDRESS OF SOME GRIEVANCES.

Die Veneris, 22 *Februarii,* 1649.

Ordered by the Parliament, That this Act be forthwith printed and published.

HEN. SCOBELL, *Cleric. Parliamenti.*

LONDON,

PRINTED FOR FRANCIS TYTON, FOR THE USE OF THE COMMISSIONERS OF WALES. 1650.

---

1 *Authorities—*
  (i) Collection of Acts and Ordinances—Folio Black Letter—London, 1650. pp. 697-706. [British Museum ; Press Mark—506. d.9. (81) Catalogue.]
  (ii) Firth and Rait : Acts and Ordinances of the Interregrum, Vol. II, pp. 342-348.
  (iii) Collection of Tracts (29th Jan., 1648—8th April, 1653) B. Museum, E. 1060. (Referred to by Gardiner : Hist. of the Commonwealth and Protectorate, Vol. II, p. 194).
  (iv) N.L.W. copy , same as (i). Catalogue, p. 51, No. 150.
  (v) Cymdeithas Llên Cymru Reprint (1908) of the special copy printed for the use of the Commissioners, pp. 9-17.
  (vi) Rees : Protestant Nonconformity, Second Edition, Appendix : Note D, pp. 511-516.
  (vii) St. Asaph : Landmarks in the History of the Welsh Church, Appendix F, 294-300. Same as (v.).

The Parliament of England taking into their serious consideration the great Duty and Trust that lies on them to use all lawful ways and means for the propagation of the Gospel of Jesus Christ in this Commonwealth : in order thereunto, Do Enact and Ordain, and be it Enacted and Ordained by this present Parliament, and by the Authority thereof,

That Col. Thomas Harrison, Col. Philip Jones, Col. John Jones, Sir John Trevor Knight, Henry Herbert, Esq. ; William Herbert, William Packer, William Blethin, Christopher Catchmay, Reece Williams, John Nicholas, Edward Herbert, Robert Jones, Bussy Mansell, Edward Prichard, John Price, Rowland Dawkins, William Boteler, Edward Stradling, John Herbert, Richard Jones, Jenkin Frainlin,[1] John James, Wroth Rogers, John Herring, Stephen Winthrop, Esquires ; Sir Erasmus Phillips, Sampson Lort, Henry Williams, Silvanus Taylor, Richard King, John Williams, John Dancy,[2] Thomas Watkins, James Phillips, John Lewis, William Barber, Esquires ; John Daniel, John Bowen, Gent., John Puleston, one of the Justices of the Court of Common Pleas, Humphrey Mackworth, William Littleton, Robert Duckenfield, Thomas Baker, Hugh Price, Evan Lloyd, Richard Price, Robert Griffith, Edward Owens, George Twisleton, John Carter, Thomas Mason, Leighton Owens, Rice Vaughan, Thomas Ball, Hugh Courtney, Edward Taylor, Roger Sontley,[3] Esquires ; Daniel Lloyd, David Morris, William Wynne, Gentlemen ; Thomas Swift, Esq. ; Hugh Prichard, Gent., John Sadler, John Peck, Luke Lloyd, Andrew Ellis, Ralph Crechley, Esquires ; Lewis Price of Llanwnog, Henry Williams, John Browne, Gent., are hereby constituted and appointed to be Commissioners in the Counties of Montgomery, Denbigh, Flint, Carnarvon, Merioneth, Anglesey, Monmouth, Glamorgan, Pembroke, Carmarthen, Cardigan, Brecknock, and Radnor, and every of them, to put in execution the several powers and authorities hereinafter mentioned and directed (that is to say)

That they the said Commissioners or any five or more

1 ' *Franklin* ' in Calendars of the Committee for Compounding (passim) ; also in Lamb. 1072, f. 49, and in ' Humble Representation and Address,' p. 11.
2 Danzy (Firth and Rait : Acts and Ordinances. Vol. II., p. 15) ; Dantsey (Examen et Purgamen, '' To the Reader '' [3]) : Dauncy (Commonwealth Exch. Papers 251).
3 ' Sonllye ' (Lamb 1027, f. 34 (d)).

of them shall have full power and authority, and are hereby enabled and authorised to receive all Articles or Charges which shall be exhibited against any Parson, Vicar, Curate, Schoolmaster, or any other now having or shall have any Ecclesiastical benefit or promotion within the said counties, or any of them, for any Delinquency, Scandal, Malignancy, or non-Residency ; and upon such articles so exhibited, to grant out Warrants in writing under the Hands and Seals of the said Commissioners, or any five or more of them, to be directed to the party against whom such Articles shall be exhibited, requiring his appearance before such Commissioners, at a certain day and place in the said Warrant mentioned, to answer the said Charge or Articles respectively ; and after notice of the said Warrant personally made or given to the said party Articled against or left at his dwelling House or ordinary place of abode, and that notice proved by Oath to be made by the space of ten days before the day of appearance in the said Warrant mentioned (no just Cause being made and proved to excuse the not appearing) and likewise after answer made by such as shall appear according to summons,

Then the said Commissioners, or any five or more of them, are hereby enabled and authorised to proceed to examination of witnesses upon Oath ; the said examinations and Depositions of such Witnesses to be put in writing, as well on the behalf of the Commonwealth to prove such Charges and Articles, as on the behalf of the parties articled against to make good their Answers ; which Oaths the said Commissioners or any two or more of them, have hereby power to administer.

And after due examination and proof made by confession of the party complained of, or by the Oath of two credible Witnesses, actually to amove, discharge and eject all such Ministers and other persons from their respective Cures, Benefices, Places and Charges, as they the said Commissioners or any five or more of them, upon such hearing shall adjudge to be guilty of any of the Crimes aforesaid, in the said Articles contained and comprised ; and after such Judgment given, in case any person shall find himself aggrieved with such Judgment so given, Then it shall and may be lawful, to and for any twelve or more of the said Commissioners, upon Petition preferred to them by the party grieved, to review, examine and reverse the same, if they or the greater part of them see just cause so to do :

And if notwithstanding the said ejected person shall not find relief within six Weeks after his Petition so preferred, Then the said Commissioners, or any five or more of them, shall at the request of the parties so aggrieved respectively, certify the respective Proceedings and Proofs in such cases respectively to the Committee of Parliament for Plundered Ministers ; who are hereby authorised upon the return of such Certificates, and view of such Proceedings and Proofs, without further examination of Witnesses in such cases, to examine the Grounds of the said respective Judgment appealed from, and to affirm or revoke the same, as they shall find it most agreeable to Justice, and the tenor of this Act.

And be it further Enacted and Declared, That the said Commissioners or any five or more of them, have hereby power and authority to allow the Wife and Children of such Minister or Ministers so ejected and amoved, for their main tenance, a proportion not exceeding a fifth part of the Living, Parsonage, Benefice, Vicarage, Charge or other place, out of which the said Ministers shall be respectively removed (all Parish Charges, Public Taxes, and other Duties being first deducted out of the whole).

And be it further Enacted by the Authority aforesaid, That if any Parson or Vicar holdeth or enjoyeth, or which shall hold or enjoy plurality of Benefices or Ecclesiastical Promotions (one or more of which being within the Counties aforesaid) and upon a Warrant directed to him under the Hands of the said Commissioners or any five of them, requiring him at a certain day and place in the said Warrant mentioned, to make choice and elect which of the said Benefices and Ecclesiastical Promotions he desires to hold : and upon notice of the said Warrant, shall not within forty days after the said notice, make his Election, testified under his hand before five or more of the said Commissioners, which of the said Benefices or Promotions he desires to hold, then from and after such default (no just cause being proved to excuse the same) all his right, title or interest in and to all such Benefices and Promotions to cease, determine, and to be utterly void.

And to the end that godly and painful men, of able gifts and knowledge for the work of the Ministry, and of approved conversation for Piety, may be employed to preach the Gospel in the counties aforesaid (which heretofore abounded in Ignorance and Profaneness) And that fit persons of approved Piety and Learning may have encouragement to employ themselves in the education of Children in piety and good literature, Be it Enacted by the Authority aforesaid, That the said Commissioners, or any five or more of them, be and are authorised and enabled to grant Certificates by way of approbation to such persons as shall be recommended and approved of by Henry Walter, Walter Cradock, Richard Symonds, Roger Charnock, Jenkin Lloyd, Morris Bidwell, David Walter, William Seaborn,[1] Edmond Ellis, Jenkin Jones, George Robinson, Richard Powell, Robert Powell, Thomas Ewins,[2] John Miles, Oliver Thomas, Doctor John Ellis, Ambrose Mostyn, Stephen Lewis, Morgan Lloyd, William Jones, Richard Edwards, Vavasor[3] Powell, Richard Swain, Rowland Nevett, Ministers of the Gospel, or any five or more of them, for the preaching of the Gospel in the said counties, as well in settled Congregations and Parochial Charges, as in an Itinerary course, as the said Commissioners (by the advice of such the said Ministers as shall recommend and approve of the said persons respectively) shall adjudge to be most for the advancement of the Gospel, or for the keeping of Schools, and education of Children :

And to the end that a fitting maintenance may be provided for such persons as shall be so recommended and approved of, as also for such others approvedly godly[4] and

---

1 ' Sebborne ' (Walk. c. 13, f. 17).

2 ' Ewins ' is the spelling throughout in the Broadmead Records, Calamy's ' Account,' and the Episcopal returns of 1665 ; there is a variant ' Evenes ' in the Tenths Accounts of 1657-58 quoted by Shaw (Vol. II, App. IX, p. 594). The ' Owen ' suggestion of Archdeacon Thomas (Dioc. of St. Asaph, p. 109, First Ed.) seems to be a desire to make a man look a Welshman who was really a genuine Saxon.

3 ' Valvasor ' always in Walker's ' Sufferings,' in the Propagation Treasurer's account for Brecon (Walk. c. 13, f. 60), and in the latter of Challenge addressed to Powell in 1652 by Alex. Griffith (Petition of South Wales, p. 17). The latter playfully reads his name as ' Value for ' in quoting Vavasor's letter to ' A Perfect Diurnall ' (Petition, p. 6.)

4 Rees : Hist. Prot. Nonconformity, App., p. 513, makes this context to read ' approved *by* godly,' which would mean the setting up of a dual system of approving. It has no authority whatsoever.

painful Ministers now residing within the said Counties, for whose support and maintenance there is little or no settlement made or provided ; Be it therefore Enacted and Ordained by the Authority aforesaid, That in order to the said maintenance, and in the regulating, ordering and disposal thereof, they the said Commissioners, or any twelve or more of them, are hereby authorised and enabled by themselves, or others deriving authority from them, to receive and dispose of all and singular the Rents, Issues, and Profits of all and every the Rectories, Vicarages, Donatives, sinecures, Portion of Tenths, and other Ecclesiastical Livings, which now are, or hereafter shall be in the disposing of the Parliament, or any other deriving Authority from them ; as also to receive and dispose of the Rents, Issues and Profits of all Impropriations and Glebelands within the said Counties, which now are, or hereafter shall be under Sequestration, or in the disposal of the Parliament, by virtue of any former Statute, or any Act or Ordinance of this present Parliament.

And be it further Enacted by the Authority aforesaid, That the said Commissioners, or any twelve or more of them, shall and may out of the said Rents, Issues and Profits of the said Rectories, Vicarages, Donatives, sinecures, Portione of Tenths, and other Ecclesiastical Promotions ; as also out of the Rents, Issues and Profits of the said Impropriations and Glebelands, order and appoint a constant yearly maintenance for such persons as shall be recommended and approved of as aforesaid, for the work of the Ministry, or the Education of Children ; provided that the yearly maintenance of a Minister do not exceed one hundred pounds, and the yearly maintenance of a Schoolmaster exceed not Forty pounds :

And that godly Ministers (who have or shall have Wife or Children) may not too much be taken off from their duties in the Ministry, with the care and consideration of maintenance for their Wives and Children after their decease, but that some care thereof may be had by others, whereby a greater encouragement may be given to them to set themselves the closer to the work of the said Ministry ; Be it Enacted by the Authority aforesaid, That the said Commissioners, or any twelve or more of them, are hereby enabled and authorised to make such yearly allowance to the Wife and Children of such godly Minister after his decease, as to the said Commissioners or any twelve of them shall seem reasonable, for the necessary support and maintenance of such Wife or Children, or any of them, Provided always, That such allowance so to be made to such Wife and Children, do not exceed the yearly sum of thirty pounds :

And if any person or persons being Tenant or Occupier of any Lands, tenements or Hereditaments, liable and subject to the payments of any Tenths or other Duties in right payable or belonging to any Parsonage, Vicarage, or any the abovesaid Ecclesiasticall Promotions, shall refuse payment thereof, Then the said Commissioners or any two or more of them, are hereby authorised and enabled to put in execution against every person and persons so refusing, the powers and authorities vested and settled by this present Parliament in the Justices of the Peace, for the relief of Ministers from whom such Tenths and Duties are detained and subtracted.[1]

And be it further Enacted by the Authority aforesaid, That the said Commissioners or any twelve or more of them, out of the said Tenths, Rents, and Profits by them receivable by force of this Act, shall and may allow such moderate salary or wages to such person or persons who shall be employed in the receiving, keeping, and disposal thereof, as they shall conceive to be necessary and reasonable.

And be it further Enacted by the Authority aforesaid, That all and every person and persons qualified and approved of as abovesaid, for the preaching of the Gospel as aforesaid, who shall be vested and settled by the said Commissioners or any twelve or more of them, in any Rectory, Vicarage, or Parochial Charge, which the said Commissioners or any twelve or more of them have hereby power to do, shall be deemed and adjudged to be seized of the same, as fully and amply, to all intents and purposes, as if such person and persons were presented, instituted and inducted to and in the same, according to former Laws in such cases used and provided.

And whereas the remoteness of the said Counties from

---

1 Scobell : Acts and Ordinances, Vol. I, p. 129, 9th Aug., 1647 ; Ibid., Vol. I, p. 180, 27th Oct., 1648.

the Courts of Justice at Westminster occasioneth˙ many
acts of high Misdemeanours, Oppression and injury to be
committed there, which often times escape unpunished,
and the persons aggrieved thereby, for want of means to
seek relief by due course of Law, left remediless ; To the
end therefore that such Misdemeanours, Oppressions and
Injuries may the better be enquired after, and the parties
aggrieved thereby without much expense of monies or loss
of time, may be in some way of relief, Be it enacted by the
Authority aforesaid, That the said Commissioners or any
five or more of them, shall have, and hereby have full Power
and Authority to receive all Complaints which shall be
brought before them, of any such Misdemeanours, Oppression
or Injury committed by any person or persons within the
said Counties, or any of them ; and by Warrant directed to
the party complained of, under the Hands and Seals of the
said Commissioners or any five or more of them, to appear
before them at a certain day and place in the said˷Warrant
mentioned, requiring an Answer to the said Complaints ;
and after answer made, then with the consent of both parties,
testify under their Hands and Seals, to proceed to hear and
determine the same.

And whereas sufferings of that nature generally fall upon
persons well-affected to the Parliament, and such as have
acted in and for their service, which said persons are not
of ability to travel to London, to be relieved by the Committee
of Parliament, commonly called the Committee of Indemnity,
Be it therefore Enacted and Ordained by the Authority
aforesaid, That the said Commissioners, or any five or more
of them, shall be, and are hereby made and constituted a
Committee of Indemnity, to all intents and purposes, within
the Counties aforesaid, for the hearing and determining of all
matters and things properly relievable and determinable by
the said Committee of Indemnity. Provided always, That
if any person or persons shall find him or themselves aggrieved
at the proceedings of the said Commissioners, acting as a
Committee of Indemnity, then the said person or persons so
aggrieved shall and may prosecute his or their Petition or
Appeal for relief, in such manner and form as in and by this
Act is prescribed in the case of ejected Ministers, and bring

the same to a final determination before the said Committee of Indemnity sitting at Westminster ; which said Committee are hereby authorised to hear and determine the same, as they shall see just cause.

And be it further Enacted, That all Power and Authority formerly vested in any Committee within the said Counties, or any of them, for the placing of Ministers in Ecclesiastical Livings or Promotions, be from henceforth determined ; and that no person or persons shall be from henceforth vested and settled in any Rectory, Vicarage, or Ecclesiastical Promotion within any of the said Counties, unless such person or persons so to be vested or settled be recommended and approved of for the work of the Ministry, according to the tenor and true meaning of this Act : And that this Act shall continue and be in force for the space of Three years, from the Five and twentieth day of March, One thousand six hundred and fifty and no longer.

VII.

COMMISSIONERS[1] AND APPROVERS.

The Commissioners had perforce to be enthusiastic adherents of the Parliament, and the great majority had already enjoyed experience in various phases of administration. Out of the eight Monmouthshire men five were members of the Committee of the County which kept up a grimly humorous correspondence with the old Earl of Worcester prior to the surrender of Raglan in 1646[2]; three of the Denbighshire group figure on the Committee of Sequestrations which granted the tithes of Bettws to John Holland in 1648[3]; Hugh Price of Gwernygo, Richard Price of Gwynly, and Lewis Price of Llanwnog were members of the Committee of Accounts for the County of Montgomery, and Robert Griffith was 'solicitor' for sequestrations[4]; Richard King, Henry Williams, and John Williams were Commissioners for the Militia in the county of Radnor[4]; and four had acted on the Committee to provide salaries for the South Wales itinerants appointed in 1646.[5] Forty out of the seventy-one Commissioners had already been Commissioners to raise 'moneys' in their respective counties for the army under Fairfax in 1647[6]; thirty-eight were named in the ordinance for raising £20,000 a month for the relief of Ireland[7]; thirty-nine in a further ordinance for the military assessment of 17 March in the same year[8]; sixteen out of the twenty-eight North Wales representatives were deputed to carry out the associating ordinance of 21 August, 1648,[9] and twenty to

1 The editor of the Calendars of the Committee for Compounding continually refers to the Commissioners as the " Society " for the P.G.W. on analogy, presumably, of the S.P.C.K.
2 The Committees answer thereunto (" A letter from the Earl of Worcester to the Committee of Parliament sitting in the County of Monmouth "). Printed June 9, 1646. (N.L.W.).
3 Supra, p. 47.
4 Commonwealth Exchequer Papers, No. 251 [sheets not numbered] containing Orders and Correspondence of various County Committees.
5 Supra, p. 61.
6 Firth and Rait : Acts and Ordinances, Vol. I, pp. 962-980.
7 Ibid., Vol. I, pp. 1072-1098, 16th Feb., 1647-8.
8 Ibid., Vol. I, p. 1112.
9 Ibid., Vol. I, pp. 1183-1184.

levy the composition fine of 10 August, 1649[1] ; twenty out
of the thirty-one South Wales Commissioners had similar
duties to execute the fine levied on 23 Feb., 1648-9[2] ; forty-six
figured in the ordinance for raising £90,000 a month for six
months towards the maintenance of the forces (7 April,
1649)[3] ; and sixty-seven in a further ordinance of assessment
passed in December of the same year.[4] Irretrievably committed to the interests of Parliament were John Lewis, who
had explained its cause to Wales in a tract of 35 pages ; Henry
Herbert, member of the Long Parliament since 1642 and
for a time one of its Commissioners residing in the Scots
Army[5] ; John Puleston who, when a barrister of the Middle
Temple, had assisted William Prynne and others in ' regulating ' the University of Oxford in 1647[6] ; Sir John Trevor,
who had been member of the Derby House Committee since
2 June, 1648[7] ; and Philip Jones of Llangyfelach, who had
hardly entered Parliament before he was named additional
Commissioner in the Act for Maintenance of Ministers.[8]
Even more extreme cases were Duckenfield, Harrison, and
John Jones, who had " heard, tried and adjudged "
Charles I,[9] while the two latter had signed the death-warrant.
More than a dozen of the Commissioners held responsible
military posts. Edward Prichard was Governor of Cardiff,
Philip Jones of Swansea, Rowland Dawkins of Carmarthen
and Tenby, John Nicholas of Chepstow, Hugh Price of Red
Castle, John Sadler of Holt, Andrew Ellis of Hawarden,
George Twisleton of Denbigh, John Carter of Conway, Thomas
Mason of Carnarvon, Thomas Swift of Holyhead, and also
superintendent of the postal packet to Ireland.[10] Within the
year 1650 Sampson Lort is made responsible for the victualling
of ships sailing from Milford Haven for the pacification of
Ireland,[11] and Hugh Courtney is Quarter-master General and
Deputy Governor of Beaumaris.[12] Some of the Commissioners

1 Firth and Ralt : Vol. II, p. 212.
2 Ibid., Vol. II, p. 15.
3 Ibid., Vol. II, pp. 24-47
4 Ibid., Vol. II, pp. 294-315.
5 W. R. Williams : Parl. Hist. of the Principality of Wales, p. 123.
6 Firth and Rait : Acts and Ordinances, Vol. I, pp. 925-927—" Master John
Pulizton."
7 D.N.B., Vol. LVII, p. 221.
8 C. J. VI, 365 (15th Feb., 1649-1650) ; admitted to sit for Brecknock, 6th Feb.
(C. J. VI, 358).
9 Firth and Rait : Acts and Ordinances, Vol. I, pp. 1254-1255.
10 Calendars of State Papers, Dom. 1649-1660, passim.
11 Cal. St. Papers, Dom. 1650, p. 454, Dec. 3.
12 Ibid., p. 312, Aug. 30.

had performed services during the Civil Wars worthy of special mention. Philip Jones had been 'in many ways helpful' before and during the battle of St. Fagans[1]; Edward Taylor had actually unhorsed and made prisoner the redoubtable Sir John Owen at the battle of Llandegai[2]; Richard Price had prevented the arrival of succour from Denbigh at a critical moment in the siege of Ruthin Castle[3]; General Mytton had spoken in the very highest terms of the services of Thomas Mason at the same juncture[4]; to S. R. at the siege of Carnarvon John Carter was " a very pritty gentleman, full of action "[5]; and Mason, Ball, and Richard Price had been granted the sum of £2,000 between them out of the composition fine of North Wales for " their good and faithful services to the Commonwealth," and as " a reparation towards their Arrears, Disbursements and Sufferings."[6] Bussy Mansell acted as Commander-in-Chief of the Parliaments' forces in Glamorgan until the arrival of Horton,[7] and John Jones of Maesygarnedd had negotiated the surrender of Anglesey both in 1646 and 1648.[8]

As their names suggest, many of the Commissioners were not Welshmen. Twisleton came originally from Yorkshire,[9] Carter from Buckinghamshire,[10] Courtney from Cornwall.[11] Thomas Mason had lost a command in Ireland because he had refused to bear arms against the Parliament,[12] and Thomas Swift first came into notice in the affrays before Welshpool as one of the Earl of Denbigh's captains of cavalry.[13] Eleven of the Commissioners came from the

1 A Letter from Col. Horton to his Excellency the Lord-General (St. Fagons, May 6, 1648), p. 9 (N.L.W.).
2 Narrative together with Letters presented by Captaine Taylor to the Honourable House of Commons . . . p. 5. [June 5, 1648.] [N.L.W.]; A Letter from Chester of the Great Victory against . . . Sir John Owen, p. 6. [8th June, 1648.] [N.L.W.]
3 A Letter to the Honorable William Lenthal, Esq., Concerning the Surrender of Ruthin Castle, pp. 3, 4. N.L.W.
4 Ibid., p. 5.
5 The taking of Carnarven . . . . p. 6. N.L.W.
6 Firth and Rait : Acts and Ordinances, Vol. II, p. 212.
7 W. R. Williams : History (Parliamentary) of the Principality of Wales, p. 99 ; J. Hobson Matthews : Cardiff Records, Vol. V, p. 493.
8 D.N.B., Vol. XXX, p. 125 ; An Exact Relation of the Whole Proceedings of Gallant Col : Mittou in North Wales. p. 7. N.L.W.
9 Williams : Parliamentary History, p. 4.
10 Ibid., p. 74.
11 Simpkinson : Life of Harrison, p. 214 [quoting Sec. Thurloe's letter of February, 1655-6 to General Monk re imprisonment of Harrison and followers. Ultimately, they had to retire to *their own counties* . . . Courtney to *Cornwall.*]
12 A Letter to the Honorable William Lenthal, Esq., concerning the Surrender of Ruthin Castle [from General Mytton]. Printed April 14th, 1646, p. 5 (N.L.W.).
13 Collonel Mittons valiant Exploits certified . . . . Pr. Aug. 14, 1644, p. 3. (N.L.W.).

English Border : Wroth Rogers, once a tailor of Llanfaches,[1] was Governor of Hereford, Humphrey Mackwòrth Governor of Shrewsbury, and Robert Duckenfield Governor of Chester[2] ; John James, John Herring and Stephen Winthrop were Herefordshire men[3] ; so also was William Littleton, Justice of Great Sessions for Carnarvon, Anglesey and Merioneth[4] ; John Browne, Leighton Owens, and Thomas Baker of Swinney all came from the county of Salop.[5] Out of the thirteen Commissioners who had their homes in the *Wrexham* district four had English names.[6] The five most distinctively Welsh counties supplied only two between them : one from Carmarthenshire (James Phillips of Tregibby), one from Cardiganshire (John Lewis of Glasgrug), *not one* from either Merioneth, Carnarvon, or Anglesey.[7] Thus the personnel of the Commissioners illustrate the territorial range of the Puritan interests and the thoroughly *English* atmosphere of the Puritan conquest.[8] The Anglesey poetaster, John Griffith of Llanddyfnan, waxes satirical over the ' dim Cymraeg ' of the plebeian officers of the Parliamentary army[9] ; to the constable of Corwen the Commissioners who sequestered livings in the Vale of Edeyrnion were all " strandgers."[10] Even John Lewis rejoices that God had providentially designed the pacification of Cardiganshire for men " of our own bowels."[11] Morgan Llwyd, on the other hand, finds precedent for the rise of originally obscure men to greatness in the stories of Gideon, Saul, and David.[12] The arrival of ' strange ' men and the intense Royalist bias of the native gentry account for the very few representatives of old Welsh families among the Commissioners. Such were Sampson Lort of Stackpole Court, Sir Erasmus Phillips of Picton Castle, Sir John Trevor of Trefalun, and John Puleston of Emral ; some important families find a place through collateral members. William Herbert of Coldbrook,

---

1 The Diary of Walter Powell of Llantilio Crossenny (ed. Bradney), p. 42, n. 1.
2 Calendars of State Papers Domestic (1649-1660), passim.
3 Names appear as Commissioners for *Herefordshire* under various ordinances.
4 Cal. St. Papers, Dom. 1654, p. 102. Died 1652.
5 Under ' Salop ' in various ordinances for assessment, etc.
6 A. N. Palmer : Hist. of the Older Nonconformity of Wrexham, pp. 4-31.
7 *I.e.,* excluding *Englishmen* in command of garrisons.
8 This is more especially true of *North Wales.*
9 Addit. MS. 14891, folio 7 ; 14874, folio 131b.
10 Lamb. 1027, fol. 34, Report [d].
11 The Parliament Explained to Wales, Part III, p. 31 ; Phillips : Civil War, Vol. I, pp. 355-356.
12 Gweithiau, Vol. I, " Llyfr y Tri Aderyn," p. 169.

his son Henry, and Edward Herbert of Grange were
descendants in the second line of the Sir William Herbert
who fell at Banbury[1] and who had secured a good share of
the plunder of their ancient home ; John Herbert, mayor
of Cardiff in 1650,[2] and steward of his father's manor of
Llystalybont,[3] was the seventh son of the fourth Earl of
Pembroke[4] ; Edward Stradling of Roath was the grandson
of a natural son of Sir Edward Stradling of St. Donats[5] ;
and Bussy Mansell was the heir of a third son of Sir
Thomas Mansell of Margam.[6] The bulk of the Commissioners,
barring successful soldiers of fortune, were country squires
like Richard Price, prosperous yeomen like Roger Sontley,
or aspiring lawyers like Christopher Catchmay of Trelech
in Monmouth,[7] and Robert Griffith and Rice Vaughan of
Montgomery.[8] Wales during the Propagation regime was
governed by a military middle class.

Some, like Philip Jones, had been enthusiastic for the
Parliament from the beginning, while the ' good affection '
of others was a later development. The elder Herbert of
Coldbrook did not begin to ' hinder ' the Royal cause until
the Abergavenny conference in September, 1645[9] ; Edward
Prichard of Llancaiach had entertained the King at his
house in August, 1645[10] ; the family of Picton Castle had
occasionally lapsed in their loyalty to the Puritan cause[11] ;
Sampson Lort was charged with supplying Poyer with
thirty-six bushels of corn in April, 1648[12] ; and James Phillips
of Tregibby is described after the Restoration as " having
the good fortune to be in with all times."[13] Like the latter,
a large proportion of the surviving Commissioners took the
line of least resistance and " made their peace " in 1660 :
Bussy Mansell ' early repenting '[14] ; John Nicholas was one

1 G. T. Clark : Limbus Patrum Morganiæ et Glamorganiæ, p. 293.
2 Cardiff Records, Vol. V, p. 513.
3 Ibid., Vol. V, p. 547.
4 Ibid., Vol. II, p. 53.
5 G. T. Clark : Limbus Patrum, p. 439 (Stem IXb, should be VIIIb).
6 Ibid., p. 496. [Edward Prichard had married Mansell's sister Mary, p. 496.]
7 Diary of Walter Powell, p. 43, n. 3 ; Lamb. 1027, No. 23.
8 Cal. State Papers, 1653-54, p. 34 [rival for office of prothonotary in Counties
Mont. and Denbigh].
9 J. R. Phillips : Hist. of the Civil War, Vol. II, Doc. LXXX, p. 268.
10 Ibid., Vol. I, p. 314.
11 Ibid., Vol. II, Doc. XXIV, C. p. 85.
12 Cal. Committee for the Advance of Money, Vol. II, p. 1019. (He was discharged,
however, 15th March, 1649-50, and on March 14, 1649-50, the Admiralty Comm.
term him ' an able man.' C.S.P., 1649-1650, p. 39.).
13 Williams : Parl. Hist., . 30.
14 State Papers, Dom. Carp II, Vol. 396, No. 140.

of those whom the King " wanted to call home '" from exile[1] ;
John Carter became Steward of the manor of Denbigh in
July, 1660, and Governor of Holyhead in November of the
same year[2] ; and even Philip Jones is confident of a successful
appeal against some of his lands being given to the Earl
of Worcester "because he has as good and firm an estate
therein as the laws can give."[3] He became High Sheriff of
Glamorgan in 1671,[4] and managed to hand over his acquired
estates almost intact to his successors at Fonmon Castle.[5]
That there were among the Commissioners uncompromising
Puritans of a more genuine type is proved by the attitude
of some of them towards the Protectorate of Cromwell and
the fortitude of others under the Anglican supremacy that.
set in with the Restoration and the Clarendon Code. William
Blethin kept a conventicle at Dinham in 1669[6] ; Rice
Williams the same at Newport[7] ; Richard King was one of
the justices of New Radnor who countenanced Vavasor
Powell in his opposition to the Protectorate in 1654[8] ; John
Williams and Thomas Watkins are accused of having left
the 'service' at the Quarter Sessions of Radnor to hear
Morgan Llwyd's "dangerous and seditious sermons against
the Protector" at the same crisis[9] ; eleven of the Commissioners subscribed the "testimony on truth's behalf
against wickedness in high places" at the end of 1655[10] ;
Lewis Price was imprisoned at Welshpool in 1660,[11] and
soon afterwards is said to have left the country[12] ; and
Hugh Courtney, after suffering various terms of imprisonment for disaffection towards the Cromwellian regime, had
to leave England early in 1661 never to return.[13] John

1 Williams : Parl. Hist., p. 125.
2 Ibid., p. 74.
3 House of Lords MSS. Comm. Reports, Appendix I, p. 160. Date of petition;
17th Feb., 1661-2; Further petition, March 10, 1661-2 (p. 162).
4 Williams : Parl. Hist., p. 98.
5 Grant Francis : Swansea Charters, Appendix VIII, pp. 167-207.
6 Lamb. 639 (Codices Tenisoniani), fol. 186b.
7 Ibid., fol. 188.
8 Thurloe State Papers : Vol. II, 128. Letter of Capt. Halle to Alex. Griffith,
2nd March, 1653-4.
9 Ibid., Vol. II, 129. Letter of Chas. Roberts to John Gunter (no date).
10 *A Word for God* (Thomason Tract B.M.), pp. 8-11. ["A paper newlye
exhibited . . . by *Vavasor Powell.* Thurloe to Henry Cromwell, Jan. 1, 1655-6].
Names:—Richard Price, John Williams, Henry Williams (1), Edward Owens, Lewis'
Price, John James, John Browne, Hugh Pritchard, Henry Williams (2), William
Wynne, Hugh Price.
11 Letter of High Sheriff of Mont. to Privy Council, 24th June, 1660: Quoted in
Spluther James : Hanes y Bedyddwyr, pp. 395-397.
12 Letter of High Sheriff of Mont. to Privy Council, 22nd Aug., 1660. Quoted in
Spinther James : Hanes y Bedyddwyr, pp. 395-397.
13 Williams : Parl. Hist., p. 3.

Browne, again, is reported to have broken the terms of the Conventicle Act in 1669[1] ; the house of Luke Lloyd at Bryn[2] in English Flint and that of William Wynne at Cristionydd[3]- near Ruabon are ' meeting-places ' under the 1672 Declaration of Indulgence ; and Richard Price of ' Groynly ' is described as a ' teacher '[4] during that short-lived period of Puritan freedom. And the religious outlook of these and others is further attested in manifold ways. John Herring welcomed at his house the Quaker preachers Camm and Audland on their journey northward from Bristol in September, 1654[5] ; Hugh Price and Lewis Price are among the eleven signatories to the glowing tribute of Vavasor Powell's labours affixed to his " Life " in 1671[6] ; Robert Duckenfield was a patron of the extreme Independent Samuel Eaton[7] ; Sir John Trevor had provided a refuge for William Jones after his ejection from Denbigh[8] ; Judge Puleston and his lady had invited Philip Henry to Emral and Worthenbury in 1653[9] ; the latter speaks with great respect of Edward Taylor,[10] John Sadler,[11] and especially of Luke Lloyd, " the top branch in all respects of our small vine "[12] ; Edward Prichard became a zealous Baptist[13] ; and Daniel Lloyd, John Browne, Edward Taylor, and David Maurice were important members of Morgan Llwyd's ' gathered ' church at Wrexham.[14] Finally, Thomas Harrison and John Jones suffered death as regicides in 1660. Powell's opinion was that " most of them are really godly."[15]

Men of such type would naturally enter upon their new duties in 1650 with zest, but hardly any of them were able to devote their attention exclusively to them. The head of

1 Lamb. Codices Tenisoniani, Vol. 639. fol. 192b. [" teacher " at Milford in Salop].
2 State Papers, Dom. Car. II, Entry Book 38A, p. 244.
3 Ibid., p. 201. [' Christionate.'] Licence issued 22nd July, 1672.
4 Ibid., p. 262. Licence issued 28th Oct., 1672.
5 Braithwaite : The Beginnings of Quakerism, p. 119, n. 3 ; p. 168, n. 2.
6 p. 123.
7 Burrage : The Early English Dissenters, Vol. I, p. 328 ; Urwick : Historical Sketches of the County Palatine of Cheshire, p. 11.
8 State Papers, Dom. Car. II, Entry Book 38A, p. 261. [' Plosteake,' —Plas Teg, Flintshire.] Lic. issued October 28, 1672 ; Calamy : An Account of the Ministers . . . . Vol. II, 713. [" Allowed Land to the value of £20 per annum."]
9 Philip Henry : Diaries and Letters, ed. Matthew Henry Lee, p. 15.
10 Ibid., pp. 75, 77, 252, 260.
11 Ibid., p. 118.
12 Ibid., p. 374.
13 Joshua Thomas : Hanes y Bedyddwyr (Pontypridd ed.), p. 176.
14 Gweithiau : Vol. II, " Llythyrau." IV, p. 250.
15 A Perfect Diurnall (May 3-10, 1652). His accompanying remark that " they were all faithful to the Parliament from the beginning " is disproved by the facts cited on p. 94.

the Commission had to leave South Wales in June, 1650,[1] to become Commander-in-Chief of the home forces during the absence of the Lord General ; in July of the same year[2] he was made Lieutenant of the Ordnance, and until the battle of Worcester in 1651 the Council of State ply him with orders varying from the defence of Lancashire[3] to the prevention of robberies in the neighbourhood of London.[4] John Jones served on the first Council of State[5], and in July, 1650, he was appointed one of the Commissioners to assist the Lord Deputy of Ireland for two years[6], being re-appointed in 1652 for another term.[7] Harrison and Sir John Trevor were members of the Third (1651)[8] and Fifth (1652-3) Councils of State[9] under the Commonwealth. Puleston was kept busy by his ordinary duties at the Common Pleas, the trial of John Lilburne the Leveller[10], and the judicial commission to deal with disturbances in the eastern counties.[11] The general unrest of the spring and summer of 1651 caused urgent messages to be sent from the Council of State to all men holding military posts in Wales to redouble their vigilance, recruit troops, and march with them to certain specified points. More than half the Commissioners were in command of troops at this juncture as Captains, Cornets, or Lieutenants.[12] Courtney's duties at Beaumaris were especially onerous.[13] Rowland Dawkins had to suppress an insurrection in Cardiganshire.[14] Affairs in Ireland continually called for more troops : William Barber was ' one of the Commissioners out of the Countrey ' for that purpose,[15] and there is a record that £34 18s. 0d. was paid to Capt. John Dancy for ' raising, Impresting, and Conducting ' fifty foot-soldiers out of the

---

1 Cal. St. Papers, 1650, pp. 207, 222.
2 Ibid., p. 261.
3 Calendar of State Papers, 1650, p. 288, Aug. 15.
4 Ibid., p. 442, Nov. 26.
5 Firth and Rait : Acts and Ordinances, Vol. II, p. 2. (attended 172 out of a possible 319, C.S.P., 1649-1650. Preface, lxxv.).
6 C. S. P., 1650, p. 228.
7 C. J. VI, 434 ; VII, 167 ; C. S. P. 1652, p. 365, Aug. 12 ; John Jones was present at a meeting of the *South* Wales Commissioners at Roath on March 6, 1652-3 (Lamb. 1006, fol. 53), probably on his way *to* or *from* Ireland.
8 C. S. Papers, 1651, Preface xxxv. Possible attendances, 248 (Harrison, 46 ; Trevor, 169.).
9 Ibid. 1653, ,, xxxiii. ,, : ,, 122 (Harrison, 32 ; Trevor, 77.):
10 C.S.P., 1650, p. 335. Oct. 10 (nominated one of Judges).
11 Ibid., pp. 463-4. Dec. 9 (nominated one of Judges).
12 *Especially* Cal. St. Papers, 1650 pp. 505-512.
13 Ibid., 1651, p. 303.
14 Williams : Parly. History, p. 45,
15 Walker MS., c. 13, fol. 8b,

H

county of Radnor to Milford for the ' Recrewt ' of regiments
in Ireland.[1]   Duckenfield was made responsible for the
subjection of the Isle of Man,[2] and Parliament ordered the
Council of State to present Humphrey Mackworth with a
chain of gold and a medal worth £100 for his services at
Shrewsbury.[3]   And the vast expense of the Army's upkeep
led to heavy assessments ; practically all the Commissioners
were nominated in the ordinance of 25 Nov., 1650, to raise
' £120,000 per mensem ' for four months,[4] and in a further
ordinance to the same purpose passed on 10 Dec., 1652.[5]
Others were kept busy by the Committee for Compounding.
Jenkin Franklin was one of the Sequestration Commissioners
for South Wales appointed on February 7, 1650[6], and
eleven of the North Wales Commissioners performed similar
duties there.[7]   Rice Williams and Christopher Catchmay
were appointed to hold courts on various sequestered manors
committed to the care of the Committee of Monmouth,[8] and
Andrew Ellis was made steward of the sequestered estates
of the Earl of Derby in Flintshire.[9]   Some, like Philip Jones
and Henry Herbert, were members of the Rump up to its
dissolution, while the office of High Sheriff in the thirteen
counties from 1650 to 1653 was almost always filled by one
or the other of the Commissioners.[10]   The more active of the
Commissioners, especially during 1650 and 1651, could only
act during relaxation from more imperative duties ; others,
especially those engaged in the service of the state in London,
did so but very occasionally.[11]   These considerations notwithstanding, Philip Jones was the leading spirit among the
South Wales Commissioners.   It was against him that the
jealous well-affected and Royalist pamphleteers concentrated
their attacks ; whatever his ' creatures ' might decide,
" Collonel Jones was always beside the curtain."[12]   His

1 Commonwealth Exch. Papers 251 (papers not numbered)—order of Commissioners of Militia for Radnor.
2 C. S. Papers, 1651, p. 448, Sept. 25.
3 Ibid., pp. 373, 374, Aug. 27.
4 Firth and Rait : Acts and Ordinances, Vol. II, pp. 467-483.
5 Ibid., Vol. II, pp. 653-680.
6 Cal. Comm. Compounding, Vol. I, p. 172.
7 Ibid., Vol. I, p. 173.   Appted. Feb. 13, 1650.
8 Ibid., Vol. I, p. 265   July 2, 1650.
9 Ibid., Vol. I, p. 258.   June 26, 1650.
10 List of Sheriffs, Record Office.
11 The author of a critical pamphlet on the jurisdiction of the Commissioners—
" Certain Seasonable Considerations . . . . ." places those " all that meet to act
by virtue thereof [the Act] " in a special category (p. 2) ; also " *those that act* " (p. 5).
N.L.W.
12 Walker, c 4, fol 69b.

brother-in-law, John Price of Gellihir and Cwrt-y-carnau in Gower,[1] was the Treasurer of sequestered revenues. His detractors were continually referring to the man " who made Hay while the Sun shin'd," and " increased his Interest from £17 or £20 a year to £3,000."[2] The most aggressive members in North Wales were the English group headed by Twisleton and the compact band who hailed from the Wrexham district. Of the twenty-seven recorded meetings of the North Wales Commissioners eleven were held at Wrexham[3]; of the six who sat at Carnarvon on 7th May, 1652, and sequestered Robert Jones from the rectory of Llandwrog, four came from Wrexham, together with Hugh Courtney and Thomas Swift.[4]

The large experience of the Commissioners in the administration of somewhat complex ordinances, demanding a general business capacity, diverts the criticism that, not having been bred to the law, they were unfit to sit as a Committee of Indemnity under the Act[5]; it also prepared some for still more exacting posts and a wider sphere of responsibility. Rice Williams of Newport became one of the six Commissioners for Compounding appointed by the Protector in 1654[6]; James Phillips became a member of the Army Committee of the Kingdom in the same year[7]; and Philip Jones became one of the most influential members of the most important committees of later Councils of State,[8] Cromwell's Comptroller of the Household, and a member of the 1657 House of Peers.

Of the twenty-five Approvers, fourteen were already at work in Wales as nominees of the Parliament and its Committees[9]; Ewins was one of the All-Hallows' missionaries[10]; Rowland Nevett had taken the place of the dispossessed

---

1 G. T. Clarke: Limbus Patrum Morganiæ, p. 85; Cardiff Records, Vol. V; pp. 491, 492.
2 *Especially* " A Second Narrative of the Late Parliament (so-called), p. 7. Printed . . . . 1658." (N.L.W.).
3 Bodl. Rawlinson, c. 261. [Cymdeithas Llên Cymru Reprint. 1908]; cp Major-General Berry's remark to Sec. Thurloe in 1656—" *Wrexham* . . . . the onely place in this countrey where any thing may be done." (Thurloe State Papers, Vol. IV, p. 287.)
4 Lamb 1027, Case 29. Report of William Pridchard, Petty constable of Llandwrog, June 6, 1662.
5 Certain Seasonable Considerations . . . . p. 5. Observation 2. (N.L.W.).
6 Cal. Comm. Comp., Vol. I, p. 668. Feb. 10, 1653-4.
7 Williams : Parl. Hist., p. 40. 24th June, 1654.
8 Capt. John Poyntz' appeal to Jones, re petition—" Strickland will put his hand to what you agree to."—C.S.P., 1655, p. 294, Aug. 21 ; the cover of *Bodl. Walker, MS. e* 13 is part of a Latin parchment deed empowering Col. Philip Jones to act as arbitrator in a matter of dispute between English merchants and the King of Portugal.
9 Supra, Chapters III and IV.
10 Supra, p. 77.

Humphrey Wynne at Oswestry,[1] and it is probable that
Oliver Thomas acted in collaboration with him as " an able
and godly Welsh minister preaching to the Welsh there "[2] ;
Theophilus Jones records a tradition that " Jenkin Jones
was a preacher before the Wars "[3] ; there is a theory that
John Miles had settled down in Gower during the Civil War,
and had even taken an active part in it[4] ; of Charnock,
Robinson, Bidwell, Seaborn, Swain, and Richard Powell
there is no surviving evidence connecting them with evangelical work in Wales before the promulgation of the Act.
Six were itinerants pure and simple ; Llwyd both preached
itinerantly and had charge of a gathered church ; William
Jones acted as chaplain to the Denbigh garrison,[5] and as
minister of the parish church in the town ; Jenkin Jones,
the heir of Tymawr in Llanthetty,[6] worked on independent
lines, outside the purview of the Committees ; Ewins over-
looked a gathered church, and seems to have depended upon
voluntary support[7] ; the others had been settled in parochial
charges. And the duties of ' approving ' conjoined with the
work of ' preaching the Word ' were far from measuring the
activities of the more versatile among them. Thomas Ewins
was induced by a letter of 14th July, 1651[8] to become a
' faithful dispensor of y[e] word of y[e] Gospell ' in Bristol, for
which special provision was made by an ordinance of the
Commons[9] ; Jenkin Lloyd was named, with Dr. John Owen
and others, a Trustee upon whom lands and ecclesiastical
revenues were vested for the ' advance of the Gospel and
Learning ' in Ireland,[10] and on 18th February, 1651-2, his is
one of the twenty-seven names suggesting certain proposals
for the Propagation of the Gospel throughout the country to
the consideration of Parliament[11] ; and Vavasor Powell,
Jenkin Jones, and Walter Cradock, though " he had no skill

1 House of Lords MSS. *W*. [Petitions of ejected clergymen at the Restoration—
Humphrey Wynne, 23rd June, 1660] ; House of Lords MSS. Comm. Report, Appendix
I, p. 108.
2 Cp. Shaw : Hist. of the English Church during the Civil War, Vol. II, Appendix IIIb, p. 408, and Lamb. 978, fol. 519.
3 History of Breconshire, Vol. II, p. 525. (1805 Ed.)
4 Cymdeithas Hanes Bedyddwyr Cymru, Trafodion (1910-11) ed. T. Shankland,
p. 10.
5 Calamy : An Account of the Ministers . . . . (1713). Vol. II, 713.
6 Rees : Prot. Nonconformity (Sec. Edition), p. 111.
7 Erbery · The Sword Doubled, p. 7.
8 Letter printed in full—Broadmead Records (ed. Haycroft), p. 32.
9 C. J. VI, 388. 29th March, 1650.
10 Firth and Rait : Acts and Ordinances, Vol. II, p. 356.
11 C. J., VII. 259. Proposals reported to the House by a Special Committee, 11th
Feb., 1652-3·

in war,"[1] are found in actual command of troops recruited by Harrison[2] from the 'congregations' in the troublous times of 1651. Jenkin Jones raised a troop of 100 men in May[3], and on a certain Thursday in August Cradock was organising a rally of the Parliament's sympathisers at Chepstow to the number of 6,000.[4] On November 29th, 1651, warrants were issued by the Treasurers-at-War to pay Cradock £803 12s. 0d. for one month's pay of a troop of 200 horse, and £907 4s. 0d. to Powell for two months' pay of a troop of 100 horse.[5] Morgan Llwyd, marching northward with Harrison's army, saw the hills of Scotland,[6] and he and his friends were enjoined by the members of the church at Wrexham to put on the whole armour of God if they wished to be ' shot-free.'[7]

There was no effort at an equitable distribution of the approvers among the thirteen counties : Anglesey, Carnarvon, Flint, Pembroke, and Carmarthen have not a single representative ; Merioneth 2, the Wrexham district 2, other parts of Denbighshire 2, Cardiganshire 1, Brecknock 2, Monmouthshire 3 ; Vavasor Powell's· sphere of labour lay mainly in Radnor and Montgomery ; Richard Swain ultimately settled down in Radnor,[8] but came originally from Shrewsbury[9] ; Richard Powell was a Herefordshire man,[10] but made his home at Penywern in the parish of Glasbury[11] ; two were engaged at Oswestry beyond Offa's Dyke, one of whom was a native of Salop[12] ; David Walter and Morris Bidwell worked in Glamorgan[13] ; so also did Miles and Seaborn,[13] though the former came from Newton by Clifford in Hereford,[14] and the latter bears a Border sur-

---

1 *Divine Drops Distilled*, p. 108.
2 Cal. St. Papers, 1650, p. 280, Aug. 10. Council of State to Harrison.
3 Cal. St. Papers, 1651, p. 175 (May 2) ; 187-188 (May 9) ; 195 (May 12).
4 Ibid., p. 339, Aug. 18. Council of State to Lord Grey.
5 Cal. St. Papers, 1651-2. Appendix, p. 579.
6 Gweithiau, Vol. I. Song XXIX, p. 62. '· Gwel fy llygaid, frynniau Scottiaid "';
                   Credwch, chwi welwch yn wir
               Mae'r Scottiaid a yscyttir. Stanza [2] ;
reference to *Carlisle* in MS. of Llwyd's Diary at Cardiff Free Library (Gweithiau, Vol. II, Introd. xxvi.).
7 Gweithiau, Vol. II, Attodiad V. Letter dated Sat., July 12 [1651].
8 At Clyro. Lamb. 972, fol. 366.
9 Probably of the same family as the *Swaine* whose land had to some extent been used up for the fortification of Shrewsbury Castle—Calendar of St. Papers, 1652-3, pp. 344, 363 ; 1655, pp. 317, 607.
10 Foster : Alumni Oxonienses (1500-1714). Vol. III, 1193.
11 Lamb. 1027. Report " Glasbury," Answer 6.
12 Foster, Al Oxon., Vol II, 866.
13 Walker MS. c. 13, fols. 17-32 (Glamorgan Disbursements under Act).
14 Cymdeithas Hanes Bedyddwyr Cymru : Trafodion (1910-11), pp. 8, 9.

name[1]; Ewins, Charnock,[2] and Edmond Ellis[3] came from London, while Robinson came from the North Country.[4] More diverse still were the approvers' ideas about doctrine and church government. One critic makes Richard Symonds a warm defender of ' antipædobaptists,'[5] another that he was a ' Sceptick in his religion '[6]; John Miles had already paid his historic visit to the Baptist brethren at the Glasshouse in London, where he was baptised by immersion[7]; Ewins later became the founder of the Baptist community at Broadmead in Bristol[8]; Jenkin Jones was a Calvinistic Baptist who believed in open communion[9]; Morris Bidwell was the ' priest ' who seized the Quaker John ap John by the collar at Swansea, and delivered him to a constable[10]; the more tolerant spirit of Llwyd had made John a Quaker in 1653 by sending him and another to ' try ' George Fox[11]; Dr. John Ellis kept on friendly terms with the ardent Royalist of Caergai[12]; Jenkin Lloyd deprecated ' differences about holy things '[13]; and Rowland Nevett and Oliver Thomas had in 1647 been named as " Ministers fit to be of the Second Classis " in Shropshire.[14] The great majority would be described in the loose terminology of the time as ' Independents.' It would be impossible with such approvers to subsidise unduly any particular sect or to impose new canons of uniformity. All of them would agree with Vavasor Powell that there should be no toleration for ' corrupt or damnable opinions,'[15] and with Cradock's ideal " to make union and communion with God their main worke . . . .

1 Benedict *Seaborn* and George *Seaborn* were names of prisoners taken at *Raglan* n " A Perfect List of the names *off* the Colonels, Majors, Captains. Lieutenants and other officers therein " (N.L.W.) ; Mr. *Seabourne* was one of prisoners taken at *Hereford.* " Severall Letters from Colonell Morgan . . . ." (N.L.W.).
2 Foster : Al. Oxon., Vol. I, p. 264.
3 Calamy : An Account of the Ministers . . . . (1713), Vol. II, p. 731
4 Foster : Al. Oxon., Vol. III, p. 1267.
5 Edwards : Gangræna, Part III (1646), pp. 241, 242.
6 Bodl. Walker MS. c. 4, fol. 67 (Mansell to Walker). There is, however, no corroboration of either statement in the records of the time.
7 Joshua Thomas : Hanes y Bedyddwyr (Pontypridd Ed.), p. 35 : Trafodion, p. 11.
8 Broadmead Records (ed. Haycroft), p. 43.
9 Broadmead Records (ed. Underhill), p. 513. Letter of Henry Maurice to Edward Terrill (1675).
10 Besse : Sufferings of the Quakers, Vol. I, p. 735.
11 George Fox : Journal, Vol. I, p. 188 (1891 Ed.) ; Braithwaite . The Beginnings of Quakerism, p. 123.
12 Rowland Vaughan : Yr Arfer o Weddi yr Arglwydd . . . . Gan Ioan Despagne (1658). Llythyr Annerch I'r gwir anrhydeddus *Sion Elis* . . . . wir barchedig fugail . . . . llywydd anrhydeddus . . . . (quoted Ashton : Hanes Llenyddiaeth Cymru ; 1650-1850, p. 25).
13 Valedictions (1658), p. 28 (Brit. Mus. Thomason).
14 Shaw : Hist. of the English Church. Vol. II, Appendix IIIb, p. 408.
15 God the Father Glorified (1649), p. 141

to Love, Honour, Receive Saints qua Saints."[1] Neither
Erbery, with his ever-increasing catalogue of dangerous
opinions, nor Christopher Love, with his ultra-Presbyterian
bias and reputed intriguing with the Scots, found a place
among the Approvers.[2]
Episcopal antecedents proved no ground of exclusion.
Rowland Nevett had once been vicar of Stanton in Shropshire[3]; Richard Powell had already held two livings in
Herefordshire[4]; Dr. John Ellis had been rector of Wheat-
field in Oxfordshire[5] before he was instituted to Dolgelly;
and even Oliver Thomas in his conformist days had laid
great emphasis on the exclusive right of ordained clergymen
to the work of exposition.[6] Two had no difficulty in conforming at the Restoration : Jenkin Lloyd,[7] who had prepared
the way by his defence of the Three Creeds in 1658,[6] and
Dr. Ellis, whose ' Defensio Fidei ' published in 1660 pur-
ported to be an answer to the arguments by which the
Anglican system was customarily assailed.[9] With these
exceptions, the genuine Puritanism of the main body of the
survivors stood the most exacting tests at and after the
Restoration. Robert Powell passed from the scene in the
summer of 1650,[10] Seaborn very probably in 1651,[11] Richard
Powell in 1658,[12] Llwyd and Cradock both in 1659, Bidwell
" before the Restauration."[13] Henry Walter is keeping a
conventicle at Caerleon in 1669[14] and takes out a licence
under the Declaration of Indulgence three years later[15];
Edmond Ellis was ejected[16]; likewise Jenkin Jones, who is
a ' teacher ' in 1672 at Cilgerran in Pembrokeshire[17]; likewise George Robinson,[18] who appears in a similar capacity
at Llantrisant in Monmouthshire[19]; John Miles migrated

1 The Saints' Fulnesse of Joy (1646), Dedication p. 3.
2 Love enjoyed a salary of £150 a year since 1648 as minister of St. Bartholomew,
Exchange. (Shaw : Hist. of the English Church, Vol. II, 149, n. 1.).
3 Foster : Al. Oxon. (1500-1714), Vol. II, 866. Instituted 1636.
4 Ibid., Vol. III, 1193 ; Morton Jeffray, inst. 1634 ; St. Dubritius, inst. 1637.
5 D.N B., Vol. XVII, p. 283.
6 Carwr y Cymru (1630), p. 85
7 13 Car. II (presentations to livings), Patent 47, No. 146.
8 Sermon on Christ's Valedictions, p. 35.
9 D.N.B., Vol. XVII, p. 283.
10 Walk, c. 13, f. 60 (inference from nature and amount of payment).
11 Vide Note at end of Chapter.
12 Lamb. 1027, Glasbury Report.
13 Walk, c. 4, f. 72.
14 Lamb. Cod. Ten., Vol. 639, f. 186b ('Cavelion ').
15 S. P. Dom., Car. II, 38A, p. 169. Licence received June 17th, 1672.
16 Calamy : Account, Vol. II, 731.
17 S.P. Dom., Car. II, 38A, p. 85.
18 Calamy : Account, p. 473.
19 S.P. Dom., Car. II, 38A, p. 203. Licence issued, June 22, 1672 (' Lantrissa ')

to America in 1663[1]; Ambrose Mostyn, after his ejection from Wrexham, became for a time chaplain to the Puritan Lord Say and Sele[2]; William Jones settled at Plas Teg with Sir John Trevor[3]; Richard Swain returned to his native Shrewsbury, where he keeps a conventicle in 1665[4] and takes out a licence in 1672[5]; Thomas Ewins was a conventicler at Bristol in 1665,[6] and suffered imprisonment from time to time[7]; Rowland Nevett also offended against the Clarendon Code in 1669,[8] and is described as 'teacher'[1] in 1672 both at Bolas, Weston, and Oswestry[9]; finally, Vavasor Powell spent ten years after the Restoration in the Fleet and Southsea prisons, but during one of his two short-lived spells of freedom is found in 1669 'teacher at Llan-vylling' to a number of conventicles.[10] Of the small knot of Approvers still unnoticed the Restoration records are silent.

Nor were the Welsh 'triers' lacking in academic distinction. Seventeen were alumni of the University of Oxford. Henry Walter was a Bachelor of the Civil Law[11]; Symonds a B.A. from Exeter College[12]; Robinson an M.A. from Christ Church[13]; Richard Powell an M.A. from Brase-nose[14]; Ambrose Mostyn a B.A. from the same College[15]; John Ellis was a Fellow of Jesus and a D.D. of St. Andrews[16]; Oliver Thomas,[17] Stephen Lewis,[18] and William Jones[19] were all M.A.'s from Hart Hall; Swain an M.A. from Oriel[20]; Rowland Nevett likewise from St. Edmund Hall[21]; and Jenkin Lloyd an M.A. from Jesus[22] who was made a Doctor

1 Trafodion, p. 16.
2 Calamy : Account, p. 714.
3 supra, p. 96.
4 Lamb. Cod. Ten. Vol. 639, ff. 337, 338 · Calamy : Account, p. 734.
5 S.P. Dom., Car. II, 38A, p. 244. Licence issued, Sept. 5, 1672.
6 Lamb. Cod. Ten., Vol. 639, f. 317.
7 Broadmead Records (ed. Haycroft), pp. 50-52.
8 Lamb. Cod. Ten., Vol. 639, f. 139b.
9 S.P. Dom., Car. II., 38A, p. 215 (Oswestry and Weston), p. 274 (Bolas). Licences issued July 25, 1672.
10 Joshua Thomas : Hanes y Bedyddwyr (Pont. Ed.), pp. 45, 46; Lamb. Cod. Ten. Vol. 639. f. 139b.
11 Foster : Al. Oxon., Vol. IV, p. 1564. 22nd Oct., 1633. Jesus.
12 Ibid., p. 1451. Feb. 5, 1628-9.
13 Foster : Al. Oxon., III, 1267. 9 July, 1635.
14 Ibid., 1193. 10th May, 1631; Heberden : Brasenose College Register (Oxford Hist. Soc. Pub. LV), I, p. 149.
15 Foster : Al. Oxon., Vol. III, p. 1041; Brasenose Coll. Reg. I, p. 154, 28th Jan.. 1629-1630.
16 D.N.B. Vol. XVII, p. 283. Fellow of Jesus (1628); D.D., St. Andrews (1634).
17 Clark : Registers, Sect. III, p. 387. 8th July, 1628.
18 Foster : Al. Oxon., Vol. III, p. 909. 27th June, 1633.
19 Ibid., Vol. II, p. 832 ; Clark : Registers, Sect. III, 357. 19th June, 1620.
20 Clark : Registers, Sect. III, p. 414. 21st June, 1625.
21 Foster : Al. Oxon., Vol. II, p. 866. 19th Jan., 1635-6
22 Ibid., Vol. III, p. 925; 14th April, 1648.

of Divinity in 1661.[1] Roger Charnock matriculated at Magdalen Hall,[2] Jenkin Jones at Jesus,[3] Robert Powell at St. Mary Hall,[4] Miles at Brasenose,[5] and Richard Edwards at Hart Hall[6] ; but there is no evidence of their proceeding further towards a degree. Vavasor Powell was reputed to have been a student at Oxford, and the strength of the tradition induced Wood, though with evident reluctance, to include him among his ' Athenae.'[7] He had from ' Childhood been brought up a Schollar,'[8] though his halting Latinity compares very unfavourably with that of Dr. George Griffith in the correspondence preceding the Newchapel Conference.[9] Cradock describes Oxford as the University he ' had formerly known,'[10] but the records of the various Colleges have been searched in vain for his name. Bidwell, Ewins, Seaborn, David Walter, Edmond Ellis,[11] and Morgan Llwyd do not seem to have had any University education ; it is likely that the latter laid the foundation of his evident learning during his stay at Brampton Bryan,[12] whose rector, Stanley Gower, had been Chaplain to Archbishop Ussher[13] and became a member of the Westminster Assembly.[14]

NOTE.—WILLIAM SEABORN.

Nothing definite is known of him except that he is named in the Propagation Act as one of the Approvers, and that he received £130 16s. 9d. " for his sallary in 1650 and in parte for 1651 " from the Glamorgan Treasurer. (Walker c. 13, f. 17). His name does not occur in the ' Liber Institutionum ' ; nor as one approved or appointed by the C.P.M. for evangelical work in Wales before the Act ; nor in the Lambeth MSS. as one finding favour with the ' Triers.' He is not among those who received hortatory letters from Erbery or marks of contumely from Alexander Griffith ; nor does his name figure among the 322 who supported Vavasor Powell in regretting the Protectorate, nor among the 762 who agreed with Cradock and Miles in accepting it. This hiatus made Archdeacon Thomas (Hist. Dioc. St. Asaph, 1906, p. 109) half-suggest that ' *Seaborn* ' could be equated with ' *Morgan* ' ; and curiously enough, though Seaborn passes out

1 Wood : Fasti Oxoniensis (ed. Bliss). Vol. II, Pt. 2, p. 258. Sept. 12, 1661.
2 Foster : Al. Oxon., Vol. I, p. 264. 31st Jan., 1639-1640.
3 Ibid., Vol. II, p. 822. 29th March, 1639.
4 Ibid., Vol. III, p. 1193. 9th July, 1641.
5 Ibid., Vol. III, p. 1012. 18th March, 1635-6 ; Brasenose College Register, Vol. I., p. 171.
6 Foster : Al. Oxon., Vol. II, p. 450. 11th Dec., 1640.
7 p. 344 (old edition).
8 Life, p. 120.
9 A Bold Challenge of an Itinerant Preacher Modestly Answered [containing correspondence, pp. 1-7.] (N.L.W.).
10 Saints Fulnesse of Joy, p. 30.
11 ' Edmund Ellis was a Skinner from London.' (Calamy II, 731).
12 Supra, p. 26.
13 Gweithiau Morgan Llwyd, Vol. II, Introd. xxiv.
14 Firth and Rait : Acts and Ordinances, Vol. I, p. 180. [Ordinances for summoning Assembly of Divines. 12th June, 1643.]

of the records after 1650, a 'William Morgan' appears in those of 1651. But the Treasurer has written not *Seaborn* but *Sebborne* and in any case, there were such surnames as Seaborn or Seabourne, for in addition to those mentioned above (p. 102, n. 1) there appears the name of a 'Mr. Richard Seabourne a delinquent of Hereford,' unless he be the same man as the prisoner referred to (Shaw : Vol. II, p. 494). Further, the accounts undoubtedly show William *Morgan* to be an itinerant in Glamorgan and Monmouth, receiving £10 in each county for his work. The latter account describes him specifically as 'a preacher amongst the Welsh people,' while the probability is that Seaborn could not preach in the vernacular at all. And the sums received by Morgan were quite incommensurate with the dignity and duties of an Approver, and contrary to the general custom of the Treasurers in paying them. It is also curious that the entry of Seaborn's payment is worded very similar to Erbery's, which carries with it another hypothesis that both retired from the official propagation on conscientious grounds. But there is no reference to Seaborn in any of the very numerous works of Erbery. Thus the records can only barely justify the statement that Seaborn hailed from the Border, was English in speech like Erbery, did the work of an Approver-Itinerant in Glamorgan for one-and a-quarter years, and presumably died in the spring or summer of 1651.

VIII.

MANUSCRIPT SOURCES

(ON WHICH THE CONCLUSIONS OF THE FOLLOWING CHAPTERS
ARE MAINLY BASED).

(i) *Bodl. Rawlinson MS. c.* 261[1] (Cymdeithas Llên Cymru
Reprint, 1908), pp. 18-32. This contains the
" proceedings of the Commissioners for *North
Wales* " from 9th May, 1650, to 19th November,
1651. Even for this period, however, it is not
complete, since the Exchequer returns for Montgomery (infra) declare that John Davies of Garthbeibio and William Jones of Llangadfan were both
ejected on 23rd April, 1651, a meeting unrecorded
in the Rawlinson MS.

(ii) *Bodl. Walker MS. e.* 7, *fols.* 206-215*b*. (Vide infra
Chaps. XVI-XVIII.) This contains an *extract* of the
" Account from y[e] Commission by Act of Parliament
for propagacion of the Gospel in Wales of all y[e]
sequestered tithes, Church livings, and impropriations within y[e] counties of South Wales and y[e]
county of Monmouth together with all y[e] proceedings made in obedience to y[e] said Act of
Parliament by y[e] said Commission drawn up y[e]
20th of April, 1652." The actual ' Account ' seen
by Walker " among a very great Heap that were
confus'd and unsorted and seem to be neglected
on the Floor of an Outer Room there "[2] [Lambeth
Palace Library], has been lost. This Extract was
made by Walker's correspondent and scribe,

---

[1] This is the same MS. as is referred to in a letter (address and signature torn)
sent to Walker after his " Sufferings " was published. The writer desires the ' learned
Author ' to know that he has in his possession a MS. ' containing about 3 sheets, and
giving a short account of what ye Committee for y[e] Propagation of y• Gospell in
North Wales transacted at their severall meetings from ye 9th of May, 1650, to Nov.
the 19th, 1651." (Walk. c. 7, f. 117).
[2] Sufferings, Part I, p. 151.

John Bear, and gives the names of the clergy
'ejected before the Act,' 'ejected since this Act,'
adding, in some cases, the specific cause of ejection.
(iii) *Bodl. Walker MS. c.* 4, *fols.* 65-72*b*. This contains
an " Account of the hard Usages of the Clergy . . .
during the miserable Confusions of our Nation
since the Martyrdom of King Charles the first till
the Restauration " supplied to Walker in 1709
by Edward Mansell of Henllys, for the compilation
of the " Sufferings." Folios 65-70 refer to those
livings lying in the Diocese of Llandaff in the
county of Glamorgan ; 70-72*b* in the Diocese of
St. David's. The account is highly coloured,[1]
very inaccurate in its terminology, but includes
facts gleaned from the descendants of the ejected,
which are also supported by reliable contemporary
evidence.

(iv) *Bodl. Walker MS. c.* 13, *folios* 5-69*b*. This contains the
accounts[2] of the Treasurer of South Wales furnished
to the Commissioners sitting at Neath according
to the ordinance of 30th August, 1654. (Firth
and Rait : Acts and Ordinances : Vol. II, pp. 990-
993). They were ' taken and allowed ' on 10th
August, 1655.

(v) *Exchequer Returns (First Fruits)* for all the counties
of North Wales except Flint. They contain the
names and surnames of the ministers of the several
rectories, vicarages, donatives, and curacies within
the various ' bailiwicks ' supplied in obedience to
a writ of the Barons issued 28th November, 1651,
with schedules annexed to be returned by 3rd
February, 1651-2. The Record Office contains no
similar returns for the South Wales counties. (A
Guide to the Public Records (1908) : Scargill
Bird, p. 132.)

1 Mansell writes at the end of folio 72b :—
  " Si quid novisti Rectius
     Candidus Imparti : Si non, his utere mecum."

2 The accounts which have come down are not by any means complete. Only
the ' disbursements ' for 1650 are given for Cardiganshire, and only those for 1651-
1652, grouped together, for Carmarthenshire. The Pembrokeshire account takes
together the same years, and specifies only the *total* sums paid out to officials, ministers
and schoolmasters.
Vide infra, Chap. XVI.

(vi) *Exchequer Returns (First Fruits) for County Mont-gomery*—the results of Inquisitions held before the Sheriff and twelve Jurors on

(a) *7th February*, 1657-8, giving particulars of the men who had held livings in the county since 8th June, 1649 (folios 114-116).

(b) *28th April*, 1658, to the same effect, but in some cases containing additional information (folios 117-119).

No similar returns have been discovered for any other Welsh Counties.

(vii) *Lambeth Palace MS.* 902, *folios* 38-57 ; 915, *folios* 87-182. These contain parochial inquisitions made under the " Act for Maintenance of Preaching Ministers, and other Pious Uses," 8th June, 1649. (Firth and Rait : Acts and Ordinances, Vol. II, p. 147). Commissions under the Great Seal were issued to every county in England and Wales to inquire, ' by the Oathes of good and lawful men and by all other good ways and lawful means,' of the true yearly value of all parsonages and vicarages presentative, the names of the present incumbents, proprietors, and possessors, etc.—all to be certified into the Court of Chancery. The above include the returns from *Anglesey* and *Pembroke* only ; no other returns from Wales are known to exist either at Lambeth Palace or the Record Office. (Scargill Bird : A Guide to the Public Record Office, p. 80 ; Shaw : Hist. of the English Church during the Civil War, Vol. II, App. XI, pp. 605-6 ; Todd : Guide to the 1837 Report of the Commissioners on Records, pp. 397-411).

(viii) *Lambeth Palace MSS. 902, folios 1-35 (St. Asaph) ; 59-66 (Bangor) ; 904, fols. 124, 142 (Coventry and Lichfield) ; 905, fols. 1-67 (St. David's) ; 910, fols. 35, 43, 226-230, 278-288 (Gloucester) ; 913, fols. 735-779 (Llandaff) ; 917, fols. 72, 100, 103 (Hereford).* These are the Surveys of the possessions of the Bishops, Deans and Chapters ordered

by the Acts of 9th October, 1646 (L. J. VIII, 513)
and 30th April, 1649 (C. J. VI, 237), which contain
a description of the premises, an account of leases,
and the names of the incumbents.

(ix) *Lambeth, Palace MSS.* 966-1005 ; 1007-1021. *Augmentation Books.* These volumes, as their title
suggests, contain the orders of the Trustees for
Maintenance of Ministers appointed by the
ordinance of 8th June, 1649, for the ' augmentation '
of salaries recommended by the C.P.M. or the
ʟommittee for the Reformation of the Universities
after April, 1650 (C. J. VI, 388), or after 2nd
September, 1654, by the Commissioners for the
Approbation of Public Preachers (Firth and Rait :
Acts and Ordinances, Vol. II, 1025-1026). The
orders of the Trustees during the period of Propagation hardly ever concern Wales ; some volumes,
notably 975 and 976, have not the slightest
reference to the Principality ; others, however,
since *all* ministers after the ordinance of 1654
had to receive the approbation of the ' Triers,'
contain orders of the latter based on previous or
' original ' orders of the C.P.M. or of the Commissioners under the Propagation Act ; or, in some
cases, of both. This, in many cases in South
Wales, is the only method of ascertaining who held
a particular living during, or during some part,
of 1650-1653.

(x) *Lambeth Palace MS.* 1006. This is numbered among
the Augmentation Books, but really contains in
a very miscellaneous way the orders of the Propagators of the Gospel in Wales (among those of
the Four Northern Counties of England), some
confirming those found in Bodl. Rawl. c. 261 for
North Wales, and some otherwise unknown orders
for South Wales.

(xi) *Lambeth Palace MS.* 1027. This contains a series of
very imperfect returns from constables in Wales
to a demand for information about the proceedings
of 1649-1660 by what are called the " Commis-

sioners for Sequestration of Ministers and of Value of Livings." The writ was issued on 15th May, 1662. This MS. is in parts badly mutilated.

(xii) *House of Lords MSS.—Petitions,* 1660. These are lettered J, L, O, P, S, T, W, Y, are fifty-one in number, and were petitions presented in pursu-ance of two orders of the House of Lords on 22nd and 23rd June, 1660, for securing the tithes and other profits of sequestered livings in the hands of the churchwardens or overseers of the poor of the several parishes until the titles of the sequestered clergy and of the men in possession should be determined. The petitions are all practically couched in the same terms, occasionally specifying the *date* of sequestration by the ' late pretended powers.' The names are given in the *House of Lords MSS. Commission Report, Appendix I, pp.* 104-107, 121.

(xiii) *Liber Institutionum, Series A, Vol. IV,* 1556-1660 (Record Office). This contains the names of clergymen instituted to benefices, the date in each case being based on the bishops' certificates. The four Welsh dioceses are separately paginated. It also includes some, *but not all,* of those ordered to be inducted and instituted by the Lords after the downfall of the bishops.

(xiv) *Sion College MS.* marked A.R.C. $\overline{\text{L40. 2}}$ $\overline{\text{E. 16}}$ *styled " Acts of the Committee for Plundered Ministers,"*

but this is an incorrect description. It contains the entries of the Committee for the Reformation of the Universities from July, 1650, to 14th April, 1652, which took over a large part of the old duties of the C.P.M. (p. 39). There is not a single refer-ence to Wales, and the document is only important as illustrating the complete independence in ecclesiastical matters enjoyed by the Principality under the Propagation Act,

(xv) *Bodleian MS.* 330 (but lately lettered Rawl. D. 711)—
" a register of those ministers who subscribed the
Engagement " before the C.P.M. in London or
J.P.'s' in the country. It once contained 145
numbered pages, but pp. 23-134 and 137-140 are
lost. Only one or two ministers from Wales are
found in the surviving list, but it contains the
names of some of those ministers sent to Pembrokeshire from London in 1650 by Hugh Peters, and of
whom otherwise little is known.

(xvi) *Bodl. Walker MS. c.* 6, *ff.* 39-43. " The names of those
who took the Ingagement." With occasional
variants as regards dates and the spelling of names,
this list agrees with the alphabetical list placed at
the inverted end of Rawl. D. 711 (surnames from
M to Y).

(xvii) *Lambeth Palace Library, Vol.* 639 (*Codices Tenisoniani*).
1669 Returns of Conventicles, ff. 139-140 (St.
Asaph and Bangor) ; 186-188b (Llandaff) ; 1665
Returns, f. 303b (St. Asaph) ; ff. 331, 336b, 337
(St. David's), concerning the whereabouts of
" non-subscribers."

(xviii) *Domestic State Papers, Car. II,* 38 *A.* contains dates
of licences granted under the Declaration of
Indulgence (1672).

IX.'

THE NEW EJECTIONS—FORTUNES OF THE EJECTED.

Notwithstanding the distractions of the year 1650,[1] the Commissioners set to work without delay. Before 2nd October of that year[2] fifty clergymen had been ejected in Pembrokeshire, and by November 22nd[3] practically the whole of Anglesey had been denuded of the old order. By the end of the year the ' executioners '[4] had done their work, and the second Puritan revolution was in full working order ; fifths were being paid, and the collector for Monmouthshire was drawing up a list of ' the parishes togeather with the persons ' who were in arrear with their rents.[5] In the absence of anything like a complete record of the transactions of the Commissioners, an approximately exhaustive list of the ejected clergy is only made possible by eliminating the names of those who were undoubtedly ejected *before* the Act, by supplementing the evidence of Bodl. Rawl. c. 261 for North Wales by the Exchequer Returns of 1652, 1657, and 1658, and by reference in some cases to the ' Liber Institutionum ' for the clergy in possession at the beginning of 1650. For South Wales a similar list is arrived at by supplying the manifest deficiencies of Walker MS. e. 7 regarding clergy ejected *since* the Act from the names of the clergy actually receiving fifths according to Walker MS. c. 13, and by collating the full list of sequestered livings in the latter document with the testimony of the ' Liber,' the ' present incumbents ' on Bishop and Chapter lands found by the Surveyors in 1647-1649, and with the ' men

1 Supra, pp. 96-98.
2 Commissioners of 1649 at the Guild Hall, Haverfordwest. (Wed., 2nd Oct., 1650). Lamb. 915, fols. 87-182.
3 Commissioners of 1649 at the Shire Hall, Beaumaris. (Nov. 22, 1650). Lamb. 902, fols. 36-57.
4 Alexander Griffith : Strena Vavasoriensis, p. 1 [1653]; Alexander Griffith Mercurius Cambro-Britannicus, p. 3 [1653.].
5 Walker, MS. c. 13, f. 47.   ▲

who supplied the cure' in Pembrokeshire in the very recent reports of the Commissioners under the Maintenance Act of 1649. Further evidence is supplied by the personal notes of the petitioners of 1660, by the recollections of the country constables in 1662, and by reference to an 'Abstract[1] of some of ye Constabels returns for this shire' (Carmarthenshire), the originals of which are not now discoverable at Lambeth.

1 This was made by John Bear, one of the scribes who were serviceable to Walker in compiling the " Sufferings." This 'abstract' is found in Walk. e. 7. ff. 219-219b. Similar Monmouthshire entries on the upper part of f. 219 are in the handwriting of Walker himself.

NORTH WALES.

NAME OF CLERGYMAN.	STATUS: RECTOR, VICAR OR CURATE.	LIVING OR LIVINGS FROM WHICH EJECTED.	CAUSE OF EJECTION (WHEN SPECIFIED OR ASCERTAINED).	MS. REFERENCE.
ANGLESEY				
Chedle, Rowland Dr.	R.	Llandegfan and Llanfihangel	Pluralist[1]	Rawl, c. 261, 20.[2]
Evans, Henry	R.	Llanfechell		Ibid., 21.
Evans, Owen	R.	Heneglwys		Ibid., 21.
Jones, On	R.	Llangefni	[3]	Exch. Ret., 1652 (Anglesey); Lamb. 902, f. 15.
Lloyd, Evan	R.	Rhoscolyn	Pluralist; said to keep Llanbeulan	Rawl. MS. c. 261, 21.
Lloyd, Robert	R.	Llanfachreth		Ibid., 21; Lords' Petitions, L. 60.
Lloyd, Wm	R.	Llanfair Pwll Gwyngyll.	Pluralist: allowed to keep Llandisilio.	Rawl. c. 261, 21.
Lloyd, William	R.	Llanfihangel Ysceifiog		Ibid., 21.
Lloyd, Wm	R.	Llaneigrad		Ibid., 21.
Payne, John	R.	Penmynydd, Llangeinwen and Llanbedr yn Niwbwrch.		Ibid., 21.
Wve, Robert Dr.	R.		Pluralist	Ibid., 20.
Whs, Hugh Dr.	R.	Llanrhuddlad and Llantrisant.	Pluralist, delinquency, and scandal	Ibid., 20; Cal. Comm. Comp. III., 1725.

1 The Rawlinson MS, only in very few cases assigns the *cause* of ejection. The Bulkeleys of Beaumaris describe Chedle as a "swearer and drunkard and regardless of his word." [Calendar of Committee for the Advance of Money, Vol. II, pp. 1163-1164].
2 No. of page in the Reprint of 1908.
3 Line signifies cause not ascertained, contemporary records being absolutely silent on the point.

NORTH WALES—continued.

NAME OF CLERGYMAN.	STATUS: RECTOR, VICAR OR CURATE.	LIVING OR LIVINGS FROM WHICH EJECTED.	CAUSE OF EJECTION (WHEN SPECIFIED OR ASCERTAINED).	MS. REFERENCE.
ANGLESEY (con.)				
Wms, Lewis	R.	Llanidan	—	Rawl. c. 261, p. 21.
Williams, Thomas	R.	arn	—	Ibid., 21.
CARNARVON				
Evans, Godfrey	C.	Eglwys Rhos.	—	Rawl. c. 261, p. 20.
Evans, Michael	R.	Llanllyfni	—	Exch. R, 1652, Carn.
Gethin(g), John	R	Criccieth	Pluralist; allowed to keep Llangybi	Exch. Ret., 1652, Carn.; Lords' Petitions,1660, W.
Griffith, William	R.	Llanddeiniolen	—	Exch. Ret., 1652, Carn.
Wms, Evan	V.	Conway	—	Rawl. c. 261, 20.
Jones, Robert	R.	Llandwrog	—	Exch. R, 1652, Carn.; Inab, 1027, No. 29.
Owen	R.	Rhiw	Scandal	Rawl. c. 261, p. 30.
Parry, is	V.	Llangystenyn	—	Ibid., p. 20.
Robinson, Hugh	R.	Llanbedr and Trefriw	—	Ibid., p. 20.
Thomas, Henry	V.	Dwygyfylchi	—	Exch. Ret., 1652, Carn.
id, William	R.	Llanberis	Ignorance and scandal	R awl. c. 261, p. 30.
DENBIGH				
Hill, Wm Dr.	V.	Llanrhaiadr yng Nginmeirch	—	Ibid., p. 23.
is, Richard	V.	Llansilin	—	Ibid., p. 18.
Jones, Humphrey	V.	Llangollen	—	Ibid., p. 18.
Lloyd, id Dr.	Warden of Christ's Hospital.	Ruthin	—	Ibid., p. 23.

	Name		Place	Note	References
DENBIGH (*con.*)	Lloyd, Foulke	R.	Efenechtyd	—	Lords' Petitions, L.1660.
	Lloyd, Humphrey	V.	Ruabon	—	Rawl. c. 261, p. 20; Lords' Petitions, L. 1660.
	Lloyd, Robert	V.	Chirk	—	Rawl. c. 261, p. 23; Exch.Ret.,1652,Denb.
	Maurice, Oliver	R.	Llanbedr	—	Rawl. c. 261, p. 18.
	Meyrick, Griffith	C.	Llansannan	—	Ibid., p. 29.
	Mos, Hugh	R.		—	Ibid., p. 32.
	Owen, Ellis	V.	Llanarmon yn Ial	Delinquency	Ibid., p. 28.
	Powell, William	R.	Llandegla	—	Ibid., p. 20.
	Roberts, John	C.	Bryneglwys	—	Ibid., p. 20.
	Rogers, William	V.	Denbigh	—	Exch. Ret., 1652,Denb.
	Williams, John	V.	Llanrhaiadr-ym-Mochnant	—	Rawl. c. 261, p. 18.
FLINT [1]	Fogg, Robert	Chapelry	Overton	Pluralist: allowed to keep Bangor on Dee.	Ibid. p. 26.
	Jones, Humphrey	V.	Hope	—	Ibid., p. 19.
	Rogers, William	R.	Cwm	—	Ibid., p. 19.
MERIONETH	Atkins, Thos	R.	Bews Gwerfil Goch	Scandal	Ibid., p. 28.
	Hughes, John	V.	Towyn		Lamb. 1027, fol. 33a.
	Roberts, Edward	C.	Corwen		Rawl. c. 261, p. 20.
	Roberts, Mr.	V.	Llanfachreth	Scandal	Ibid., p. 29.
	Roberts, Theodore	C.	Llanfor	Scandal	Ibid., p. 29.
	Swayne, John	R.	Pennal	Resignation of living	Ibid., p. 20.
	Nil, Maw	R.	Llandderfel		Ibid., p. 28.
	Nye, Edward	R.	Llanymawddwy	Scandal	Ibid., p. 29.

[1] This agrees in the main with Vavasor's declaration to a London newspaper—" the are not two ministers cast out by vertue of this Act in all Flintshire." (A Perfect Diurnall: May 3—10, 1652).

NORTH WALES—*continued.*

NAME OF CLERGYMAN.	STATUS: RECTOR, VICAR OR CURATE.	LIVING OR LIVINGS FROM WHICH EJECTED.	CAUSE OF EJECTION (WHEN SPECIFIED OR ASCERTAINED).	MS. REFERENCE.
MONTGOMERY · ·				
Bayly, William · ·	R.	Penstrowed	· ·	Rawl. c. 261, p. 9; Exch. Return, Mont., 116, 119.
Bray, David · ·	V.	Llandisilio		aRawl. c. 261, p. 18.
Davies, John · ·	R.	Garthbeibio		Exch. Ret. Mnt, 115, 118.
Davies, John · ·	R.	Gllin		Ibid., 115.
Edwards, William · ·	R.	Llanfihangel yng Ngwynfa		Ibid., 115; Rawl. c. 261, p. 19.
Ellis, Edward · ·	V.	Guilsfield	———1	Ibid., 115; Rawl. c. 261, p.19.
E ...s, ...w	R.	Penegoes	· ·	Ibid., 115.
Griffith, Alexander · ·	V.	Llanwnog	· ·	Ibid., 114.
G ...h, ...ge Dr. · ·	R.	Llandrinio	'Resigns for pluralities'; allowed to keep Llanymynech in Salop2	Ibid., 115; Rawl. c. 261, p. 18; Exch. Return, ..., 1652; ...is Petns., 1660, W.
Griffiths, ...th · ·	V.	Llanwyddelan		Exch. Ret, Mont., 114.

1 Probably for the causes referred to on p. 32.

2 Entry in Rawl MS.: " Doctor George Griffith Elected Llanymynech in the County of Salop " (9th May, 1650), *i.e.*, *elected Llanymynech and surrendered Llandrinio.* The significance of this word 'elected' throughout the Rawl. MS. is active, not passive—Griffith was not *appointed* 'de novo,' but simply *approved* by the Commissioners. He became Bishop of St. Asaph in 1660.

MONTGOMERY.. (con.)					
Hughes, John	R.	Hirnant	:		Rawl c. 261, p. 21.
Hughes John	V.	Llansantffraid	:		Ibid., 19.
Humphreys, Richd.	R.	Aberhafesp	:		Exch. Ret., Mont., 115.
Jones, Richard	V.	Llanfair Caereinion	:		Ibid., 115 ; Rawl. c. 261, p. 19.
Jones, Roger	R.	Llanerfyl	:		Exch. Ret., Mnt., 115.
Jones, William	R.	Llangadfan	:	Delinquent	Ibid., 115, 118.
Kyffin, John	R.	Manavon	:		Bid., 116, 119. ; Rawl. c. 261, p. 19.
Langford, Wm.	V.	Welshpool	:	Resignation	Exch.Ret., Mnt., 119 ; Lrds Petitions, 1660, W.
Lawrence, Wm.	C.	Churchstoke	:		Exch. Ret., Mnt., 115 ; Rawl. c. 261 [21].
Lewis, Eubule	R.	Newtown	:		Exch.Ret., Mnt., 116 ; Rawl. c. 261, p. 24.
Ll yd, Thomas	R.	Llanbrynmair	:	Pluralist, *Berriew.* Used to hold	Exch. Ret., Mnt., 114, 118.
Lloyd, Elias	R.	Llangerniew	:		Ibid., 115.
Parry, Griffth	V.	Bettws	:		Ibid., 114, 118.
Price, John	R.	Llangynog Bala	:		Ibid., 116.
Roberts, David	V.		:	Disaffection and scandal, probably. [Bodl. 325, f. 164.]	Rawl. c. 261, p. 19 ; Exch. Ret.,Mont.,114.
Rogers, Oter	C.	Buttington	:		Rawl. c. 261, p. 20 ; Exch. Ret.,Mont.,115.
Tudor, Evan	V.	Darowen	:		Ibid., 114.

1 *Contemporary evidence in this case conflicting, e.g.,—*
(a) "*Hiernant.* Parsonage—John Hughes parson there, and hath continued there (MS. defaced) yeares, and *still continueth.*" (Exch. First Fruits Return, 1657, slip 114). (Montgomery).
(b) Also 'Johannes Hughes . , per XI. an. Rector.' (Epitaph). (Thomas: St. Asaph, p. 739) ; ' Vicar there 40 years' (p. 557, Ibid).
The testimony of the Rawlinson MS. is quite explicit :—
"At ye Bala, 16th Oct., 1650, Mr. John Hughes, Rector of Hiernant, was then Elected."
It was possible that he was restored on appeal, but there is no hint of this in the surviving records of the time.

NORTH WALES—continued.

NAME OF CLERGYMAN.	STATUS: RECTOR, VICAR OR CURATE.	LIVING OR LIVINGS FROM WHICH EJECTED.	CAUSE OF EJECTION (WHEN SPECIFIED OR ASCERTAINED).	MS. REFERENCE.
MONTGOMERY (con.)				
Thompson, Thos.	V.	Llandyssil	—	Rawl. c. 261, p. 21; Exch. Ret., Mont., 114, 118.
Williams, Edward	V.	Llanbrynmair	Scandal	Ibid., 114, 118.
Williams, Thos.	V.	Llanllwchaiarn		Rawl. c. 261, p. 19; Exch. Ret., Mont., 114.
Wynne, Rees	R.	Gtell aGreinion		Ibid., 116, 118; Lords Petns. 60, W.

SOUTH WALES.

NAME OF CLERGYMAN.	STATUS: RECTOR, VICAR OR CURATE.	LIVING OR LIVINGS FROM WHICH EJECTED.	CAUSE OF EJECTION (WHEN SPECIFIED OR ASCERTAINED).	MS. REFERENCE.
BRECKNOCK				
Cecil, Thomas	R.	Llanbedr Patrisho	Enemy to the Parliament, and a common drunkard.	Walker e. 7, 213 b.
Dennis, Thomas	V.	The Hay	—	Lib. Inst., Men., 57; Walker c. 13, f. 61.
Edwards, Wm. Dr.	R.	Llandefaelog		Lib. Inst., Men., 45; Walker c. 13, f. 60.
Griffith, John	R.	Llanfihangel Talyllyn	Drunkenness, and being in arms against the Parliament.	Walker e. 7, 213b.
Habberley, Richard	R.	Talgarth and Llyswen	Common swearer, malignant and scandalous.	Walker e. 7, 213b.

	Name		Parish		Charge	Reference
BRECKNOCK (con.)						
V.	Hatley,[1] Griffith	..	Abereskir	..	..	Walker e. 7, 214.
R.	Herbert, Hugh	..	Llanvillo	..	Illegal induction.	Lib. Inst. Men., 52; Walker c. 13, f. 61.
R.	Lewis, William	..	Maesmynus	..		Walker c. 13, f. 62b.
R.	Lewis, Walter	..	Talachddu	..		Lib. Inst. Men., 46; Walker c. 13, f. 61.
R.	Perrott, John	..	Cathedine	..	Common swearer; drunkard; assisting the King in the War.	Walker e. 7, 213.
R.	Prichard, Roger	..	Llanddew	..		Lib. Inst., Men., 47; Walker c. 13, f. 61.
R.	Prichard, Samuel	..	Llanynys	..		Lib. Inst., 55, Men.; Walker c. 13, f. 61.
R.	Prytheroh, Samuel	..	Llanhamlach	..	Drunkenness, fornication, lying and 'Quarreling.'	Walker e. 7, 213b.
R.	Thos, Hopkin	..	Ystradgynlais	..		Lib. Inst., Men., 45; Walker c. 13, f. 62b.
V.	Thos, James	..	Llanwrthwl	..	Railing, swearing, simony.	Walker e. 7, 213.
V.	Vaughan, Thomas	..	Llansantffread	..	Common drunkard, common swearer, no preacher, in arms against the Parliament.[2]	Walker e. 7, 213b.
V.	Williams, Charles	..	Bronllys	..	Delinquency	Walker e. 7, 213b.
V.	Williams, David	..	Cwmdu	..	Simony and illegal induction.	Walker e. 7, 214.

1 'Audley' in Constable's report in 1662 (Lamb. 1027, 3); 'Hartly' in Walker, e. 7, f. 214; 'Hatley' in 'True and Perfect Relation,' p. 50.
2 Notwithstanding all this, there is hardly any doubt that this is the 'Thomas Vaughan, *gentleman*,' referred to in the Brecon Accts for 1651-2 (Walk. c. 13, f. 63). Theophilus Jones has an interesting account of this brother of the Silurist (Hist. Breck. (1898), pp. 435-6).

SOUTH WALES—*continued.*

BRECKNOCK (con.)	NAME OF CLERGYMAN.	STATUS: RECTOR, VICAR OR CURATE.	LIVING OR LIVINGS FROM WHICH EJECTED.	CAUSE OF EJECTION (WHEN SPECIFIED OR ASCERTAINED).	MS. REFERENCE.
	Williams, Richard	R.	Llanthetty	—	Lib. Inst., Men., 46; Walker c. 13, f. 61. "True and Perfect Relation" pp. 38-39.
	Williams, Matthew	V.	Llangattock	"Delinquency and Scandal" ostensibly, really because of strained relations with friends of the Commissioners, infra, Chap. XVIII.	
	Williams, William	R.	Llanafanfawr	Delinquency	Walk. e. 7, 214.
	Watkins, Andrew	R.	Penderyn	Illegal induction	,, e. 7, 214.
	Watkins, Walter	V.	Devynnock	Resigned "upon charge given in articles against him."	,, e. 7, 214.
	Wood, Jacob	V.	Llandevally	Malignancy, assisting the King, praying for his success in public, common drunkard and swearer.	, e. 7, 213, 213b.
	1Wrench, Simon	V.	Llangammarch	—	, e. 7, 213b.

1 The Surveyors of Dean and Chapter Lands on 19th Oct., 1649, report the incumbent as 'Symon Mirrick' (Lamb. 905, f. 57).

CARDIGAN				
Daies, John	R.	Cellan	Drunl ness	Walk. e. 7, 213.
vales, Dad	R.	Tremaen		,, c. 13, f. 36.
Evans, David	V.	Llandyfriog	Steal and my	,, e. 7, 213.
Bus, ...th	V.	Llanrhystyd	Scandal, my, drunk-r ness, and keeping a non alehouse.1	,, e. 7, 213.
Evans, Mgan	R.	isle Acron	Drunkenness	,, e. 7, 213.
Foulkes, Lewis	V.	Tregaron	Drunkenness and incest.	,, e. 7, 213.
Herbert, Edward	V.	Idle	Insufficiency, non for-son, delinquency.	,, e. 7, 213.
Lewis, Mis	R.	Pdse	Insufficiency	,, e. 7, 213.
Idd, Ryn	R.	Jan	Drunkenness	,, e. 7, 213.
dMh, Rees	V.	Iddr pnt t efan	Drunkenness and keeping a non house.	,, e. 7, 213.
Mr, William	V.	Silian and Llanwnen	Drunkenness and using the non Prayer Book.	,, e. 7, 213.
oMgan, Gfith	R.	Bangor and Henllan	Insufficiency, non-ess, iny.	Walker e. 7, 213; Lords' Petns., W. 1660.
Powell, Mis	R.	flys Bledrws	Keeping a non ale-house, using the non Pr. Book.	Walker, e. 7, 213.
Psi, David	V.	Llanfihangel y	D ness	,, e. 7, 213.
Price, Evan	R.	cdgho	D ness, non, using the Prayer Book.	,, e. 7, 213.
Prichard, Roger	R.	gdlo		Lib. Inst., Mon., 27; Walker c. 13, f. 36.

1 The allegation against some of the Cardiganshire clergy of 'keeping a common ale-house' loses some of its pungency when it is remembered that, even after the Knoxian Reformation in Scotland, it was decreed that ministers or readers who kept an 'open tavern' should observe decorum [reference to the General Assembly of 1576 in 'Politics and Religion in Scotland', Vol. I, p. 215 (W. Law Mathieson) quoting Calderwood iii. p. 377].

SOUTH WALES—*continued.*

NAME OF CLERGYMAN.	STATUS: RECTOR, VICAR OR CURATE.	LIVING OR LIVINGS FROM WHICH EJECTED.	CAUSE OF EJECTION (WHEN SPECIFIED OR ASCERTAINED).	MS. REFERENCE.
CARDIGAN (*cont*)				
Roberts, Humphrey	V.	Llansantffraid	Drunkenness, insufficiency	Wer. e, 7, 213.
Roberts, John	R.	Aberporth	Drunkenness	,, e, 7, 213.
Thomas, Wm.	V.	Penbryn	——	diocs' Trans, T. 1660.
?his, John	R.	Llandyssul	——	Inab. 1027, No. 32; Walr c. 13, f. 36.
CARMARTHEN				
Prydderch, H ?ry	R.	Llanfihangel-ar-Arth	Drunkenness and malignancy.	Wlk. e. 7, f. 212; Wlk. c. 13, f. 40b.
?has, Griffith	R.	Llanstephan	——	Wlk. e. 7, f. 218b.
Evans, William	V.	Merthyr	Drunkenness and malignancy.	,, e. 7, f. 212.
Evans, Walter	R.	St. Clears	——	,, f. 212.
Griffith, Rees	V.	Myddfai	Insufficiency, sc adel and delinquency.	,, f. 209.
Hughes, William	V.	Llanarthney	D ?hss and malignancy.	,, f. 212.
Jenkins, Morgan	V.	Abernant	ditto	,, f. 212.
Jones, ?has	V.	Llangain	ditto	,, f. 212.
J ?es, William	V.	Llanegwad	Malignancy and refusing "Engagement."	,, f. 209.
Lewis, ?has	R.	Henllan Amgoed	——	,, f. 212.
Maylard, Wm.	V.	Pembrey	——	,, f. 218b.
Nicholson, ?n.	V.	Llandilofawr	Malignancy and refusing "Engagement."	,, f. 209.

1 Date of ejection uncertain; most probably *before* the Act; vide Puritan nominee to Penbryn (p. 66).

			Parish	Cil-		Reference
CARMARTHEN (con.)	Gn, William	..	V.	Kidwelly	..	Lords' Petitions, 1660.
	Hps, dger	..	R.	Meg and maenllwyd.		Walk. e. 7, f. 212.
	Price, Hias	..	V.	lile	Scandal and delinquency.	„ „ f. 209.
	Fmrd, oge	..	R.	Idel	Malignancy, insufficiency, refusing "Engagement."	„ „ f. 209.
	Rees, John	..	V.	Llangunnor	Scandal, insufficiency	„ „ f. 209.
	Puleston, Wn.	..	R.	oake		Lords' Petitions, 1660.
GLAMORGAN ..	Bevan, Wm.	..	R.	Loughor	Delinquency	Walker c. 4, 72b.
	lgls, Bard	..	R.	Eglwys Brewys		L.I., Llandaff, 15; Walk. c. 13, f. 29b.
	Btler, John	..	V.	Penmark	Insufficiency and delinquency.	Walk. e. 7, f. 208.
	Davies, David	..	V	Llangynwyd		Walker c. 4, 70; c. 13, f. 21.
	Davies, Meredith	..	V.	Aberavon	Insufficiency	„ c. 4, 70.
	Davies, Rees	..	V.	Pentyrch		Lamb. 913, f. 752; Walk. c. 4, f. 65b.
	aEis, Jenkin	..	R.	St. Gs	Insufficiency and delinquency.	Walk. c. 7, f. 208.
	age, Edward	..	R.	sly	Delinquency	„ e. 7, f. 208.
	fh, Isaac	..	V.	Llangyfelach	Malignancy and refusing "Engagement."	„ e. 7, f. 208.
	J nes, Lewis	..	R.	Myr Mvr		Imb. 913, f. 751; Walker c. 13, f. 21b.
	Galen, Tohn	..	R.	Coyty		Walker e. 7, f. 208.
	Kinge, William	..	C?	faiff ?		Mk. c. 13, ff. 17b, 26b, 31.
	Mk, Lmd	..	V.	St. yhns		L.I., faff, 12; Walk. c. 13, f. 29b.
	Mn, fin	..	V.	St. Mry's, Swansea	Insufficiency	Walk. c. 4, 72b.
	Prohard, G.	..	R.	aidnnor	Delinquency	„ e. 7, 208.

SOUTH WALES—*continued.*

NAME OF CLERGYMAN.	STATUS: RECTOR, VICAR OR CURATE.	LIVING OR LIVINGS FROM WHICH EJECTED.	CAUSE OF EJECTION (WHEN SPECIFIED OR ASCERTAINED).	MS. REFERENCE.
GLAMORGAN (con.)				
Reynolds, Christopher	V.	...iff	Delinquency	Walk. c. 4, 6b.
Swinglehurst, Richd.	R.	...as	Delinquency and refusing "Engagement."	„ e. 7, 28.
Williams, Henry	R.	Flemingstone	——	„ c. 4, 68; Walk. c. 13, f. 29b.
Williams, John	V.	...arn	——	c. 13, f. 29; Lamb. 913, f. 749.
Wilson, John	R.	Porthkerry	——	Wlk. e. 7, 208.
Barry, Daniel	R.	Llanhenog	——	Bab. 913, f. 771; Wlk. c. 13, f. 44.
MONMOUTH [1]				
Brabourne,[2] Robt.	V.	...nth	My ... ad delin-quency.	Walker, e. 7, 215.
Clarke, William	R.	Dixton	Malignancy, drunkonness.	War e. 7, 215.
Clegg, John	R.	Igby	...cy, ...ng habitation v ...n Parliamentary ...ces near, ...lility to ...ph in ...sh.	Walker e. 7, 12b.
Cragge, John	R.	Llantilio Portholey	——	Lamb. 913, fol. 779; Walker c. 13, f. 44.

1 *Monmouth*: "The Ministers *in general* who made their appearance before the Commissioners at *Chepstow* were ejected and shortly after sequestered" (quot. from a constable's report in 1662). (Walk. e. 7, f. 218b). But it must be carefully noted that the evidence for some of the Monmouth ejections is purely circumstantial.
2 Brabourne (Walk. e. 7; C.S.P., 1654, p. 173);
Brabourne (Bodl. D. 711, f. 9), Exch. Pap. 251; Bodl. 326, f. 206);
Braband (Walk. c. 13, f. 57);
Brabant (Lamb. 979, i., f. 12).

MONMOUTH (con.)						
pd, George	..	V.	Trelech	..	——	Lib. Inst. Llandaff,121; Walker c. 13, f. 43b.
Davies, W.	..	V.	Raglan	..	——	L.I., Llaff, 121; Wlk. c. 13, b.
Dr, Garnons	..	V.	Llanover	..	——	Lamb. 913, fol. 774; Walk. c. 13, f. b.
Dobbin, John	..	R.	Llangattock Vibon Avel	..	Using the Prayer Book; inability to preach.	Walker e. 7, 215.
Edwards, John	..	R.	Langstone	..	and prosecution of the godly in the neighbourhood.	Walker e. 7, 215.
Edwards, John	..	R.	Llanmartin	..	——	L.I., Llaff, 127; Walker c. 13, f. 43.
ld, Pl ffgir	..	R.	Penhowe	..	Using the Prayer Book, and inability to ph.	Wer e. 7, 215.
Harris, Wr	..	R.	Wolvesnewton	..	Drunkenness; in arms against the Parliament.	Wer e. 7, 12b.
Hawes, Richard1	..	R.	Llangua	..	——	Walk. c 13, f. 51b (arrears of fis ?).
Hayward, Tos.	..	R.	Bedwas	..	——	Walk. c.13, f. 57b (ffis).
Heath, Richard	..	R.	Grosmont	..	——	Walk.c. 13,f. 57b (fifths ad).
Hughes, William	..	V.	Abergavenny	..	Drunkenness and induction.	Walk. e. 7, 215.
Hughes, Michael	..	V.	Usk	..	Publishing the l King,drunken-es, and ng Common Prayer Book.	„ e. 7, 214b.
Jeffreys, Howell	..	V.	Matherne	..	and drunken-ness.	Walk. e. 7, f. 215.

1 Col. Bradney makes no reference to Hawes in his list of Llangua incumbents (Hist. Mon., Pt. I, p. 92).

SOUTH WALES—continued.

NAME OF CLERGYMAN.	STATUS: RECTOR, VICAR OR CURATE.	LIVING OR LIVINGS FROM WHICH EJECTED.	CAUSE OF EJECTION (WHEN SPECIFIED OR ASCERTAINED).	MS. REFERENCE.
MONMOUTH (con.)				
Jones, J hro	R.	Llanfoist	Drunkenness	Walker e. 7, 215b.
?, Lewis	V.	Llanddewi Skirrid	Ill ???	Walk. e. 7, 215.
?s, Rice	R.	Michaelstone-y-Vedw	??? insufficient.	„ e. 7, 215.
?s, William	V.	Dingestow	D ??? ard igno-rance.	„ e. 7, 214b.
Lewis, Charles	V.	Llanllowell	Drunkenness—Sat in the Stocks at Chepstow.	„ e. 7, 215.
M?, John	V.	Llangwm	Drunkenness	„ e. 7, 214b.
M?, Thomas	R.	Wilcrick		L.I., Llandaff, 126; Walker c. 13, f. 50.
Morgan, —	V.	Magor		Walker c. 13, f. 57b (fifths).
?s, ?gn	R.	Wonastow	Drunkenness and insufficiency.	Walker e. 7, 215.
Hs, John	R.	Skenfrith		„ c. 13, f. 51b (fifths).
Price, ?n	V.	Llanfihangel Crucorney	Malignancy and drunkenness.	Walk. e. 7, 215.
Price, Wi lliam	V.	Cwmyoy	Using the Prayer Book and inability to preach.	„ e. 7, 215
Price, ?n	R.	Llanhilleth		L.I., Llandaff, 112; Walker c. 13, f. 43; Walk. e. 7, f. 219.

MONMOUTH (con.)				Malignancy and drunkenness.	
Pri ▮▮l, David ..	V.	Llanfihangel-juxta-Usk. ▮n	..		Walk. e. 7, 215.
Price, Daniel ..	V.		..		Lamb. 19, f. 759; Walk. c. 13, f. 57b.
Pye, Moore ..	R.	Llanva p▮y	..		Walk. c. 13, f. 53; Lamb' ▮▮, W. 160.
▮ell, George ..	R.	▮▮in	..		▮, diff, 111; L.I., Walker c. 13, f. 53.
▮ R▮, ▮▮y ..	R.	Mynyddislwyn	..		Bodl. 325, f. 168; Walk. c. 13, 49b.
Roberts, J hno ..	R.	Bihton	..		Lamb. 19, f. 769; Walk. c. 13, f. 44.
Rogers, Owen ..	V.	Lantilio Crossenny	..	Malignancy and drunkenness.	Walk. e. 7, 25.
▮s, A▮n ..	V.	I▮ellen	..	Using Prayer Book, inability to preach.	,, e. 7, 215.
▮▮s, ▮e ..	R.	Bassaleg	..	Using Prayer Book and malignancy.	,, e. 7, 215.
ki▮, William ..	V.	Llanarth	..		Lamb. 913, f. 777; Walk. c. 13, f. 43b.
Williams, Edward ..	R.	Gwernesney	..	Frequently tippling, swearing, and using the Prayer Book.	Walk. o. 7, 214b.
▮s, John ..	R.	Penyclawdd	..		Lamb. 913, f. 776; Walk. c. 13, f. 43b.
Williams, William ..	R.	Cwmcarvan	..		Walk. c. 13, 57b (fifths).

1 *Geo.* in Liber Inst., Llandaff, p. 111. *James* in Walker e. 7, 1. 219.

2 It is very probable that this *Henry Rees* ('*Rice*' in MS.) had become unsatisfactory to the C.P.M. in Dec., 1649, *i.e.*, before the Act. "It is ordered that 5*l.* a yeare be paid unto *such* Minister as the Committee . . . shall approve of to officiate ye Cure of the said Church provided that he first subscribe ye Ingagement" (Bodl. MS. 326, f. 206b).

K

SOUTH WALES—*continued.*

NAME OF CLERGYMAN.	STATUS: RECTOR, VICAR OR CURATE.	LIVING OR LIVINGS FROM WHICH EJECTED.	CAUSE OF EJECTION (WHEN SPECIFIED OR ASCERTAINED).	MS. REFERENCE.
PEMBROKE				
Barwicke, Mael	R.	Nash	Pl ist; d to ld R. of Herbrandston	L.I., Men., 8, 18; Lamb. 915, fol. 96.
Brookes, Richard	R.	Noulton	Drunkenness	Walk. e. 7, 2b.
Browne, as	R.	Loveston	Insufficiency	,, e. 7, 212b.
Burgess, Edward	C.	Prendergast		,, e. 7, 212b.
Carre, Mark	V.	Llanstadwell	Hist: ld to ld V. of Gase.	c. 13, f. 7b (fine) L.I., Men., 17, 20; Lamb. 915, fol. 88.
Collyer, Edward	R.	Llanbedr Efelfre	Drunkenness	Wlk. e. 7. 212b.
n, James	V.	St. Twinnells	Malignancy	,, e. 7, 212b.
Elliott, Lewis	R.	Castlebigh	Drunkenness	,, e. 7, f. 212b.
Evans, Richard	R.	Jordanston		L.I., Men., 2; Walk. c. 13, f. 9b.
Griffith, Henry	R.	Gumfreston	Pluralist: allowed to hold R. of St. Petrox; "an aged minister"	L.I., Men., 7, 5; Lamb. 915, f. 36.
ane, Lewis	R.	St. Brides	Insufficiency	Wlk. e. 7, 21 2b.
Hayward, s.	V.	Moelgrove	Insufficiency	e. 7, 21 2b.
Hudson, Francis	V.	Penally	Pluralist; d to ld R. of Rudbaxton.	L.I., 915, f. 121.
Hughes, Trevor	V.	Ludchurch	Drunkenness	Wlk. e. 7, 212b.
Humphreys, Rod.	R.	Llanfihangel Penbedw	Insufficiency	,, e. 7, 2b.
James, David	R.	Briddell		Lords' Petitions, J,1660; Wlk. c. 13, f. 9.

PEMBROKE (con.)

Name		Parish		Reason	Reference
¹Jewell, [Bid]	..	Tenby	R		..	Lamb. 915, f. 104; Walk. c. 13, f. 5.
[Js], Thomas [this]		St. Laurence	R.		..	Insufficiency	Walk. e. 7, 212b.
Jones, [this]		Pontvaen	R.		L.I., Men., 40; Walk. c. 13, f. 9b; Lamb. 915, f. 162.
[nJs], William		Cosheston	R.	Malignancy	Walk. e. 7, 212b.
King, [Ann]		Fresthorp	R.	Insufficiency	,, e. 7, 212b.
[Yd], Richard		[swifi]	R.	Malignancy	,, e. 7, 212b.
Love, Edward		Talbenny	V.	Malignancy	,, e. 7, 212b.
Loveling, [Mhew]		Castlemartin	R.	Insufficiency	,, e. 7, 212.
Matthias, John		[Wh]			Lamb. 915, f. 159; Wlk. c. 13, f. 11.
M[aen], Edward		Mathry	V.	Malignancy	Walk. e. 7, 212b.
Meyrick, William		Llanychaer	R.	Alehouse Keeper	,, e. 7, 212b.
Miles, Henry		Dinas	R.	Insufficiency	,, e. 7, 212b.
[Md], John		Marletwy	V.	Drunkenness	,, e. 7, 212b.
[Np], Eymon		Lambston	C	Drunkenness	,, e 7, 212b.
²Onacre, Paul		St [r Me]	V.	Insufficiency	Inab 915, f. 145.
Owen, Francis		Hodgeston	R.		Wlk. e. 7, 212b.
O[wn], [Ge]		B[gelly]	R.		Mr: Suff, II, 325; Walk. c. 13, f. 5.
Owen, John		Rosemarket	V.	Drunkenness	,, e. 7, 212.
Phillips, John		[Ideloy]	V.	Drunkenness	,, e. 7, 212b.
Phillips, John		[Mil]	R.		L.I., Men., 41; Lamb. 915, f. 166; Walk. c. 13, f. 9.

1 He must have subscribed the Engagement, which is expressly laid down as a condition by the C.P.M. before paying up his arrears of salary early in 1650 (Bodl. 327, f. 185).

2 The *name* is derived from Walker (Sufferings: Pt. II., p. 325).

Three entries, one in the Lamb. MS. and two in the Walk. MS. :—

1650 { (a) St. Florence—vicarage—minister ejected." (915, f. 145).
      (b) " St. Florence vicarage : £10 given to ye children's order". (Walk. c. 13, f. 5).
      (c) " £10 given by the Commissioners to ye children of *the late vicar*". (Walk. c. 13, f. 8b.).

However, in face of the evidence (p. 69) that Waller was made both rector and vicar of this living in 1648, it must be inferred that Onacre was ejected *before* the Act.

SOUTH WALES—*continued.*

NAME OF CLERGYMAN.	STATUS: RECTOR, VICAR OR CURATE.	LIVING OR LIVINGS FROM WHICH EJECTED.	CAUSE OF EJECTION (WHEN SPECIFIED OR ASCERTAINED).	MS. REFERENCE.
PEMBROKE (con.)				
Phillips, Robert	R.	Henry's Moat	Pluralist; also Rector of Stackpole.	L.I., Men., 6,39; Walk. c. 13, f. 5b.
Pardoe, Marmaduke	V.	St. David's	Drunkenness	Walk. e. 7, 212.
Price, John	V.	Llanwnda	Drunkenness	Lords' Petitions,P.1660; Walker e. 7, 212b.
Pro and, Edward	V.	St. Dogmells	Pluralist: allowed to hold R. of Cilgerran.	Men., 2, 35; Lamb. 915, f. 147.
Rees, Morgan	V.	Llandisilio 1	Insufficiency	Wlk. e. 7, 212b.
Rees, William	V.	Maenclochog	Insufficiency	,, e. 7, 212b.
Thomas, Morgan	V.	Roch	Drunkenness	,, e. 7, 212b.
fhs, Oliver	P.	Lawrenny	Malignancy	Lords' Petitions,P. 1660; Walk. e. 7, 212b.
Vaughan, Morris	R.	Penrieth	Pluralist: allowed to be V. of Clydey.	L.I., Men., 35; Imb. 915, f. 151; Walk.c.13, f. 5.
White, Nicholas	V.	St. Issells	Insufficiency	,, e. 7, 212b.
Williams, David	V.	Ambleston	Drunkenness	,, e. 7, 212.
Williams, Henry	V.	Carew	Drunkenness	,, e. 7, 212b.
Willi ms, Howell	V.	Llanrhian	Drunkenness	,, e.7, 212b.
Williams, Rlp	R.	Robeston	Malignancy	Lamb. 1027, No. 49; Wlk. e. 7, 212b.
Williams, Richard	R.	Trefgarn	Insufficiency	Wlk. e. 7, 212b.
	R.	Spittal		Imb. 915, f. 172; Wlk. c. 13, f. 8b.

1 Partly in Pembroke and partly in Carmarthen. 2 The name of this incumbent is not found in any contemporary record.

County	Name	Type	Parish	Charge	Reference
PEMBROKE (con.)	———1	V.	Wiston	———	Lamb. 915, f. 145.
RADNOR	Browne, Charles	V.	Llangunllo	———	Lamb. 905, f. 28; Walk. c. 13, f. 65.
	Griffith, Alex.	V.	Glasbury2	Drunkenness and lasciviousness	Lamb. 1027, Glasbury Report; Walk. e. 7, 214.
	Jones, David	R.	Llanbadarnfawr		Walk. c. 13, ff. 66, 68.
	Jones, Richard	V.	Llandegley		Lamb. 905, f. 22; Walk. c. 13, f. 67.
	Jones, David	V.	Llanfihangel Nantmelan	Drunkenness	Walk. e. 7, 214b.
	Mellin, Henry	R.	Aberedw	Common swearing, adhering to & assisting the King.	Lords' Petns. 1660; Walk. e. 7, 214.
	Morgan, Morris3	V.	St. Harmons		Lamb. 905, f. 36; Walk. c. 13, f. 65.
	Owen, Hugh	C.	Hyeopp	Scandal	Ibid. e. 7, 214b.
	Phillips, John	R.	Diserth	Drunkenness and enmity to the Parliament.	Ibid., 214.
	Price, Humphrey	R.	Bryngwyn	Drunkenness, love of litigation, enemy to the Parliament	Ibid., 214.
	Rea, John	R.	Bledifa		Lib. Inst., Men., 63; Walk. c. 13, f. 67.
	Vaughan, John	V.	Llowes		Walk. e. 7, 214b.
	Waller,4 Phineas	R.	Whitton	Drunkenness	Walk. Suff., II, p. 410; Walk. c. 13, f. 66.
	Williams, William	V.	Llansantffraid-in-Cwmtoyddwr	———	Lords' Petns. 1660; Walk. c. 13, f. 65.
	Winston, Walt.	R.	Newchurch	———	Lib. Inst., Men., 61; Walk. c. 13, f. 65.

1 The name of this incumbent is not found in any contemporary record.
2 This place is really in Brecknock, but has been included in the Radnor list (Walk. e. 7).
3 'Morgan Morice' (Walk. c. 13. f. 68b).
4 'Waler' in Walk. c. 13.

The Commissioners did not shrink from exercising to the full their independent powers of revision. Among the ejected are twenty-nine men who were satisfactory to the Puritan authorities of the pre-Propagation period. No less than thirteen nominees of the Lords are sequestered ; Henry Miles of Dinas and Lewis Gwynn of St. Brides in Pembrokeshire, both approved by the Assembly, are found ' insufficient,' William Jones of Llanegwad has become a malignant, and four in Cardiganshire are deprived for gross misdemeanours, only three of them being able to preach.[1] Ten who had found favour with the C.P.M. are removed, including John Phillips of Diserth in Radnor, who had emerged victorious from the competition instituted before the examining committee of the Assembly in 1647.[2] The pluralists of Anglesey, connived at by the Lords, find no mercy, and friends of the Parliament suffer the same fate : the great services of Robert Fogg do not suffice to keep him the chapelry of Overton in addition to the rectory of Bangor-on-Dee,[3] and Edward Thelwall was compelled to relinquish his living of Llanynys when appointed to the mastership of Ruthin School.[4] Matthew Evans of Penegoes finds in the new Commissioners sterner inquisitors than the old Committee of Montgomery[5] ; old charges of disaffection and scandal, obscured from the notice of the Assembly and found unproven by the C.P.M.,[6] see David Roberts excluded from the vicarage of Llandinam ; successful appeals to the Barons of the Exchequer is no bar to the ejection of the clergymen of Brecon and Eubule Lewis of Newtown[7] ; and the sequestration of Edward Ellis of Guilsfield, though still the subject of inquiry by the central authorities,[8] seem sufficient grounds for his definite dismissal from that cure. Men who had been found satisfactory by well-affected patrons, ' preaching ministers ' in Monmouthshire appointed under the express terms of capitular leases,[9] higher clergy who had hitherto succeeded in saving some living or other

1 Walker e. 7, f. 213.
2 Supra, p. 45.
3 Rawl. c. 261, p. 26.
4 Ibid., p. 19. He did not become Head Master of the Grammar School there, but of the ' free school ' established by the Commissioners.
5 Supra, pp. 42, 71.
6 Bodl. 325, f. 164.
7 Supra, pp. 51, 52.
8 Cal. Comm. Compounding, Vol. IV, p. 3056.
9 p. 19 supra. John Roberts of Bishton and Daniel Barry of Llanhenog.

interest from the devastating force of ordinances of plurality and sequestrations,—all failed to satisfy the new Puritan tests. The ignorance and lax moral standard which had inevitably arisen out of the problems and obsessions of the episcopal system, the loyalty to King and Bishop and Prayer Book, illegal induction by the Bishops upon the presentation of delinquents,[1] and refusal to swear the necessary oath of obedience to the new republican government, cannot be tolerated by these Commissioners of " piety and integrity."[2] Pluralists were ruthlessly eliminated ; some were dispossessed of all their livings, while others were suffered to retain one. Dual influence in various localities came to an end : William Jones was rid of the presence of William Rogers at Denbigh, Oliver Thomas of the vicar John Williams at Llanrhaiadr, and Henry Rees[3] was not deemed ' godly ' enough to minister at the Puritan stronghold of Mynyddislwyn. Anomalous cases, however, still remained : Hugh Bonner was not formally ejected from Llanwenarth and Aberystruth, but no tithes were paid him by the parishioners[4]; and Nathan Jones, never actually deprived, found the bells sold, the Bible taken from the pulpit, and the services interrupted by drink-loving and tobacco-laden Puritans at Merthyr Tydfil.[5]

Generally speaking, the lot of the ejected was undoubtedly hard. Though the accounts of South Wales show that £1,866 7s. 5d. were paid in fifths during 1650-1653, the allowances to wife and children were far from being regularly or universally granted.[6] Many causes operated.[7] Such were the hostile attitude of some clergymen, the extent of their personal means, the slow payment of tithes, the frequent arrears of the men who farmed the sequestered livings, and the consideration whether the ejected was married or no, whether families were large or small, and whether death

1 Walker MS. e. 7, f. 215—definition given in the case of Lewis Jones of Llanddewi Skirrid.
2 Vavasor Powell : A Brief Narrative . . . prefixed to " Bird in the Cage." p. 3.
3 There are reasons for the belief that he was sequestered before 1650 (vide p. 129, Ref. 2). But his name is not included among the eighteen so described in Walk. e. 7, f. 215b.
4 Walker MS. e. 7, fol. 215b ; Ant. [onȳ] Bonner in Lib. Inst., Llandaff, p. 17. The author of the ' Sufferings ' confuses ' Aberystruth ' with ' Aberystwyth,' (Part II, p. 212).
5 Wilkins : History of Merthyr Tydvil, pp. 94, 95.
6 The allowances were made to those ejected *before* the Act as well as to those ejected *under* it.
7 Fuller ; The Church History of Great Britain (1655) ed. Brewer (1845), Vol. V, p. 333, has an exhaustive analysis of the reasons advanced for withholding fifths during the regime of the C.P.M.

ensued after sequestration. In the case of pluralities, one living only, and that often the poorest, carried fifths. Thomas Bassett, once rector of the inordinately large parish of Llantrisant, obtained fifths only for Leckwith,[1] and that after "continual teazing of the Rulers."[2] Of undoubtedly surviving clergymen, some, like Edmund Gamage of Llanharry, received no allowance whatsoever[3]; some, like Jenkin Lewis of Llancarfan, for one year only[4]; some, like the old incumbents of Llangorse and Llansantffread in Brecon, received the three years' fifths in one instalment[5]; and others, like Richard Swinglehurst of Llanmaes in Glamorgan, were told that they were rich men "and did not want."[6] Nor was the basis of calculation consistently adhered to. Some, as in the case of Merthyr in Carmarthenshire, were based on the rent received and not the rent set[7]; some received the exact allowance in total disregard of the deduction of public charges[8]; some fifths were far below the instruction of the Act[9]; some, on the other hand, were very generously treated[10]; others, including the North Wales beneficiaries, received the grant duly prescribed,[11] while some only approximately so.[12] Again, the various counties greatly differed in their attitude. Cardiganshire was by far the most generous and consistent[13]; no fifths were paid at all during 1650 in Carmarthenshire[14]; of the large number of sequestered clergy in Glamorganshire $(20 + 35)$[15] only twenty-nine are in receipt of fifths in 1650, six in 1651, and nine in 1652; of the still larger number sequestered in Monmouth $(18 + 45)$[16] twelve only get

1 Walker c. 13, ff. 25, 25b.
2 Walker c. 4, f. 65b.'
3 Walker c. 13, f. 15. [For convenience, the names of the *clergymen* in this paragraph represent the *wife and children*, to whom *only* the grant was made.]
4 Walker c. 13, f. 15.
5 Walker c. 13, folios 61, 61b.
6 Walker c. 4, f. 69.
7 Walker c. 13, f. 40 ; Rent set, £20 ; received, £18. Fifths = £3 12s. 0d.
8 *E.g.*, Sully in Glam. Rent set, £70 ; Assessments, £9 14s. 6d. Fifths = £14 (c. 13, f. 15).
9 *E.g.*, Pendoylan in Glam. Rent £60. Fifths = £7 4s. 0d. (c. 13, f. 15) ; Matherne in Mon. Rent £45. Fifths = £1. (c. 13, f. 43b).
10 *E.g.*, Ilston in Gower. Rent £60. Assessments £3. Fifths = £20 (c. 13, f. 16); Porteynon in Gower. Rent £40. Assessments £3. Fifths = £11 (c. 13, f. 16).
11 *E.g.*, Llanafanfawr in Brecon. Rent £55. Assessments £3 9s. 0d. Fifths = £10 6s. 0d. (c. 13, 59b).
12 *E.g.*, Cilie Aeron in Card. Rent £13 6s. 8d. Assessments £2 0s. 0d. Fifths = £2 15s. 0d. (c. 13, f. 33).
13 Walker c. 13, ff. 33—36b.
14 Walker c. 13, f. 37.
15 Twenty ejected *under* the Act, thirty-five before.
16 Forty-five ejected *under* the Act, eighteen before.

allowances in 1650, ten in 1651, twenty-two in 1652 ; Radnor paid out during the first year £67 18s. 0d.,[1] and for the last two years together only £63 13s. 0d.[2] Of the forty-six clergymen whose ejection is recorded in the Rawlinson MS. orders for fifths were made in eleven cases only. Under such conditions the ejected clergy had to seek for other means of subsistence. Nathaniel Gamage of Eglwysilan,[3] Hugh Gore of Oxwich,[4] and Francis Davies of Llangan[5] kept private schools ; Hopkin Thomas of Bishopston was maintained by his brother, Wm. Thomas of Swansea[6] ; William Lewis of St. Fagans,[7] Thomas Morgan of Colwinstone[8] and Edmund Gamage of Llanharry[9] had to live on some small pittances of their own ; and Henry Williams of Flemingston lived by his poetry, he ' being a witty man and good company.'[10] Others left their old quarters. Edward Gamage of Rhossilly, having in vain turned farmer, crossed to Ireland[11]; Dr. Gordon of Porteynon died in Kent[12]; William Bayly of Penstrowed retired to Llanegryn in Merioneth,[13] and John Hughes, late vicar of Llansantffraid, moved his home to Meifod in the same county.[14] Rowland Owen of Wrexham became " an Artist in Patience."[15] Of a more virile type was Dr. Hugh Williams of Llanrhuddlad, who was reported for disturbing the tenants of the rectories from which he had been ejected[16] ; John Edwards of Tredunnock in Monmouth, who translated Edward Fisher's " Marrow of Modern Divinity " into Welsh[17] ; Thomas Powell of Cantref in Brecon, who crossed over to the Continent, where probably he composed " Cerbyd Jechydwriaeth " for the purpose, he says, of directing some, and supporting others, in the right way and the true gospel[18] ; Richard

1 Walker c. 13, f. 66.
2 Ibid., f. 68.
3 Walker c. 4, f. 65b.
4 Walker c. 4, f. 72.
5   Ibid.   f. 69b.
6   Ibid.   f. 72b.
7   Ibid.   f. 67.
8   Ibid.   f. 68.
9   Ibid.   f. 67b.
10   Ibid.   f. 68.
11   Ibid.   f. 72.
12   Ibid.   f. 72.
13 Exch. Returns, Mont., 1658.   Slip 118.
14   Ibid.   Slip 119.
15 David Lloyd : Memoires (1668), p. 570.
16 Cal. Comm. Comp., Vol. III, p. 1725.
17 Madruddyn y Difinyddiaeth Diweddaraf. O cyfieithiad J. E. Dedication (July 20, 1650) subscribed " Sion Tre-redyu " (C.F.L.).
18 Ashton : Hanes Llenyddiaeth Gymreig o 1650 i 1850, pp. 51, 52.

Jones of Llanfaircaereinion, who wrote out a mnemonic summary in verse of the New Testament and a similar epitome of the book of Genesis[1] ; Dr. George Griffith who, in weak health, crosses over from his Border ' pastorate ' of Llanymynech to defend his ' mixt ways ' against the ' ways of separation ' advocated by Vavasor Powell[2] ; and Alexander Griffith, the ejected of Glasbury and Llanwnog, whose ' Hue and Cry,' ' Strena Vavasoriensis,' and ' Mercurius Cambro-Britannicus ' contained virulent criticism of the policy of the Propagators. The strength of Anglican sentiment is represented in the will of Sir Marmaduke Lloyd of Maesyfelin, who wished to die in the true faith in which he had been nurtured,[3] and the dark days which had befallen lay and cleric Cavaliers find expression in Rowland Vaughan's statement in 1658 that for the last seven years he had lived like " a pilgrim in a cell."[4]

For the clergy, however, the troublous times had some redeeming features. Robert Jones of Llandwrog, John Gumbleden of Coyty,[5] and Roger Jones of Llanerfyl were restored to their livings upon *appeal*, the first by the Commissioners themselves[6] and the last by the Committee for Plundered Ministers.[7] The fact that four Merionethshire clergy are still in possession of the livings in February, 1652, from which they had been duly ejected in 1650-1651, that Henry Thomas is paying first fruits for his plurality of Maentwrog, and that the ejected curate of Pennal is now styled ' Vicar of Towyn,' points to considerable leniency on the part of the county agents of sequestration.[8] Some of the clergy secured appointments as schoolmasters under the Act,[9] and the South Wales accounts record many acts of generosity towards them. Constantine Smith, ' a poore chorister at Llandaff,' receives £13 6s. 8d. towards his relief

1 Testûn Testament Newydd ein Harglwydd a'n Iachawdwr Iesu Grist yu Benhillion Cymraeg mewn Egwyddoraidd Drefn. Dedication written at ' Llanfair ynghaer *Eingnion*, Kalend. Jonawr, 1652 (= 1653). (B' Mus.).
2 A Bold Challenge . . . , p. [3] ; Animadversions on an Imperfect Relation . . . p. 21 ; Exchequer Return, Salop, 1652.
3 Lloyd Records and Pedigrees, ed. Theakston and Davies (1912), p. 30. Will dated 1651. " I hope onlie to bee saved in vera fide Christiana Ecclesiae Anglicanae in qua natus fui *puer* in eadem vera fide *morior senex*."
4 Yr Arfer o Weddi yr Arglwydd (1658). Gan Ioan Despagne. Dedication, p. 26—" megis pereryn mewn cellan " [quoted in Ashton : Hanes Llen. Gymreig.]
5 Walker MS. e. 7, f. 208.
6 Lamb. 1027, Report 29. Sequestered at Carnarvon, 7th May, 1652. Re-admitted at Bala, 7th July, 1652.
7 Exch. Return, Mont., 1657, Slip 115. *The only recorded case.*
8 Exchequer Return, Merioneth, 1652.
9 Infra, Chap. XV, pp, 226-230.

in 1650,[1] and the wife of Charles Lewis of Llandegfedd a donation of £20 towards the support of herself and her children, ' being very poor '[2]; the same reason finds Edward Williams of Llanbrynmair restored to his vicarage ' for one year only ' in 1653[3] ; likewise John Owen, the vicar of Llanbadrig in Anglesey, ' a very poor man, charged with a wife and many children,' is allowed to officiate that cure.[4] Robert Lloyd, the author of " Llwybr Hyffordd," and ejected from the vicarage of Chirk, is given £20 a year ' out of the profits of the said vicarage.'[5] Philip Williams of Robeston in Pembrokeshire admits that he received the ' harvest ' upon petition in 1650.[6] And there are many cases of North Wales clergymen being allowed to enjoy the profits of their sequestered livings, some ' freely,' one of ' wool and lambs,' and the eleven Anglesey rectors who were all ejected on 18th September, 1650,[7] for practically nominal sums to be paid to the Treasurer with the proviso, however, that this was to hold good for one year only.[8] There are instances, again, of ejected clergy being permitted as tenants of the sequestered premises as ' set and let ' under the provisions of the Act. Such were Charles Herbert at Llanvillo and Walter Watkins at Devynnock in Brecon,[9] David Powell at Clemenston in Glamorgan,[10] Morgan Jenkins at Abernant and Thomas Price at Llandebie in Carmarthen,[11] Edward Williams of Gwernesney,[12] John Clegg of Llangibby,[13] Daniel Price of Caerleon[14] and Charles Lewis of Llandegfedd[15] in Monmouth, William Jones of Llangadfan and John Davies of Garthbeibio in Montgomery,[16] Maurice Robins at Llanbeblig in Carnarvon[17] and Henry Evans at Llanfechell in Anglesey.[18] During 1651 and 1652

1 Walker MS. c. 13, f. 17.
2   Ibid.   ff. 45b. 51b.
3 Exch. Return, Mont., 1657. Slip 114.
4 Exch. Return, Anglesey, 1652 [not numbered].
5 Rawl. c. 261 [26].
6 Lamb 1027 Report 49.
7 Rawl. c. 261 [20, 21].
8   Ibid.   [24, 25].
9 Walker c. 13, f. 61.   (1651).
10   Ibid.   f 21   (1652).
11   Ibid.   f. 37.   (1650).
12   Ibid.   f. 43.   (1650).
13   Ibid.   f. 50.   (1651).
14   Ibid.   f. 50.   (1651).
15   Ibid.   f. 50.   (1651).
16 Exch. Return, Mont., 1658, Slip 118.
17 Rawl. c. 261 [30].   The entry suggests that he was ejected before the Act.
18 Exch. Return, Anglesey, 1652. This list is not exhaustive. John Edward at Tredunnock and Henry Prydderch at Llanfihangel-ar-Arth may be added (c. 13, ff. 40, 50).

Margaret Griffith becomes tenant of the vicarage of Llangyfelach at her husband's death,[1] and Elizabeth Phillips
of Skenfrith farms that living in 1650 though her husband
is still living.[2] And it may be safely inferred that the
Hugh Powell who farmed Cantref in Brecon for 1650-1652
(c. 13, ff. 59, 61), and the John Field who farmed Penhowe in
Monmouth in 1652 (f. 55), were somehow related to the
clergymen ejected from those livings. The same privilege was extended to the widows of clergymen who
do not seem to have been ejected : ' Jayne ' Middleton
at Steynton in Pembrokeshire,[3] Elizabeth Limm at
Witston in Monmouthshire,[4] and ' Widow Powell ' at
Llanelieu in Brecon.[5] Jane Griffith of Llanddulas is
allowed £15 out of the first profits arising from the rectory,[6]
and Anne Vaughan is not only tenant of the ' prebendship '
of Mochdre in Montgomery but is also allowed to enjoy the
profits arising therefrom.[7] And notwithstanding the ordinances of Parliament, the old services of the Church of
England were still performed more or less secretly. Henry
Nicholls of Coychurch beheld multitudes of the ' Prelatick
Judgment ' flocking to private houses to hear ' private
Expositions and teachings,'[8] and Mansell refers to Rees
Davies of Pentyrch conducting services according to the
discarded liturgy, ' by stealth.'[9] Some Breconshire clergy
ejected in the spring of 1653 for ' taking the boldness to
preach the word of God,' were sent prisoners to ' Chepstow
Garrison,' and others were pulled out of their pulpits [10]
But notwithstanding the close surveillance of the Parliament's
officers,[11] Llwyd admits that worshippers " in many places "
carefully observed some of the minutest directions of the
Prayer Book.[12] George Griffith at Newchapel openly defended
' set prayers ' and referred to the Directory in contemptuous

1 Walker MS. c. 13, f. 19 (1651) ; f. 21 (1652).
2   Ibid.   f. 43 (1650) ; cp. f. 57.
3   Ibid.   f. 9b (1651) ; death of " the late minister " referred to—
                        Lamb. 915, fol. 98.
4   Ibid.   f. 55 (1652).
5   Ibid.   f. 61 (1651 and 1652).
6 Rawl. c. 261 [29] : Order made 30th July, 1651.
7   Ibid.   [22] :   „   „   11th June, 1650.
8 The Shield Single against the Sword Doubled, p. 26.
9 Walker MS. c. 4, f. 65b.
10 True and Perfect Relation, p. 50 ; probably the same incidents are referred to
in Gemitus Ecclesiæ, p. 11.
11 Llwyd : Gweithiau, Vol. I, " Llyfr y Tri Aderyn," p 164—" mae milwyr a
chynghorwyr yn spio am danom, i'n dal, ac i'n difetha " (Raven).
12 Gweithiau, Vol. II, " Gair o'r Gair," p. 172 —" yn eu sefyll " ; Llyfr Gweddi
Cyffredin a Gwenidogaeth y Sacramentay, pp. 19, 23. [1630]. C.F.L.

words,[1] and both he[2] and William Salesbury of Bachymbyd[3] are warmly praised by a Royalist historian for " keeping up the offices and Ceremonies of the Church " during the times of usurpation. Such, no doubt, is the point of R.H.'s remark that the scholar of Caergai was ' abundans pietatis,' and the reason that he and Salesbury were, with the learned Dr. William Brough, addressed as ' tres Religionis *propagatores.*'[4] Vavasor Powell distinctly admits that some of the clergy after their ejection did occasionally preach ' to please their old parishioners, some of which would hear none else[5] ' : thus did David Roberts at Llandinam,[6] John Davies at Garthbeibio,[7] Oliver Rogers at Buttington,[8] and Richard Jones of Llanfair kept on terms of friendship with Oliver Thomas the approver,[9] and " did frequently preach and teach and perform all the offices of a minister there."[10] The same remark applies to two ejected clergymen in Anglesey, Henry Evans at Llanfechell and Owen Evans at Heneglwys.[11]

After all, out of the scores of sequestered clergy, the number who in divers ways found favour with the Propagation authorities were very few, and the celebration of the prohibited service was only made possible by the ineffective supervision of remote country districts, the failure to provide a sufficient preaching ministry, and the strong under-current of public sympathy with the ejected. The sentiments of the average Commissioners and the average Approver are summarised in the savage ' dog ' comparisons of Morgan Llwyd.[12] And the severity of the three years' regime stands out in bold relief against the comparatively tolerant times which set in after the expiry of the Act. By June, 1653, John Cragge is once more ' dispenser of the Gospel ' at Llantilio Pertholey[13] ; in June, 1654, Edward

---

1 Animadversions on an Imperfect Relation . . . pp. [13], [20].
2 David Lloyd : Memoires . . . (1668), p. 600.
3   Ibid.   p. 660.
4 Pregeth yn erbyn Schism . . . . Cyfieith. R. V. ; End of Dedication—" In opus egregium Eruditum amici Charissimi Rowlandi Vaughan." R. H.
5 Bird in the Cage Chirping . . . prefaced by A Brief Narrative of the former Propagation (1661), p. 4.
6 Exch. Return, Mont., 1657, Slip 114.
7   Ibid. .   1658, ,, 118.
8   Ibid.   1658, ,, 119.
9 ' Carwr y Cymry ' (Q. T.) writes three stanzas as ' Encomiastica ' to " Testûn Testament Newydd " (1653).
10 Exch. Return, Mont., 1658, Slip 118.
11   ,,   ,,   Anglesey, 1652 (not numbered).
12 Gweithiau, Vol. I, Song xliv, p. 85, especially stanza 1.
13 The Light of God's Countenance . . . . Set out in a Sermon preached . . . . June 5, 1653 (N.L.W.).

Wynne of Llanymawddwy, in company with Dr. John Ellis and others, is attesting the certificate of Humphrey Thomas to the living of Llandanwg according to the terms of the Ordinance passed in March of that year[1] ; in July of the same year David Jones is once more put in possession of Llanbadarn in Radnor[2] ; and William Jones is restored at Llangadfan ' by an especial Act of Grace ' of the Lord Protector.[3] In the same county David Roberts received the profits of Llandinam during 1654 and 1655,[4] John Davies gets the tithes of Garthbeibio ' without control,'[5] and Thomas Lloyd becomes a pluralist again by entering upon his old rectory of Llanbrynmair.[6]   Three Brecknock clergymen on March 6th, 1653-4, acquaint Jenkin Jones, the erstwhile Approver, that they ' adventure to bestow their paines ' among their old parishioners, and ' put ourselves upon the candor and clemency of our present Governour,[7] from whom we do expect (and doubt not to find) better measure than you forbad us.'[8] And even the bitter critic Alexander Griffith is found schoolmaster at the Hay during the latter years of the Protectorate.[9]

NOTE.—THE ANOMALY AT CONWAY.

On July 4th, 1649, Jeffrey Oldfield was ' minister ' of Conway (Bodl. 326, f. 50), and the ' vicar ' Evan Jones was ' ejected ' by the North Wales Commissioners on July 2nd, 1650 (Rawl. c. 261 [20]). These facts presuppose that both officiated in the same town in differ-ing capacities at one and the same time, which is a situation somewhat more peculiar than that of Laudian rector and Puritan vicar, and *vice versa* (p. 135 supra).   The suggestion made here is that Oldfield was chaplain to the English garrison of the Parliament stationed at Conway under Col. John Carter, and that he remained there until that garrison was disbanded by the re-arrangement of the country's forces made by the Council of State (July 12th, 1655—C. S. Papers, s.a., pp. 229-30).   It is to be noted also that the £50 augmentation granted to him by the C.P.M. in 1649 came not from the ordinary revenue of an unsequestered living, but from that of the sinecure rectory of Clynnog Fawr.   It is also consonant with the foregoing theory that on 12th March, 1656-7, Roger Wynne is described as Minister of Conway.   (Lamb. 977, f. 71).

1 Lamb. 980, liber ii, f. 88 ; Firth and Rait : Acts and Ordinances, Vol. II, p. 857.
2 Lamb. 980, liber iii, f. 161.
3 Exchequer Return, Mont, 1658, Slip 115.
4   ,,   ,,   ,,   1657,   ,,   114.
5   ,,   ,,   ,,   1658,   ,,   118.
6   ,,   ,,   ,,   1658,   ,,   118.
7 The Lord Protector.
8 True and Perfect Relation, p. 52.
9 Lamb. 987, f. 322.

X.

NEW MINISTERS—ITINERANT SYSTEM— MAINTENANCE.

It was well that some proportion of the clergy survived even the new ejections. To Alexander Griffith they were renegades, 'ignorant and illiterate.'[1] On 20th April, 1652, 127 of the 'old ministers' were still in possession in South Wales—Glamorgan 17,[2] Carmarthen 19,[3] Pembroke 31,[4] Cardigan 13,[5] Brecon and Radnor together 14,[6] and Monmouth 33.[7] Types of these were William Ormond, rector of Walton[8] in Pembroke, in October, 1650, described as 'clerke and *preaching* minister[9]'; Giles Nicholas of Llansoy in Monmouth, whom family influence kept in the living through all the vicissitudes of the times[10]; and Evan Griffith, who not only kept his rectory of Oxwich in Gower,[11] but received in addition an augmentation of £50 per annum during the period of Propagation.[12] In North Wales twelve remained throughout in the county of Montgomery[13]; thirteen in Carnarvonshire in February, 1652,[14] including Roger Wynne, curate of Llandudno,[15] who survived to become 'minister' there in 1655,[16] and minister of Conway in 1657[17]; a very small proportion in Denbighshire[18] and a

1 Mercurius Cambro-Britannicus, p. 4.
2 Walker e. 7, f. 209.
3   Ibid.   f. 212.
4   Ibid.   f. 212b.
5   Ibid.   f. 213.
6   Ibid,   f. 214b.
7   Ibid.   f. 215b.   Surely an exaggerated figure in face of the evidence on pp. 126-129.
8 Lib. Inst , Meneuen, fol. 19 ; Inst. 2nd Nov., 1619.
9 Lamb. 915, fol. 91.
10 Diary of Walter Powell (ed. Bradney), p. 21, n. 2.
11 Lib. Inst., Meneuen, fol. 77 ; Instituted 12th Jan., 1638 ; most probably he is the 'John' Griffith of the 1665 Return (Cod. Ten., 639, f. 336).
12 Walker c. 13, ff. 17, 20, 22b.
13 Examen et Purgamen Vavasoris, p. 15. This statement is not strictly true. Of the twelve whose names are mentioned, *six* had been approved by the C.P.M. or instituted by the Lords, and also remained unejected under the Propagation Act.
14 Exchequer Return for First Fruits, 1652.
15 Found in possession of curacy by Surveyors in Sept., 1649, at salary of £10 (Lamb. 902, f. 62).
16 Lamb. 968, f. 4 ; 972, f. 126.
17 Lamb. 977, f. 71.
18 Exch. Return, 1652.

large proportion in Flintshire[1] ; and the district of Ardudwy in Merioneth was practically unaffected.[2]   In Anglesey the old order was represented by Richard Wynne, curate of Penmynydd who had the small tithes (value £8) for his salary[3]; Robert Hughes, rector of Llanddeusant, ' able but sickly '[4] ; Thomas Hughes, rector of Aberffraw, ' an approved preacher '[5] ; Thomas Maurice of Llangristiolus, who had his salary of £16 confirmed by the Commissioners[6] ; Thomas Jones of Trefdraeth, a ' good preaching minister '[7] ; Hugh Humphreys of Amlwch, ' a good divine and constant preacher '[8] ; and the poor vicar of Llanbadrig.[9]   Here, and in all the counties, there remained approved pluralists confined to one living, and the doubly commended nominees of Parliament and its Committees.

The Commissioners found the work of pulling down much easier than the work of building up ; of *new* appointments to ' settled congregations and parochial charges ' there is but scanty evidence in the Rawlinson MS., the payments in South Wales, or the retrospective testimony of the Lambeth MSS. Humphrey Prichard is appointed to Guffin,[10] a certain ' Johnes ' to Carnarvon,[11] and William Bodurda, B.D., is given the rectory of Aberdaron[12] ; Oliver Thomas leaves Oswestry and ' elects ' Llanrhaiadr,[13] to carry the torch of dead Evan Roberts[14] ; Randall Proudlove officiates at Holt,[15] one of the Eytons at Overton,[16] Richard Steele at Hanmer,[17] and William Fowler[18] is paid £25 by the Treasurer for North Wales for his work at Beaumaris in 1650-1651 for eighteen weeks.[19]   Thomas Carter, having relinquished

1 Vavasor Powell in " A Perfect Diurnall," May 3–10, 1652 [5].
2 Lamb. 1027, ff. 33b, 37a.
3 Lamb. 902, f. 40.
4   Ibid.   f. 47.
5   Ibid.   f. 50.
6   Ibid.   ff. 51, 52 ; Rawl. c. 261 [25], [31].
7   Ibid.   f. 52.
8   Ibid.   f. 54.
9 Supra, p. 139.
10 Rawl. c. 261 [30] ; Lamb. 1017, f. 47.
11   Ibid.   [29].
12   Ibid.   [31].   It was very natural that a Welshman and a Fellow o St. John's College, Cambridge, should have received the living (P. 3, supra ; Walk. Suff. Pt. II, p. 148.)
13   Ibid.   [18].
14 Provision made for Roberts's wife and children [26].
15   Ibid.   [29].
16   Ibid.   [26].
17   Ibid.   [28].
18 Rawl. c. 261, p. 30.
19 Very probably as Courtney's chaplain, p. 97.

his other ecclesiastical promotions,[1] sees well to 'elect' the rectory of Abergele.[2] Such appointments are still fewer by comparison in South Wales. Robert Williams becomes minister at Llanbadarn in Cardigan[3] at the death of another Evan Roberts[4]; Roger Seys is minister at Loughor in 1650,[5] a certain Mr. Davies at Margam,[6] John French of Cardiff[7] at Wenvoe, Joshua Miller of London at St. Andrew's[8] in Glamorgan; in Pembroke are Edward Carver at Tenby,[9] Richard Harris at Manordeifi,[10] Stephen Love at Cosheston,[11] William Jones at St. David's[12] and Thomas Warren at Carew[13]; Mr. Lambe is lecturer at the town of Brecon[14]; and Thomas Haughton is settled minister at Gladestry in Radnor.[15] Letters were sent and visits paid to London and the Universities in search of suitable men, only to find that many had betaken themselves to the North of England,[16] and of the others, many were ignorant of the Welsh tongue.[17] Some, again, ' waived the Employment.'[18] Hugh Peters also lent his powerful influence. He incurred the expense of £25 in sending four ministers from London to ' the countrey ' in 1650,[19] one of whom, Stephen Young, was reputed to have borne a partisan in guarding the scaffold at the King's execution.[20] And, partly from private inclination, partly from the dearth of ministers, the new schoolmasters being ' fit persons of approved Piety and Learning,' helped in the work of preaching,[21] and at times even some of the Commissioners themselves and their officials came to the rescue. Capt. John Williams receives payment for such services in

1 Lamb. 997, f. 101, liber ii. There was a 'Thomas Carter' appointed to the living of Saltwood (Kent) on 2nd March, 1647-8 (L. J., X, 115).
2 Rawl. c. 261 [18, 28].
3 Walker c. 13, f. 34.
4 Provision made for Roberts's family (f. 34).
5 Walker Ibid. f. 17.
6 In 1652. Walk. c. 13, f. 52.
7 Walker c. 4, f. 67b.
8 Lambeth 972, f. 33 ; Walker c. 13, ff. 17, 23, 26b, 31.
9 Walker c. 13, f. 7 ; Lambeth 972, f. 6.
10 Ibid. f. 12.
11 Ibid. f. 7 ; moved to Haverfordwest 16th March, 1652-3. (Lamb. 972, 8.)
12 Lamb. 972, f. 380 ; 996, f. 420.
13 Ibid. f. 7 ; Lamb. 972, f. 10.
14 Walker c. 13, f. 63. Probably Thomas Lamb, the General Baptist of Bel Alley (supra, p. 77.)
15 Lambeth 997, liber ii, f. 153.
16 Supra, p. 89.
17 Vavasor Powell : Bird in the Cage . . . A Brief Narrative, p. 4.
18 Examen et Purgamen, p. 39—'' those of *greatest* eminency and learning.''
19 *Pembrokeshire*, from which Peters had just returned to London. Walker c. 13, 7, 7b. But vide infra, pp. 165-166.
20 Palmer : Nonconformist Memorial, Vol. II, p. 632.
21 Examen et Purgamen, p. 17.

L

Radnor,[1] and Walter Powell heard the Governor of Hereford preaching at Llantilio Crossenny on September 1st, 1650, and Sequestrator John Morgan of Tintern on May 22nd, 1651.[2] Rice Williams of Newport has been described as an 'able preacher.'[3] Under these circumstances it somewhat savoured of irony that Ireton had sent a Mr. Boone to Monmouthshire 'to gaine preachers' for the conversion of Catholic Ireland.[4]

The Commissioners' remedy for this 'famine of the Word' lay primarily in the continued activities of the itinerant approvers. Henry Walter received payment in Glamorgan and Monmouth[5]; Walter Cradock in 1652 was decrying mere humane learning as far north as Presteign[6]; Seaborn and Symonds seem to have confined their activities to Glamorgan[7]; David Walter worked mainly in the Swansea and Neath district,[8] though at times he delighted to exercise his faculty in Llandaff Cathedral[9]; Jenkin Jones, though mainly associated with Brecon,[10] was preaching at Llantilio on July 7th, 1650, and also on September 29th[11]; George Robinson was there on May 22nd, 1651[12]; John Miles managed to dovetail his duties as Approver with organising Baptist churches from the borders of Hereford to the town of Carmarthen[13]; Ambrose Mostyn, with his headquarters at Wrexham, was preaching at Welshpool on July 25th, 1652, and at Oswestry on August 1st in the same year[14]; Richard Powell passed sometimes from Brecon to his native Herefordshire[15]; Morgan Llwyd 'lost his voice' in the peninsula of Lleyn[16]; lastly, Vavasor Powell was styled the 'metropolitan of the itinerants,'[17] ranging over Brecon, Radnor, and Montgomery.[18] The latter is described as often preaching

1 Walker c. 13, f. 66.
2 Diary (ed. Bradney), p. 42.
3   Ibid.   p. 40 (Col. Bradney's footnote).
4 Walker c. 13, f. 51; *John Jones* also suggested in his Letters to Morgan Llwyd that he and Vavasor Powell should come over to Ireland " to divulge the bridegroom's message." (Gweithiau : Vol. II., pp. 289, 298).
5 Walker c. 13, ff. 17, 52; preaching at Llantilio on June 30, 1650 (Diary, p. 41).
6 Mercurius Cambro-Britannicus, p. 7.
7 Walker c. 13, ff. 17, 31.
8 Walker c. 4, f. 70.
9   Ibid.   f. 66.
10 Walker c. 13, ff. 60, 63b.
11 Diary of Walter Powell, pp. 41, 42.
12   Ibid.   p. 42.
13 Joshua Thomas : Hanes y Bedyddwyr (Pontypridd Ed.), pp. 75—89.
14 Animadversions upon an Imperfect Relation . . . . . p. 11.
15 Alex. Griffith : Strena Vavasoriensis, p. 8.
16 Gweithiau : Vol. I., Song xxxiv., stanza [3], p. 68.
17 Alex. Griffith : Strena Vavasoriensis, p. 1.
18 Examen et Purgamen Vavasoris, passim.

in two or three places a day, as being seldom two days a week throughout the year out of the pulpit, as sometimes riding a hundred miles in a week, and as taking every opportunity, especially of ' Fairs, Markets, or any great Concourse of Peoples,' to propagate the Gospel.[1] And in addition to these came a large *extension* of the itinerant system as deduced from the names of persons in the South Wales accounts who receive payment in two or more counties, and the mention of other ' preachers ' or ' ministers ' not associated with any particular church, from definite orders of the North Wales authorities and the implied significance of other appointments recorded in the Rawlinson MS., from the list of itinerants given in the ' Examen et Purgamen Vavasoris,' and from references in the Lambeth MSS., the ' Account ' of Calamy, the Ilston Records and the writings of Erbery. The following is a list of such names who were at work in Wales during all, or some part of, the Propagation period.

1 Life, p. 108.

ITINERANT.	MAIN SPHERE OF ACTIVITY.	MS. REFERENCE OR OTHER AUTHORITY.
Abbott, John	Brecon and Monmouth	Walker c. 13, ff. 45, 63.
Barnes, Thomas	Monmouth	" " f. 45. "Preacher" (not definitely settled).
1 Bowen, Evan	Brecon and Radnor	" " ff. 62, 66.
Broadway, Thomas	Cardigan	" " f. 34.
Davies, David	Glamorgan, Brecon and Carmarthen	" " f. 26b; Ilston Records (quoted by Joshua Thomas: Hanes y Bedyddwyr, Pontypridd Ed., pp. 85-86); Erbery: Call to the Churches, p. 4.
Davies, Griffith	Glamorgan and Carmarthen	Walker c. 13, ff. 22, 39.
Davies, Meredith	" "	" " ff. 22, 39.
Davies, John	Brecon, Radnor and Montgomery	" " ff. 63b, 66, 68b; Examen, p. 14; Strena Vavasoriensis, p. 8.
Delemayne, Mr.	Brecon	Walker c. 13, f. 63. "Minister" (not definitely settled).
Corbett, Mr.	North Wales	Rawl. c. 261 [24].
Edwards, Charles	North Wales	" " [26].
Hall, John	Pembroke	Walker c. 13, f. 7.

1 *Evan Bowen.*
(a) *Evan Bowen:* inst. to vic. of Llangurig, 16th March, 1625-6. (Lib. Inst., Bangor, p. 6).
(b) *Evan Bowen:* inst. to vic. of Abereskir, 30th Oct., 1631 (Lib. Inst., Menev., p. 46).
(c) "*Evan Bowen* of Llanafanfawr ... a Mason, being untaught in the English tongue ... had not read the Primmer." (Walk. Suff., I, 161; II, 409).
(d) "We know but one who hath not perfect English, but he is a man of such excellently gifts and dexterous faculty in his own language that the Lord hath made him instrumental in the conversion of divers Welsh people." (Examen et Purgamen, p. 17).
(e) 'To *Mr. Evan Bowens*, £20.' (Radnor Accts. 1650—Walk. c. 13, f. 66). 'To *Mr. Evan Bowens*, Minister, for the years 1651, £30.' (Brecon Accounts—Walk. c. 13, f. 62).

It is practically certain that (a) and (b) are the same man; equally so that (c) and (e) refer to the same person; that the (d) statement is predicated of (c) and (e) is conjectural, but very probable (Shankland: Seren Gomer, July, 1901, p. 189); but that all five are the same Bowen is very unlikely. The first Evan Bowen had probably died before the institution of Griffith Hatley to the vicariate of Abereskir. (Vide supra, pp. 52, 121).

Name	District	Reference
Hanmer, John	Bron and Radnor	Walk. c. 13, ff. 62, 68; Examen, p. 14.
Harris, John	Brecon, Radnor and Logan	" " " ff. 17, 63, 68b.
Herbert, Geo	'Teacher about Abergavenny'	" " " f. 51.
Higgs, Daniel	Glamorgan and Carmarthen	" " " ff. 22, 39.
Hodson, Mr.	North Wales	Rawl. c. 261 [26].
Hughes, William	Pembroke	Walker c. 13, f. 7.
Edward, George	'Preacher amongst the Welsh people'	" " " f. 51.
Erbery, William	Glamorgan, at Bridgend, Llantrisant, &c. Headquarters at Cardiff.	"Call to the Churches," passim.
Evans, Hugh	Brecon and Radnor	Walker c. 13, ff. 62, 66, 68.
Griffith, Maurice	Bron and Radnor	" " " ff. 62, 68; Examen, p. 14.
Griffiths, Cambor	Pembroke	" " " f. 7b.
Hunt, Richard	with	" " " f. 45.
Ible, Nathaniel	Glamorgan and Carmarthen	" ," " ff. 17, 22b, 26b, 39.; Lamb. 977, f. 36—Minister in the Town and County Carmarthen in July, 56.
Jackson, Christoper	Pembroke	Walker c. 13, f. 7.
Jenkins, Edward	Brecon and Glamorgan	Rawl. c. 261 [27].
Jones, Richard	North Wales	Mer c. 13, f. 39; Lamb 977, f. 36—described on July 31, 56, as Minister in Carmarthenshirr.
1Jones, Samuel	Carmarthen	Walker c. 13, f. 39. 'Minister' merely (not definitely settled).
Jones, James	Carmarthen	Wer c. 13, ff. 20, 39.
Jones, Watkin	Glamorgan, Monmouth and Carmarthen	" " " ff. 63b, 66.
Knollys, Hanserd	Brecon and Radnor	" " " f. 7. (not definitely settled).
Knowles, Daniel	Pembroke	ah. 1027, f. 34(d).
Llewellin, Thos	Vale of Edeyrnion	Walker c. 13, ff. 66, 68, 68b; Examen, p. 14.
Lucas, Richard	Radnor	" .. " ff. 17, 34.
Mell, Mr.	Glamorgan and Cardigan	
Nicholls, Henry	Glamorgan	" " " ff. 17, 26, 31b; c. 4, 69b.
Ch, Edward	Radnor	" " " ff. 68, 68b; Examen, p. 14.

1 To be distinguished from Samuel-Jones, *Llangynwyd.*

ITINERANT.	MAIN SPHERE OF ACTIVITY.	MS. REFERENCE OR OTHER AUTHORITY.
Owen, Richard	Brecon and Cardigan	Walker c. 13, 62; Lamb. 1008, f. 250.
Morgan, Owen	Radnor	„ „ 68, 68b; Examen, p. 14.
Morgan, William	Glamorgan and Monmouth—" Preacher amongst the Welsh people "	„ „ 20, 27, 51.
Parry, Henry	Montgomery	Examen, p. 14.
Price, Charles	Radnor	Walker c. 13, f. 68 ; Examen, p. 14.
Powell, J hro	Glamorgan and Carmarthen	„ „ 20 ; 1 th 977, f. 36.
Proud, Thomas	Glamorgan and Brecon	„ „ 17, 20, 22 ; Joshua Thomas: Hanes y Bedyddwyr (Pont. Ed.), p. 79.
Prosser, Walter	Glamorgan, Brecon and Carmarthen	Walker c. 13, f. 62 ; Ilston Records quoted by hdia hdias, Pont. Ed., pp. 81, 82.
Quarrell, James	Montgomery	Examen, p. 14; Lamb. 989, f. 58.
Rosser, Edmund	Brecon and Monmouth—" Preacher in the Mountains "	Walker c. 13, ff. 51, 60, 62.
Rogers, Hugh	Monmouth	Walker c. 13, f. 57.
Richards, William	Monmouth	„ „ f. 51b.
Richards, Benjamin	North Wales	Rawl. c. 261 [27].
Roberts, John	gn and Carmarthen	Wer c. 13, ff. 17, 20, 39.
Roberts, Jonathan	gh Wes	Rawl. c. 261 [27].
Roberts, Richard	North Wales	Rawl. c. 261 [26].
Seys, Roger	Morgan and Carmarthen	Walker c. 13, ff. 17, 39.
Bs, Edward	gh and Carmarthen	„ „ ff. 20, 39.
Bs, Howell	Vale of Edeyrnion	nb. 1027, ff. 34 (d).
Townesend, Mr.	gn and Carmarthen	Walker c. 13, ff. 17, 20,.39.
West, —1	Pembroke	„ / „ f. 7.
Willi nas, Evan	gh and Carmarthen	„ „ ff. 20, 39.
Willi nas, Henry	Montgomery	„ „ f. 60 ; Examen, p. 14 ; thy: cent, II, p. 712.
Wi ns, Walter	Glamorgan	A lk. c. 13, ff. 26b, 31b ; True and Perfect Relation, p. 33.
Young, Stephen	Pembroke	Walker c. 13, f. 7 (not definitely settled).

1 Christian name uncertain. A Robert West subscribed the 'Engagement' on Jn29, 1649-50 (Bodl.:D. 711, f. 9b) and a Tho. West on Nov. 9, 1649 (ibid. f. 11).

Only a slight degree removed from these were the Approver Thomas Ewins, who, prior to his departure to Bristol in 1651, combined the supervision of the church at Llanfaches with preaching at Chepstow[1] ; Francis Symes, who in 1650 officiated both at Trelech and Tintern[2] ; Thomas Ellis, who was minister at Dixton in 1650[3] and Grosmont in 1651[4] ; and Philip Williams, whose pastoral work lay at Skenfrith in 1650[5] and at Dixton in the latter year.[6] Nor does the above list include the 'godly members' of the churches of Mynyddislwyn and Llanfaches,—seventeen in 1650,[6a] twenty in 1651,[7] an unspecified number in 1652,[8]—who received altogether £978 18s. 10d. from the Commissioners for 'exercising their gifts and promoting the work of the Lord' mostly among the *Welsh* in the highlands of Monmouth and Brecon, whose arrival enabled Vavasor Powell in turn to send four ministers from the latter county on a preaching crusade to Cardiganshire.[9] Even this depletion did not exhaust the resources of the gathered church of Mynydd-islwyn, for £50 is given to Henry Walter in 1651 to pay the 'teachers' who were stationary there.[10] Thus far had the early labours of William Wroth and the Parliament's ordinances of 1645 and 1646 succeeded in creating a Puritan atmosphere in south-eastern Wales. And both the itinerant system in itself and the exceptional character of its personnel derived inspiration from the somewhat loose terminology of contemporary Confessions of Faith and the practice of the more advanced Puritan bodies. The Particular Baptist in England held that 'disciples,' defined as men 'able to preach the gospel,' could administer the ordinance on which they laid most especial stress[11] ; his prototype in Wales found authority in Scripture for sending out 'helps,' 'prophets' and 'apostles' to gather churches from the

---

1 Walker c. 13, f. 45.
2   Ibid.   f. 45.
3   Ibid.   f. 45.
4   Ibid.   f. 51.
5   Ibid.   f. 45.
6   Ibid.   f. 51.
6a   Ibid.   f. 45b.
7   Ibid.   f. 51.
8   Ibid.   f. 57.
9   Ibid.   ff. 62-63.
10   Ibid.   f. 52.
11 Crosby : History of the English Baptists, Vol. I, App. II, Article xli. in 1644 Confession of Faith (pp. 20-21); McGlothlin : Baptist Confessions of Faith, p. 185.

▲

world[1]; the General Baptist had already despatched his ' messengers ' to the Welsh border[2]; so had the Independent Church of All Hallows to Monmouthshire[3]; the cautious minds who drew up the Directory allowed those who intended the ministry to read the Word and, like the Llanfaches propagandists, exercise their gifts in preaching[4]; finally, the Savoy Conference of 1658, harking back to the Independent polity of the Propagation era, declared that preaching was not ' peculiarly ' fitted to either ' pastors ' or ' teachers.'[5] Responding to these favourable influences and affording a natural solution to the problems that arose on the morrow of the ejections, the itinerant system bade fair even to absorb the energies of the settled ministry. *E.g.*, Roger Seys, minister at Loughor,[6] is preaching in Carmarthenshire in 1651 and 1652[7]; Charles Price, placed by the C.P.M. at Glascwm in Radnor,[8] becomes an itinerant in the same county,[9] ultimately settling down in Cardiganshire[10]; Richard Owens, minister of Verwick in Cardigan in 1649,[11] receives payment in Brecon for 1651,[12] and is back in the former county in 1652[13]; Henry Nicholls, formerly at Bedwas in Monmouth,[14] crosses over to preach within a radius of twelve or fifteen miles in the Vale of Glamorgan, and is called the " Bishop of those places "[15]; while David Davies, who succeeded to the living of Gelligaer on the death of Robert Covy,[16] and Walter Prosser of Llanigon,[17] are both pressed into the Baptist movement of John Miles. Nor is there any record that the Approvers Bidwell, Swain, and Charnock had the care of any particular congregation during the first two years, and the wording of the Rawlinson MS. suggests that Richard Edwards, to whom the living of

---

1 Joshua Thomas : Hanes y Bedyddwyr (Pontypridd Ed.), pp. 213-214; and esp. J. T.: A Hist. of the Baptist Association in Wales, pp. 12-13. Definition of *duties of Church officers* by Miles and his fellow-ministers.
2 Supra, p. 77.
3 Supra, p. 77.
4 Reliqniæ Liturgicæ, Vol. III, p. 23.
5 Dale : Hist. of English Congregationalism, p. 387, Article xiii.
6 Walker c. 13, f. 17.
7   Ibid.   f. 39.
8 Supra,   . 69.
9 Walker c. 13, f. 68.
10 Lamb. 1006, f. 55.
11 Shaw : Hist. of the English Church during the Civil War, Vol. II, App. VII, p. 526.
12 Walker, c. 13, f. 68.
13 Lamb. 1006, f. 55.
14 Supra, p. 68.
15 Walker c. 4, f 69b.
16   Ibid.   f. 65.
17 Joshua Thomas : Hanes y Bedyddwyr (Pont. Ed.), p. 79.

Llanfair D.C. had been sequestered, was also asked to " officiate [generally] in the work of the Gospel."[1]

Under the itinerant system the wondering hillsides of Wales enjoyed a variety of tongues. There arrived Charles Edwards, a brilliant Oxford scholar[2] and the later author of " Hanes y Ffydd " ; Richard Jones, the future translator into Welsh of Baxter's " Call to the Unconverted "[3] ; Jonathan Roberts, whose learning and gospel-labour fitted him to measure swords, in company with Philip Henry, against Bishop Lloyd of St. Asaph at Oswestry in 1681[4] ; John Abbott, who was to second the still greater controversialist John Tombes in the Baptist dispute held at St. Mary's, Abergavenny, on 5th September, 1653[5] ; and more noteworthy still, Hanserd Knollys, the pupil of Richard Sibbes at Cambridge, contemporary there with Thomas Goodwin, John Lightfoot and William Spurstow, religious exile, public disputant, successful propagator of the Gospel, and the most prominent Baptist of the times[6]. Of somewhat lesser fame were Daniel Higgs, who came from Chadwitch in Worcestershire,[7] and Francis Symes and Thomas Proud, the expenses of removing whose families from London was borne by the treasury of Monmouthshire, £4 in the case of the latter[8] and £40 in the case of the former.[9] It is improbable that such men had to undergo the period of probation reserved for the ordinary itinerant. The Rawlinson MS. refers to three ' public preachers ' upon trial in North Wales in November, 1650[10] ; £20 was paid by order to some that were probationers for defraying of their charges in travelling to preach the gospel in Brecon, Cardigan and Carmarthen under Vavasor Powell[11] ; and £4 18s. 6d. was paid at ' ye Inne in Cheps*toll* ' to defray the expenses of four ministers that came to offer themselves to preach, but were not found fit.[12]

1 Rawl. c. 261 [26].
2 D.N.B., Vol. XVII, p. 13: Scholar, Honorary Fellow. Bible Reader.
3 Galwad i'r Annychweledig. Date of Preface—June 15, 1659. (Brit. Mus.).
4 Calamy : Account, Vol. II, p. 716 ; Life of Philip Henry, p. 155.
5 Public Dispute . . . . touching Infant baptism [by I. W.]. B.M.
6 James Culross : Hanserd Knollys (Baptist Manuals, Vol. II), pp. 13. 29, 30, 36, 44, 67 ; D.N.B., Vol. XXXI, pp. 279-280 ; Crosby : Hist., Vol. I, 337-339.
[Neither Culross nor Crosby nor Alexander Gordon in D.N.B. make the slightest reference to his sojourn in Wales at *this* time.]
7 Calamy : Account, Vol. II, p. 729.
8 Walker c. 13, f. 45b.
9 Ibid. f. 45.
10 Rawl. c. 261 [27].
11 Examen et Purgamen Vavasoris, p. 13.
12 Walker c. 13, f. 45b.

It does not seem that the period of probation was duly
defined by express order, for Dr. George Griffith asks Vavasor
Powell at Newchapel how many sermons would be sufficient
for ' triall ' and who was to judge, adding that some had
already served as probationers for two or three years.[1]
The greater number of the itinerant preachers were not
learned men, and the registers of the Universities are silent
about them. Some, like Stephen Young, were old soldiers
of the Parliamentary army[2]; Henry Williams of Ysgafell
near Newtown was a substantial farmer[3]; and various
trades and occupations were represented amongst them.
Benjamin Richards was a weaver,[4] William Morgan was
probably a shoemaker of Abergavenny,[5] and Vavasor Powell
was accompanied to London in March, 1653, by ' a cap-
maker, who was his fellow-preacher.'[6] Even David Walter
the Approver is dubbed both ' weaver ' and a ' common
country Thatcher ' by Mansell in the same paragraph.[7]
This, together with the fact that they knew not the ordination
of a bishop nor even the sanction of a Presbyterian classis,
coupled with their unconventional methods of preaching,
made the travelling preachers the especial objects of attack
to Cavaliers accustomed to the bohemian resident and the
careless non-resident. Derogatory epithets were applied
to them : ' new ' preachers at Llantilio Crossenny,[8] ' journey-
men ' in Montgomeryshire,[9] 'runners' in Brecon and Radnor,[10]
' rambling teachers '[11] and ' hackney preachers '[12] in
Glamorgan, ' ambulatories ' at Guilsfield,[13] ' propigators '
in Corwen,[14] and ' iterates ' at Llangattock in Brecknock-
shire.[15] Sometimes they went in danger of their lives.
A ' gifted brother ' was violently pulled out of the pulpit
at Dolgelly and had his blood ' drawne,'[16] while in the

1 Animadversions upon an Imperfect Relation . . . pp. 22-23.
2 Supra, p. 145.
3 Joshua Thomas : Hanes y Bedyddwyr (Pont. Ed.), p. 285.
4 Walker e. 7, f. 218.
5 Lamb. Codices Tenisoniani, Vol. 639, f. 186· Episcopal Returns, 1669.
6 Gardiner : Hist. of the Commonwealth and Protectorate, Vol. II, p. 196.
7 Walker c. 4, f. 66.
8 Diary of Walter Powell (ed. Bradney), p. 41.
9 Alex. Griffith : Strena Vavasoriensis, p. 6.
10 Thurloe State Papers, Vol. II, p. 128.
11 Walker c. 4, f. 65.
12   Ibid.   ff. 66, 68.
13 Thomas : Hist. of the Diocese of St. Asaph (1874), P. 734. [Quoting Guilsfield
Petition of June 1, 1652].
14 Lamb. 1027, f. 34(d).
15 Lamb. 1027, f. 30.
16 Animadversions . . . . . . p. 25.

summer of 1653, soon after the expiry of the Act, some of Powell's ' companions in travell ' were beaten with stones, and others wounded with ' Swords, Tucks and Clubs.'¹ Various writers, contemporary apologists of the old system, did not spare them. The author of the ' Strena ' says generally that the itinerants could not read or understand English² ; Rowland Vaughan calls them false prophets and doctrine-mongers,³ weavers who treat the Word of God as so much woollen cloth to be unravelled⁴ ; Edward Dafydd of Margam describes the fanatics as blind ones who commit grievous frauds⁵ ; and the peasant ballad-writers refer with regret to the learned Doctor who has been set aside,⁶ to the impudent churls who roar and bellow in the market-place,⁷ to the material tradesmen who have no ' call ',⁸ and the preachers of the forest who know none of the 24 letters.⁹ The works of Huw Morus abound with similar references. Nathan Jones of Merthyr pithily puts it that " preach they cannot unless they be sent, and teach they cannot what they never learnt."¹⁰ Nor did the new preachers as a class give great satisfaction to the more conservative Puritan leaders. John Lewis of Cardiganshire looks askance at the ' simple youngelings ' in the ranks of the new preachers,¹¹ and Dr. John Ellis thinks that ' sums of maintenance could have been better bestowed ' than they were.¹² Calamy owns that several of them were ' unlearn'd,'¹³ and his continuator Palmer that " upon the downfall of Episcopacy . . . came in an unlettered tribe, who did not mind the matter at all."¹⁴ Baxter relates a story of a Welsh itinerant who came to him for counsel in 1663 " with whom it greiv'd him

---

1 Examen et Purgamen Vavasoris, p. 12.
2 p. 5.
3 Prifannau Crefydd Gristnogawl . . . . o waith Iago Usher, Escob Armagh. At y Darllennydd [5].
4 Yr Arier o Weddi yr Arglwydd . . . . gan Ioan Despagne (translated by Vaughan). Llythyr Annerch [quoted in Ashton : Hanes Llen. 1650-1850], p. 25.
5 Llanover MSS.—" Cerdd i'r Ffanaticiaid " : printed in full in " Cymru," Tach., 1901, pp. 218-219 ; in part in " Seren Gomer," Gorff, 1902, pp. 169-172.
6 Phillipps MSS. (Cardiff Free Library), No. 12453. [" Hen Gerddi Gwleidyddol." Reprint by Cymdeithas Llên Cymru, 1901]. " Can i'r Amseroedd Blin," p. 27.
7 Ibid, p. 27.
8 Ibid. " Cwyn rhyw Eglwyswr," p. 33.
9 Ibid. " Can i'r Amseroedd Blin," p. 28.
10 Wilkins : History of Merthyr Tydfil, chap. IX, p. 94.
11 " Some Seasonable and Modest thoughts in order to the furtherance and promoting the affairs of religion and the Gospel, especially in Wales." (1656) ; also Letter of Lewis to Baxter—quoted in " Wales," Vol. III, pp. 122-124, in an article by Mr. J. H. Davies on " An Early Attempt to found a National College in Wales."
12 Letter to John Lewis, p. 124 (vide Reference 11).
13 Account . . . . Vol. II, p. 735.
14 Nonconformists' Memorial, Vol. 1, Introduction, vi-vii.

to talk."[1]   Lastly, William Erbery, the supreme itinerant of the age, does not find among his fellows the ' gift of a Tongue to tell us the true Originals nor of Interpretation to Translate them aright,'[1] and with characteristic inconsistency declares that the whole system is ' not according to rule or yet to reason,' and prophesies that ' at last they will run out of the Church and Countrey too.'[3]   To the distrust of friends and the criticism of foes the moving spirits among the Approvers had their answer based on the theory of spiritual revelation—Llwyd refers the Raven to Psalm cv. 22 and Job xxxii. 9, 10[4]; Powell will not agree that God had confined his discoveries to *old* men,[5] and on the question of mere learning retorts to his opponent at Newchapel with the ' tu quoque ' argument[6] ; and Cradock had as early as 1648 protested vigorously in London against the Presbyterian practice of calling those men ' Tubpreachers, Tinkers, and Cobblers ' who were filled with the ' good newes ' and' fulfilled the conditions of Amos iii. 8, adding the proviso that no one should ' run ' before he be ' sent ' and believe his own judgment rather than the judgment of the saints.[7]

Besides the acknowledged deficiencies of many of the itinerants on the score of learning, the working system had other serious limitations.   The old evil of Anglicisation finds new expression, probably on account of the Saxon bias among the Commissioners, in the Broadways, Corbetts, and Hodsons who were at work in Cardiganshire and North Wales[8] ; a new pluralism of counties replaces the old pluralism of separate and often widely-scattered livings ;[9] the sinecure rector makes room for the fleeting preacher ' supplied with fresh horses at every stage '[10] ; and the unity of thought and uniformity of action, the usual concomitants

---

1 Catholic Communion Defended, Vol. II, p. 29.
2 The Welsh Curate, p. 11.   (N.L.W.).
3 The Idol Pastor : or, Foolish Shepherd, p. 98 (N.L.W.).
4 Gweithiau, Vol. I., " Llyfr y Tri Aderyn," p. 165.   Eagle answering Raven.
5 Saving Faith . . . . p. 75.
6 Perfect Diurnall, No. 138, Aug. 2, 1652.
7 Glad Tydings from Heaven . . . . pp. 50-52.
8 *Erbery*, though he preached in some distinctively *Welsh* districts, could ' not deliver himself in the Welsh tongue ' (Henry Nicholls : Shield Single . . . p. 10). Though proud of his ' Welsh blood ' (Ministers for Tythes . . p. 2) he had to speak in English at Llantrisant " for many of the Welsh understood." (A Call to the Churches . . . . p. 5).
9 James Wilson : Victoria Hist. of Cumberland, Vol. II, pp. 93-97—account of the Propagation in the Four Northern Counties of England.
10 Alex. Griffith : Merc. Cambro-Britannicus (1652), p. 6.

of the missionary labours of the early Christian era,[1] are
neutralised by the diverse opinions which obtained among
the Propagators. Their numbers were too few not a
single ' Itenerant Minister ' found his way to Llansantffread
in Brecon,[2] ' now and then ' only to Michelston-super-Ely,[3]
and ' once or twice a Quarter ' to Merthyr Dovan.[4] The
failure to provide an adequate ministry in point of numbers
produced a host of critics. Two officials of the Parliament
in Brecon declare in October, 1651, that there were only
two preaching settled ministers in that county of seventy-
three parishes, and the souls of the Commissioners for Compounding ' are much aggrieved at the sadness of their
relation '[5]; the Sheriff of Anglesey reports that the
unsanctioned Henry Evans of Llanfechell is the only preacher
in the hundred of Talybolion in 1652[6]; there was a petition
of the ' well-affected ' in the counties of South Wales to
Parliament in the same year " for a supply of ministers in
lieu of those that have been Ejected "[7]; a secular tourist
who visited Wales in the early months of 1653 comments
on the sparsity of regular church services[8]; and Alexander
Griffith roundly states that there were ' 700 parishes unsupplied with any recognised minister, and that one could
ride ten or twelve miles on the Lord's day where there is
twenty churches and not one door opened.'[9] The comparative failure of the Propagation system, the growing hostility
of the Rump towards the ideals of Harrison and the Army
officers generally,[10] the uncertainty whether the Act would
be renewed, saw a number of the approvers and itinerants
settled down in particular districts[11] either before its expiry,
or during the interim jurisdiction of the Welsh Commissioners
guaranteed by Cromwell's letter in April, 1653,[12] or by approval

1 M'Giffert : Hist. of Christianity in the Apostolic Age, pp. 636-672.
2 Lamb. 1027, f 36a.
5 Walker c. 4, f. 67b.
4   Ibid.   f. 68
5 Cal. Comm. Comp., Vol. I, 495, Oct. 29 and 27th Nov., 1651.
6 Exchequer Returns, 1652, Anglesey.
7 C. J., vii, p. 103 : N.L.W. Catalogue, p. 57. For a more particular account of
this Petition vide Chapters XVII and XVIII.
8 A Short Relation of a Long Journey . . . . made by John Taylor. (B. M.—
Thomason Tract).
9 Strena Vavasoriensis, p. 5.
10 Simpkinson : Life of Harrison, Chap. IX, pp. 143-160.
11 . . . " It is thought to hinder the parishes from petitioning for orthodox
ministers." (Thurloe State Papers, Vol. II, p. 128. Capt. Halle to Alex. Griffith,
Feb., 1654).
12 Calendar of State Papers, 1652-1653, pp. 293-294 ; Cal. Comm. Compounding,
Vol. I, 637.

of the ' Triers ' appointed for England and Wales in 1654,[1]
under whom the itinerant system came practically to an end.
The authoritative evidence for these settlements is of a
heterogeneous character. A few definite orders made under
the Act have been preserved in Lamb. 1006, and the Augmentation Books contain entries both of independent appointments made by the Triers and of others founded on previous
directions of the Commissioners of Wales. The silence of
the Lambeth MSS. has to be complemented by the information supplied in the next generation to Calamy by. James
Owen,[2] by the Calendars of the Committee for Compounding,
by the State Papers themselves, and by Lambeth MS. 1027.
Vavasor Powell and some of the itinerants became involved
in ʼthe movement against the Protectorate and prejudiced
their chances for State appointments[3] ; of others the records
of the time have no evidence. Hanserd Knollys only stayed
during 1650 and 1651.[4] Two, Richard Jones and Roger
Seys, became schoolmasters.

1 Firth and Rait : Acts and Ordinances, Vol. II, pp. 855-858 ; 968-990.
2 Calamy : Account, Vol. II, p. 721.
3 Subscribers to " Word for God " (1655). Marked in list [   ]
4 Cal. State Papers, 1652-1653, p. 240—March 29, 1653, resigns examinership
at Customs and Excise " for more beneficial employment " ; Walker c. 13, 63, 66—
payments only for 1650 and 1651.

SETTLEMENTS.[1]

NAME.	SPHERE OF LABOUR.	DATE OF APPOINTMENT (WHEN SPECIFIED).	MS. REFERENCE OR OTHER AUTHORITY.
I. APPROVERS.			
Bidwell, Morris ..	Swansea ..	17 March, 1652-3 ..	Lamb. 972, f. 366.
Charnock, Roger ..	Monmouth ..	6 April, 1653 ..	Lamb. 997, lib. i., f. 12; Calendar of State Papers, 1654, p. 173; S. P. Dom. Interr., G. 22, f. 1486a.
Cradock. Walter ..	Usk ..	25 March, 1652-1653 ..	Lamb. 972, f. 120.
Edwards, Richard	Llanfair D.C. ..	Minister—1652 ..	Exchequer Returns, 1652, Denbigh.
Jones, Jenkin ..	Llanthetty ..	Admitted to Rectory ...18 Nov., 1657; "pastor of a congregated church"	Lamb. 998, f. 137; An Alarum to Corporations .... Narrative of some of the Anabaptists at the Town of Brecknock ... 1659 (N.L.W.).
Llwyd, Morgan[2] ..	Wrexham ..	16 Oct., 1656 ..	Lamb. 977, f. 42.
Mostyn, Ambrose	Holt ..	16 Oct., 1656 ..	Lamb. 977, f. 42.
Powell, Richard ..	Glasbury ..	Easter, 1653 ..	Lamb. 1027, "Glasbury" Rpt.,Answer 6.
Robinson, George	Llangibby ..	9 Feb., 1652-3 ..	Lamb. 997, ii. 237.
	Llangattock (Mon.) ..	25 Oct., 1654 ..	Lamb. 986, f. 524.
Swain, Richard ..	Clyro (Radnor) ..	22 Nov., 1655 ..	Lamb. 983, f. 9; 987, ff. 209-210; 996, f. 404.
Symonds, Richd...	Lecturer at Llandaff Cathedral ..	19 March, 1657 ..	Lamb. 995, f. 113.
Walter, Henry ..	Newport ..	25 March, 1652-3 ..	Lamb. 972, f. 119.
Miles, John ..	Lecturer at Llanelly ..	Previous to July 31, 1656 ..	Lamb. 977, f. 36.

1 Many of these appointments fall outside the purview of the Propagation Act, but are inserted more especially to illustrate the *breakdown of the Stat-paid itinerant system.*
2 Llwyd had been associated with Wrexham long before, but this is the first record of his being 'settled' there.

SETTLEMENTS—continued.

NAME.	SPHERE OF LABOUR.	DATE OF APPOINTMENT (WHEN SPECIFIED).	MS. REFERENCE OR OTHER AUTHORITY.
II. ITINERANTS AND QUASI-ITINERANTS.			
Abbott, John	Abergavenny	25 March, 1652-3	Lamb. 972, f. 120.
Barnes, Thomas	Magor	1651	Walker c. 13, f. 51.
Davies, David	Neath	March 23, 1654-5	Lamb. 972, f. 379; 907, iii, f. 217.
Davies, Griffith	Gelligaer	24 Oct., 1655	Lamb. 986, f. 300.
Davies, John	Llandevally	1 Feb., 1654-5	Lamb. 997, iii, f. 138.
Davies, Meredith	Llannon (Carm.)	Previous to July 31, 1656	Lamb. 977, f. 36.
Edwards, Charles	Llanrhaiadr-ym-Mochnant	1653	D.N.B., Vol. XVII, p. 13.
Ellis, Thomas	Grosmont	Before expiry of Act	Cal. Comm. Comp., Vol. IV, p. 3137.
Hall, John	Steynton (Pemb.)	Before 15 Dec., 1654	Lamb. 997, iii, f. 73.
Hanmer, John	Llanfihangel-y-Creuddyn		Lamb. 1006, f. 56; 968, f. 8.
Harris, John	Tregaron	16 March, 1652-3	Calamy, II, p. 716; Lambeth, 639, f. 337.
Higgs, Daniel	Rhossilly		Walker c. 4, f. 72.
Hughes, William[1]	Begelly (Pemb.)	Before 1653	Calamy, II, p. 717.
Ible, Nathaniel	Carmarthen		Lamb. 977, f. 36.
Jackson, Christopher	Lampeter Velfrey	Before July 31, 1656	Calamy, II, p. 717.
Jones, James	Llangyfelach		Lamb. 986, f. 441.
Jones, Richard	Denbigh—Schoolmaster	24 Dec., 1655	Lamb. 997, f. 63.
Jones, Samuel	Llanegwad	Before 17 Feb., 1656	Lamb. 996, f. 313; 977, f. 36.
Lucas, Richard	Presteign	Before 30 Oct., 1655	Firth and Rait, Vol. II, p. 984.
Nicholls, Henry	Coychurch	Before Aug., 1654	Walker c. 4, f. 69b; Lamb. 996, ff. 300, 312.

1 Calamy's exact entry is ' Bily : Mr. Thomas Hughes.'

Name	Location	Date	Signatory / Reference
[Owens, Edward	Llanrhystyd	Before 1653	Signatory.—'Word for God,' p. 9.]
Owens, Richard	Llanfetherin	18 Aug., 1654	Lamb. 1008, f. 250.
Morgan, Owen			Lamb. 997, ii, 142 ; S. P. Dom. Interr., G. 22, f. 1486a.
Parry, Henry	Cemmes (Mont.)	28 Sept., 1654	Lamb. 997, ii, 208.
Price, Charles	Cardigan	26 March, 1652	Lamb. 1006, f. 55.
Powell, John	Llangyndeyrn	Before July 31, 1656	Lamb. 977, f. 36.
Prosser, Walter	Tredunnock	3 July, 1657	Lamb. 998, f. 94.
Proud, Thomas	Cheriton (Gower)		Calamy, II, p. 731.
Quarrell, James	Forden	Before 1653	Lamb. 989, f. 58.
[Griffith, Maurice¹			Signatory. "Word for God," p. 9.]
[Rosser, Edmund			Signatory. "Word for God," p. 9.]
Rogers, Hugh₂	Newtown	Before Feb., 1658	Exch. Ret. Mont., 1658 ; Cal. II, 712.
Roberts, John	Loughor₃	Before Oct., 1655	Lamb. 996, f. 300 ; Walk. c. 4, f. 72b.
Roberts, Jonathan	Llanfair D.C.		Calamy, II, p. 716.
Roberts, Richard	Moreton-Corbet₄ (Salop)	Before Nov. 4, 1659	Lamb. 987, ff. 59, 60.
Seys, Roger	Schoolmaster at St. Fagans	Sept. 5, 1653	Lamb. 1006, f. 186.
Symes, Francis	Chepstow	26 March, 1652	Lamb. 972, f. 120.
Williams, Philip	Llanvapley	12 May, 1654	Lamb. 997, i, f. 53.
Young, Stephen	Rosecrowther (Pem.)	Before 14 Feb., 1659-1660	Lamb. 987, f. 238 ; Calamy, II, 718.

1 Accompanied Vavasor Powell to Cardiganshire on a preaching tour against new Government (1654). (Thurloe State Papers, Vol. II, p. 93.)—Intercepted Letter of John Phillips to John Gunter).

2 Calamy vaguely refers to a 'Mr. Rogers' who was ejected from Caerwent after the Restoration (II, 473), but he is probably to be found in the *Lewis* Rogers who, according to the Lamb. MSS., was appointed to Monmouth by the 'Triers.'

3 'John Roberts of Lughouse,' in the Lamb. MS.

4 The MS. reads 'Preacher of ye Gospell of & within ye chappelry of Morton within the parish of (*blank*).' As the salary ordered to him issued out of the tithes of 'Llansilin' (Llansilin) in the counties of Denbigh and Salop, it is safe to assume he settled either at St. Martin or Moreton-Corbet or Moreton-Say in Salop, no 'Morton' being found in that county.

M

The name of William Erbery is conspicuously absent from the foregoing list. After receiving £200 from the Glamorgan treasury for 1650 and 1651,[1] God began to ' roar in his spirit ' and men to ' hit him in the teeth '[2] regarding the sources of this maintenance. The months of mental stress the subject caused him, and the many cases of conscience submitted to himself by even that impressionable character before he decided to preach to ' lose a hundred a year ' and to become ' an Independent indeed,'[3] reflect the confusion of thought prevailing on the question of ministerial support. According to the Confession of 1644 the Particular Baptist ministers were ' to live by the Gospel by the law of Christ ' and the ' constraint of forced Law ' was not to be resorted to for payment[4] ; that of 1646 left the latter words out as unnecessary[5] ; while those of 1651 and 1652 left the article out altogether.[6] The Confession of the sixteen Somerset churches belonging to the same body declared that the ministry hath power to receive a livelihood of the brethren, but that it was commendable in case of necessity that they should labour with their hands.[7] The same addendum is found in the only contemporary Confession of the General Baptists, the " Faith and Practice of Thirty Congregations " in the Midlands (1651), who find it is the will of God that " preachers should have maintenance of them that receive spiritual food by them."[8] The Presbyterians of the Assembly hoped as the result of the Covenant to enter upon the full heritage of the Church of England.[9] Thomas Coleman summed up the Erastian standpoint in his sermon before the House of Commons in which he was willing to surrender Church-government to the civil authorities in return for guarantees of high learning and a sufficient competency.[10] The majority of the Independents had no scruples about the subject, as appears by the first proposal of the committee of divines, including Dr. John Owen and

1 Walker c. 13, ff. 17, 26b ; Henry Nicholls : The Shield Single, p. 10.
2 The Sword Doubled (1652) . . . . p. 3. This tract was " The sum of a letter written to one of the Commissioners in South Wales, April/ 19, 1652."
3 Ibid., pp. 14-15.
4 McGlothlin : Baptist Confessions of Faith, p. 185, Article XXXVIII.
5 Crosby · Hist. of the English Baptists, Vol. 1, App. II, p. 20, Art. XXXVIII.
6 McGlothlin : Baptist Confessions, p. 184, footnote [b].
7 Ibid., p. 211, Art. XXXII [really XXXI].
8 McGlothlin : Baptist Confessions of Faith, p. 105, Articles 59 and 61.
9 John Lightfoot : Works, Vol. XIII, pp. 281, 283.
10 W. M. Hetherington : Hist. of the Westminster Assembly, p. 310 [30th July, 1645].

the Five Dissenting Brethren, submitted for the consideration of Parliament in February, 1651-2,[1] and the Savoy Conference of 1658 takes public maintenance of ministers for granted.[2] Nor did Parliament show any disposition to disturb the customary payment of tithes. On 8th November, 1644, an ordinance was passed commanding their due exaction[3] ; on 9th August, 1647, an additional ordinance to render the rights of ' intruded ' ministers indefeasible[4] ; and impropriate tithes formed a not inconsiderable part of the fund placed under the control of the Trustees for Maintenance in 1649.[5] On the other hand, the " Agreement of the People " presented by the Army officers to Parliament in January, 1648-9, accepted the provision of a public treasury for maintenance, but had no desire that tithes should form a component part of it,[6] and there was a strong minority in the Little Parliament that believed in their utter abolition.[7] However, notwithstanding the fears of Llwyd's ' croakers ', the ' necke of Tithes ' was never ' cutt off '[8] : John ap John, the future Quaker, was threatened with ' pikyls and other waes ' for denying payment in 1653,[9] and Ralph Kynaston's riotous opposition to the collecting authorities at Llandrinio and Llandisilio in Montgomeryshire was effectually borne down.[10]

These conflicting ideas and Puritan misgivings find ample expression in Wales. Cradock had as early as 1646 declared boldly for State maintenance both as a work of piety and a work of equity,[11] and the fact that the £31 2s. 6d. rent of the living of Llanfaches did ' of righte ' belong to him[12] proved that he had no objection to an interest in which tithes played an important part. Henry Nicholls ' heartily wished ministers' maintenance might arise some other way than that of Tythes.'[13] Rowland Nevett strongly protested against the possible discharging of the C.P.M.'s order granting

1 C. J. VII, 258.
2 Dale : Hist. of English Congregationalism, p. 387, Art. XIV.
3 L. J. VIII, 53 ; Scobell : Ordinances, Vol. I, p. 74.
4 L. J. IX, 380 ; Ibid., p, 129
5 Shaw : Hist. of Eng. Church, Vol. II., pp. 214-216.
6 Ibid. Vol. II, p. 74.
7 C. J. VII, 361.
8 Gweithiau, Vol. I, Song XXV, stanza 3, p. 52.
9 Gregory Norris : Supp ement 6 [Friends Hist. Society], p. 5.
10 Examen et Purgamen Vavasoris, p. 24.
11 Saints Fulnesse of Joy, p. 34 ; Divine Drops Distilled, p. 205.
12 Walker c. 13, f. 47.
13 The Shield Single against the Sword Doubled, p. 10.

him and others the tithes of Llanyblodwel.[1] Jenkin Lloyd subscribed the 1652 report.[2] Mansell records a tradition that Richard Symonds, supported by Edmond Ellis, preached at St. Fagans from Malachi iii, 10 just before the ' Tith-Harvest.'[3] The same authority has it that David Davies, who had been given the cure of Gelligaer by the free gift of the parishioners, preached down tithes for three years, but finding that this gift did not come up to the value of the living at the 4th Harvest, began to be mutinous and to preach up the divine right of ' Tyth,' which greatly offended the parishioners.[4] After the expiry of the Act, Richard Powell, when settled at Glasbury, would not receive tithes at all,[5] nor would Jenkin Jones for his itinerant ministrations at Merthyr Tydfil.[6] Both, however, had been paid from the treasury of Brecon[7] when the Act was in force. Vavasor Powell's attitude seems particularly inconsistent. He refused the living of Penstrowed in 1647 because the profits mainly consisted of tithes,[8] accepted the provision of the C.P.M. in 1648 drawn from a portion of the tithes of six parishes in Montgomeryshire,[9] renounced all public maintenance about 1653,[10] petitions the Committee for Compounding not to alienate the above tithes from him in 1654,[11] and at the end of 1655 calls tithes a ' Popish innovation.'[12] Llwyd, though he makes the Raven feed on the ' bodies of the dead '[13] and denounces unworthy ministers who fight ravenously for tithes,[14] does not minimise the necessity of wages,[15] and though he signed the ' Word for God ' in 1655,[16] is allowed £100 a year as ' preacher of the gospell ' in Wrexham in 1656 in lieu of what was settled upon him by the ' late Commissioners for propagation of the Gospel.'[17] Hugh Evans traversed the principles of the General Baptists by accepting payment

1 Cal. Comm. Comp.; Vol. IV, 2529.　18th July, 1654.
2 Supra, p. 100.
3 Walker c. 4, f. 67 [date not given].
4　　 Ibid.　　f. 65.
5 Examen et Purgamen Vavasoris, p. 22.
6 Wilkins : Hist. of Merthyr Tydfil, p. 95.
7 Walker c. 13, ff. 60, 63, 63b.
8 Calendar of State Papers, 1656, p. 140.
9 Bodl. 325, f. 68.
10 Examen. pp. 12-13.
11 Cal. Comm. Comp., Vol. III, p. 1725, 30th Nov., 1654.
12 " Word for God," Preamble, p. 8.
13 Gweithiau, Vol. I, " Llyfr y Tri Aderyn," p. 157.
14　　 Ibid.　　Song xliv., stanza 3, last line.
15　　 Ibid.　　Song xvii., last line, p. 41 ; xxvii, 6, p. 57.
16 Page 10.
17 Lamh. 977, f. 42.

by the State, and John Miles, notwithstanding his close touch with the parent churches in London, defends public maintenance without qualifications, deriving Scriptural authority from 1 Cor. ix, 6-11 and 1 Tim v, 17, 18,[1] and while he, David Davies, Walter Prosser, and Thomas Proud are subsidised by the Commissioners, other ministers of the new Baptist communion had to depend upon special financial arrangements for their support.[2] Other 'Anabaptist' teachers of the time are described by Edward Dafydd as agonising preachers who do without pay.[3] This triple policy of the South Wales Baptists led to serious internal discord, provided a vantage-ground for attack by the Quaker invaders, and caused the Abergavenny church to pass a resolution on 11th July, 1655, that they abjured any minister who derived financial support from the civil magistrate.[4]

Thus there was an *official* propagation by approved ministers, unejected clergy, versatile Approvers and enthusiastic itinerants, both after and under probation, side by side with an *unofficial* propagation by some ejected ministers from whom tithes were detained, by sectarian ministers specially provided for, by Erbery and his friends[5] who came to look upon the authorities as 'robbing God '[6] and upon the 'churches' as 'those poor low things,'[7] and by a growing school of Baptists who deplored the relation between Church and State.

NOTE.—HUGH PETERS AND ENGLISH PEMBROKE.

That this famous Puritan did co-operate in reinforcing the personnel of the propagators in this part of the county the Pembroke-shire accounts of 1650 (Walk. c. 13, ff. 7, 7b) give unmistakeable proof ; that this county was one of the most drastic centres for ejections is probably also due to his influence (Walk. Suff. I., p. 147, quoting a 1663 ' Life '). But to arrive at the particular names of the persons recommended by him and approved by the Welsh Commissioners is a more difficult matter : in some instances contact with Peters is a matter of inference, and the exact Christian names in one or two cases have to depend upon Calamy's informant. £10 was explicitly

---

1 An Antidote against the Infection of, the Times (Reprint by Welsh Baptist Hist. Soc., Vol. I, ed. T. Shankland), p. 25.
2 Joshua Thomas : Hanes y Bedyddwyr (Pont. Ed.), p. 170.
3 Cerdd y Fanaticiaid : ' Seren Gomer ' copy, p. 172.
4 Joshua Thomas : Hanes y Bedyddwyr (Pont. Ed.), p. 215 (footnote) ; Trafodion Cymdeithas Hanes Bedyddwyr Cymru : 1910-1911, ed. T. Shankland, p. 16.
5 The Shield Single (Henry Nicholls), p. 4 ("To the Reader "). Refers to Erbery's ' friends,' ' his own party '—but there is no evidence that he started any organisation of his own.
6 The Sword Doubled, p. 10.
7 Erbery : Testimony, p. 314

disbursed by Peters in " sending *Mr.* [*Stephen*] *Love* to the Countrey " ; £10 also in sending *Mr.* [*Christopher*] *Jackson* and *Mr.* [*William*] *Hughes* ; £5 likewise in the case of *Thomas Warren.* From the wording of the entry concerning '*Mr. West* and *Mr.* [*Daniel*] *Knowles* ' and the coincidence of the sum disbursed to them by the Commissioners' Clerk, it may with some reason be inferred that Peters was the moving cause, though his name is not expressly mentioned. Nor does his name figure in the case of *Stephen Young* (or *Yonge*), though the traditional story about him enshrined in Walk. Suff., Part I, 160, col. 2, would argue a stronger probability of his being a Peters' nominee than any on the list. As a certain '*Camber Griffiths* ' subscribes the Engagement as 'Minister of the Word ' on January 16th, 1649-50 (Bodl. D. 711, f. 7), and a ' Combe 'Griffins ' is found receiving £9 14s. 0d. for unspecified work in the Pembroke accounts, and as the great majority of the ' Engagers ' in the Oxford MS. came from London and the Home Counties from which naturally Peters would draw his supplies, it is almost certain, notwithstanding the Cymric flavour in his name, that he ought to be included in the group. The names of Edward Carver and John Hall figure in the accounts in close proximity to the above names, but no evidence connects either with England or with Peters. Of the places they actually hailed from only slight hints are given, and those in two cases only. Thomas Warren probably came from Polstead or Witnesham in Suffolk (Shaw : Vol. II, pp. 423-4), which seems supported by Calamy's assertion that he retired after 1660 ' in the direction of Great Yarmouth ' (II, 718). The same authority says that Jackson died in London (II, 717). When they arrived is also uncertain ; the parochial Commissioners of 1650 (*2nd October*) refer to not a single one of the group as settled in parishes, which points to the conclusion that if some had arrived in Pembroke before that date that they were engaged in itinerant work. Of their later settlements some information has already been given (pp. 160-1) ; Love died in May, 1655 (Lamb. 972, f. 580) ; the later history of West, Knowles, and Griffiths is wrapped in obscurity. Love and Warren were ministers-assistant to the South Wales Commissioners under the Ejection ordinances of 1654 (Firth and Rait : Vol. II, p. 984). As Peters himself was such a devoted follower of Cromwell and took interest in Pembroke affairs up to 1660 (C. St. Papers, 1659-1660, p. 410), it is natural to find five of the group (Young, Warren, Love, Jackson, Hughes) subscribing the " Humble Representation and Address " (p. 9) drawn up by Cradock in support of the Protectorate ; and also natural to find two of them (Jackson and Hughes) ejected or silenced at the Restoration (Calamy II, 717). Warren was ejected but ' conform'd afterwards,' not, however, before deserving a place as a pioneer of ' gathered churches ' in Pembrokeshire in the famous letter of Henry Maurice in 1675 (Broadmead Records, ed. Underhill, Addenda B., p. 517). The interesting record of Stephen Young deserved a better fate than Calamy's bare remark—' ejected but afterwards conform'd (II, 718).

XI.

SERVICES AND SERMONS.

To scruples about State maintenance was added the contentious question of attendance at parish churches. Some objected to do so because of the old associations, while others dissented from the " Doctrine and Worship owned by the State."[1] The Dove advises the Eagle to flee from the ' parish palaces ' and ' the old rotten churches ';[2] ; Vavasor Powell wants Parliament to declare ' the places consecrated by the Bishops to have no inherent holinesse in them ';[3] ; and the word ' Saint ' is very often omitted from the designation of parish churches in the Puritan records of the time.[4] Another aspect of this attitude was the ' creeping into houses,'[5] the ' cathedral service down by the mill-stream,'[6] the idea that services held under a tree or in a barn were as sacred as those observed in a church,[7] and the quoting of Scriptures describing Christ preaching sometimes in private houses, sometimes from a boat, sometimes on a hillside, and seldom in the synagogue.[8]   Another natural consequence was the arrival of the itinerant preacher, with his Bible in his pocket or under his arm,[9] to hold forth in the open with the people assembled around him standing.[10] But it was difficult even for the zealous adherents of the ' gathered ' churches to disregard altogether the old moorings grounded on convenience and long custom : this explains why Jenkin Jones monthly broke bread to his followers in the church of Merthyr,[11] while at other times it was possible for the

1 Admitted in " proposals " for propagation of the gospel in England, reported to Parlt. 11th Feb., 1652-3. Proposal 12. C. J. VII, 258.
2 Morgan Llwyd : Gwcithiau, Vol I, " Llyfr y Tri Aderyn," pp. 207-208.
3 Saving Faith : Epistle Dedicatory.
4 E.g., Bodl. 327, f. 186. "Maries, Haverfordwest."
5 Llwyd : Gweithiau, Vol. I, " Llyfr y Tri Aderyn," p. 170. Raven's remark.
6 Phillipps MSS. (C. F. L.), " Hen Gerddi Gwleidyddol," VI, p. 27.
7 Pregeth yn erbyn Schism . . . . Cyfleith. R. V., ' Rhagymadrodd,' pp. 5-6.
8 Morgan Llwyd : Gweithiau, Vol. I., " Llyfr y Tri Aderyn," p. 186.
9   Ibid.   Vol. II, Gair o'r Gair, Sec. VIII, par. 7, p. 173.
10   Ibid.   Vol. II, Gair o'r Gair, Sec. VIII, par. 4, p. 172 ;
                       Vol. I, Llyfr y Tri Aderyn; p. 159.
11 Wilkins : Hist. of Merthyr Tydfil. p. 94, Chap. IX.
   The fact that the Collector of Pembrokeshire paid £6 to Peregrine Phillips for the repair of the parsonage house at Llangwm in 1650 seems to show that he had no objection to preach in the parish church. (Walk. c. 13, f. 7).

' brethren ' to put some one to preach ' *in* a yew-tree in the churchyard ' while the rector occupied the pulpit inside.[1] In other places the situation changed : Henry Nicholls held the living of Coychurch in Glamorgan and ministered to a ' gathered ' church at St. Mary Hill.[2]   Sometimes, again, an itinerant would preach to a mixed[3] congregation at the parish church and afterwards address the ' faction ' else-where, *e.g.*, Vavasor Powell had one service at the church of New Radnor and another at the house of one Tom Tudman.[4] On the other hand, Morgan Llwyd, though in charge of a gathered church at Wrexham, does not seem to have held any meetings in the parish church of the place.[5]   The itinerants had right of entry to all churches, both unsupplied and otherwise.   That Dr. John Ellis was rector of Dolgelly did not prevent a ' gifted brother ' ascending his pulpit[6] ; later, however, the false prophets, according to Rowland Vaughan, herded their goats within close compass of the Doctor's temple.[7]   Erbery, after his secession, when pre-vented to address the Independent congregations,[8] is holding high dispute within the ' prelatick meeting-houses,'[9] but pours contempt on the people who believe there is no teaching the people but from a pulpit.[10]   As a general rule, the Baptists kept rigidly outside the parish churches : the followers of John Miles in the neighbourhood of Llanelly met at the house of one Jane Jones of Llangennech,[11] while Captain Thomas Evans of Eglwysilan, of the same persuasion, held services at his own house.[12]   In the face of these divergent conditions three conclusions emerge with some degree of clearness— that the churches became mere places of convenience,[13] that the propagation to the catholic Anglican mind signified the complete triumph of the secular spirit, and that the more advanced Puritan, turning away from the church door

1 Wilkins : Hist. of Merthyr Tydvil, p. 93, Chap IX.
2 The Shield Single against the Sword Doubled,   " To the Reader," p. 13. (Henry Nicholls).
3 Thurloe State Papers, Vol. I, p. 124.
4 Thurloe State Papers, Vol. II, p. 123.
5 Gweithiau, Vol. II., Introd. li.
6 Animadversions upon an Imperfect Relation . . . . [25].
7 Yr Arfer o Weddi yr Arglwydd. . . . [translated by R. V.]. Llythyr·Annerch . . . . i Sion Ellis. (Ashton : Hanes Llen., 1650-1850, p. 26).
8 Letter "for Mr. Walter Cradock " in " Call to the Churches," p. 35 (= 41 really)
9 Call to the Churches, p. 6.
10 Testimony, p. 327 (C. F. L. Copy).
11 Joshua Thomas : Hanes y Bedyddwyr (Pont. Ed.), p. 508.
12 Walker, c. 4, f. 65b.
13 Described in so many words in 1652 proposals. C. J. VII, 258.

and having as yet but little opportunity to build his own chapel,[1] fell back upon the primitive expedients of the apostolic age.

The order of worship ' owned by the State ' was that prescribed in the Directory. Refusal to ' read ' it had cost many clergymen their livings, and Vavasor Powell, in the last resort, declared certain Anglican practices superstitious because they were not according to the Presbyterian service-book.[2] In this respect, again, there was no uniformity. The preacher who expounded from the ' pue ' at Cardiff because of the thin audience,[3] the smith who expounded at Llantilio before the commencement of the ordinary sermon,[4] and the prominent pastor who told Erbery that he had discontinued the practice of praying before and after sermon,[5] were all violating the strict injunctions of the Directory. Jenkin Jones, also, in distributing the bread and wine among the congregation[6] was unmindful of the spirit of the compromise arrived at in the Assembly after prolonged debate between the Independents and the Presbyterians in 1644 that the communicants were to sit " *at* or *about* the table."[7] The uniformity became still less pronounced among the ' gathered ' congregations who worshipped outside the parish churches. The Particular Baptists did not tolerate the singing of Psalms until after the expiry of the Propagation Act.[8] All the Puritan bodies, on the other hand, laid especial stress on prayers, which were apt to become inordinately long, one hour in some cases,[9] according to Erbery. Prayers were more ' common ' than ever they were in the old days.[10] He regrets ' the loose regrets and easie enlargements,'[10] the prayers which were really sermons,[11] the praying to God ' by his Attributes,'[12] and holds that this supreme duty

1 There is one reference, and one only, that suggests the building of special ' meeting-houses.' In the ' general ' reply of the Commissioners to the Petitioners' (1052) charge that churches were allowed to fall into disrepair, they say ' decayed chappells ' were neglected since the ' Inhabitants had a *more large and convenient place neare* to attend the worship of God.' (True and Perfect Relation, p. 46):
2 Animadversions on an Imperfect Relation . . . , [20].
3 Erbery : The Sword Doubled, p. 4. April 8, 1652.
4 The Diary of Walter Powell (ed. Bradney), p. 42, Sept. 1, 1650.
5 Erbery : Apocrypha, p. 10.
6 Wilkins : Hist. of Merthyr Tydfil, IX, p. 94. " Sixth Charge " of Nathan Jones.
7 Shaw : Hist. of the English Church during the Civil War, Vol. I, pp. 345-346 ; Reliquiæ Liturgicæ, Vol. III, p. 54.
8 Joshua Thomas : Hanes y Bedyddwyr (Pont. Ed.), p. 214.
9 The Bishop of London, p. 4.
10   Ibid.   p. 6.
11 Testimony, p. 333.
12   Ibid.   p. 328.

should be confined to meetings of the 'Saints' only.[1] Powell also believed that long prayers were contrary to gospel practice.[2] There was no room for set prayers in the Puritan services. "A neer saint," says Cradock, could pray when ' standing, walking, or talking,'[3] and he further states " that all the wisdom in the world could not make one spiritual petition."[4] Stephen Hughes is careful to state that Vicar Prichard's rhymed prayers were to be read only,[5] and hopes that the readers will not be offended at the use of such obsolete terms such as ' gosber ' and ' gwasanaeth pryd.'[6] Moreover, the adventurous Puritan spirit of the time, with its emphasis on subjective religion and conscious of its freedom, was not content with discarding the Prayer Book and varying the orders of the Directory, but also sought out new channels of spiritual activity. There came a greater devotion to family prayers, such as were practised at the house of the Llanfair felt-maker[7]; the writing and repeating of sermons[8]; the composition of ' extempory ' hymns[9]; the catechising of children on Sundays which was a marked feature of the evangelical work of Charles Edwards[10]; the ' conferences and bemoans ' characteristic of the halcyon days of Llwyd's gathered church at Wrexham[11]; the debating and resolving of several questions set by Vavasor Powell to his more immediate followers on his travels[12]; and the discussions and disputings and other ungodly business which shocked the feelings of Nathan Jones at Merthyr Tydfil.[13] Thus, taking a general view, the three years' Propagation saw the growth of private meeting places which appear as the conventicles of the Restoration period, the suggestive origins of church meetings, Sunday schools, and set Scriptural studies which became marked features of later Noncon-

1 The Bishop of London, pp. 6-7 ; Call to the Churches—Letter " for Mr. Ambrose Mostyn," p. 33 (misprint for 34).
2 God the Father Glorified, p. 9.
3 Divine Drops Distilled, p. 58.
4 Ibid. p. 169.
5 Mr. Rees Prichard, Gynt Ficcar Llan-ddyfri—Y Rhagymadrodd at y Cymru p. 5.
6 Ibid., p. 6.
7 Richard Davies : An account of the Convincement, Exercises, Services and Travels (1771 Ed.), p. 4.
8 Ibid., p. 4 ; Llwyd : Gweithiau, Vol. I, " Where is Christ " . . . p. 298 ; Rawl. c. 261 contains notes of sermons delivered by Welsh preachers [at Wrexham (?) church] from 1654 to 1656. [Olim liber Josephi Crichley].
9 Life of Vavasor Powell, p. 114.
10 D. N. B., Vol. XVII, p. 113.
11 Gweithiau : Vol. 1, Song xlvii, p. 90.
12 Life of Vavasor Powell, p. 116.
13 Wilkins : Hist. of Merthyr Tydvil. p. 93, " Fourth Charge."

formity, and the popular expedient of open-air preaching which was imitated by many of the Methodist revivalists of the 18th century. And notwithstanding the failure of the Commissioners to supply a settled minister for every parish, Vavasor Powell believed that ' no generation since the Apostles daies had such powerful preachers and plenty of preaching as this generation.'[1] Erbery admitted that many of his contemporaries in Wales were men of ' parts, power, policy and piety.'[2] This dictum is confirmed from many quarters. An unfriendly critic says that David Walter drew a mighty congregation wherever he went,[3] and had a vast memory for the Scriptures[4] ; Ambrose Mostyn had a genius for unravelling difficult texts and abhorred unpremeditated sermons[5] ; Rowland Nevett had perforce, on account of the destruction of the parish church in 1644 during the siege, to be content with addressing an audience of only three hundred at the Town Hall of Oswestry, while he could secure an audience of two or three thousand were there a place large enough to contain them[6] ; Cradock was the ' first of the Pastors,'[7] more potent than a panoplied knight,[8] whose eloquence was so persuasive that John Miles had to advise the new Baptists of Breconshire to read Galatians ii. 9, 14 to fortify themselves before his coming[9] ; and Vavasor Powell would not neglect for the printing of a thousand books the preaching of one sermon.[10] Erbery preached for three months at Cardiff in the spring of 1652 a course of sermons on social questions— upon the poor, the oppressed, and the lot of prisoners— taking all his texts from the Psalms and the Prophets.[11] All the preachers could not attain to these high standards. Henry Nicholls admits that he was slow of utterance,[12] John French had a defective delivery,[13] the Baptist Morgan Jones was of ' dry tongue,[14] and Morgan Llwyd had no admiration

1 A Word in Season, p. 9.
2 A Scourge for the Assyrian, p. 4.
3 Walker c. 4, f. 70.
4   Ibid.   f. 66.
5 Calamy : Account, Vol. II, p. 715.
6 Calendar of State Papers, 1657, p. 32.
7 Erbery : Call to the Churches, p. 36.
8 Phillipps MSS.—" Can i'r Amseroedd Blin," p. 28.
9 Joshua Thomas : Hanes y Bedyddwyr (Pont. Ed.), p. 138.
10 Christ and Moses Excellency : To the Reader.
11 The Sword Doubled. pp. 2-3.
12 The Shield Single, p. 13.
13 Calamy : Account, Vol. II, p. 731.
14 Edward Dafydd : Cerdd y Fanaticiaid, ' Seren Gomer ' copy, p. 171.

for those who wrote out their sermons.[1] That the more prominent among them were men mighty in the Scriptures is illustrated in their printed works with their wealth of corroborating texts and marginal references ; their skill in exposition is witnessed by their elaborate divisions and sub-divisions, imaginary objections and conclusive answers, derivative ' doctrines ' and pertinent ' uses ' ; their intimacy with theological lore by their references to Calvin and other Continental commentators, to Hooker and the Cambridge divines, and to contemporary writers of all schools ; and their appreciation, in an age of challenging inquiry, of the prime importance of originals by their quotation of Greek, Latin, and (occasionally) Hebrew texts and the glosses of the Early Fathers. They did not sin against the light.; ' it is not sufficient for a man to walk in a *good* way, unless he is convinced it is the *best* way.'[2] But the reaction against the elegant treatise and light airy sermon prevalent among the old order, and the Puritan belief in a swift regeneration of the world by ' speaking to men's very hearts '[3] set strict limits to the display of erudition. In England this spirit is represented in the saying of a Master of Caius that university teaching was useless for producing spiritual ministers,[4] and in Wales by ' a young man of Master Powell's company ' who at the conclusion of the Newchapel dispute ' drew some people after him to the side of the Common and there inveighed against Learning and all such as professe it.'[5] Powell himself had no belief in ' ancient sayings and witty sentences . . . delivered and acted like a Play,'[6] while the ' Doctor ' to Llwyd was nothing but a ' crafty creature ' and ' a bird with vain song ' unless he had a message from God.[7] It followed that a dependence on ' naturall gifts and parts ' in the eyes of such men was a legacy of Antichrist[8]; the resort to mere reason and to the wisdom of the world but the weapons of Lucifer.[9] Again, the logical symmetry which befitted ceremonial sermons before Parlia-

1 Gweithiau, Vol. I, " Llyfr y Tri Aderyn." p. 190.
2   Ibid.   p. 253.
3 Cradock : Divine Drops Distilled, p. 12.
4 Gardiner : Hist. of the Commonwealth and Protectorate, Vol. II, p. 322, n.
5 Animadversions u on an Imperfect Relation . . . [26].
6 Christ Exalted, p. 73.
7 Gweithiau, Vol. I, " Llyfr y Tri Aderyn," p. 252.
8 V. Powell : Christ Exalted. p. 74.
9 Llwyd : " Llyfr y Tri Aderyn," p. 190.

ment and the Lord Mayor would not yet be appreciated by the hillside audiences : for them ' Comparisons, Parables, Similitudes,'[1] ' learning from the creatures,'[2] stories after the manner of the Apostles,[3] imaginary dialogues,[4] and ' standing upon Truth and not by Logick.'[5]   And though Powell declares his distaste for ' peremptory Doctrine '[6] and pictures of ' might and cruelty,'[7] it is probable that the Principality rang with denunciations of the way of the world and with the terrors of a coming judgement.   George Robinson preached ' damnac'on ' at Llantilio,[8] and Richard Jones of Denbigh in a review of the preaching activities of that generation only referred to the Boanerges who took their texts from minatory verses and to the disciples of Apollos who uttered warnings with great power.[9] Courage and straightforwardness the propagators did not lack. *E.g.*, Erbery in his dramatic letter to one of the Commissioners dilates upon Puritan notables who had reared buildings at the expense of Cavalier fortunes[10] ; Powell was bold enough to object to some of the Commissioners' proceedings,[11] and even in his sermon before Parliament in 1650 waxed sarcastic concerning those ' polititians that came in at the end of the worke for their own ends '[12]; Cradock frankly advocated calling 'a Spade a Spade,'[13] and hoped the Puritan authorities, before whom he was preaching, and who were then in course of setting up a new national church-system, would not " step up in the stead of the Cavaliers '"[14]; and John Miles bracketed with racking landlords, merciless usurers, and treacherous guardians of infants, the ' covetous ' ministers who most probably belonged to his own restricted persuasion.[15]   This virtue sometimes led them to serious lapses from good taste : the fact that Erbery in answering the charge of heresy brought

1 Life of Vavasor Powell, p. 109.
2 Cradock : Divine Drops Distilled, p. 39.
3   Ibid.   p. 7.
4 General inference from Llwyd's methods.
5 Actual remark of Ambrose Mostyn in sermon at Welshpool, June 25, 1652. [Animadversions . . . 11].
6 Spiritual Experiences [included in " Bird in Cage "], p. 139.
7   Ibid.,   p. 83.
8 Diary of Walter Powell (ed Bradney), p. 42.   May 22, 1651.
9 Galwad i'r Annychweledig, " Y Llythyr at y Cymru." [3-4].   There is a good example of the phraseology of this type of sermon in pages 11-12.
10 The Sword Doubled, p. 4.
11 A Perfect Diurnall : May 3-10, 1652.
12 Christ Exalted, p. 81.
13 Divine Drops Distilled, p. 23.
14 Saints Fulnesse of Joy, p. 32.
15 An Antidote against the Infection of the Times, p. 34.

against him before the C.P.M. denounced the churches as 'whores of Babylon,' and used that term no less than seven times in four lines,[1] implies that his sermons also contained many patches of crude realism. Sometimes they let drop unguarded expressions,[2] which, together with other delinquencies, were carefully noted and chronicled by the ejected and their sympathisers. A common accusation was that they wandered from their texts, ' like so many squirrels jumping from branch to branch,' remarked the Raven[3]; another was the ' potting of texts ' from which conclusions were ' wrested '[4] without any regard to the context, or ' urging Scriptures to serve their turn,' as when Vavasor Powell quoted Num. xvi, 24, 26, 1 Cor. v. 11, and 2 Tim. iii, 5 as encouraging ' separation '[5]; and the bards write with much scorn of the beating of pulpits, the wild eyes,[6] the pious ranters who seem ready to fly bodily to heaven,[7] and the confident but lack-learning itinerants who, with their large talk of miracles, are unable to cope with the profound doctrines they essay to explain.[8] Erbery, after he became ' a man of wrath '[9] to all the Churches, draws up a special catalogue of the shortcomings of their ministers : choosing their texts exclusively from the New Testament,[10] sitting to hear one another's sermons,[11] even selling their sermons at the highest rate,[12] dwelling on ' commonplaces of the *nature* of Faith '[13] instead of directly preaching the gospel of Christ, and ' frothy fellows ' that they were,[14] ' dressing up the language of old writers in a new dress.'[15] To his support of the Cavalier charge that they gave their own glosses upon the texts,[16] Henry Nicholls pointedly retorts

1 Testimony, pp. 326-327. [He had to appear before the Committee for preaching various ' heresies ' across the Border].
2 *E.g.*, Vavasor Powell at Welshpool—" he taught that Christ was to reign a thousand years upon the earth and that HE (= Powell) was to sit next unto him." Alex. Griffith : Hue and Cry, p. 19.
3 Morgan Llwyd : Gweithiau ,Vol. I, " Llyfr y Tri Aderyn," p. 186.
4 " His neck looks like a wrested Text " [remark about a Wrexham Puritan in " A New Ballad of the Plague " (Transcript by A. N. Palmer—N.L.W.)] ; " wrestio'r fengil "—Phillipps MSS., VIII, p. 33. " Cwyn rhyw Eglwyswr."
5 Animadversions . . . . [23-24].
6 Phillipps MS. 12453, Reprint, Song viii, p. 33.
7 Huw Morus: " Drych yr Amseroedd " [quoted in Gweithiau Llwyd, Vol. II, Introd. xlv. (lines not included in the " Gwallter Mechain " Collection)].
8 Phillipps MS. 12453, Reprint, vi, p. 28.
9 The Welsh Curate, p. 14 ; Apocrypha, p. 4.
10 Call to the Churches, p. 6.
11   Ibid.   p. 11.
12 A Scourge for the Assyrian, p. 54.
13 Call to the Churches, p. 11.
14   Ibid.   p. 13 (misprinted 12).
15 A Scourge for the Assyrian, p. 53.
16 The Honest Heretique, p. 312 (C.F.L. Copy).

that neither do the prophecies of the Old Testament ' bear a private interpretation,'[1] which was Erbery's own common practice. The latter also, probably conscious of his own good record on the matter,[2] rails at the ministers for disregarding the poor in their sermons,[3] always showing partiality for the rich and strong,[4] and forgetting the claims of the oppressed in their desire to ' serve Tables ' and follow the way of the world.[5] That this was generally true is indirectly disproved by the emphasis on equality running through the political programme outlined for the Eagle in " Llyfr y Tri Aderyn,"[6] the generous hospitality awaiting all-comers at Powell's home at Goetre,[7] and the fact that part of George Robinson's salary for 1650 and all of Cradock's salary for 1650 and 1651 was distributed among ' divers godly Poore People ' in the county of Monmouth.[8] On this point it is curious to note that Erbery " had it once in his thoughts to take the hundred pounds he received from the Glamorgan Treasurer in 1650] and give it as a publique stocke for the poor of Cardiffe " ; but he naively consoles himself for not doing so by adding that " God will shortly provide for the poor though man will not."[9]

1 The Shield Single, p. 19.
2 Supra, p. 171.
3 A Scourge for the Assyrian. p. 52.
4 The Idol Pastor [contained in the ' North Star,'] pp. 93-94.
5 The Welsh Curate, p. 12.
6 Gweithiau, Vol. I, pp. 262-265.
7 Life, p. 111—" he had room for twelve in his beds, a hundred in his barns, and a thousand in his heart."
8 Walker c. 13, ff. 45, 51.
9 The Sword Doubled, p. 15.

XII.

DOCTRINE.

" Be steadfast in those truths which you have been taught concerning God and his Attributes, Christ and his Offices, the Holy Spirit and its manifestations, the decrees of God before time, the two Covenants (viz., the Law and the Gospel), the wretched state of all men by Nature, and out of Christ ; the freeness of God's grace, in opposition to man's free will ; the Doctrine of Justification by the imputed Righteousness of Christ, apprehended and received by Faith, Sanctification (distinct from Justification) wrought by the Spirit in us, Perseverance, Assurance, and growth in Grace by vertue of our union with Christ, and his spiritual in-dwelling and working in us."[1]   This comprehensive outline of high Calvinism drawn up by Powell for the benefit of his immediate followers after the Restoration marks a very great advance on the somewhat amorphous body of doctrine professed by the Puritans of Wales before the outbreak of the Civil War. The effort of Oliver Thomas, in explaining to ' Cymro ' the true import of Phill. ii, 12, is singularly jejune in combating the Arminianism supposed to be latent in that text[2] ; the ' six points ' emphasised by Wroth on his visits to Bristol were a mere catalogue of simple Gospel truths admitted by all schools[3] ;   according   to   Erbery,   Wroth's   immediate successors at Llanfaches contented themselves with negative denunciations of hypocrisy, ' great professors ', and material ' performance of good duties '[4] ; and Vavasor Powell's early preaching on the Border alternated between ' shaking and terrifying doctrines ' contained in Luke xi, and the extremes of Antinomianism, ' destroying and utterly denying the use of the Law.'[5]   This state of flux denoted men in need of

1 The Bird in the Cage :, Epistle Dedicatory, pp. 7-8.   Exact words of writer quoted.
2 Car-wr y Cymru :   " Ymddiddan rhwng Car-wr a'r Cymro," p. 54 (1630).
3 Broadmead Records (ed. Haycroft), p. 23.   [Circa 1640].
4 The Wretched People [contained in the " North Star "], p. 117.   [Circa 1642-3.]
5 Life—" Mr. Powell's Account of his Conversion and Ministry " prefixed, p. 14. [Mentions specifically Luke xi. 21.] [Ante 1642.]

more light and coherent leadership by contact with great formative movements and with minds severely disciplined who were bent upon reducing theology into an exact science. The sojourn in England coincided with the arrival of the political heirs of the " Lords of the Congregation " to redress the disasters which had befallen the Puritan arms and with the mission of the spiritual descendants of Knox to bring order out of the chaos which had befallen English divinity. They were to apply to the ' low legall ' tendencies of Perkins and Bolton, to the doctrine of free grace as taught by Sibbes and Crisp, and to the emphasis on the letter of Scripture characteristic of John Goodwin,[1] the rigid standard of belief inspired from Geneva ; it was in this work of theological redaction, indeed, that the Presbyterians were to find their one point of agreement with the Independent divines who had newly returned from their exile among the Calvinists of Holland. Their joint product, the Westminster Confession of Faith, found one of its most valiant defenders in the Vavasor Powell whose corpus of theology had been so undeveloped on the mountains of Radnor. At the end of December, 1649, he enters the lists against the greatest living exponent of universal redemption[2] and asserts that the term ' world ' in John iii, 16 connotes the professing Gentiles only, and not all the posterity of Adam.[3] A few weeks before he had declared unhesitatingly before the Lord Mayor that man is saved by grace alone,[4] and in the printed version devotes 58 pages to an exhaustive treatment of the subject,[5] finding in the Scriptures forty types of promises for those that are ' elected.'[6] Similarly, Cradock at All Hallows holds, in his analysis of ' naturall religion,' that man's unaided graces are ' morall virtues of old Adam gilded over,' and that the performance of his quasi-spiritual duties depends either upon the imitation of others, or upon the influence of education, or upon ' the power of the letter preached.'[7] He approves of the remark that man in con-

---

1 A Scourge for the Assyrian, pp. 30-31.—Erbery's account of the divergent strands of thought in English theology (1600-1645).
2 Supra, p. 75.
3 Reference of Henry Nicholls to the debate.   [The Shield Single, p. 56.]
4 Christ and Moses Excellency, pp. 154-156.
        Ibid.   pp. 109-167.
5   Ibid.   pp. 259-268.
7 Divine Drops Distilled, p. 132.

version is merely passive,[1] and naively says that the
quickening spirit of God in the work of sanctification can
make ' a Schollar ripe ' sometimes ' in a quarter of a year,
even in a moneth almost.'[2]   Again, faith to him is the
' mysticall art ' by which the afflicted are borne up.[3] Concerning fall from grace, Vavasor Powell solemnly adjures
his people not to entertain such a heresy,[4] and Cradock's
opinion is that though a saint may sometimes miss the *will*
of God the *Spirit* can not forsake him except in very rare
cases, as when it left Christ to be tempted in the wilderness.[5]
On their return to Wales, the propagation of such unqualified
Calvinism was reinforced by such men as Henry Nicholls,
episcopally ordained,[6] ' but a new modeled minister,'[7] who
declared that the doctrine of Personal Election was ' the very
Truth of the Gospel,'[8] and by the " Particular " Baptists
who had subscribed to Articles III-VI of the London Confessions of 1644 and 1646.[9] These find an echo in the
' Antidote ' of John Miles whose ' considerations to sinners '
emphasise original sin,[10] that ' Adam was not a private man
in that act of his fall,' and that there existed no inherent or
habitual righteousness.[11] Nor were the Welsh Puritans
oblivious of the dangers that attended the profession of
extreme Calvinism. Cradock especially denounces men
who are ' puffed up with spiritual pride, flying too high above
the Gospel,' making the doctrine of justification a pretence
for ' swagger, and even looseness and wantonness.'[12] Nicholls
utters a warning that Election should be taught ' wisely
and warily.'[13] And the difficulties which have always
attended the logical exposition of the ' decrees of God before
time ' are represented by the failure of Jenkin Lloyd to
explain how one of the thieves on the Cross was ' inspired by
saving grace ' and the other not except by the fatalist

1 Divine Drops Distilled, p. 172.
2 Divine Drops Distilled, pp. 171-172.
3   Ibid.   p. 128.
4 Spiritual Experiences, p. 132.
5 Divine Drops Distilled, p. 168.
6 Walker c. 4, f. 66.   There is no reference, however, to Nicholls in the ' Liber
Institutionum.'
7 Erbery : A Dispute at Cowbridge, p. 45 [included in " Call to the Churches "].
8 The Shield Single, p. 54.
9 Crosby : Hist. of the English Baptists, Vol. I, App. II, pp.8-9, for " 1644 " ;
McGlothlin : Baptist Confessions of Faith, p. 175, for " 1646."
10 pp. 1-2.
11 pp. 11-12.
12 Divine Drops Distilled, pp. 203, 204, 215, 226.
13 The Shield Single, pp. 56-57.

argument that God's plans were " occult and not unjust "[1] ; and by the explanation of Matth xx, 16 and xxii, 14 in one place by Llwyd on the basis of free-will,[2] and in another by suffusing high Calvinism with the ideas of the mystic.[3] The distortion to which the dominant creed was liable in the minds of simple men made Powell to deprecate ' hard thoughts of God,'[4] and to labour his five ways of preaching the Gospel ' to suit the idea of Election.'[5] For this doctrinal aspect of the Propagation had brought forth critics of diverse schools. The Raven, echoing the Arminian leanings which made the Laudian regime on the intellectual side so repugnant to the reformers, inquires whether the self-conceit of the Puritan outweighed the necessity for ' good works,'[6] and the country rhymester wishes to be saved from the preachers who place ' hypocrisy and all our sins ' at the door of the Almighty.'[7] Over against the ' Particular ' came the ' General ' Baptists, and in a class of its own came the uncompromising opposition of Erbery. Faith, according to him, was the ' Protestant's God,'[8] and universal redemption was ' nearest the Gospel indeed.'[9] He summarily evaded the significance of the Calvanistic texts in the four Gospels by the startling theory that Christ was only a "minister of the Circumcision,' ' a legall teacher,' and that the truths he taught were preached only to the Jewish Church and not to the world in general.[10]

This was not the only strange doctrine that emanated from the fertile brain of Erbery. Even as chaplain in the Army he had been accused of corrupting the minds of the soldiers by his Antinomian leanings[11] ; he was charged before the C.P.M. in 1652 with blasphemous denial of the divinity of Christ[12] ; he argued in a dispute with Henry Nicholls that ' God is in union with mankinde '[13] ; in some of his works he displays especial sympathy with the Quakers of

1 Christ's Valedictions, p. 61.
2 Gweithiau, Vol. I, " Llyfr y Tri Aderyn," p. 173.
   Ibid.   pp. 216-217.
4 Spiritual Experiences, p. 132.
   Christ and Moses Excellency, pp. 142-145.
6 Llwyd : Gweithiau, Vol. I. " Llyfr y Tri Aderyn." p. 168.
7 Phillipps MS. 12453.   " Y Letani Newydd," Song vii, p. 31.
8 The Children of the West, p. 15.
9 A Scourge for the Assyrian, p. 34.
   10 A Call to the Churches, p. 4.   This was the argument adopted at Llantrisant when asked to explain John i. 12 by one of the henchmen of John Miles.
   11 D.N.B., Vol. XVII, p. 384
   12 Testimony, p. 316.
   13 A Dispute at Cowbridge—" Letter to Mr. Davy Walter " in " Call to the Churches," pp. 50-51 ; Apocrypha, pp. 3-4.

the North of England,[1] and his daughter Dorcas became involved in the chequered career of James Naylor[2]; but the sect to whom he approximated most closely were the Seekers, who were patiently waiting for a new commission from heaven. This is especially the case with his theory of the Three Dispensations. The first was that of the Law, the second of Gospel-Order; God as Father in the one, as Son in the other; appearing through 'forms' in the first, through flesh in the second.[3] Christ's first day in the grave corresponded to the former, his second to the latter.[4] The second dispensation lasted in its primitive purity only for about 250 years, when the Apostacy came,[5] described by Erbery in vivid terms derived from the thirty-seventh of Ezekiel.[6] The Churches then came into Babylon, lay down in the open valley with the dry bones, fell into divided forms and defiled worship, became as the 'two sticks divided and dry.'[7] The Spirit departed, and its place was taken by childish catechisms and confessions of faith, the dictates of Fathers and the decrees of Councils, limping liturgies and mouldy manuscripts,[8] coupled with a slavish adherence to ordinances, instituted in Gospel-times for the sake of the weak ones in the Churches only.[9] The genuine saints were scattered, 'bewildernessed,' and the so-called 'gathered' churches only served to scatter them the more,[10] for 'now there is less love and more offences.'[11] The Independent Church-fellowship was continually building Babylon anew.[12] But in the latter days, in the fulness of time, God would appear as pure Spirit, and would be All in All; the New Jerusalem would come down from heaven, 'a city without walls,' for the Christian Church would revert to the tradition of apostolic unity. Abundance of 'savages' will come in, and the hearts of men will be enlarged to accept them.[13]

1 A Whirlwind from the South, p. 38 ; The Children of the West, p. 63 ; The Welsh Curate, p. 8.
2 Braithwaite : The Beginnings of Quakerism, pp. 247, 252 [disproves statement in D.N.B. that Dorcas was his *wife*.]
3 A Scourge for the Assyrian, p. 23.
4 Henry Nicholls : The Shield Single, p. 42. This he heard Erbery deliver 'in the pulpit.'
5 Call to the Churches, p. 9.
6 The Idol Shepherd, p. 89 [especially quoting verses 1, 2, 11, 13, 16, 17.]
7 The Bishop of London, p. 8.
8 A Scourge for the Assyrian, p. 34 ; A Whirlwind from the South, p. 28.
9 The Welsh Curate, pp. 3-4.
10 The Idol Shepherd, p. 92.
11 The Wretched People, p. 107.
12 Call to the Churches, p. 50.
13 Call to the Churches, p. 36 (misprint for 43) ; The Sword Doubled, p. 12.

Ordinances will be finally swept away,[1] and the Spirit will be manifested as in pentecostal times in manifold gifts. This new order will be ·a state of the saints on *this* earth ; indeed some of them, but not the churches, are under ‚it already.[3] However, it comes not by the strength of reason nor the reading of the Scriptures, but by the revelation of God's mighty power to each of His children.[4] Nor, Erbery is careful to add, will the third dispensation be due to " the outward force and strength of *man*, which has attended great acts in these latter times."[5] These were his main theses, indulging in their development in long digressions and fantastic interpretations of Old Testament texts, *e.g.*, in equating the Isles of Britain with the " Isles of the Sea" mentioned in Isaiah, Jeremiah, and the Psalms.[6] Other collateral views were that Wales would lead the way in crushing schisms and all shibboleths,[7] that the growth of sects in Southern Britain was due to the softening influences of the climate,[8] that liberty should be allowed ' honest Papists,'[9] that the ' Priests and Prelates were nearer to the ordinances ' than the ministers of the day,[10] that the Mohammedans were ' only misbelieving Christians,'[11] and that an alliance with the Turks ' from the east side ' should not be impossible.[11] To his criticism of the itinerant system[12] and his opposition to State maintenance[13] he added a contempt for the militant ministers, like Cradock and Powell,[14] who delighted in ' pieces of silver and a fortnight's pay '[15] ; and, contrary to the growing hostility among the Welsh Puritans to the Rump,[16] Erbery was disposed to deal leniently with a body ' clouded under particular corruptions and crouching under its own greatnesse,' but, nevertheless, one ' in whom

1 The Welsh Curate, pp. 3-4.
2 The Bishop of London, p. 21.
3 A Dispute at Cowbridge (in " Call for the Churches "), p. 47.
4 A Scourge for the Assyrian, p. 35.
5 Call to the Churches, pp. 8-9.
6 A Whirlwind from the South, p. 38 ; Apocrypha, p. 4 ; The Children of the West, p. 49.
7 Apocrypha, pp. 7-8.
8 A Whirlwind from the South, p. 39.
9 Testimony, p. 333.
10 The Children of the West, p. 54.
11 Testimony, p. 334.
12 Supra, p. 156.
13 Supra, p. 162.
14 Supra, p. 101.
15 The Woman Preacher : or The Man of War, p. 83 [included in " The North Star."]
16 " The Humble Representation and Address," [1656], to Cromwell by Cradock and others refers to the ' weariness of its doings ' that had set in (1649-1653), p. 5.

God hath so visibly appeared.'[1]   With all his Ishmaelite
tendencies, he kept up a friendly correspondence with the
'idol pastors,' commiserates with Ambrose Mostyn on the
death of his wife,[2] begs Vavasor Powell to accept his 'large
affections,'[3] fails to understand the point of some of Llwyd's
queries,[4] and prints the mystic's letters without his
permission.[5]   Under the circumstances, however, he had
to become 'a private Christian,'[6] to be of no Religion *with
men*,'[7] and by 'the hand of God to become mad for the
Churches' sake.'[8]   A friendly critic of the next generation
describes him as 'taken ill of his whimsies,'[9] and a historian
of Nonconformity says that several years before his death
he was visited by a sore affliction which to some degree
deranged his mind.[10]   On the other hand, Erbery's answer
to the charges before the C.P.M. is full of the subtle arguments of a master of controversy,[11] and his criticisms of
Vavasor Powell's fierce diatribe at Christ Church against
the new Government a few months before his death show
unwonted moderation and betray no diminution of mental
power.[12]   Rather should it be said that his was a wonder-
fully versatile but somewhat unbalanced mind whose high
ideals set up impossible standards for an age of transition.

Erbery's theory of the last dispensation, with no fixed
date and confined to the pervading power of the Spirit in the
souls of men, made him apply to the calculating Christians
who were looking forward to the personal reign of Christ on
earth for a thousand years the fulminations of Jeremiah
against the false prophets who beguiled the Jews in Babylon.[13]
This conception, however, appealed with immense force to
the imaginations of men towards the latter part of the reign
of Charles I.   It fitted in with the generally accepted idea
that the four beasts of Daniel's vision[14] signified the great

1 A Scourge to the Assyrian, p. 63 ; Testimony, p. 338.
2 Call to the Churches—" Letter to Ambrose Mostyn," pp. 35-36.
3   Ibid.   " Letter to Vavasor Powell," p. 36 (= 41).
4 The North Star—" Letter to Morgan Lloyd," p. 19.
5   Ibid.   ibid. (previous letter), pp. 14, 17
6 The Honest Heretique ; or, Orthodox Blasphemer, p. 310.
7 The General Epistle to the Hebrews, p. 6.
8 The Mad Man's Plea, p. 3.
9 A Winding Sheet for Mr. Baxter's Dead (1685), p. 3.
10 Rees : Hist. of Prot. Nonconformity (Sec. Ed.), p. 43 [no authority is given].
11 Testimony, esp. p. 337.
12 An Olive-Leaf : Or, Some peaceable Considerations to t he Christian Meeting
at Christs-Church in London, Munday, Jan. 9th, 1653 [-- 1654].
13 Jeremiah xxviii. 8 ; **xxix.** 8, 9 ; Testimony : " To the Christian Reader,"
p. '9].   Signed by J. W. [= John Webster, Erbery's apologist].
14 Daniel vii, 4-7.

empires of Assyria, Persia, Greece and Rome, that Charles I was ' the little horn,'[1] and that the High Court of Justice was the throne of the Ancient of Days,[2] and it received added force from the comparative impotence of the Papacy and the events of the Thirty Years' War. Many ordinary citizens welcomed the new gospel because it presaged an era of peace and goodwill and an end to the bitter political and religious controversies which threatened to rob the Puritan Revolution of its glory. And this Fifth Monarchy was said to be close at hand ; how close depended upon the varying interpretations[3] given to the time of the ' taking away of the daily sacrifice ' and ' the setting up of the abomination ' (Daniel xii, 11), to which 1,290 days mentioned in the same verse and the 1,260 days (Rev. xi. 3), both resolved into terms of years,[4] were indiscriminately added. Some reckoned from the apostacy of Julian[5] ' in 360 or 366 ' (+ 1,290 = 1650 or 1656)[6] ; others started from the ' end of Paganisme in 395 ' (+ 1,260) and made the commencing date to be 1655 ; others summed up the lives of the patriarchs from the Creation to the Flood (Genesis v), and inferred the year to be 1656, ' because it must be as in the days of Noah ' ; others added to the date of the Council of Nice (325) twice the number of the beast (666) in Rev. xiii, 18, and found it to be 1657 ; others started to calculate at ' the downfall of the Roman Empire either in 400 or 406 ' (+ 1,260) and arrived at 1660 or 1666 ; last of all, another quite unscientific method decided also upon the latter date, ' because of the number 666.'[7] To these vagaries of calculation was added a vital difference concerning political action,—whether to adopt the quietist attitude and wait calmly for the dispensations of Providence, or to hasten the advent of the Millennium by combating earthly powers

---

1 Daniel vii. 8.
2   Ibid.   9.
3 Some of the calculations given below seem to take no cognisance whatsoever of the accepted meaning of the base in the Daniel text.
4 " What if those days be not years ? "—" The Revelation Unrevealed," p. 27 [anonymous], Jan. 17th, 1649-50.
5 Julian died in 363—Gibbon : Decline and Fall [cd. Bury], Vol. II, p. 515.
6 Archer : Personall Reign of Christ on Earth (1642), p. 51.
7 The evidence for these various theories is contained in—
    (i) Henry Archer : Personall Reign of Christ on Earth, pp. 47, 51.
    (ii) Thurloe State Papers, Vol. IV, March, 1655, containing a summary of Fifth Monarchy ideas supplied to the Secretary of State by Pell, *Retrospectively*, they form good evidence for the period 1642-1655.

that occupied the place the saints were destined to fill.[1] The latter point of view, naturally enough, had its strongest supporters in the Army, among men who had been accustomed to look to the Scriptures for the justification of every act, and who regarded the coming kingdom of Christ as a natural climax to the victories they had won by the direct hand of God. Harrison is looked upon by some historians as the leader of this advanced wing, and the theory has been adumbrated that his engineering of the Propagation Act was meant to make Wales the venue of a great theocratic experiment as a preparation for the rule of the saints.[2] But, notwithstanding the undoubted Millenarian trend of his arguments before the Council of Officers in June, 1649,[3] the tone of his letters to John Jones in 1652,[4] and the emphasis he laid upon ' men feareing God ' being appointed as officials of Parliamentary committees,[5] the weight of evidence favours Gardiner's opinion that even in the early days of 1653 he was only ' drifting ' into the ranks of the *aggressive* Fifth Monarchy party.[6] Among this evidence is the anti-Millenarian tenor of the propagation proposals submitted by him and others to the Parliament in 1651-52[7] and the doctrinal attitude of the Welsh approvers.

Comparatively few of the propagators were guilty of " measuring the word of God with their fingers "[8] ; there was hardly one in all South Wales. David Walter wandered from Genesis to Revelations,[9] but there is no evidence that he paid any particular attention to the mystical books ; Henry Nicholls did expect to see his Saviour " not in the Spirit only, but in the flesh also," but the context proves that he is referring to the day of judgment[10] ; Hanserd Knollys would go no further than that ' the saints were to govern

---

1 Gooch : English Democratic Ideas in the Seventeenth ;Century, Chap. vii, p. 261.

2 Simpkinson : Life of Harrison, Chap. vi., p. 101.

3 Supra, p. 79.

4 Simpkinson : Life of Harrison. Appendix, pp. 293-296.

5 Commonwealth Exchequer Papers : Committees of Accounts, Bundle 259 [loose sheet—not numbered]. Recommendation of Thomas Jefferson to be Registrar-Accountant to the Comm., his " Lov. ffreindes," 5 Nov., 1652.

6 Hist. of the Commonwealth and Protectorate, Vol. II, p. 181.

7 C. J. VII, 258-259. [It is of this Committee that *Jenkin Lloyd* was also a member.]

8 Phillipps MS. 12453. Reprint, Song vi, " Can i'r Amseroedd Blin," p. 28. [This is assumed to be a gibe at the " calculators."]

9 Walker c. 4, f. 66 ; Erbery gives no clue in his letter to Walter in his " Call to the Churches," pp. 45-46.

10 The Shield Single, pp. 43, 59.

the Nations by Christ's *law* and by his *commission* '[1]; John Miles in referring to the Second Coming quotes texts whose evidence were never summoned by the orthodox Millenarians[2]; and Walter Cradock maintained the old-fashioned exegesis of " the last days " given at All Hallows[3] up to the time he was accusing Vavasor Powell and his party of ' running before God in prescribing wayes and times for the bringing forth the merciful dispensations he hath promised.'[4] It was not at once that Powell became a thoroughgoing propagator of the new ideas. At the beginning of 1650 he puts down as controverted questions whether Christ will come to reign on earth, whether *all* the Saints shall reign with Him, or only those that suffered under Antichrist, or ' the people of the Jews ' alone[5]; at the same time he states that most godly writers upon Daniel named that current year as the time of Jubilee.[6] He hopes also that Parliament will see well to abolish the heathen names of the days and months—a particularly punctilious matter with the Millenarians—" that so the people may learn the language of the Scriptures and not of Ashtaroth."[7] That Powell had a clearer vision on these ' controverted questions ' during the Propagation period is proved by specific instances of sermons on the subject as described by Alexander Griffith,[8] by the testimony of another hostile critic that ' he was a giddy-headed parson . . . and chief holder forth to that dangerous people called the Fifth Monarchy,'[9] by his own ' confident ' letter to Erbery on the subject,[10] and especially by his impassioned outbursts, nine months after the expiry of the Act, upon the iniquities of the men who had temporarily delayed the Millennium by dissolving the Little Parliament.[11] In his sermon at

1 Culross: Hanserd Knollys [Baptist Manuals, Vol. II], pp. 97-98.
2 Antidote against the Infection of the Times, Section I, p. 8.
3 Divine Drops Distilled, pp. 152, 210; Saints Fulnesse: Ded. [4].
4 The Humble Representation and Address (1656), p. 4.
5 Christ Exalted, pp. 51-52; the date of this sermon effectually dissipates Miss Brown's vague doubt that Powell held Millenarian ideas in 1652 (Baptists and Fifth Monarchy Men, p. 22).
6   Ibid.   pp. 91-92.
7 Saving Faith Set Forth in Three Dialogues.—" Epistle Dedicatory."
8 Hue and Cry (1654), pp 5-10. The authors of the ' Examen ' assert that '' he never made it the subject of one whole sermon, and doth very seldom, and then sparingly, touch upon it " (p. 19). Their argument, however, is unconvincing, when compared with their defence of the doctrine on the previous page.
9 Quoted by Simpkinson in " Life of Harrison," p. 101.
10 Referred to as such in Erbery's " Letter to Vavasor Powell " (Call to the Churches, p. 36). Powell's letter has not survived.
11 " A small matter should fetch him [= Cromwell] down, with little noise "— Powell's sermon, 19 Dec, 1653, at Blackfriars. [C. S. Papers, 1653, pp. 305-306.]

Blackfriars he poured scorn on the idea that Oliver Cromwell should usurp the place of Jesus Christ, especially when the latter's kingdom was in the process of being set up[1] ; on his return to Wales he declared absolutely that he would never submit to any government that was not according to God's word[2] ; and even went so far as to ' list troops ' in opposition to the men whose ideals were embodied in the " Instrument of Government."[3]

But though it is with Powell that the new doctrine finds its most fierce and persistent[3a] defender in Wales, it is in the works of Llwyd that it receives its fullest expression. With him, again, the actual date of the fateful event is quite uncertain : his song in 1648 veers between 1650, 1656, and 1665[4] ; in the early days of 1650 he calls his little daughter ' Peace ' in celebration of the peaceful days that are on the point of coming[5] ; at the end of the same year he bids men prepare for 1660[6] ; in " Llyfr y Tri Aderyn " he adopts the patriarchal calculation[7] ; in any case, it will be ' within man's age.'[8] He follows the English Millenarians in drawing a distinction between Christ's coming and the end of the world, and in making the last judgment fall within its limits.[9] Then will come for the world a Sabbath day of rest,[10] that one day which will be as a thousand years[11] ; a glowing Summer will succeed a long Winter of ignorance and persecution[12] ; there will be but one Temple for all the sons of God,[13] one Tree where all birds will make their nests[14] ; and the great Reality will supersede the shadowy ordinances.[15] But these wonderful days will be immediately preceded by civil commotions and convulsions of nature and by a grim struggle with the ' beast ' as typifying the ' last times ' of

1 Calendar of State Papers, 1653-4, p. 305.
2 Thurloe State Papers, Vol. II, p. 93.
3   Ibid.   Vol. II, p. 174.
   3a His faith in it remained undimmed even after the Restoration.   [The Bird in the Cage : Epistle Dedicatory [9] ; A Word in Season, p. 83 (= 38).]
4 Gweithiau, Vol. I, Song, 1648, " The Spring," v, 8, p. 22.
5   Ibid.   Song xiii, " 1650," p. 36.
6   Ibid.   Song xxvii, " Hanes Rhyw Gymro." v. 22, p. 60.
7   Ibid.   Llyfr y Tri Aderyn, p. 198.
8   Ibid.   Song viii, " The Spring," v, 8, p. 22, Llythyr i'r Cymru
                         Cariadus, p. 121 ; Ll. T. A., p. 262.
9   Ibid.   Song viii, " The Harvest," v. 2, p. 30 ; Ll. T. A., pp. 196-8.
                         (cp. with Archer : Personall Reign, p. 5).
10   Ibid.   Ll. T. A., p. 197.
11   Ibid.   Song viii, " The Summer," v. 26, p. 27 (converse also true).
12   Ibid.   Song viii, pp. 19-20, 23-30.
13   Ibid.   Llyfr y Tri Aderyn, p. 231.
14 Gweithiau, Vol. II, Gair o'r Gair, cap. 1, sec. 9, p. 136.
15 Gweithiau, Vol. I, Song lii, v. 4, p. 9.

the forces of reaction.[1] 'Those deep suspicious birds,'
the Dutch, must be fought ' on Christ's score '[2]; Britain
will lead the van against the Papacy, which will be buried
in its own ruins[3]; the domination of the Turk will come to
an end in Eastern Europe[4]; and Llwyd does not forget to
cry woe upon all the unregenerate survivals of the old Wales
from the proud descendants of princes to crafty lawyers
and all ' worshippers of the letter.'[5] Nor were the saints to
be inactive during this eventful period, for there was necessity
for much and proper preparation. The Jews were to be
converted,[6] the propagation of the gospel was to be carried
on with ever-increasing zeal, and there was a call for
redoubled spiritual energy among the churches, especially
in practising the humbler and more unobtrusive Christian
virtues[7]; finally, Llwyd recommended to the ruling powers
the adoption of certain standards of political morality which
would make the existing State merge naturally into the
chiliastic era.[8] These were to some extent put in practice
by the Parliament which ' looked to God,'[9] and Llwyd's
indignation was equally deep as Powell's at the seeming
selfishness of those who, like Cromwell and Lambert, '
wrapped
up Christ's interest, as one that will fold up a stalking horse
after he hath shot the bird.'[10] The old fear that ' men and
means ' would fail had been thoroughly justified.[11] In the
foregoing outline the ' teacher of North Wales '[12] followed,
generally speaking, in the steps of English Millenarianism.
There is some evidence that he had no great sympathy with
the ' fleshly measurers,'[13] and in developing some aspects of
the doctrine he virtually discounts the conclusions of the
calculators. *E.g.*, differences among Christians may mean
a new triumph for Antichrist[14]; conversely, a growing

1 Gweithiau, Vol. I, Song iii, v. 5, p. 9 ; xl, v. 5, p. 79 ; xlii, v. 2, p. 83.
2   Ibid.   Song xxxix, vv. 1, 4, p. 77.
3   Ibid.   Song viii, " The Spring," v, 9, p. 22.: xxvii, vv, 22-23, p. 60.
4   Ibid.   Song xlii, v. 4, p. 83.
5 Llyfr y Tri Aderyn, pp. 220-221. 30 types of unregenerates are mentioned.
6 Vol. I, Song xx, v. 5, p. 44; xxv, v. 14, p. 54; xlii. v. 4, p. 83; Llyfr y Tri Aderyn. p. 177.
7 Llythyr i'r Cymru Cariadus, pp. 121-122 :· Llyfr y Tri Aderyn, p. 239.
8 Llyfr y Tri Aderyn, pp. 262-265.
9 Calendar of State Papers, Dom., 1653-1654, p. 11. Declaration of Saints' Parliament, July 12th, 1653.
10 Gweithiau, Vol. II, " An Honest Discourse Between Three Neighbours," p. 216 [" Goodman Future "].
11 Vol. I, Song xxvi, v. 8, p. 56.
12 Erbery's description of Llwyd in Apocrypha, p. 9.
13 Llyfr y Tri Aderyn, p. 226.
14 Vol. I, Song viii, " 1648 " : The Summer, v. 45, p. 29.

spirit of accommodation may hasten the coming of what was above all else a time of peace and good-will among men[1] ; nor is there any suggestion in his works of a possible postponement of the Millennium for forty-five years even after the completion of the ' 1,290 days.'[2] Further, there · existed in Llwyd's mind a strong vein of mysticism derived from studying the extant works of Jacob Boehme. The influence of the " Teutonic Philosopher "[3] is evident in his distinction between God as Spirit that cannot be realised and God as revealed in Nature,[4] in the idea that Nature itself is a compact of Fire and Light,[5] in the belief that the Eternal Nature is the source and fount of the Temporal Nature,[6] in the conception that the Divine Trinity maketh its home in every man,[7] and in the dictum that men are ' signing ' themselves from within in fixed forms for ever present in their physical appearance.[8] Boehme himself had no faith in the Sabbath of the chiliasts, asserting that the Sabbath of Rebirth and the Sabbath Eternal were all-sufficient for the children of God.[9] As these ideas developed and deepened in Llwyd's mind they led to a considerable qualification of the orthodox Millenarian theories. He moves away from Archer's definition of Paradise as a quasi-purgatorial region from which the souls of the saints emerge to appear with Christ on earth,[10] and declares it to be the heavenly nature and to exist in all places where the love of God is made manifest[11] ; and he advises his readers to look for Christ, not at a distance of even a few years, but even on the hearth of their own hearts.[12] " The true Sabbath is within '[13] ; ' there are flowers in our own gardens '[14] ; ' there

1 Vol. I, Song viii, " 1648 " : The Summer, v. 44, p. 29.
2 Daniel xii, 12.   1335 days.
  Daniel xii, 11   1290 days.
  _____
  45 days.

3 *Erbery* was also a reader of ' Behme, the Teutonick *Theosopher.*' [Testimony p. 333].
4 Vol. I, Song xxvii, " Hanes Rhyw Gymro," v. 19, p. 59.
5 Encyclopædia of Religion and Ethics, " Boehme " (G. W. Allen), p. 780.
6 e . Whyte : An Appreciation of Behmen, p. 71 ; Llyfr y Tri Aderyn, p. 199Al x
7   Ibid.   p. 61 ; Llyfr y Tri Aderyn, p. 187.
8   Ibid.   pp. 40-42 ; Llythyr i'r Cymry Cariadus, p. 119 ; Llyfr y Tri Aderyn, p. 224.
9 W. Hobley : Art. II on Jacob Boehme [quoting letter of Boehme to Paul Keym] in " Traethodydd," May, 1900, p. 172.
10 Personall Reign of Christ upon Earth, pp. 24-25.
11 Llyfr y Tri Aderyn, pp. 213, 215.
12 Gwaedd Ynghymru, p. 145.   .
13 Llyfr y Tri Aderyn, p. 265.
14 The North Star, " Letter for Mr. William Erbery," p. 12 [May, 1653].

is a golden mine in our own fields.'[1]   Even in this mystic environment the Millenarian outlook is not wholly surrendered. But in his later works the coming of the Fifth Monarch is only occasionally dilated upon, and then cautiously, as when he advises men not to profess more concerning it than is warranted by the unequivocal words of Scripture.[2]

Contemporary criticism in Wales of Fifth Monarchy opinions is practically confined to Erbery. Much as there was of common ground between his theory of the Third Dispensation and the current conception of the Millennium,[3] he could see in it "no just discerning of the seasons."[4] There was great work yet to do, and many prophecies were still unfulfilled.[5]   He held that the reign of Christ, 'held forth in a fleshly pretence,' would hinder saints from seeking the Spirit, and conduce to a repugnant form of spiritual pride ; "some of your followers," he writes to Vavasor Powell, "have begun to reign already as Kings, but not with Christ."[6]   To the same correspondent's citation of Acts i, 11 as his 'foundation' that Christ would appear again on earth 'in the like manner' to that in which he had ascended, Erbery rejoined that the disciples, obsessed with his fleshly presence and with their sorrow at his departure, did not notice the 'fulness of the Spirit dwelling in that flesh after it was raised.'   Hence he would appear the second time in the *Spirit* only, a conclusion strengthened by the fact that God's appearances since the beginning assumed more and more a spiritual aspect.[7]   On another occasion he said he could not understand the second appearance of Christ in a fleshly body, and that, as some Millenarians declared, to all the saints at once.   "For," added the critic, "such a body can be but circumscriptively in one place at once, and Christ must move swifter than the sun here and there, East to West, North and South."[8]   Before the C.P.M. in 1652 Erbery placed a gloss of his own on the four beasts, making them correspond to the four different stages of the

---

1 The North Star, " Letter for Mr. William Erbery," p. 14.
2 Gwyddor Uchod, Vol. II, v. 21, p. 104 (1657).
3 Especially on the questions of ordinances, toleration, and church unity.
4 The Testimony : " To the Christian Reader " [9].   Summary of doctrines by
                                       J. W. (1658).
5   Ibid.   [8].
6 " Letter to Vavasor Powell " [Call to the Churches, p. 36 (= 41)].
7   Ibid.   p. 36 (misprint for 37).
8 An Olive-Leaf, p. 188.

" Ecclesiastical State '—Popery to the first, Prelacy to the second, Presbytery to the third, and by a convenient transference from Daniel vii to Revelations xiii, Independency and Anabaptism to the two horns of the second of the *two* beasts mentioned in verse 11 of the latter.[1]

It was only natural that the enthusiastic[2] belief in the imminent coming of Christ on the part of Llwyd and Powell would draw around them a considerable number of kindred spirits. There runs a strong undercurrent of this conviction in the phraseology of a letter, subscribed by Llwyd and four Commissioners, sent from the ' Church of Christ ' at Wrexham to the London congregations in 1651[3]; it runs much stronger in another letter, also signed by Llwyd and four Commissioners,[4] sent to Cromwell after the dissolution of the Rump, rejoicing that the Lord General was enabled so long to follow the swift pace of the Lambe who marcheth out of Edom in these our dayes "[5]; and the three representatives to serve ' on behalfe the Saints in North Wales,'[6] nominated as they were by Powell and Harrison[7] within two months of the expiry of the Act, were declared Fifth Monarchy men.[8]   Equally definite was the attitude of. Capt. John Williams, one of the members for South Wales.[9] Nor is it likely that the stubborn attachment to the same creed in following years on the part of a still wider circle was the sudden outgrowth of political opportunism. There is no mistaking the point of Hugh Courtney's adjuration to Daniel Lloyd to ' be patient until the end ' in December, 1653[10]; the tone of the same Millenarian's letters to Colonels John Jones and Thomas Mason about the same time indirectly prove that they, too, felt the ' shame and reproach ' that came upon the ' gospel and the possession thereof ' by

1 Testimony, p. 335.
2 Llwyd's Millenarian ideas had but imperceptibly waned during Propagation times.
3 Oct. 24th, 1651. Commissioners = Daniel Lloyd, John Browne, Edward Taylor, David Maurice.   [Gweithiau, Vol. II, " Llythyrau," pp. 247-250].
4 Edward Taylor, John Browne, Roger Sontley, Hugh Prichard.
5 Gweithiau Morgan Llwyd : Vol. II, " Llythyrau," XII, pp. 264-266 : the letter was entitled " a voice out of the hearts of diverse that *waite for the Lord Jesus in Denbighshire* in North Wales."
6 In the Little Parliament (July-Dec., 1653). Hugh Courtney, John Browne, Richard Price.
7 Simpkinson : Life of Harrison : Appendix, pp. 297-298—" Letter of M ajor-General Harrison to Col. Jones," May 17th, 1653.
8 Brown : Baptists and Fifth Monarchy Men, p. 33, n. 16.
9 Thurloe State Papers, Vol. II, p. 128.
10   Ibid.   Vol. I, p. 640, 20 Dec., 1653.

interrupting the activities of the Saints' Parliament[1] ; several
sanguine spirits in the course of 1654 ' taught strange things,'
especially that the worldly Cromwellian regime would be
of short duration[2] ; twelve people in the company of Vavasor
Powell and a sister of Morgan Llwyd, strong in the belief
that ' the Lord would soon appear,' were indicted
for seditious words before the Montgomeryshire Sessions
the same year[3] ; and it is evident from the terms of the
' Word for God ' in 1655 that 322 people in North and Mid-
Wales looked upon the supporters of the Protectorate as
much ' hinderers of the Lord Christ, his kingdom, and people '
as the ' late king or his party.'[4] James Quarrell and Charles
Lloyd cite the evidence of writers, both ancient and
modern, in support of the personal reign of Christ.[5]
Lastly, it is not improbable that the assured belief in April,
1660, of Rice Jones, the schoolmaster of Llanfair Caereinion,[6] in " the Lord doing great things in righteousness "
that very month was the survival of his association with
Vavasor Powell during the Propagation era.[7] How far the
erstwhile Approvers Richard Powell, who was ' repairing
and scouring his pistols' in February, 1654,[8] and Jenkin
Jones, who was bracketed with Vavasor Powell as enlisting
troops in March of the same year,[9] moved in sympathy with
outraged Millenarian sentiments as such, apart from conscientious objections to new State developments, the records
of the time afford no clue. Nor is there any surviving
evidence to prove how far John Lewis of Cardiganshire
advanced from his point of view in 1646, which was a cautious
denial of a ' temporall and personall reign of our Saviour
upon the earth,' but an ardent belief in the ' temporall '
fulfilling of the glorious descriptions of the Church in the
latter days given by the prophets.[10] Nor, notwithstanding
the romantic peculiarity of his name, is there any satisfactory
evidence to connect the Richard Goodgroome, who figures in
the Monmouthshire accounts for 1650-1651 as usher at

1 Thurloe State Papers, Vol. I, pp. 639-640.
2   Ibid.   Vol. II, pp. 129, 501.
3   Ibid.   p. 220.
4 Preamble, pp. 1-8 : Signatures, pp. 8-11.
5 Examen et Purgamen Vavasoris (1654), p. 18.
6 Infra., Chap. XV.
7 Calendar of State Papers : 1659-1660, p. 407.
8 Thurloe State Papers, Vol. II, p. 93.
9   Ibid.   Vol. II, p. 174.
10 Contemplations upon these Times : Part I, pp 17-18.

Usk,[1] with the Fifth Monarchist of the same name who was somewhat prominent in London about nine months before the King's restoration.[2]

1 Walk. c. 13, ff. 45b, 51.
2 Brown: Bapt. and Fifth Monarchy Men, pp. 185, 190, n. 44.

XIII.

CHURCH GOVERNMENT—CHURCH ORGANISATION.

The political character of the English Reformation produced a National Church with the King as Supreme Head ; the religious basis of the Puritan Revolution gave rise to 'gathered' churches, 'distinct Commonwealths redeemed from the world,'[1] congregations of believers owning direct allegiance only to Christ himself. Their members disregarded the arguments of those who emphasised apostolic succession and historic continuity ; they refused to follow the Presbyterians in finding precedents in ancient Jewish history for a covenant of God with a whole nation[2] ; and in opposition to Erbery and the Seekers they claimed Scriptural sanction for their 'congregational' way in the will of God as already revealed. But for them congregation implied segregation, both from a corrupt Church and from an earthly State, and also from the world in the wider sense of being 'the devil's street in which his coaches trundle.'[3] And though the practical benefits of the 'via media' and a lingering desire for church unity made one generation turn aside from the ideals of Browne and the Elizabethan Puritans to try the "New England way,"[4] the forced lines of demarcation drawn by the war and the clarifying effect of the Assembly debates drove advanced thinkers from halting compromises to crystallised opinions, from tentative measures to an assured polity. This polity is represented at one end by the 'Apologeticall Narration of the Five Dissenting Brethren,'[5] and at the other by the Savoy Declaration of 1658.[6] There was no church except where the faithful met[7] ; from the decision of an assembly in which Christ was present there could be no appeal[8] ; 'there was

1 Cradock : Divine Drops Distilled, p. 178.
2 Erbery's definition (The Sword Doubled, p. 12).
3 Erbery : The North Star : remark of Morgan Llwyd in a letter to him, p. 1.
4 Supra, Chap. II.
5 Jan., 1643-4.
6 Taken to represent Independent thought and practice [1645-1658].
7 Dale : History of English Congregationalism, p. 362.
8   Ibid.   p. 274.

no power over a power '[1] ; no person could be added to the church except with the consent of the church itself[2] ; Christ had furnished each particular church with officers having full power to administer ordinances and exercise and execute censures[3] ; these censures could only be applied to members of that particular church[4] ; and civil precincts were not to determine the boundaries of any congregation.[5] The Five Brethren admitted that there were times when such a company of men might be uncertain about the will of Christ, when it would be expedient to summon synods to obtain light and leading, and that it might be advisable on occasions to appeal to the learning of great theologians or to the counsel and judgment of living men. But in no circumstances were these external factors to be allowed to determine the doctrine of the individuals.[6] Equally emphatic is the Savoy Declaration on this basal question of independence. The synods were not instituted by Christ, were only resorted to for advice on matters of *difference,* and were not entrusted with any power or jurisdiction over the churches themselves to exercise any censures.[7] In other words, this system allowed neither a hierarchy of orders nor a hierarchy of assemblies. The freedom from outside ecclesiastical control made its critics apply to it the ' scurvie name,'[8] ' the reproachful term,'[9] the ' proud and insolent title '[10] of *Independency,* a term substituted by *Congregationalism* when reference was made to the manner in which every separate congregation claiming to be a Christian church ought to be organised.[11]

This was the ideal of church government brought back with the Welsh Puritans after their English sojourn, and adopted by the great majority of the Approvers and itinerants, who ' gathered ' their members sometimes within, and sometimes without, the parish churches.[12] Powell exulted that he had left ' Church-Society,'[13] and in his three

1 Remark of Philip Nye in the Assembly, Feb. 21st, 1643-4. Dale, p. 284.
2 Article XVII (Savoy). Dale, p. 387.
3 Articles XVI and XVIII (Savoy). Dale, p. 387.
4 Article XXII (Savoy). Dale, p. 387.
5 Article XXIII (Savoy).   ibid.
6 Dale : Hist. of English Cong., p. 274.
7 Articles XXVI and XXVII (Savoy). Dale, p. 389.
8 Cradock : Divine Drops Distilled, p. 91.
9 Henry Nicholls : The Shield Single, p. 17.
10 "Apologeticall Narration "—quoted in Dale, pp. 281-282.
11 Discussion of terms ' Independent ' and ' Congregational,' Dale, pp. 375-376.
12 Supra, pp. 167-169.
13 Spiritual Experiences, p. 83.

hours' debate at Newchapel endeavoured to prove from Old and New Testament texts[1] that the ' way of separation ' was most warrantable and nearest the word of God.[2] Henry Nicholls defended the ' gathering ' of churches against Erbery's ideal of spiritual isolation in almost the identical terms adopted a few years afterwards in Article III of the Savoy Declaration.[3] Llwyd in " 1648 " advised good men to ' associate in the way and bee listed in some regiment.'[4] References to the discipline and government of the new ' gathered ' churches in Wales are exceptionally few. Chance remarks of Erbery[5] and Llwyd[6] point to the fact that they covenanted to ' live as a holy society,' a practice defended by Browne[7] and Henry Jacob,[8] adopted by the latter when organising his Independent church at Southwark in 1616,[9] by John Robinson before he and his church left for Holland, by John Cotton in New England,[10] and by Hugh Peters during his stay in Rotterdam.[11] They had their *elders*, too, as witnessed by the two Commissioners and one itinerant who acted as such in Powell's Radnor congregation,[12] by the two elders of the ' professed church of Christ ' at Llanigon,[13] and the ' ruling elder ' of the church at Llanfaches, who enjoyed the title, but not the duties, of the corresponding officer in the Presbyterian system.[14] And the spiritual basis of the churches postulated a high standard of living among the members. New members had usually undergone a period of probation, ' sometimes a yeer or two ' according to Erbery[15]; Cradock drew a distinction between attendance at prayer of ' carnall ' men and their witnessing the administration of the Lord's Supper[16]; and to those who walked ' inordinately '

---

1 Numbers xvi, 24, 26 ; 1 Cor. v, 11 ; II Tim. iii, 5 (Animadversions [23-24]).
2 A Bold Challenge, p. [3].
3 The Shield Single, p. 66 ; Dale : Hist. of Cong., p. 386.
4 Gweithiau : Vol. I, Song viii, p. 29.
5 The Welsh Curate, p. 7 ; A Scourge for the Assyrian, p. 43.
6 Gweithiau, Vol. I, Song viii, v. 41, p. 29.
7 A True and Short Declaration [quoted by Winifred Cockshott : " The Pilgrim Fathers," p. 31.]
8 Burrage : The Early English Dissenters, p. 287, Vol. I.
9   Ibid.   p. 314, Vol. I [also Vol. II, Doc. XVIII, p. 294.]
10   Ibid.   p. 289, Vol. I.
11   Ibid.   pp. 301-303, Vol. I.
12 Examen et Purgamen : " To the Reader " [2].
      Comms. = John Williams, John Dancy.
      Itinerant = Morris Griffith (' Maurice ' in Walk. MSS.).
13 Joshua Thomas : Hanes y Bedyddwyr (Pont. Ed.), p. 138. [This church went over to the Close Baptists.]
14 Erbery : The Wretched People, p. 108.
15 The Welsh Curate, pp. 7-8.
16 Divine Drops Distilled, p. 149.

there was a delivery 'unto Satan,'[1] an extreme Puritan practice which was little to the liking of the tolerant spirit of Llwyd,[2] and which was discountenanced by Cradock in his later years.[3]   Henry Nicholls contrasts the 'rebukes, reproofs and censures' which obtain among his 'Church-fellowship' with the lax discipline of the Cavaliers.[4]   Powell is more explicit in recommending excommunication after the failure of due admonition and temporary suspension,[5] And no doubt the masterful character of some of the leading Puritans gave some colour to the charges of exercising ponti-fical authority over their charges which were levelled against them.   Dr. George Griffith compares Powell's methods to those of the Jesuits,[6] and Erbery has it that the saints in Wales were 'embondaged' to their pastors and teachers.[7] On another occasion, he accuses them of 'picking and choosing their members'[8] and of showing preference for the wealthy,[9] a practice all the more indefensible because he defines Independency as a 'pure Democracy.'[10]   The critic makes one notable exception.   He finds grounds for praising David Walter for his 'unsetledness and loofness of spirit from all church-forms,' and makes him come near his own ideal of 'waiting for a high Power and Spirit to appear in all the Saints.'[11]   Though there is no evidence that Walter became a convert to Erbery's gospel of the Third Dispensa-tion, yet his attitude of the open mind was quite consonant with one of the cardinal principles of Independency.   Jacob's church in 1616 covenanted to 'walk in all God's ways as he had revealed or should make known to them,'[12] and the authors of the "Narration" distinctly laid it down that their present judgment and practice were not to be a binding law for all time ; they cautiously allowed for religious pro-gression and new revelations.[13]   This point of view led directly to the wide religious toleration which found varied

1 Henry Nicholls : The Shield Single, p. 50 ; Cradock : Divine Drops, p. 126.
2 Gweithiau, Vol. I, " Llyfr y Tri Aderyn," p. 169.
3 The Broadmead Records (ed. Haycroft), p. 47 [1654].
4 The Shield Single, p. 27.
5 The Bird in the Cage : Epistle Dedicatory [9].
6 Animadversions, p. 18.
7 Apocrypha, p. 9.
8 The Idol Pastor, p. 90.
9 The Welsh Curate, p. 8.
10 A Scourge for the Assyrian, p. 24.
11 Call to the Churches, p. 46.
12 Burrage : The Early English Dissenters, p. 314.
13 Dale : Hist. of English Congregationalism, p. 280.

expression in the gathered churches of Wales. Powell's followers differed in ' opinion and Faith '[1] ;' Llwyd's members did not ' sup with Christ in ordinances all '[2] ; Baptists and Independents worshipped together at Llanfaches before they had to flee to Bristol[3] ; Cradock was alive to the danger of putting ' carnall faction ' before " spiritual communion,"[4] of making formal confessions and the ' conjunction of opinion in any controverted point ' the conditions of church member-ship[5] ; finally, though he made his private practice on the subject perfectly clear,[6] he paid a generous tribute to the ' pious people ' who practised baptism by immersion.[7] And this prime virtue of toleration found sympathetic surroundings . in the autonomousness of the Independent churches. " The generality of our churches," declares the Preface to the Savoy Declaration in a well-sustained nautical metaphor, " were like so many ships (though holding forth the same general colours) launcht singly, and sailed apart and alone in the vast Ocean of these tumultuating times," adding a frank admission of the inherent defect in Congre-gational ideals—" exposed to every wind of Doctrine . . . . without Association among ourselves, . or so much as holding out common lights to others, whereby to know where we were."[8] The idea of holding occasional synods was not developed ; both word and policy were repugnant to Cromwell[9] ; and Cradock followed Thomas Goodwin in preferring the ' fruitfulness and power ' of the English ideal to the. ' beauty ' of discipline and government which seemed the main characteristic of reformed churches abroad.[10] But in Wales the great activity of Cradock and the itinerants must have led to some cohesion among the ' gathered ' churches, and the modicum of truth contained in the terms

1 A Brief Narrative of the Former Propagation [preface to " Bird in the Cage," p. 8.]
2 Gweithiau, Vol. I, Song xlvii, v. 1, p. 89. April, 1652.
3 Broadmead Records (ed. Haycroft), p. 26.
4 Divine Drops Distilled, p. 27.
5 Saving Faith, p. 24.
6   Ibid.   p. 28 [marginal note.]
7 Gospel Libertie, p. 100.   But these various aspects of Cradock's tolerant mind can certainly not be adduced in favour of the idea that in his later years he became a quasi-Presbyterian and " a decided friend to monarchical government." (Morrice : Wales in the Seventeenth Century, p. 50). The best corrective of such a view is the 1662 report of the " petty constable " of *Llandenny* (Lamb. 1027, Report 23, 13 June, 1662).
8 Dale : Hist. of Congregationalism, p. 384i
9 Thurloe State Papers, Vol. II, p. 67.
10 Saving Faith, p. 32.

' bishop '[1] and ' metropolitan '[2] sarcastically applied to the more prominent of the ministers implied some departure from the strictest application of Independent principles. Llwyd and his people, in their letter from Wrexham to the London congregations, judge that the Lord had ordained one church to write to another " for their common profit," and wish that such a practice were more in use among the " assemblies of God."[3]   Harrison also suggests in a letter to Col. John Jones that Powell, Jenkin Jones, and Cradock, with some other ' bretheren,' should come up as ' messengers ' from their congregations to stir up the Laodicean Rump to proceed with measures for the more effective propagation of the gospel in England.[4]   But the idea of representation contained in the Major-General's letter was not adopted for purposes of conference or federation within the Principality until, three years after the expiry of the Act, Vavasor Powell organised a meeting at Llanbadarn, where 400 representatives from " seven or eight several counties " assembled.[5] And even that assembly was summoned more for political purposes than religious.[6]

Had the rigid Presbyterian ideal designed for Southern Britain by the majority of the divines in the Westminster Assembly under the guidance of Scottish Commissioners been adopted in Wales it would present a striking contrast to the loosely-knit Independent system. And for the space of five years affairs seemed to point to such a consummation. " The breath of the Scottish army " during 1643-4 " blew great strength and favour " upon the arguments of the divines[7] ; the examining committee of the Assembly laid especial stress on all candidates being ' presbyters '[8] ; all approved ministers between 1643 and 1648 had to take the Covenant, whereby they were to further the development of religion in doctrine, worship, and government according

1 Supra, p. 152.
2 Supra, p. 146.
3 Gweithiau, Vol. II, " Llythyrau," IV, p. 249.
4 Simpkinson :   Life of Harrison :   Appendix, " Thirteenth Letter," p. 294, [Nov. 7th, 1652] ; also " Sixteenth Letter," pp. 295-296 [Nov. 30th, 1652].
5 Thurloe State Papers, Vol. V, p. 112 [information sent from Gogert*h*an, 12 June, 1656].
6   Ibid.   —" countenanced by magistrates, dissenters of the present government."
7 Shaw :   Hist. of the English Church during the Civil War, Vol. I, p. 164 [quoting remark of Robert Baillie :   Letters, Vol. II, p. 120].
8 Mitchell and Struthers :   Minutes of the Westminster Assembly, p. 324, Session 785, Feb. 4th, 1646-7.

to the word of God and the example of the best reformed churches,[1] which was only another way of expressing the Scottish ideals; in June, 1646, Parliament decided on the adoption of modified Presbyterianism, and the Second Classis in Salop included parishes in the Oswestry district right on the Welsh border, of which Rowland Nevett and Oliver Thomas were " deemed to be fit ministers "[2]; and on May 1, 1648, during the second Civil War, an Ordinance against Blasphemies and Heresies was passed, which would rivet the chains of a new uniformity as firmly as the old was in the days of Laud.[3] The Presbyterian solution commended itself to many moderate men.[4] It would afford a refuge from sectarian chaos and absorb into a new national church satisfactory members of the old order on comparatively easy terms. Henderson and the other divines from Scotland stated their case with considerable ability, and dwelt much on the propriety of bringing English church-government into consonance with the practice of the Protestant churches on the Continent. But a system born of political exigency and alien to the instincts of insurgent Puritanism could have no permanent lodgment, and the Army completed what the Erastians had begun. Even during the days of its supremacy, the application of the unqualified Presbyterian polity was found impossible in practice. Especially was this true in the case of Wales. The itinerant system introduced there by the Parliament in 1645-6 was no part of Presbyterianism, and the itinerant ministers themselves were openly hostile to it. Cradock, after ' wishing Heaven that he might go over the line '[5] from the ' Jesuiticall designs '[6] of the Assembly, eventually did so without its certificate,[7] and Vavasor Powell, after an argument with Stephen Marshall about ordination, obtained a certificate subscribed by three of the Dissenting Brethren.[8]

---

1 W. M. Hetherington : Hist. of the Westminster Assembly, p. 129, quoting Clause I of the Covenant.
2 Shaw : Hist. of the English Church, Vol. II, App. IIIb, p. 408.
3 Dale : Hist. of English Cong., p. 309.
4 Even Milton in 1641 was an enthusiastic upholder of a Presbyterianism approximating to the Scottish model, in order that England should ' come from Schisme to unity with our neighbor Reformed sister Churches ' (Of Reformation Touching Church-Discipline in England, ed. Hale, pp. 59-72).
5 Divine Drops Distilled, p. 229.
6   Ibid.   p. 52.
7 Supra, p. 46.
8 Life, pp. 15-16. [The remark of J. R. Phillips that Powell was a " *Presbyterian* minister " has no foundation whatsoever. (Hist. of the Civil War in Wales, Vol. II, Doc. CXI, p. 374)].

But neither the taking of the Covenant nor the imprimatur
of the Assembly could make a people Presbyterian who had
no Presbyterian traditions. Llwyd's references to ' entrapping oaths,'[1] ' mascked Popes,'[2] and ' Scottish hippocrits '[3]
represent the attitude of a Puritanism which found its
Elizabethan exemplar in John Penry and not in Thomas
Cartwright. No classical machinery was set up in Wales
under the ordinance of 1646 ; there is no mention of a
" voluntary association " (which took its place in several
English counties) until in 1658 Philip Henry set up such an
arrangement for the county of Flint[4] ; nor can it be definitely
predicated that there was a single Presbyterian minister
of the orthodox type during our period in Wales. Rowland
Nevett, the erstwhile member of the Salop Second Classis,
is found prompting Vavasor Powell to utter separationist
sentiments at Newchapel,[5] and an impartial moderator for
the same dispute has to be sought in the Presbyterian Samuel
Hildersham of West Felton,[6] who lived across the Border.
Ambrose Mostyn is sometimes classed as a Presbyterian,[7]
but this is discounted by the fact that he organised the
first ' gathered ' church at Swansea,[8] had ideas about the
subjects of baptism that were not Presbyterian,[9] and followed
Morgan Llwyd in the pastorate of the ' gathered ' church
at Wrexham.[10] It is sometimes stated that the Wrexham
district was at this time a stronghold of Presbyterians,[11]
for which, however, there is no contemporary confirmation.
Llwyd is silent about local followers of that persuasion ;
" A New Ballad of the Plague " affords no light on the
question ; no Commissioners hailing from the district come
under that category ; and no minister of Wrexham or its
neighbourhood are found attending either the North Shrop-

1 Gweithiau, Vol. I, Song i, v. 10, p. 5.
2   Ibid.   Song vi, v. 10, p. 16.
3   Ibid.   Song xxiv, v. 12, p. 50—" The English Triumph over
Scottish Traitors."
4 Account of the Life and Death of Mr. Philip Henry (1698), pp. 59-61.
5 Animadversions, pp. 13-15.
6 Animadversions, p. 6 ; probably he was one of ' our honored.neighbours of the
Presbytery ' referred to in the ' Examen ' (p. 41).
7 Mr. J. H. Davies is inclined to this view [Gweithiau Morgan Llwyd, Vol. II,
Introd. li.]
8 The Broadmead Records (ed. Underhill).—Letter of Henry Maurice (1675),
p. 514.
9 The Diaries and Letters of Philip Henry (ed. Matthew Henry Lee), p. 42.
10 Lamb. MS. 987, ff. 200-201.
11 A. N. Palmer: Hist. of the Older Nonconformity of Wrexham, p. 34. [circa 1651];
J. Spinther James : Hanes y Bedyddwyr, Vol. II, p. 348.

shire Classis in 1647,[1] or the Voluntary Association formed in Cheshire in 1653,[2] or the nearest highly organised classis, that of Manchester.[3] It cannot be said that Presbyterianism was a living force in the religious life of north eastern Wales until the advent of Philip Henry to Worthenbury in September, 1653,[4] and his visits to Wrexham most probably account for the presence of Presbyterians there in March, 1655.[5] Erbery and Nicholls, who between them pass in review all the religious forces at work in *South* Wales, give no room to Presbyterians; and Henry Maurice, in his letter to Edward Terrill of Broadmead discussing the rise and fortunes of Nonconformist churches in Wales up to 1675, does not assign a Presbyterian origin in a single instance.[6] This absence of Presbyterian sentiment is also witnessed by the attitude of representative laymen. John Lewis recommends the taking of the Covenant to his countrymen by the diplomatic statement that 'it propounds no church as a pattern but only the Word of God'[7]; two members of the Long Parliament associated with Wales, Recorder Glynne and Sir William Lewis of Brecon, were 'charged and impeached' by the Army in 1647 not because of Presbyterian leanings, but because they were members of a committee of the Commons which had shewn undue leniency to delinquents in Wales[8]; Sir Thomas Middleton of Chirk was a type of Puritan who was no Episcopalian and had no love for the sects, but his desire to restore the Kingship in 1651 arose from political grounds only[9]; and the fact that Col. Thos. Mytton of Halston was deemed fit to be of the Second Salop Classis in 1647 did not thereby make him a Presbyterian.[10] As far as surviving evidence goes, the same conclusion is true of his fellow-members of the Classis— Leighton Owen and Thomas Baker of Swinney[11]—and also

1 Shaw: Hist. of the English Church during the Civil War and the Commonwealth, Vol. II, Appendix IIIb, pp. 406-412.
2   Ibid.   Appendix IIIc, pp. 441-443; Urwick: Hist. Sketches of Nonconformity in Cheshire, Introd. XXXII-XXXIII.
3 Chetham Society Publications: New Series, Vols. 20, 22, 24.
4 Diaries and Letters, p. 15.
5 Thurloe State Papers, Vol. III, p. 214.
6 The Broadmead Records (ed. Underhill), Addenda B, pp. 511-519.
7 Contemplations upon these Times, Part II, p. 26.
8 A Particular Charge or Impeachment in the Name of His Excellency Sir Thomas Fairfax And the Army under his Command. 1647. (N.L.W.).
9 Calendar of State Papers, 1651, pp. 200, 201, 204, and especially p. 337—" Letter of Charles II to Sir Thos. Middleton," Aug. 17th, from *Stoke*.
10 D.N.B., Vol. XL, pp. 16-17. Article by C. H. Firth.
11 Shaw: Hist. of the English Church, Vol. II, App. IIIb, p. 408.

of Humphrey Mackworth of the First Classis,[3] all three
Commissioners under the Act.

The nearest approach to Presbyterianism in Wales was
the close organisation of the Particular Baptists in the
South under the leadership of John Miles. After a fortnight's
visit in the spring of 1649 to the London church which met
at the Glass House in Broad Street, when he was baptised
by immersion and had an opportunity to study at first
hand the faith and practice of the churches in which William
Kiffin, William Consett, Edward Heath, and Hanserd Knollys
were the chief lights, he returned to Gower to found the
Baptist church at *Ilston* ' according to the primitive pattern.'[4]
After the first baptisms there on October 1st, 1649, the new
gospel soon spread. Before January 12th, 1650, another
Baptist church had been ' gathered ' at Llanharan as a
suitable centre for those baptised at Gelligaer and St. Brides[5] ;
in the early days of February in the same year a Baptist cause
was started at the Hay in Breconshire[6] as a convenient
meeting-place for the converted Independents of Llanigon
and the Baptists who had for some years foregathered on
the other side of the mountains at Olchon in Herefordshire[7];
on January 22nd, 1651, a church was ' settled ' at Carmarthen
and another at Abergavenny previous to July in the same
year.[8] The Ilston Records bear ample witness to the
organising genius of Miles, especially in his prompt arrangements for the more effective supervision and convenience
of members scattered over a wide area. In October, 1650,
it was decided in a special church meeting that there should
be ' breaking of bread ' at Ilston on one Sunday every three
weeks for *all* the members, but that those who lived in West
Gower should meet on the other two Sundays at Llanddewi,
those in the neighbourhood of Ilston at Ilston, and those in
the adjacent " Welsh districts " of Carmarthen at the house
of Jane Jones near Llanelly. To inquire into the spiritual
welfare of the members week meetings were arranged—in

1 Shaw: Hist. of the English Church, Vol. II, App. IIIb, p. 407.
4 Joshua Thomas : Hanes y Bedyddwyr (Pont. Ed.), p. 76; J. Spinther James:
Hanes y Bedyddwyr, Vol. II, p. 280. [Letter of J. Colman, Barnstaple, to Miles,
May 9th, 1650].
5 Trafodion Cymdeithas Hanes Bedyddwyr Cymru, 1910-1911, Edited by
Thos. Shankland, ["John Myles "], p. 13.
6 Ibid.
7 The researches of Baptist historians have hitherto failed to give a satisfactory
account of the origin of this church.
8 Trafodion, p. 14.

the Welsh districts on Tuesday, at Ilston on Wednesday,
and at Llanddewi on Thursday; but church censures could
only be exercised at Ilston on Wednesday morning once
every three weeks.[1] In February, 1651, it was found
necessary to meet the convenience of Ilston members who
lived as far east as the Aberavon district : the ordinance
of baptism might be performed there, but members could be
received into full communion at Ilston itself only.[2] Later,
on April 2nd, 1651, it was decided that the Lord's Supper
should be celebrated once a quarter at Baglan or Aberavon,
that the members in those districts should partake of it at
Ilston once a quarter, and that two or more members should
attend the mother church every communion Sunday to give
a full account of the state of the good cause.[3] Similar
arrangements were made at the equally scattered church of
Abergavenny. The sacrament was to be administered there
on the first Sunday in each month ; for the convenience of
those members who lived about five miles to the north at
Llanfihangel Crucorney, service was held at the house of one
of the brethren the next Sunday after ; a general church
meeting of all the members was to be at Llanwenarth, about
two miles to the north-west, the first Thursday after communion ; and at the mother church all remaining Thursdays.
For those members who lived 14 miles to the south-east at Llangibby, a meeting was to be held every Sunday, when services
would be conducted by men duly sent from Abergavenny ;
bread would be broken once every three months ; and there
was to be a weekly church meeting every Wednesday.[4]
These local arrangements were controlled and to some extent
supplemented by the *General Meeting* of representatives
which had also the difficult task, especially so in the case of
a newly-constituted body, of arranging for ministerial supplies
and maintenance. The *first* of these was held at *Ilston* on
6th and 7th November, 1650,[5] when it was arranged that
David Davies, the new accession from Gelligaer, should
preach at Carmarthen on two Sundays every two months,
and John Miles on one. Walter Prosser, once Independent

---

1 Joshua Thomas : Hanes y Bedyddwyr, p. 80.
2   Ibid.   p. 85.
3   Ibid.   p. 86.
4 Joshua Thomas : Hanes y Bedyddwyr, pp. 209-210.
5   Ibid.   p. 81 ; Trafodion, p. 14.

elder at Llanigon, was also to visit Carmarthen once in two months. Davies was asked to minister at Llanharan as often as he could ; during his absence at Carmarthen, some brother from the Hay was expected to fill his place. At the same meeting the responsibility of each member to contribute to the support of the ministers was made clear, and £10 was specified as due from each church.[1] Of this £30,[2] £25 was to be paid to Walter Prosser, for the reason that Miles, his assistant Thomas Proud, and David Davies were already in receipt of stipends under the Act of Propagation.[3] Still more complex arrangements were made at the *second General Meeting* held at *Carmarthen* on 19th March, 1651. To supply the church at that place Prosser was to officiate three Sundays out of every eight, Davies two, and Miles one, no minister appearing there on the remaining two Sundays. Prosser's absence from the Hay was to be made good by Miles on one Sunday and by Davies on the other, on the condition that the latter was to be substituted at Llanharan by some responsible brother from the Breconshire church. And that the church at Llanharan should not be incommoded by Davies's absence in Carmarthen, his place was to be filled on one Sunday by Miles and on the other by Prosser. Details as regards time were matters of mutual arrangement among the ministers.[4] These provisions proved unsatisfactory, for at the *third General Meeting* held at *Abergavenny* on 14th and 15th July of the same year,[5] it was agreed that William Thomas, who a month before had been recommended to ' prophesy before the world ' by the church at Ilston, should for the following six months spend one week out of every three at Carmarthen and receive £10 for his services. At the same meeting the church of the Hay was asked to support Abergavenny in maintaining William Prichard, " who was shortly to be sent forth " as a recognised minister.[6] No general meetings during 1652 or early 1653 are recorded. Meanwhile difficulties other than administrative had come to confront the new organisation. Thomas Proud was

---

1 Joshua Thomas : Hanes y Bedyddwyr, p. 82.
2 Three churches were to contribute—Ilston, the Hay, Llanharan.
3 Walk{e}r c. 13, ff. 15-32.
4 Joshua Thomas : Hanes y Bedyddwyr, pp. 85-86.
5 Trafodion, p. 14.
6 Joshua Thomas : Hist. of the Baptist Association in Wales from 1650 to 17 (1795), p. 9.

dismissed from membership at Ilston during 14 weeks in 1651 for advocating mixed communion[1]; difficulties over the same subject troubled the church at Abergavenny[2]; some disorderly persons sought to rend the church at Hay, ' setting up as a distinct society, and practising in private such ordinances as are proper to the Church of Christ '[3]; the laxity of discipline at Llantrisant[4] and the somewhat tactless methods of David Davies[5] were creating a situation there which was to demand the full diplomatic energies of the general meeting at Abergavenny in 1654[6]; and there were controversies already about the singing of psalms, imposition of hands,[7] the keeping of fast days, and the number of officers and their respective duties,[8] which were not thoroughly settled at the end of the 'time of liberty.' The Baptist churches had to run the gauntlet of the unsympathetic attitude of Vavasor Powell, whose sphere of activity included Llanigon, and who preached in 1650 that it was both ' unreasonable ' and ' abusive ' to urge baptism as necessary to salvation.[9] Erbery was also hostile. He would have it that ' only the weakest of Christians fell into the waters '[10] (in other passages that ' believers should go down to the ankles ' only),[11] that they were uncharitable and narrow-minded,[12] that they were inconsistent in not obeying literally all the commands of Christ,[13] and that practical considerations precluded the words of Matthew iii, 5,6 and of Acts ii, 38,41 bearing any interpretation favourable to Baptist practice[14] Nor, naturally, could he show any sympathy with people who were " calmly dipping in the waters of Babylon, while the scattered saints were sitting down and weeping by them."[15] But amidst these diverse distractions there were powerful

1 Joshua Thomas : Hanes y Bedyddwyr, p. 87.
2 Spinther James · Hanes, Vol. II, pp. 300-301 [Letter from Ilston to .Abergavenny on the subject given in full.]
3 Joshua Thomas · Hist of the Baptist Association, p. 9.
4 This was the church that formerly met at *Llanharan.*
5 Joshua Thomas : Hanes y Bedyddwyr, pp. 170-171 ; four resolutions decided on in the case : Hist. of the Baptist Association, p. 12.
6 Ibid.
7 These two questions were brought up at the Carmarthen meeting in 1651, but were referred to the consideration of the churches. (Hist. of the Baptist Association. p. 7.)
8 Both questions discussed at Llantrisant, Aug. 30 and 31, 1654.
9 Christ and Moses Excellency, p. 49.
10 Apocrypha, p. 8.
11 Call to the Churches, p. 17 : Testimony, p. 329.
12   Ibid.   p. 12.
13   Ibid.   p. 13.   He mentions more especially the holy kiss and the feasts of love.
14 Testimony, p. 329.
15 Call to the Churches, p. 17.

influences making for solidarity. There were frequent and encouraging letters sent from church to church[1]; the mission of Hanserd Knollys to Radnor and Brecon must have neutralised to a great extent the opposition of Powell ; and, most significant of all, there was the unremitting solicitude for the spiritual welfare of the churches displayed by their fount and source at the Glass House. The records of the time contain letters sent by the latter to each of the churches and others addressed in a general way to the ' churches of Christ.' One letter, possibly referring to Erbery and his teaching, warns them not to be deceived by the high pretences and pious masquerade of vain Christians[2] ; another by propounding a series of rhetorical questions enjoins them to maintain more firmly than ever the ' closeness ' of their exclusionist communion[3]; and a third gives the wholesome advice not to multiply churches unless they were able to man them with efficient pastors.[4] Through the London connection, again, the Baptists of Wales were kept in contact with the advanced ideals of other settlements of the sect lying further afield. It was by the desire of the Baptist churches in *Ireland*, whose most prominent member was Thomas Patient,[5] that the church of Abergavenny[6] observed the first Wednesday in each month as a day of fasting and of prayer for a further manifestation of the favour of God ; it was by the inspiration of the same body that a letter was sent from the London churches to Wales asking for " full knowledge of all those that are one with us in the sound principles of truth "[7]; and when there was a question of discontinuing the appointed fast days in 1654, the General Meeting at Llantrisant decided otherwise in pursuance of an agreement to observe the same not only among the churches of England and Wales, but among those of Scotland and Ireland also.[8] Yet, notwithstanding these uniforming influences and the visit paid by John Miles to London in

1 Joshua Thomas : Hanes, pp. 89, 138-139, 168-169.
2 Ibid., pp. 83-84 [1651].
3 Ibid., p. 84 [1651].
4 Joshua Thomas · Hist. of the Baptist Association, pp. 7-8 ; Trafodion. p. 15.
5 Referred to as ' Mr. Patience ' in Col. John Jones' Letter from Dublin (15 Sept., 1652). Gweithiau Morgan Llwyd, Vol. II, pp. 300-301.
6 Joshua Thomas : Hanes, p. 210. Most probably the day was thus observed in *all* the churches, but specific evidence is wanting.
7 Joshua Thomas : Hist. of the Baptist Association, Appendix, p. 20 [24 July, 1653].
8 Joshua Thomas : Hist. of the Baptist Association, pp. 11-12.

1651,[1] Baptist polity in Wales persisted in adaptation to its own environment. Miles and his fellow-ministers inverted the teaching of II Cor. i, 24 affirmed in the 1644 Confession of Faith at the end of Article LII[2] ; by the large jurisdiction of the General Meeting they developed a keener supervision over individual churches and a freer exercise of church censures than was warranted by Article XLVII in the four London Confessions[3]; and the definition of the duties of church officers given at Llantrisant in 1654[4] and the importance attached by Miles to the eldership in the 'Antidote' of 1656[5] show closer affinity with the ideas of the Assembly divines[6] than with the standards of the seven London churches or the Savoy Declaration of the Independents. It is probable that their defence for such a bold development would be that only by the adoption of such a quasi-Presbyterian system could a community, whose tenets were peculiarly liable to perversion and who were bordered on all sides but one by other Baptists of laxer views and more attractive discipline, be kept free from the plethora of heresies and consequent danger of disintegration which to them deprived the Independent toleration of all its virtues. Such a system was not likely to be popular, but the ' close ' Baptists made up for narrowness of number by intensity of conviction, exemplified in the later careers of young men who were grounded in their doctrines during the first years of the Republic. Most notable were William Prichard, who became associated with the church of Llanwenarth through the years of persecution[7] up to his death in 1713[8]; Lewis Thomas[9] and Morgan Jones,[10] upon whom devolved the supervision of the cause in the Swansea district after the departure of Miles to America ; Howell Thomas[11] and Thomas Joseph,[12] who

1 Trafodion, p. 14.
2 McGlothlin : Baptist Confessions of Faith, p. 189.
3   Ibid.   pp. 175-198 ; Crosby : Hist. of the English Baptists, Vol. I, App. II. p. 23 (1646).
4 Joshua Thomas : Hist. of the Baptist Association, pp. 12-14.
5 p. 23, II Section. " Admonitions to Saints."
6 Shaw : Hist. of the English Church during the Civil War, Vol. I, p. 161.
7 State Papers Dom., Car. II, 38 A, p. 232, Licence issued under Declaration of Indulgence on Aug. 10th, 1672.
8 J. Spinther James : Ḥanes y Bedyddwyr, Vol. II, p. 480.
9 Lamb. (Codices Tenisoniani), Vol. 639, f. 187b—taught conventicle at Newton Nottage ; S. P. Dom., Car. II, 38A, p. 251, Licence issued to preach at Swansea, Sept. 30th, 1672.
10 Joshua Thomas : Hanes, pp. 311-312; Spinther James, Hanes, Vol. II, pp. 461-3.
11 Calamy : An Account of the Ministers . . . (1713), II, p. 732, ejected (1660) from Glyncorrwg, (but preaches at *Newton Nottage* in 1672—S. P. Dom, 38A, p. 188).
12 Calamy : Account, Vol. II, p. 732 ; S. P. Dom., Car. II, 38A, p. 188, Licence to preach at *Bridgend*.

preached the doctrine of believers' immersion in the Afan
and Ogmore valleys respectively; and William Jones of
Cilmaenllwyd,[1] to whose energies later Baptist causes in the
three south-western counties trace their beginnings.
Different views about admission to the Lord's Supper
on the one hand and Arminian tendencies on the other kept
various bodies of Baptists in Wales outside the pale of Miles's
organisation. First came Jenkin Jones, a Catabaptist,[2]
a term used to describe those who 'dyd speake and hold
oppynyon agaynst the baptisme of children.'[3] He was
Congregational in church-government, practised *free communion*,[4] and in 1650 tried to dissuade the Independents
of Llanigon from going over to the 'close' Baptists.[5]
Another body of Baptists, with William Thomas as pastor,
had taken 'deep root'[6] at Llangwm and Llantrisant in
Monmouthshire. At a time when 'there was no talk of
ordinances,'[7] they had been used to worship with the other
Puritans of Llanfaches, but came back as a separate body
from the Bristol and London exile to be 'in judgment for
free communion with saints as saints.'[8] Very probably,
William Milman, the schoolmaster of Magor,[9] dubbed a
'Sabbatharian Anabaptist,'[10] threw in his lot with them.[11]
Further north came the isolated case of John Abbot of
Abergavenny, who is distinctly stated to have been 'dipped'
before September, 1653,[12] but probably, like his friend John
Tombes,[13] he subscribed to the whole doctrine 'set forth
by the State' except on the one point of the proper *subjects*
of baptism.[14] The Arminian Baptists counted adherents

1 Joshua Thomas: Hanes y Bedyddwyr, esp. pp. 318-321 and passim. Probably he ought not to be included here, as there is not sufficient evidence that he
was a Baptist before the Restoration.
2 Calamy: Account, Vol. II, p. 732.
3 This is a sixteenth century definition given by John Veron in "An Holsome
Antidotus . . . agaynst the pestylent heresye of the Anabaptists" (1548) [quoted
in Burrage: Early English Dissenters, Vol. I, p. 56.]
4 The Broadmead Records (ed. Underhill), p. 513—Letter of Henry Maurice (1675).
5 Joshua Thomas: Hanes y Bedyddwyr, p. 138.
6 Edward Dafydd of Margam: Cerdd i'r Fanaticiaid—Reprint in 'Seren Gomer,'
July, 1902, p. 170—" yn fonog yn Sir Fyno."
7 Erbery: Apocrypha, p. 9. [This statement is probably extravagant, as E.'s
point in the context is to show the utter uselessness of all ordinances.]
8 The Broadmead Records (ed. Underhill), pp. 515-516.
9 Infra, p. 229.
10 So described in Lamb. Codices, Vol. 639, f. 186b—returns of conventicles.
11 Named in association with William Thomas at Llangwm in 1669 (Vol. 639,
f. 188b).
12 John Cragge: Arraignment and Conviction of Anabaptism (1656), p. 29.
[Account of the Abergavenny Dispute.]
13 D.N.B., Vol. XIX, pp. 929-930.
14 Joshua Thomas: Hanes y Bedyddwyr, p. 211, says definitely that Abbot
favoured *free communion*.

in Radnor, Brecon, and South Montgomery, looked to the General Baptist church at Coventry as their original and to Jeremy Ives, one, of the most noted champions of adult baptism in his generation, as their first 'gatherer.' They were quite as strict as regards communion as the Particular Baptists, but had a much looser organisation. Their contemporary Confession of Faith[1] merely enumerates church officers, enjoins 'the laying on of hands for the Ordaining of Servants and Officers to attend about the Service of God '[2] and devotes especial attention to the needs of the poor[3]; it was only when the individual churches. were unable to cope with this duty or when particularly serious disputes arose within them that they were to seek the counsel of ' some other society.'[4] Nor does the Confession of 1651 give any intimation of anointing the sick with oil, washing the feet of the saints, abstaining from the ' eating of blood,' solemnisation of marriages among themselves, or of the censorious ' messenger ' who went from church to church, which their most reliable historian specifies as some of their later characteristics.[5] Their outstanding leader in Wales at this period was Hugh Evans of Llanhir, for some time an itinerant under the Act of Propagation,[6] who, after spending some time as clothier's apprentice in Worcester, moved to Coventry, joined the church there, and understanding that ' his native country of Wales did not receive the proper ministration of the ordinance of Jesus Christ,' returned thither about 1646, accompanied by Ives, who stayed for some time.[7] With him were associated Daniel Penry, Rees Davies, Evan Oliver, and John Prosser ; also John Price of Maes-y-gelli near Nantmel, and William Bound of Garthfawr near Llandinam, from whose joint pamphlet[8] defending the memory of Hugh Evans against the calumnies of the Quakers is principally derived what

---

1 The Faith and Practice of Thirty Congregations (Midlands), 1651—McGlothlin : Baptist Confessions of Faith, pp. 95-109. [. . . . address to all the Saints and Churches of God who walk according to the commands of Jesus Christ in England, *Wales,* Army, or elsewhere, p. 96.]
2 McGlothlin : Confessions, Art. 73, p. 108.
3   Ibid.   Art. 65, p. 106.
4   Ibid.   Art. 70, p. 107.
5 Taylor : Hist. of the General Baptists, pp. 413-414, 449-455.
6 Supra ; p. 149.
7 The Sun Outshining the Moon, p. 9. B. Mus. [Thomason] ; The Broadmead Records (ed. Underhill), p. 518—Letter of Henry Maurice (1675).
8 " The Sun Outshining the Moon " (1657). Evans died in 1656. John *Moon* was the Quaker critic.

P

little facts there are known of the beginnings of the General
Baptist persuasion in Wales.

And even this latter body did not exhaust the divergencies
of opinion among the Baptists of Wales. In 1650, both in
London and on the Brecon highlands, Vavasor Powell was
avowedly hostile to the Baptist creed[1]; in 1652 he was more
than sympathetic, since in May of that year Alexander
Griffith was ready in a public debate to defend against him,
and as the first thesis to be discussed, "the Necessity of
Baptism, and the lawfulnesse of Pædobaptism."[2] Some
time in the fall of 1655 he was 'rebaptized,'[3] and he who
in the London of the Civil War stated that "outward
partaking of Ordinances is one of the least things in
Religion"[4] advocated in the London of 1661, the using of
the same 'carefully and conscientiously.'[5]   But all this
notwithstanding, Powell's practice differed widely from the
'particularist' standpoint of Miles: even in 1661 he gives
no distinctive prominence to the ordinance of baptism[6];
and during a somewhat mysterious visit in the summer of
1669 he resorts, not to the company of the strict Baptists of
Glamorgan and Monmouth, but to Llanfyllin[7] in Montgomery,
to be the coadjutor of John Evans of Oswestry, one of the
most prominent Independents of the second Puritan generation. Evidently, as Crosby puts it, Powell and the followers
who adhered to him, refused to make adult immersive baptism
' the boundary of their communion.'[8] It is quite consonant
with this dictum that George Griffiths ' minister of the
Gospel at the Charterhouse ' should in 1658 send an invitation
to Powell to attend the Savoy Conference of the Independents, and that he should express himself ' free and desirous
to come,' provided the Assembly did not go upon " political
and worldly accounts."[9]

1 p. 205 supra.
2 The Petition of the Six Counties of South Wales (' For Mr. Valvasor Powell '),
p. 19 (misprint for 21).
3 Thurloe State Papers, Vol. IV, p. 373.
4 Spiritual Experiences, pp. 62, 63, 134.
5 Bird in the Cage . . . Epistle Ded., p. 3.
6 Ibid.
7 Lamb. Cod. Ten., Vol. 639, f. 139b.
8 Hist. of the English Baptists, Vol. I, p. 378.
9 Peck: Desiderata Curiosa (1779), Lib. X, No. XXV, pp. 507-508.

APPENDIX.

(A) *Llanover MS. c. 4, ff. 281-282.*

[" Cân i Ladron Morganwg.''']

Hardly anything is known of the activities of Miles between his departure from Oxford and the visit to the Glass House in 1649. But in the above MS., a Welsh song of poor quality alleged to be the work of Jenkin Richards, the Cavalier poet of Blaenau Gwent, the Baptist crusade was in full fervour as early as 1646. Miles, David Davies, and other members of the Ilston school are mentioned amongst those who are desirous of ' sending us to have a thorough dip in a river ' (stanza 20). The song, however, is full of inaccuracies :· Erbery was no longer a Cardiff ' offeiriad ' (st. 5) ; certain lines (st. 19) imply that Cradock and the Independents were opposed to all sorts of baptism ; and the epithet ' penwan ' (st. 13) describes Miles much less accurately than the ' pe(n)gam ' of Edward Dafydd in ' Cerdd y Fanaticiaid.' Yet the ' englyn ' which concludes the thirty-eight stanzas unmistakably states that Richards composed the work in the summer of 1646. But the reminiscence of Edward Dafydd in the first line of the ' englyn ' (cp. Llanover MS. c. 31, No. 23), the haphazard location of the song in the MS., the notorious inaccuracy of Iolo Morganwg in copying and collating, and the practical certainty that the stanzas refer to a state of affairs *after* 1650, force the conclusion that the ' englyn ' is divorced from its proper context. Miles's words are so explicit that he was the '' first in these parts to preach the glorious ordinance of baptism '' in the spring of 1649, that they must be controverted by stronger evidence than the vague and inexact lines of the bard of Gwent.

(B) *The Particular Baptists in Wales : Sources of their History.*

    (i) Joshua Thomas : Hanes y Bedyddwyr Ymhlith y Cymry o Amser yr Apostolion hyd y flwyddyn hon [1778.]

In the composition of this work he depended mostly on

    (a) old traditions gleaned in the Olchon district ;

    (b) manuscript records of some of the oldest Baptist churches, especially Abergavenny.

(ii) Joshua Thomas : A History of the Baptist Association in Wales From the year 1650 to the year 1790 [1795]. Here he is able to correct and supplement (i) by the Records of the church of Ilston (October 1st, 1649—August 12th, 1660) taken to America by John Miles. Extracts from these were made by Dr. Isaac Backus, the historian of New England, and sent to Joshua Thomas in 1792.

(iii) Joshua Thomas : Hanes y Bedyddwyr (1885), edited by the Rev. Benjamin Davies, Pontypridd, which is a translation of the manuscript " Materials towards the History of the Baptists in Wales " at which Thomas was busy during the year of his death (1797). These ' materials,' which make fuller use of the Ilston " Extracts " than was called for by the circumscribed character of (ii), are kept in the library of the Bristol Baptist College.

(iv) J. Spinther James : Hanes y Bedyddwyr, Vol. II, chap. III. [1899].

(v) Thomas Shankland : Articles in review of " Diwygwyr Cymru " (Beriah Evans) in " Seren Gomer " (1900—1902).

(vi) Thomas Shankland : Article on " John Myles " in " Trafodion Cymdeithas Hanes Bedyddwyr Cymru, 1910–1911." (iv), (v) and (vi), were able to make use of photographic reproductions of the " Ilston Records."

XIV.

LIMITATIONS—ABIDING EFFECTS.

This diversity of church organisation distracted men accustomed to uniformity, and the vagaries of doctrine bewildered a country-side unequipped for their assimilation by the discriminating power of education. Even the cultured[1a] Henry Nicholls could not understand the ' Delphick riddles '[1] of Erbery, his ' quirks and quillets worthy of the old Popish schoolmen,'[2] which were ' so many arrows shot over the heads of his hearers.'[3] At the end of eighty-seven verses sung in 1648 and transfused with his mystical-millenarian ideas, Llwyd has a fear of his reader getting ' tyred,'[4] advises him in 1653 to read his words over a second time,[5] and even in 1655 has doubts whether the Welshman's ear is ' sunk deep enough ' to appreciate the abstruse involutions of his arguments.[6] The preaching of the famous Baptist John Tombes on a visit to Abergavenny offended some and shook others in the faith, while many were in a dilemma what to think of their own salvation, their children's and their ancestors. [7] A certain I. W. piquantly remarked that the ' poor simple people ' who believed him were under the delusion that they could understand in half seven years the mysteries of divinity when in seven years they could scarce learn the mysteries of the lowest profession.[8] The reaction in favour of a simple faith was representative. The ' richer sort ' of Powell's congregations refused to accept his ideas of the Fifth Monarchy,[9] and the ' sober part of Christians ' assured Cromwell they expected no other ' visible ' govern-

1a Foster : Alumni Oxonienses, Vol. III, p. 1068.
1 The Shield Single, p. 48. " Capiat, qui capere potest."
2   Ibid.   p. 49.
3   Ibid.   p. 47.
4 Gweithiau, Vol. I, " 1648'" The Harvest, v. 8, p. 31.
5   Ibid.   " Llythyr i'r Cymru Cariadus," p. 122.
6 Gweithiau, Vol. II, " Cyfarwyddid i'r Cymru," Sec. 3, p. 86.
7 J. Spinther James : Hanes y Bedyddwyr, Vol. II, p. 304.
8 Public dispute touching infant baptism, the 5th of September, 1653, in the Church of St. Maries, Abergavenny, Epistle Ded.
9 Thurloe State Papers, Vol. II, p. 124.

ment but his own.[1]   John Jones of Maesygarnedd speaks
the mind of a level-headed Puritan.   Babes must be fed
with milk[2] ; the ordinances are not to be advanced either
above or below their right latitude[3] ; plain Scripture
expressions are the more useful[4] ; and he confesses that
one of his friend Llwyd's 'papers' was good and spiritual
according to his understanding, wishing, however, that it
had been penned in language less 'parabolicall.'[5]   Dr. John·
Owen, speaking in special reference to Wales, regrets that
over-much zeal had hurried the people with violence beyond
their principles and probably beyond the truth, almost
destroying the whole flock by over-driving the cattle and
young ones.[6]   The Cavaliers dwell on another aspect of the
problem.   The people follow the new preachers in crowds,
but have no belief in them,[7] and so many 'separations'
are there that the ordinary man is at a loss whom to follow.[8]
Nor did the *public disputes* tend much to clear up the fundamental questions of controversy.   The three hours' event
at Newchapel consisted of a little solid argument interspersed
with abusive personalities, quibbles of logic, and interruptions
from the audience[9] ; Erbery brought the 'shew' at Llantrisant to an end by consigning his opponent, the Baptist
David Davies, to the 'Fire '[10] ; the debate at Cowbridge did
not regain its dignity after the immoderate laughter caused
by Henry Nicholls perverting Erbery's 'private interpretation' of Zech. ii, 4 to mean that there would be 'cattel' in
heaven,[11] and soon the latter left the field because he saw an
'ambush' laid by his opponent with the contention that
God's union with mankind was *gracious* but not *saving*[12] ;
finally, in the Abergavenny debate between John Tombes

1 Thurloe State Papers, Vol. IV, p. 505 ; The Humble Representation and
Address, pp. 3-4.
    2 Gweithiau Morgan Llwyd, Vol. II, p. 302,—" Llythyrau"—John Jones to
Llwyd, 30 Sept., 1653.
    3   Ibid.   To Morgan Llwyd, Aug 23rd, 1652, p. 297.
    4 Vide 2.
    5 Gweithiau Morgan Llwyd, Vol. II, p. 302.
    6 Sermon before Parliament, 30 Oct., 1656. [Quoted in Rees : Hist. of Prot.
Noncon. in Wales, pp. 95-96.]
    7 Phillipps MS. Reprint, Song vi, " Can i'r Amseroedd Blin," p. 28.
    8   Ibid.   p. 29.
    9 " I wish Mr. Powell would leave his disputeing " (Vol. II, p. 298). [John
Jones to Morgan Llwyd from *Drogedah*, Aug. 23rd, 1652.]   Powell, indeed, seems to
have evaded the challenge (dated from Glasbury, 9 May, 1652) from Alexander Griffith
to debate publicly four specified points, ' either at the University of Oxford or in any
place within ten Miles of my aboad.'   (Petition of the Six Counties of South Wales,
pp. 18-19, misprint for 20-21). N.L.W.
    10 Erbery : Call to the Churches, p. 6.
    11 Erbery : A Dispute near Cowbridge [in " Call to the Churches," p. 47].
    12   Ibid.   [ibid.   p. 51].

and John Cragge, there was a succession of elaborate enthy-
memes and quotations from Ambrose of Milan made before
an audience ' who had no more capacity to pry into them
than a bat into the third heaven.'[1] Over against the barren
results of such disputings and the tendency in a time of
unfettered liberty following a long period of repression for
men ' whose hearts were as tinder or gunpowder to catch
at every spark of false light '[2] came an inchoate desire for
church unity, more especially on the part of Llwyd and
Erbery. With the former it led to a perceptible hardening
of his ideal of toleration[3]; both looked upon the followers
of the ' baptism of John ' as evanescent worshippers of the
letter[4]; and with both the idea of unity was only a part
of prepossessed opinions about the future. And the after-
math of war did not allow the defeated Royalists to have
any room in that ' God's house which was a larger building
than the gathered churches had set up.'[5] In the main they
took up an attitude of sullen discontent in a land where the
festivities of Christmas were officially banned,[6] where the
death of the King was defended from the pulpit,[7] and where
continually heavy assessments were levied for the upkeep
of the Navy and for furthering the interests of the Parliament
in Scotland and Ireland.[8] They took refuge in enigmatic
songs,[9] enjoyed the gibes of Erbery at the expense of the
gathered churches,[10] and confidently awaited a day of
retribution.[11]

Under these adverse conditions the hopes of those who
expected a universal transformation were not realised.
The pages of Llwyd's " Llyfr y Tri Aderyn," written about
the close of the Propagation era, contain abundant testimony
to the moral chaos which accompanied the moving of ancient
moorings and to the hypocrisy and selfishness which had.
made too much of a home in the gathered churches themselves. He compares their members to the variegated

1 Arraignment and Conviction of Anabaptism (John Cragge), pp. 25-27 ; Public
Dispute . . . . Epistle Ded. (I.W.).
2 Henry Nicholls : Shield Single, p. 37.
3 Gweithiau, Vol. I, " Llyfr y Tri Aderyn," p. 182.
4   Ibid.   pp. 201, 214.
5 Erbery : The Sword Doubled, p. 12.
6 Rowland Vaughan : Blodeugerdd Cymru, p. 52.—" Adroddiad fal y bu gynt."
7 Phillipps MS. Reprint, Song vii, '" Y Letani Newydd," p. 30.
8 R. Vaughan : Blodeugerdd, p. 53, v. 6 ; Phillipps MS. Reprint, Song vii, p. 31.
9   Ibid.   Song v, " Ymddiddan rhwng yr ha' a'r gaua'," p. 36.
10 Henry Nicholls : The Shield Single, p. 33.
11 Phillipps MS. Reprint, Song viii, " Cwyn rhyw Eglwyswr," p. 33.

flocks of Laban[1] ; they have the twin accents of Israel and of Ashdod ; and what to Erbery is a Babylon is to Llwyd a Babel.[2]   Powell came to look upon the dark days of the Restoration as ' preventing Physick ' for the ' dangerous disorders ' which were too evident among many of the ' saints.'[3]   And colour is given to these general attacks by the numerous excommunications from the church at Ilston for moral offences, by the Royalist taunts at Newchapel, and by the accusation against the ' New Lights ' of Llwyd's own church of persuading a defective person, a Mistress Brewin of Stapleford in Cheshire, to confer the main part of her £800 fortune upon their community.[4]   The Raven pointedly says that many of the new professors were as desirous of the world's good things as the old, and displayed equal craft in getting them.[5]   Nor is this suggestion without some amount of corroborating evidence.   Cradock bought a farm in the parish of Llangwm from the Treason Trustees out of the sequestered lands of the Earl of Worcester,[6] and was afraid that the 1652 Act of Sale would make void a seven years' lease of some land forfeited to the State and granted him by the County Committee of Monmouth[7] ; Powell was resolved to send a party of soldiers to distrain upon a certain Price who refused to pay rent due to him at New Radnor[8] ; and Llwyd himself died possessed of the ' Kynfell ' patrimony in Merioneth and of a tenement at Trefalun near Wrexham, besides being able to divide between his children ' gold, silver, plate, household stuffe and catell.'[9]   The labours of some of the itinerants did not prevent their farming some of the sequestered livings on behalf of the Commissioners : George Edwards that of Llanwern,[10] and Watkin Jones and Evan Williams that of Mynyddislwyn.[11]   Jenkin Lloyd's experience in matters of State[12] saw him M.P. for Cardigan-

1 Llyfr y Tri Aderyn, p. 206.
2   ,,   p. 207.
3 A Word in Season, p. 12.
4 Mercurius Britannicus, July 26th—Aug. 2nd, 1652. [Quoted in Gweithiau, II, p. 209.]   There is no further reference to the matter in any of the records.
5 Gweithiau, Vol. I, p. 161.
6 Calendar of the Committee for Compounding, Vol. III, p. 1714.   3 June, 1652.
7   Ibid.   Vol. IV, p. 3066 [lands forfeited by Henry Morgan, of Pentrebach.]
8 Thurloe State Papers, Vol. II, p. 118.
9 Gweithiau, Vol. II, " Morgan Lloyd's Will," pp. 279-280.
10 Walker c. 13, ff. 47, 50, 54.
11   Ibid.   f. 47.
12 Supra, p. 100.

shire in the first Protectorate Parliament.[1] And it is possible that he was one of the three 'Itinerant Approbationers' who appeared 'at the Parliament door, Friday, 25th of March, 1653, to beg the renewing of the Act' and to 'solicit the continuance of their own power and advantage.'[2] The hostile critics thought it became them better to preach the word in Wales, 'where there is a scarcity of preachers.'[2]

The doctrinal advance, the loose organisation, the secular spirit which had crept in amidst the spiritual activities of the preachers, all are retrospectively illustrated by the success of the *Quaker missionaries* from October, 1653, onwards. These 'railing Rabshakehs'[3] denounced tithes[4] and their payment, forced John Miles to make out a defence for the 'hireling ministers,'[5] and by presenting a direct negative to the efficacy and necessity of ordinances, captured many lukewarm members of the Close Baptist community. The churches of the '[General] babtis' in Radnorshire they 'broke in peeses,'[6] and in this county George Fox was to get his largest audiences in 1657.[7] The divided flocks of Monmouthshire afforded them an excellent field for their operations, as witnessed by the establishment of a Quaker society at Pontymoyle,[8] the conversion of an Independent minister in George White of Ystern Llewern,[9] and even of an Episcopalian in the son of a former incumbent of that living.[10] They challenged the 'man-made' ministry of the Independents in John ap John's question to a Swansea minister if he was really a minister of Christ,[11] and Richard Hubberthorne 'laid judgment' upon the minister of a church in the neighbourhood of Wrexham.[12] On the other hand, a Welsh itinerant could easily gravitate into a Quaker

1 W. R. Williams : Parl. Hist. of the Principality of Wales, p. 30 ; John Hughes Hist. of the Parly. Repn. of the County of Cardigan (p. 14, u.i.) ; Lamb. 1027, f. 35— " *he sitting in Parliament was excepted against as a Minister.*"
2 Certain Seasonable Considerations, p. 4.
3 John Miles : Antidote against the Infection of the Times, " To the Reader," p. 1.
4 Esp. embodied in George Fox's " Great Mistery " which contained an answer to the ' Antidote.'
5 Supra, p. 165. In Feb., 1655-6, a bitter attack upon the Cardiff Quakers was made by Joshua Miller, minister of St. Andrew's in Glam. (vide p. 145) in " Antichrist in Man the Quakers' Idol." (Civil War Tracts, N.L.W., Cat., pp. 65-66).
6 Friends' Hist. Soc. Supplement No. 6 [John ap John], p. 22. [Letter of Thomas Holme from *Cardife*, 27 day, 12 month, (1654)]
7 Braithwaite : Beginnings of Quakerism, p. 348.
8   Ibid.   p. 347.
9 Lamb. 639 (Codices Tenisoniani), f. 186.—Episcopal Returns, 1669.
10 Diary of Walter Powell (éd. Bradney), p. 37, n. 2.
11 Besse : Sufferings of the Quakers, Vol. I, p. 735.
12 Braithwaite : Beginnings of Quakerism, p. 123.

" publisher of truth," and men who said that Christ was in them,[1] and preached that the time would soon come when there would be no need of Scripture[2] were not far removed from the Quakers' belief in ' openings,' ' indwelling light,' and lack of Scriptural finality. The phenomenal success of the movement in the North had afforded examples in a typical Calvinist like John Burnyeat,[3] an Independent like Richard Farnsworth,[4] a rover among the sects like William Dewsbury,[5] and a Seeker like Thomas Taylor,[6] becoming indoctrinated with the gospel of the ' Friends '; Fox had in his sermon at Pendle Hill uttered sentiments hardly distinguishable from those of the Fifth Monarchists[7]; and in his sermon at Lancaster[8] he had displayed a very close affinity with the mystic element in Llwyd and the theory of God's immanence preached by Erbery. Llwyd later admitted that a large part of the truth lay with the Quakers[9]; Erbery would most probably have joined them if he lived; Powell, however, resolutely refused to abjure the Puritanism which found the inspiration of its faith and practice in the primitive church.[10]   But some aspects of his thought had a potential Quaker element; many of his followers and those of Llwyd became converts; and, no doubt, the declamations of Erbery had prepared men's minds for the coming of the ' sarves of the lord in chemorgenshir.'[11]

The success of the Quakers had another significance. The fact that that body from the first activities of Fox among the General Baptists of Mansfield[12] up to his assimilation of the Seekers of Preston Patrick[13] had thrived most among men who had already devoted much thought to religious matters and who had moved far from the Anglican standards was indirect evidence of a great spiritual awakening in Wales

---

1 Braithwaite: Beginnings of Quakerism, p. 123. [Saying attributed to members of church at Wrexham, probably Llwyd's.]
  2 Richard Davies: An Account of the Convincement . . . p. 5. [remark in sermon of a " great Scripturian " heard by Davies.]
  3 Braithwaite : Beginnings of Quakerism, p. 120.
  4   Ibid.   p. 59.
  5   Ibid.   pp. 63-64.
  6   Ibid.   p. 93.
  7   Ibid.   p. 107 (18 Oct., 1652).
  8   Ibid.   p. 80 (May. 1652).
  9 Gweithiau, Vol. II, " Llythyrau," XV, (at ci ' fam '), p. 269.
  10 The authors of the ' Examen ' ask what monument Powell deserved for ' carrying the flag ' from, among others, ' Dæmonaick Quakers ' (p. 41).   Date = 1654.
  11 Friends' Hist. Soc. Suppt. No. 6, p. 22. [Letter of Thomas Holme to George Fox, 27 day, 12 month, 1654.]
  12 Braithwaite : The Beginnings of Quakerism, p. 42.
  13   Ibid.   pp. 81-93.

notwithstanding its many limitations. It is true that the
' understanding ' of John ap John was ' opned ' by George
Fox[1] and not by Morgan Llwyd, that Richard Davies thought
the praying of Powell's followers ' dry dead formality,'[2]
and that Morgan Evan left the ministers of South Wales to
seek consolation elsewhere.[3] But the gospel of the propagators had produced characters equally noteworthy :
e.g., in South Wales the Edward Bowen who writes from
the ship ' Laurel ' in the Downs of the absence of ' the former
music, the melody of experienced saints ' which had been his
share in Monmouthshire,[4] and in North Wales the Morris
William Powell, ' a blind man who could see miracles and
a poor man full of song.'[5] The dark sayings of Erbery and
Llwyd were welcomed by some choice spirits. Members
of the church at Llanfaches came to hear the former preaching
at Newport,[6] and the tone of the letter sent by his friends
to Llwyd when following the army of Harrison[7] and the
phraseology of a letter sent from Wrexham to John Jones[8]
show that the Mystic's influence had permeated his more
immediate followers. And though the land transactions of
Cradock did not escape the vigilant eye of his old vicar,[9]
yet his evident sincerity and the great impression he made
during the Propagation found him invited to preach before
the Parliament in April, 1653,[10] asked by the Trustees for
Maintenance to suggest the names of men likely to assist
them with the revenue of Wales,[11] and invited to act with
Dr. Owen and others to discuss the question of admitting
the Jews with a committee of the Parliament.[12] The
exemplary life of a pious minority eventually reacted upon
the every-day life of the people : Henry Nicholls is able to
rejoice at the abated drunkenness of the people of Glamorgan,[13]
and Vavasor Powell is willing to let his enemies be judges
as to whether there was any working, playing, or travelling

1 Friends' Hist. Soc. Suppt. 6, p. 5.
2 An Account of the Convincement (1771), p. 33.
3   Ibid.   p. 9.
4 Calendar of State Papers, 1652-1653, p. 293, April 25th, 1653 ; Calendar of
the Committee for Compounding, Vol. I, p. 507.
5 Gweithiau Morgan Llwyd, Vol. I, Song xlix, pp. 94-95.
6 Erbery : The Idol Pastor, p. 88.
7 Mercurius Politicus : July 10-17, 1651 [quoted in Gweithiau, II,§ App. V, p. 322]¡
8 Thurloe State Papers, Vol. III, p. 214.   ●
9 Erbery : The Welsh Curate, p. 12.
10 C. J. VII, 274. [He was excused from doing so, however].
11 Lamb. 1008, f. 183.
12 Calendar of State Papers, 1655-6, p. 23.
13 The Shield Single, p. 33.

on Sundays in Powys.[1] Cromwell's opinion was that God
'had *kindled a seed* there, hardly to be paralel'd in the
Primitive times.'[2] The latter's encouraging letter of April,
1653,[3] the appointment of Cradock as one of the new ' triers '
of 1654,[4] and the nomination of sixteen out of the twenty-
five Approvers as ' assistants '[5] to the new County Commissioners appointed in the same year, prove that Puritan
opinion endorsed the work of the propagators and had no
desire to resort to the Rump's idea of replacing, more especially the Approvers of North Wales, by ' more moderate
men.'[6] It is true the itinerant system was gradually discontinued and more favour was shown to some of the ejected, but
the old appointments were practically all confirmed, and reinforced by new men, particularly Stephen Hughes of Mydrim,[7]
Marmaduke Matthews of Swansea,[8] Samuel Jones of Llangynwyd,[9] David Jones of Llandisilio in Carmarthen,[10] Henry
Maurice of Llanordineio[11] and Philip Henry of Worthenbury.[12]
But the years 1653-1660 brought divisions among old friends,
and little new territory was annexed by the Puritan forces.
It was when the troublous times of the Restoration came
to weed out the self-seekers who had brought discredit upon
the faithful, to see English immigrants like Benjamin Flower
of Cardiff[13] and Thomas Warren of Narberth[14] forsaking the
land of their adoption, and old nominees of the Assembly
like Thomas Freeman of Llanddewi Efelfre[15] conforming
with the times, that the great personalities of the Propagation
stood out in bold relief in company with the loyal followers
they had gathered amidst passive opposition, widespread
ignorance, and the distractions of a time of liberty. The
extraordinary number of conventiclers at Merthyr Tydfil

1 A Brief Narrative of the former Propagation, p. 8.
2 The Lord General. Cromwel's Speech delivered in the Council Chamber upon
the 4th of July, 1653. [Opening of the Little Parliament.] N.L.W.
3 Calendar of State Papers, 1652-3, pp. 293-294, 25 Ap., 1653.
4 Firth and Rait : Acts and Ordinances, Vol. II, p. 856, 20 March, 1653-4.
5   Ibid.   pp. 978-984, 23 Aug., 1654.
6 Gardiner : Hist. of the Commonwealth and Protectorate, Vol. II, pp. 196-197—
on authority of the " Newsletter," April 8/18, 1653. [No reference in the Commons'
Journals.]
7 Lamb. 977, ff. 7-8; 972, f. 433; 996, f. 312. [But vide pp. 260-261, infra].
29 Jan., 1655-6.
8 Lamb. 972, f. 379. Dec. 25th, 1655 ; after his return from New England
(Rees : Hist. Prot. Non., p. 53).
9 Lamb. 988, f. 68. 4 May, 1657.
10 Lamb. 980, f. 186 ; 995, f. 179.
11 Lamb. 995. f. 229.
12 Diaries and Letters (ed. M. H. Lee), p. 15. Sept. 30th, 1653.
13 Walker, c. 4, f. 67, from Gloucestershire ; from ' Wiltshire' (Calamy II, 731).
14 Calamy : Account . . . Vol. II. p. 718—Norfolk. Great Yarmouth.
15 Lamb. 639 (Codices Tenisoniani), f. 336b. Episcopal Returns, 1665.

bore witness to the labours of Jenkin Jones[1]; the
'schismaticks many' at Wrexham[2] to the irradiating
influence of Ambrose Mostyn and Morgan Llwyd; the 20
Baptist licences in Glamorgan, Carmarthen, and Monmouth
to the genius of John Miles[3]; the eight conventicles in
Montgomeryshire to the energy of Vavasor Powell[4]; and
the twenty-six conventicles found in Monmouthshire in 1669[5]
and the 30 licences granted there in 1672[6] to the abiding
inspiration of the simple gospel of William Wroth and his
spiritual descendants at Llanfaches and Mynyddislwyn.

1 Lamb. 639 (Codices Tenisoniani), f. 187.   1669 Returns.
2   Ibid.   f. 139b. 1669   ,,
3 State Papers, Dom. Car. II, 38 A. passim.
4 Lamb. 639, ff. 139, 139b.   1669 Returns.
5   Ibid.   ff. 186, 186b, 188.
6 State Papers, Dom., Car. II, 38 A. passim. The number of licences is arrived
at by counting those of ' teacher ' and ' meeting-place ' *separately.*

XV.

SCHOOLS.

Though the Puritan thought of the time was resolutely opposed to the obscuring of the power of the Spirit by man's ' natural parts ' or by the authority of Reason, there was no wish to derogate from learning as an aid to godliness and as a solvent for some of the material difficulties which retarded the progress of the new reformation. The encyclopædic studies proposed for the Academy in Milton's " Tractate " would not only conduce to ' a compleat and generous education ' but " bring forth renowned and Perfect Commanders in the service of their country as well "[1]; Hartlib's ' Agency of Learning ' was meant to bring divinity into line with science, industry, and school reform for the joint ' spread of salvation '[2]; the College shadowed forth in the 1644 petition of the London ministers to the Assembly was to apply the touchstone of light to the new heresies that were growing apace[3]; and the Parliamentary Visitation of the two universities was designed to purify the stream of learning at its source. The attitude of Parliament was made evident in other ways also. As early as June, 1641, the Commons sitting in Grand Committee over the Root-and-Branch Bill had suggested that the revenues of the hierarchy should be devoted to the advancement of learning and piety,[4] and in June, 1649, £20,000 out of impropriations and tithes were definitely allocated for this purpose, in the proportion of £18,000 for clergy and schoolmasters and £2,000 for the universities.[5] The Propagation Act for New England in the following month made provision for maintaining schools and nurseries of learning for the better education of the children of the natives,[6] and the Trustees under the

1 J. W. Adamson : Pioneers of Modern Education, pp. 122, 123.
2   Ibid.   p. 101.
3 W. M. Hetherington : Hist. of the Westminster Assembly, p. 173.
4 C.J. II, p. 176.
5 Scobell : Ordinances, Vol. II, p. 40.
6 Firth and Rait : Acts and Ordinances, Vol. II, p. 199.

Ireland Ordinance of March, 1650, were to settle further maintenance on Trinity College, erect a new college in Dublin, and establish a free school there.[1] Revenues arising from the estates of delinquents and hitherto devoted to the support of colleges or schools were exempted from sequestration under the ordinance of March, 1643[2]; the same principle was applied in the ordinance for the ' receiving and collecting ' of the Royal revenues in September of the same year[3]; and a similar proviso was made to govern the assessments levied for the upkeep of the forces in June, 1647,[4] Feb., 1647-8,[5] 7th April, 1649[6] and 7th December of the same year.[7] The C.P.M., also, gave strict injunctions that the salaries of the master and usher of Christ's College at Brecon should be punctually paid by the tenants of the premises from which they were drawn[8]; and in 1649, as a reason for increasing his maintenance by £100 per annum, the same Committee expected Dr. Harding, the minister of Wrexham, to bestow some of his " labours and paines in the Carefull training up and Educating of the youth there."[9]

Nor was it the policy of the Propagation Commissioners to impair the efficiency of the educative forces in the shape of grammar schools set up in Wales by philanthropic men in the reigns of Elizabeth and James. No doubt the government of these schools had been already assimilated to the Puritan standard by the inquiry set up by the Committee of *Scandalous Ministers* into the state of such schools in 1641, especially as to ' misemployment or abuse of revenue,'[10] by the jurisdiction over delinquent schoolmasters given to the C.P.M. in 1643,[11] and by asking all masters of schools to subscribe the Engagements in January, 1650[12]—a policy all the more necessary because of the strong ecclesiastical bias given to all educational institutions by the Canons of 1604.[13] This is indirectly proved by there being no record of a schoolmaster ejected

---

1 Firth and Raith : Acts and Ordinances, Vol. II, p. 356.
2   Ibid.   Vol I, .p. 110.
3   Ibid.   ,,   pp. 302-303.
4   Ibid.   ,,   p. 984.
5   Ibid.   ,,   p. 1077.
6   Ibid.   Vol. II,   p. 57.
7   Ibid.   ,,   p. 318.
8 Bodl. 324, f. 20b.
9 Bodl. 326, ff. 73-73b.
10 C. J. II, 121. April 16th.
11 C. J. III, 270. Oct. 9th.
12 Firth and Rait : Acts and Ordinances, Vol. II, p. 325.
13 Wilkins : Concilia, Art. LXXVII, " De paedagogis sive ludemagistris," pp. 393-394.

by the Commissioners, nor of any interference[1] in the affairs of Bangor (1561), Beaumaris (1609), Bottwnog (1616), Carmarthen (1576), Hawarden (1608), Llanrwst (1610), Monmouth (1615), Northop (1606), Presteign (1565), Ruabon (before 1632), Usk (1621) or Ruthin (1595),[2] which at this time was in a particularly flourishing condition under the mastership of Thomas Challoner.[3] Side by side with these schools were the free school founded at Llandovery by the terms of Vicar Prichard's will,[4] the grammar school founded at Llanegryn in Merioneth in 1652,[5] and the free school 'found and maintained' at Aberhafesp by Humphrey Jones of Garthmel in the same year[6]; nor is there any evidence that the school which was held in "the room or lofft at the lower end of the parish church of St. Asaph" had been discontinued.[7] There were in addition the schools more or less surreptitiously taught by some of the ejected clergymen,[8] and such institutions as the 'Arethmetique' school to which the young Walter Powell was sent to at Abergavenny,[9] but it is probable that the school kept by William Wyatt and William Nicholson at Newton Hall in the parish of Llanfihangel Aberbythych where "young men were most *loyally* educated for the Universities" did not proceed far into the Propagation era.[10]

The distinctive contribution of the Commissioners to the advance of learning in Wales, which was to remove 'ignorance and prophaneness' and thus complement the regenerating activities of the preachers, was the establishment of more than sixty free schools, placed principally in the larger towns and the market towns. The evidence for the following list is to be found in the official minutes of the North Wales Commissioners, confirmed in some cases by Lamb. MS. 1006 and the "Examen et Purgamen" (for the

---

1 Unless a suggested inquiry (21 Nov., 1650) 'into the state of all *free* schools in Anglesey and Carnarvon' had some effect. (Rawl., c. 261, p. 28). No mention is made of any consequences to the Friars' School at Bangor (Barber and Lewis : Hist., p. 37).
2 The authority for these dates is the Rev. Thos. Shankland's article in 'Seren Gomer,' Nov., 1901 (based on the evidence submitted to the Schools Enquiry Commission (Report, Vol. I, Appendix IV, pp. 48-61).
3 Thomas : Hist. of the Diocese of St. Asaph, p. 454.
4 Canwyll y Cymry (Llandovery Ed., 1867, Rice Rees), p. 317.
5 Vide Ref. 2.
6 Thomas : History of the Diocese of St. Asaph (1874), p. 315.
7   Ibid.   p. 275.
8 Supra, p. 137.
9 Diary of Walter Powell of Llantilio Crossenny (ed. Bradney), p. 46.
10 D.N.B., Vol. LXI, p. 27 (" Collegium Newtoniense "); D.N.B., Vol. LXIII, p. 190 ; David Lloyd : Memoires, p. 703.

County of Montgomery), in the retrospective testimony of the Lambeth Augmentation Books, and in the names of schoolmasters in receipt of salaries among the accounts of the South Wales treasurer. Even when this is supplemented by an appeal to the Domestic State Papers, in some cases the name of the school is known, but not that of the appointed schoolmaster; in other and more numerous instances the latter is given, but not the school to which he was attached. It should be said that two schoolmasters are included on the single testimony of the " True and Perfect Relation,"[1] and that two others find a place on account of the exceptionally strong circumstantial evidence afforded by Walk. c. 13.[2]

1 Vide infra. pp. 228, 229.
2 Thomas Cecil and Steven Dare. The evidence regarding William Kinge of Llandaff is too indefinite to warrant his inclusion in the list of schoolmasters (Walk. c. 13, ff. 17b, 26b, 31). And even in Dare's case, it must not be forgotten that a ' Stephen Deare ' is referred to in Oct., 1657, by the Lamb. Aug. Books as a late member of the Llandaff Cathedral choir (992, ff. 55, 65 : 993, f. 21), and as receiving £3 out of arrears due to him before 6 Jan., 1649–50, the date when the revenues of the Bishops and Chapters were invested in the Trustees for Maintenance of Ministers (Shaw, II, pp. 214–216). If Dare and Deare be the same man, it is rather unlikely that a some-time Llandaff chorister would find such favour with the rigid Glamorgan Commissioners as to be appointed schoolmaster.

NORTH WALES.

	SCHOOL.	SCHOOLMASTER.	SALARY PER ANNUM.	DATE OF APPOINTMENT (WHEN KNOWN).	MS. REFERENCE (OR OTHER AUTHORITY).
ANGLESEY	Amlwch	——1	£20	——1	Lamb. 1006, f. 320; 972, f. 449.
CARNARVON	Carnarvon	Rowland Lloyd (Master)	£20	18 Sept., 1650	Rawl. c. 261, pp. 24, 30; Lamb. 972, f. 16; 1006, f. 320.
		Sampson Morton	£6	30 July, 1651	Rawl. c. 261, p. 30.
DENBIGH	Abergele	Robert Boyle	£30	7 May, 1652	Lamb. 972, ff. 218, 529; 1006, f. 131.
	Denbigh	David Eyton	£30	19 Nov., 1651	Rawl. c. 261, p. 32; Lamb. 1006, ff. 132, 322.
	Glynceiriog	Edward Wynne	£10	4 March, 1652-3	Lamb. 972, f. 496; 980, f. 218; 1006, f. 319.
	Holt	——	£26		Lamb. 1006, f. 319.
	Llandegla	Richard Hughes	£15	21 Nov., 1650	Rawl. c. 261, p. 27; Lamb. 972, f. 388; Lamb. 1006, f. 322.
	Llanfair D.C.	——	£10		Lamb. 1006, f. 322.
	Llangollen	David Wynne	£20	19 Nov., 1651	Rawl. c. 261, p. 32; Lamb. 972, f. 217; Lamb. 1006, f. 132.
	Llanrwst	Hugh Owen	£8	30 July, 1651	Ibid. p. 30; Lamb. 1006, f. 132.
	Llansilin	Robert Edwards	£20	16 March, 1652-3	Lamb. 972, f. 127.
	Ruthin	Edward Thelwall	—	11 June, 1650	Rawl. c. 261, p. 19.
	Wrexham	Ambrose Lewis (Master)	£40	29 April, 1651	Ibid. p. 22; Lamb. 972, f. 9; 1006, ff. 131, 289; 1008, f. 161.
		Daniel Barnard2 (Master)	£25	19 Nov., 1651	Rawl. c. 261, pp. 31-32.
		Andr. Maddocks (Usher)1	£25	24 March, 1652-3	Lamb. 972, f. 9; 1006, f. 290.

1 It must be remembered that the horizontal line signifies that the name or date is not ascertained.
2 All that is known of him is that he had left before the appointment of *Maddocks.* A certain 'Mr. Parry' seems to have been schoolmaster at Wrexham before Lewis (Rawl. c. 261, pp. 25, 27).

FLINT	Hanmer	Thos. Beddoes	£15	19 Nov., 1650	Rawl. c. 261, p. 21; Lamb. 972, f. 218; 1006, f. 319.
MERIONETH	Bala	John Evans	£35	23 March, 1652-3	Imb. 972, ff. 129, 147; 1 06, f. 32.
	Gwen	Edward Roberts[1]	£10	30 July, 1651	Rawl. c. 261, f. 30; Imb. 106, f. 32.
	Dolgelly	John Griffith (M.) / ...th odes (U.)	£60	19 Nov., 1650	Rawl. c. 261, p. 21 C.S. ...; Imb. 972, f. 12; pp. 221-22.
	Ffug	—	£30	—	Imb. 106, f. 319.
MONTGOMERY	Ll ... fair	Rice Jones[2]	£20	23 ...	bld., 320; E ..., p. 14.
	Llanfyllin	—	£26	20 ..., 1652-3	Imb. 106, f 319.
	Llanidloes	Humphrey Thomas	£25	19 ..., 60	Rawl. c. 261, p. 22.
	Llansantffraid	William Hughes[3]	£25	18 June, 1651	bld. p. 2; Imb. 106, f 319.
	Montgomery	James Hydock (Master)	£20	19 ..., 30	Imb. 106, f. 30.
		Thos. ... (Vir)	£30	ore 1 63	Rawl. c. 261, p. 21; Imb. 106, ff. 30, 31; ... p. 14. ...b. 972, f. 68; ... p. 14.
	Newtown	John ... (M.)	£25	—	S.P. Dom. Interreg. G. 27, f. 123.4; Ibid. f. 1484; Lamb. 1006, f. 320.
	... Wol	Thos. Williams (U.) / ... (M.)	£20 / £40	19 Nov., 1650	Rawl. c. 261, p. 21; Lamb. 972, f. 67.
		Nath. Raven (U.)	£20	18 June, 1651	Ibid. p. 29.

1 Ejected clergyman, p. 117.
2 To be distinguished from Richard Jones, the ejected vicar.
3 Son of the ejected vicar of Llansantffraid. [Exch. Returns, Mont., 1658, slips 115, 119].
4 Claims to arrears of salary after expiry of Act. Williams was probably the ejected vicar of Llanllwchaiarn (p. 120).

SOUTH WALES.

SCHOOL	SCHOOLMASTER	SALARY PER ANNUM.	DATE OF APPOINTMENT (WHEN KNOWN).	MS. REFERENCE (OR OTHER AUTHORITY).
BRECKNOCK				
Brecon	Philip ⸢⸣rns (M.) Hugh Powell (U.)	£40¹	1650 1652	⸢⸣lk. c. 13, ff. 62, 62b. ⸢⸣lie and ⸢⸣l Relation, pp. 32, 40 ; Walk. c. 13, f. 62b.
Builth	John Williams	£25	1650	Ibid. f. 62.
Llanbedr	Thos. Cecil	£20	1650	Ibid. f. 60b.
Llanbister	⸢⸣ns Williams	£30	1650	Ibid. f. 62.
Llangorse	— Smith⁴	£40		Cal.St. Pap., 1656-57, p. 31.
	Jerome Perrott	£10	1650	⸢⸣lk. c. 13, f. 63b.
Llanigon	Eynon Pryce	£20	1650	Ibid. f. 62.
Llanthetty	John Griffiths	£22 10s.	1650	Ibid. f. 62.
Talgarth	John Prosser⁵	£20	1650	Ibid. ff. 62, 63b.
	Rice Powell	£33	16 March, 1652-3	⸢⸣b. 972, f. 164 ; 980, f. 81.
Talybont	John Griffiths	£10	1650	⸢⸣lk. c. 13, f. 62b.
Tretower	David Williams	£15	1650	⸢⸣id. f. 62b.
CARDIGAN				
Cardigan	Roger Owens (M.)	£40	6 March, 1652-3	Lamb. 972, f. 185 ; 1006, f. 53.
	Owen Picton (U.)	£20	17 March, 1652-3	Lamb. 1006, f. 54.
Lampeter	Thomas Evans	£20	2 Aug., 1652	Lamb. 972, f. 584 ; 1006, f. 56.

1 How the £40 was · ided ⸢⸣en ⸢⸣m in 1652 is uncertain ; ⸢⸣he ⸢⸣eed £24 in 1650 (f. 60) and £25 in 1651 (f. 62b), besides a £20 ' charged formerly upon the Prebend of St. David's ⸢⸣ds the free-schoole of Brecon.' (f. 62).

2 The ⸢⸣ame of the ejected ⸢⸣tor is entered ⸢⸣b, although the word is indistinctly written in the MS. and no details whatever are given of the £20. It is ⸢⸣nd, ⸢⸣ev ⸢⸣er, that this is too high a ⸢⸣th to ⸢⸣ay out of the £74 rent of the living for 1650 (f. 59) ; besides, the Brecon officials were in the ⸢⸣tom of specifying particularly what clergy ⸢⸣eed ⸢⸣ase ⸢⸣gs.

3 ⸢⸣it ⸢⸣tion in MS.

4 It is open to ⸢⸣ubt ⸢⸣her Smith was at Llangorse ⸢⸣th Perrott ; if so, they must ⸢⸣ve been ⸢⸣nter and ⸢⸣ter respectively.

5 Powell ⸢⸣ds Prosser. However, from an entry on f. 60, it seems that in 1650 Powell and Prosser ⸢⸣re both ⸢⸣nd with the Talgarth school. In 1651 ⸢⸣nd 1652 the ⸢⸣or is ⸢⸣ted as a 'minister' with a salary of £20 per ⸢⸣num (ff. 62, 63b) ; in 1653 he ⸢⸣kes ⸢⸣it once more.

	Place	Name	Salary	Date	Reference
GLAMORGAN	Cardiff	new Bancroft1	£40	1650	Walk. c. 13, ff. 17b, 22b, 26b, 31; Imb. 972, f. 388
	...ge	Wm ...has	£40	1650	Ibid. 17b, 31b.
	...it Major	...ie	£20	1651	Ib. f. 22b.
	Merthyr	William / Mrs2	£20	1650	Ib. ff. 18, 26b, 31, 31b.
	...th	Lewis Williams3	£30	1650	Ib. ff. 17b, 20, 22, 22b.
		...by Smith	£30	1650	Ib. ff. 20, 22b, 31.
	Penmark	John Butler4	£20	1650	Ib. ff. 26b, 31b.
	St. Mary Hill	Rice Daies	£20	1651	Ib. f. 22b.
		...Bright	£10	1650	Ib. f. 20.
		...sen Den5	£10	1652	Ib. f. 31b.
		Peter Day6	£50 2s.	1651	Ib. f. 20.
	Swansea	Hugh Jones	£38	1650 or 1651	True and Perfect Relation p. 32.
		Mor Pye7 (After)	£38	17 Mh, 5263	Imb. 00, f. 184; Walk. c. 13, f. 22.
		Ines Williams (U.)	£26	17 Mch, 1652-3	Ibid. f. 185; Walk. c. 13, f. 22b.
MONMOUTH	Abergavenny	Henry Vaughan (M.)...	£20	17 Mh, 1652-3	Lamb. 1006, f. 211; Walk. c. 13, ff. 62b, 63b.
	Chepstow	William Davies (U.)	£10	1651	Walk. c. 13, f. 51b.
		...w Lewis	£40	6 pril, 1650	Lamb. 1006, f. 211; Walker c. 13, ff. 51b, 57.
	Magor	W. Milman	£40	1650	Walk. c. 13, ff. 45, 51, 57.

1 'Ambrose Barcroft' in ... MS., 'Andrew Bancroft' in Lambeth MSS.
3 ... Jones in his 'First ... fers to 'Schoolmasters,' but the plural
p. 93).
3 (... ed as 'joynt schoolmasters.' A 'Humphrey Smith' was ...ale ' ...an (p. 125).
5 Not specifically described as a 'schoolmaster.' But the MS. places his ... dnt of Penderyn in 1662 ... mst be taken to be a ...
is £40.
6 Name not ...aly ... ... ame side-by- ...de with ... those of two schoolmas' ...rs, ...nd his ...dary
7 Evil from ...by in ... (p. ...) ... He was the seconder of John Crugge in the great ...om ...ate with John ...les
8 Evil from Panteg ... fore the Act' (Walk. c. 7, f. 215b). ... final flourish (Wilkins: Hist. Merth., ...qes : Breck. (1898), p. 482).
at ...by (5 Sept., 1653).

SOUTH WALES—continued.

	SCHOOL	SCHOOLMASTER	SALARY PER ANNUM.	DATE OF APPOINTMENT (WHEN KNOWN).	MS. REFERENCE (OR OTHER AUTHORITY).
MONMOUTH (con.).	Newport	Wm. Pierce } Wm. Poiskine }	£60	..	Walk. c. 13, ff. 45, 51, 57.
	Usk ⸺	Rich. Goodgroome1	£10	1650	Ibid. ff. 45b, 51.
		Henry Jones	£10	1652	Ibid. f. 57.
PEMBROKE	Carew	Henry Williams2	£20	29 June, 1652	Lamb. 972, f. 165; 1006,f 292.
	Tenby	James Picton	£40	26 March, 1652	Lamb. 972, f. 6; 980, f. 381; 1006, f. 92.
RADNOR	Bleddfa	John Harris	£25	1650	Walk. c. 13, ff. 62, 63b.
	Clyro	Dd. Jenkins	£30	1650	Ibid. ff. 62b, 66, 68, 68b.
	Llangunllo	Chas. Browne3	£26	1651	Ibid. f. 68.
	Nantmel	Griffith Evans	£30	1650	Ibid. ff. 63, 6, 68, 68b.
	New Radnor	David Evans	£25	1650	Walk. c. 13, f. 62b; True and Perfect Relation, p. 32; S. P. Dom., G. 27, f. 165.
	Rhayader	Evan Powell	£25	1650	Walk. c. 13, f. 62.
		Walter Bengough4	£8	1651	Ibid. f. 68b.

1 He is described as 'usher'; and as no 'master' is referred to in any of the Monmouth accounts, it seems certain that G. was a Propagation reinforcement to the one 'Master,' provided for the school founded at Usk in 1621.
2 Ejected from Carew (p. 132).
3 Ejected vicar (p. 133).
4 'Bengouh' in MS.

That these schools were ' free ' in the usual meaning of the term is suggested by the terms of Roger Seys' appointment to the school at St. Fagans a few months after the expiry of the Act[1]; that in *some* schools, at least, both sexes were admitted is evident from the wording of the Abergele order[2]; and that their curriculum was more akin to the ordinary grammar school of the time than to the modern primary school is proved by the Commissioners' specification of the particular subjects to be taught in some cases, by the employment of ' master ' and ' usher ' in some schools, and by the phraseology of the Act itself.[3] Some, like that at Wrexham,[4] were to ' educate Schollers in the Greek and Latin tongues,' thus conforming to the almost universal syllabus of similar schools in England[5]; others, like that at Lampeter, were to lay emphasis on the rudiments of the Latin and *English* tongues,[6] assigning an importance to the latter that was not customary with pedagogues across the Border[7]; while others, like that of Carew, were to be content with preparing their pupils ' for greater schools,'[8] a condition which in the nature of things applied to the free schools at Llanrwst, Ruthin, Brecon, and Usk, places already furnished with more or less flourishing institutions. Whether any use was made of the vernacular, or whether in the inner working of the schools any advance was made on the methods described in the ' Ludus Literarius ' of John Brinsley,[9] or any acquaintance with the ideas of John Dury in his " Reformed School " (1649),[10] or any approximation to the elaborate system in use with Charles Hoole at his school ' in the Tokenhouse in Lothbury '[11] are questions impossible to answer with the surviving evidence. The schools did not last long enough to have a distinctive history ; at the Restoration all seem to have automatically disappeared ; and Hugh Lloyd, Bishop

---

1 Lamb. 1006, f. 186.
2 Lamb. 1006, f. 131: the Lampeter order distinctly specified ' YOUTHS ' (Lamb. 1006, f. 56). The references to these schools by Charles Edwards [Y Ffydd Ddiffuant, 1677, p. 206] and in Whitelocke's Memoirs, p. 518, throw no light on this question.
3 p. 85 "Text of the Act " ; " in piety and good *literature*."
4 Lamb. 1006, f. 289.
5 Foster Watson : The English Grammar Schools to 1660, chapters XIX, XXX.
6 Lamb. 1006, f. 56.
7 Adamson : Pioneers of Modern Education, p. 25.
8 Lamb. 1006, f. 292.
9 Foster Watson : The English Grammar Schools, pp. 157, 277, 360.
10 Adamson : Pioneers of Modern Education. pp. 138-156.
11   Ibid.   pp. 156-174.

of Llandaff, describes Glamorgan as 'utterly destitute of schools' in 1662.[1]

It is certain, however, that the new schools would have a strong Puritan bias, giving much attention to the Bible and to books of devotion, and apt to look upon the classics in a favourable but new light as enabling the pupils to get a closer acquaintance with the original Scriptures and the earlier times of the Christian Church.[2] And though eight of the ejected clergymen and the son of another were appointed as schoolmasters 'to get them a livelihood from mere pity,'[3] the distinct instruction of the Act was that they should be men of 'approved piety.' The names of those among them who assisted in the propagation[4] of the gospel have not been preserved, but this can with tolerable certainty be asserted of Edward Thelwall of Ruthin, who had for three years held the living of Llanynys[5]; of John Prosser, one of the most prominent of the General Baptists[6]; of the Cardiff schoolmaster, who is stated in one of the Lamb. MSS. to have received £10 in 1655 for 'supplying the vakancy' at Llancarfan ; of Martinus Grundman[7] and Nathaniel Raven[8] who in 1655 became ministers at Llandyssil and Welshpool respectively ; of Andrew Maddocks, who was one of the six signatories of the letter sent from Llwyd's church at Wrexham to the London congregations[9]; of Ambrose Lewis, the Wrexham headmaster, Philip Henry's 'ancient friend,'[10] who is definitely described as a preacher during the later years of the Commonwealth[11]; of Griffith Jones, usher of Dolgelly, who is described as a 'minister' in 1659,[12] probably of the 'gathered' church in that place which roused the ire of Rowland Vaughan[13] ; of the William Milman already referred to[14]; of David Jenkins of Clyro, afterwards minister of Bryngwyn and Newchurch in the same county of Radnor[15]

1 Wood : Athenae Oxonienses (ed. Bliss), Vol. IV, p. 835.   Oct. 29th, 1662.
2 Foster Watson : English Grammar Schools, p. 536.
3 Examen et Purgamen Vavasoris, p. 18.
4   Ibid.   p. 17 [General Statement].
5 Supra, p. 63.
6 Supra, p. 209.
7 Exch. First Fruits Returns (1657-8), Montgomery, slips 115, 119.
8   Ibid.   ,,   115, 119.
9 Gweithiau Morgan Llwyd, Vol. II, p. 250.
10 Diaries and Letters (ed. M. H. Lee), p. 83.
11   Ibid.   pp. 42, 44, 61.
12 Calendar of State Papers, 1658-9, p. 110.
13 Yr Arfer o Weddi yr Arglwydd . . . Llythyr Annerch i Sion Elis [quoted by Ashton : Hanes Llenyddiaeth Cymru, p. 26.]
14 Supra, p. 208.
15 Calamy : An Account . . . Vol. II, p. 735.

of Thomas Quarrell, who is 'teaching' in various conventicles on the borders of Glamorgan and Monmouth in 1669, and in 1672 takes out a licence at Shirenewton[1]; and especially of John Evans of Bala, afterwards of the Oswestry Free School, 'a person of great sobriety and godliness,'[2] a friend of Vavasor Powell,[3] holder of conventicles in 1669 both at Oswestry, Llanfyllin, and Llanfechain,[4] and later Independent minister at Wrexham, where he takes out a licence under the Declaration of Indulgence.[5] Such high Puritan standards could hardly be expected of an old Raglan prisoner like William Poiskine,[6] or of future conformists like Walter Bengough and Jerome Perrott, who were appointed to the livings of Builth[7] and Cathedine[8] respectively after the Restoration.

Thus the propagation period saw introduced into Wales the new type of Puritan preaching schoolmaster, State subvention of learning, schools free for all classes, and a restricted experiment in the co-education of the sexes. It had dawned upon some sanguine minds that these developments should be supplemented by establishing a *College* for the more especial purpose of qualifying young men for the ministry. Dr. George Griffith speaks with contempt of the recent 'talk' of having a 'University' in Welshpool, and adds that when either Ambrose Mostyn or Vavasor Powell will be made Professor of Logic there, he will teach the young sophisters the unrevealed secret of making good negative syllogisms in Barbara.[9] A little later, some such institution, 'derivative and subordinate to the two mother Universities'[10] and 'situated in a equidistant town on the confines of North and South Wales,'[11] finds favour with John Lewis of Cardiganshire and Dr. John Ellis of Dolgelly. The dead hand of the Restoration was laid on these aspirations, and the ideal of a College maintained by the State had to be

---

1 Lamb. 639 (Codices Tenisoniani). ff.187, 188; S. P. Dom. Car. II, 38 A, p. 209.
2 The Broadmead Records (ed. Underhill), p. 513.
3 Thurloe State Papers, Vol. II, p. 226.
4 Lamb. 639, f. 139b
5 State Papers Dom., Car. II, 38 A, p. 129. May 22nd, 1672.
6 Phillips : Civil War ,II, Doc. XCV D, p 323.
7 Theoph. Jones : Hist. Brec. (1805), Pt. I, p. 292. [Porskin.]
8 Ibid., p. 362.
9 Animadversions . . . [p. 10]. It is probable that the 'talk' had emanated from either Mostyn or Powell.
10 John Lewis : Some Seasonable and Modest Thoughts (1656), p. 122.
11 Dr. John Ellis : Letter to John Lewis, p. 123 [Both remarks are quoted from an article in " Wales," Vol. III, pp. 121-124, on " An Early Attempt to found a National College in Wales " (J. H. Davies)]. Lewis had already suggested founding ' solemn places ' for the training of ministers in his famous tract of 1646 (pp. 34-35).

content with the pious wish of Charles Edwards[1] and the school of Samuel Jones at Brynllywarch.[2]

NOTE : A CONTRIBUTORY AREA.

The anomalous lie of a region comprising the head waters of valleys which open out to other counties, coupled with the economic law that leads men to seek the world by the line of least resistance, have from time to time furnished Brecknock with some complex matters for arrangement in the domain of education. The Propagation commissioners solved their problem by causing the Brecon officials to pay £147 10s. 0d. to the upkeep of four schoolmasters who taught outside the borders of the county, evidently because pupils came to them from the upper reaches of the Nedd and the two Taffs, and from the land along the middle Usk. Walters of Merthyr Tydfil gets £15 in 1650 (Walk. c. 13, f. 60) and £20 in 1651 (f. 63b) ; the Neath ' joynt schoolemasters ' share £87 10s. 0d. between them (ff. 63, 63b) ; the remaining £25, £20 in 1651 and £5 in 1652 (ff. 62b, 63b), went to Henry Vaughan, the master of the school at Abergavenny.

1 Y Ffydd Ddiffuant (1677), p. 212—" byddai yn gymhorth nid bychan iddi pe cyfodai ei blaenoriaid *g·leds* neu ddau ynddi . . ."
2 Rees : Hist. of Prot. Nonconformity, p. 493.

XVI

MATTERS OF ADMINISTRATION.

For the purposes of this Act the Commissioners of North and South Wales acted quite separately. The former seem to have invariably met in a body, their places of meeting being Wrexham, Welshpool, Llanfyllin, Bala, Ruthin, Conway, Beaumaris and Carnarvon.[1] Those of South Wales had also general meetings of this kind, such as that at Haverfordwest, with Jenkin Franklin of Carmarthen in the chair, when Philip Williams of Robeston was ejected,[2] and the Roath meeting of March 6th, 1652-3, which numbered present (among others) Thomas Watkins of Brecon, John Williams of Radnor, and John Daniel of Pembroke.[3] The usual rendezvous, however, was Swansea.[4] But the growth of business, especially in Glamorgan, Monmouth, and Pembroke, saw a delegation of the duties of ejecting and appointing to the Commissioners resident in those counties, since the constables' report of 1662 give the names of livings sequestered in Monmouthshire by Monmouthshire men only,[5] and Mansell records a tradition that there was a ' court of tryers ' meeting once a fortnight at Llantwit Major.[6] After one year's experience Glamorgan was divided into two separate districts, that of the west taking into its purview portions of East Carmarthen ; conversely, Brecon and Radnor in some respects worked together. The ensuing administrative work called for a large number of officials, " more," says Erbery somewhat illogically, " than ever Christ commanded . . a thing which neither Law nor Gospel nor former Ages ever heard of."[7] There were appointed for *each* county, at a salary of £40 per annum, a

1 Rawl. c. 261, passim.
2 Lamb. 1027, f. 49.
3 Lamb. 1006, f. 53.
4 Certain Seasonable Considerations, p. 2.
5 Lamb. 1027, f. 23.
6 Walker, c. 4, f. 69b.
7 The Sword Doubled, p. 10. He is referring particularly to the officials *under* the *Act.*

sequestrator or agent to 'set & let' the sequestered livings and a collector[1] to gather in the rents and profits. And in South Wales there were special solicitors and clerks for both general and particular meetings, besides door-keepers and messengers. One clerk sufficed for Brecon and Radnor together[2] ; one also for all North Wales,[3] and two joint solicitors[4] ; while Commissioner Rice Vaughan did duty for both North and South as solicitor in London, ' attending appeals there.'[5] Each county kept separate accounts, supervised by a central treasurer, one for North Wales (£100 salary per annum)[6] and one for South Wales (£200 per annum).[7] Cradock's influence is apparent in some of the Monmouthshire appointments : Thomas George the door-keeper was involved in his land speculations at Pentrebach,[8] and Richard Creed the clerk was one of his most intimate friends.[9] Naturally, services to the Parliament and Puritan attachments recommended men for the new posts. *E.g.*, Edward Vaughan, one of the North Wales solicitors and also agent for Montgomery, had been governor of the Abermarchnant garrison, and also active under the Committee for Sequestrations of that county[10] ; Thomas Nicholls, his partner, was a captain in the army,[11] and had been deemed ' fit to be a member ' of the First Shropshire Classis in 1647[12] ; Christopher Price, solicitor for Monmouth, was a prominent Baptist layman of Abergavenny[13] ; and both Sequestrator and Collector in Carmarthenshire were closely connected with Stephen Hughes, since the former, David Morgan, was to be his later patron to the living of Mydrim, and the latter was his own elder brother John.[14] And there was strong presumptive evidence that the central funds would be in safe hands in that the one treasurer was

1 John Lewis in Cardiganshire was styled " *High* Collector " (Walker, c. 13, f. 33).
2 Walker c. 13, f. 60.
3 Rawl. c. 261, p. 28.
4   Ibid.   p. 27.
5   Ibid.   p. 26 ; Walker. c. 13, f. 45b.
6   Ibid.   p. 28.
7 Walker. c. 13, f. 23 and passim.
8 Calendar of the Committee for Compounding, Vol. IV, p. 3066.
9 Lamb. 1027, f. 23: son-in-law according to Dr. Rees (Prot. Nonc., pp. 50-51).
10 Commonwealth Exch. Paper, No. 251 [not paginated]—Orders and Corr. of County Committees.
11 Rawl. c. 261, p. 27.
12 Shaw : Hist. of the Eng. Church during the Civil War, Vol. II, App. IIIb, p. 40⁷.
13 Joshua Thomas : Hanes y Bedyddwyr, p. 212, footnote†.
14 *Inference* from " Stephen Hughes " by Rev. Thos. Shankland in " Beirniad," Vol. II, No. 3, pp. 175, 177. [Oct., 1912.]

Llwyd's leading member at Wrexham,[1] and that the other was one of Miles's staunchest supporters in Gower.[2] The sequestrators and collectors were not popular with the countryside. Edward Davies of Eglwyseg, especially active in the Vale of Edeyrnion,[3] became known as the 'shearer,'[4] and Jenkin Williams of the eastern hundreds of Glamorgan was deemed capable of 'every villainy and barbarity.'[5] Still, besides allowing some clergymen to farm the livings from which they had been ejected,[6] the same privilege was extended to notorious Cavaliers who had been discharged from sequestration as lay delinquents. Such were Sir John Stepney at Prendergast,[7] the Earl of Carbery at Llanarthney,[8] Sir Charles Somerset at Monmouth[9]; and Hugh Johnson of Clynnog, a friend of the old order, and once lessee of the tithes of Penmynydd from Archdeacon White,[10] was allowed to 'enjoy' the tithes of Llanllyfni.[11] But in the majority of cases they were let to well-tried friends of the Parliament—for example, Sir John Meyrick paid the rent for the rectory of Llanwnda in Pembrokeshire,[12] Edward Price of Ffynnogion answered for the comportionary tithes of Llansannan,[13] and Edmund Meyrick of Ucheldre farmed the sinecure rectory of Corwen.[14] Puritans of a deeper dye are found as tenants in Monmouthshire: Anthony Harry, one of the elders of the Baptist church of Abergavenny,[15] at Llanvapley[16]; Hopkin Rogers, who lived to keep a conventicle there in 1669,[17] at Caldicott[18]; and Nicodemus Symonds, who a few years later became one of the first "approved capital burgesses" of Abergavenny,[19] at Llantilio

1 Gweithiau Morgan Llwyd, Vol. II, p. 250. First signatory of the letter to London.
2 J. Spinther James : Hanes y Bedyddwyr, Vol. II, p. 283. Price was of Gellihir and *Cwrt-y-carnau* ; Historical Sketches of Glamorgan, Vol. I, p. 33. [Art. "A Hero of Glamorgan," by W. Llewelyn Williams, M.A.]
3 Lamb. 1027, f. 34 (d).
4 Thomas : Hist. of the Diocese of St. Asaph, p. 499; " Y *Cneifiwr Glas.*"
5 Walk c. 4, f. 66.
6 Supra, pp. 138-140.
7 Walk. c. 13, ff. 5, 9b.
8 Ibid. ff. 37b, 38b.
9 Ibid. ff. 43b, 49b, 54b.
10 Lamb. 902, f. 59.—Report of Surveyors, 7 Sept., 1649.
11 Rawl. c. 261, p. 24.
12 Walk. c. 13, f. 6.
13 Rawl. c. 261, p. 24.
14 Ibid. p. 23.
15 Joshua Thomas : Hanes y Bedyddwyr, p. 212.
16 Walk. c. 13, f 55.
17 Lamb. 639, (Codices Tenisoniani), f. 186b.
18 Walk. c. 13, f. 54.
19 Calendar of State Papers, 1656-7, p. 224. Probably a relative of *Richard Symonds,* the Approver.

Crossenny.[1] In a few cases, some of the Commissioners themselves were farmers—William Blethin at Undy in Monmouth,[2] and William Herbert at Llanarth[3] in the same county. John Lort, brother to one of the Commissioners, is down as tenant of the vicarage of Castlemartin in Pembroke.[4] How far this semi-nepotism had proceeded in North Wales is not ascertainable from the Rawlinson MS., but the fact that an effort was made in 1651 to allow Hugh Price of Welshpool to retain in his own hands the demesne of Red Castle in contravention of his oath as sequestration Commissioner under the London Committee for Compounding[5] suggests that such a policy was far from impossible there. Again, it was natural for the sequestrators to drive hard bargains with their political foes and give easy terms to their political friends. As an example of the latter, the living of Glasbury, valued at £100 per annum, was let at £50 a year to Evan Thomas, who was carpenter to the clerk of the Brecon and Radnor Commissioners.[6] Such a practice gave rise to much criticism,[7] it being further true, according to some, that not only were the livings let to the Commissioners' 'own friends and creatures,' but also underlet by these to the parishioners at rack-rents.[8] Probably in response to such reflections, the custom grew, more especially in Brecon and Monmouth, to tender the tithes to the parishioners direct: in the former county there are four such cases in 1650[9] and 22 in 1651 and 1652,[10] and in the latter 26 in 1650,[11] 38 in 1651,[12] and 47 in 1652.[13] Powell's letter to a London newspaper states that the same policy obtained in North Wales, ' but some are either so malignant or fearfull of their priest, that they would not, nor dare not, to take them in severall parishes.'[14] The same spirit finds expression

1 Walk. c. 13, f. 43b.
2   Ibid.   f. 43.
3   Ibid.   ff. 43b, 50.
4   Ibid.   f. 9.
5 Calendar of the Committee for Compounding, Vol. I, pp. 431, 444. Major-General Berry's opinion of Price was favourable—" he is a very honest, trusty fellow, and deserves incouragement," 23 July, 1650. (Thurloe State Papers, Vol. V, p. 242.)
6 Walk. c. 13, f. 61; Lamb. 1027—" Glasbury." Thomas is described as " carpenter throughout the whole parish."
7 Alexander Griffith : Mercurius Cambro-Britannicus, p. 5.
8 Cal. Comm. Comp., Vol. I, p. 495.
9 Walk. c. 13, ff. 59-59b.
10   Ibid.   ff. 61-61b.
11   Ibid.   ff. 43-44.
12   Ibid.   ff. 49-50b.
13   Ibid.   ff. 53-54b.
14 A Perfect Diurnall (May 3-10, 1652).

in Monmouth in 1652; 'none would ingage' both at Portskewet and Rogiett, and £30 tithes were not gathered at all.[1]

Whichever system was adopted, the rents and profits were continually in arrear. To account for this, the disaffection of Cavalier parishioners counted for much; so also did a growing Puritan feeling against payment of tithes even to Puritan farmers; besides, there was the poverty caused by the war and the inefficient 'stocking' of the countryside.[2] Other circumstances, general and local, unfavourably affected the Commissioners' exchequer. Such were the outbreak of the plague in Tenby and its liberties in 1650[3], the charging of 'a horse and rider' upon sequestered parsonages in Radnor and Brecon by the Commissioners for the Militia,[4] the acquisition of valuable interests in two sequestered Gower rectories by the University of Cambridge,[5] a repetition of the C.P.M. difficulty in the matter of leases of church lands granted under the old dispensation,[6] and arrears of salaries left unpaid by the Trustees for Maintenance of Ministers and the local committees for sequestrations. £90 were due to Powell and Mostyn under the order of 7th June, 1648,[7] and in three cases—those of Thomas Field of Lawhadden,[8] Jenkin Lewis of Puncheston,[8] Richard Jewell of Tenby[9]—the Trustees ordered their final payment up to March 1st, 1650, *and not up to March 25th*. And though Parliament was very punctilious in excluding Wales from the operation of two acts passed in 1650,[10] yet in other directions the old conflict of jurisdiction that to some extent impaired the efficiency of the C.P.M. had its counterpart during the early days of the Propagation. The local Commissioners of (lay) sequestrations in Brecon question the authority of the Collectors to gather the profits, asserting that that

---

1 Walk. c. 13, f. 54.
2 This point is made much of by Vavasor Powell. (A Brief Narrative of the former Propagation, p. 6).
3 Walk. c. 13, f. 5b. £14 was excused from the rent on this score.
4 Ibid. ff. 65, 65b
5 Calendar of State Papers, 1654, p. 335 [referring to a transaction of 9 May, 1650).
6 Calendar of the Comm. for Compounding, Vol. III, p. 1710 ; Walk. c. 13, f. 58.
7 Rawl. c. 261, p. 25.
8 Lamb. 979, f. 315.
9 Ibid. f. 316. Jewell was ejected soon after (supra, p. 131).
10 Firth and Rait : Acts and Ordinances, Vol. II, 377, 5 April, 1650, " An Act for Maintenance for Ministers and other pious uses " ; Firth and Rait : Acts and Ordinances, Vol. II, p. 391, 31 May, 1650, " An Act for the better payment of Augmentations."

duty was incumbent on themselves[1] ; at the end of the year 1650 the Central Commissioners for Compounding are inquiring about the disposal of the profits of certain rectories lately belonging to the Earl of Worcester[2] ; and for some reason the *tenths* of North Wales continued to be received by the Receiver-General in London and not by Daniel Lloyd, the Treasurer.[3] By the end of the first year's working, however, matters are going more smoothly. The great majority of the unejected clergy go on as of old ; some favoured few have augmentations granted them ; the ecclesiastical profits in the hands of the local sequestrators have been handed over to the Commissioners, whose agents pay out to *approved* nominees[4] of the C.P.M. and the Lords the salaries and augmentations heretofore settled upon them ; the Trustees for Maintenance have also transferred the impropriate revenues of the bishops and chapters, from which Walter, Cradock, and Symonds used to draw their maintenance[5] ; and to this fund has been added the rents received from newly sequestered livings and also the profits of livings whose incumbents have lately deceased, but to whom no successors have been appointed.[6] From these sources were paid the salaries of the various officials, approvers, ordinary itinerants, and schoolmasters. The South Wales approvers, sarcastically described as 'gifted' persons both spiritually and financially,[7] each received £100 a year, while the itinerants, being ' Ethiopians kept at a low diet,'[8] received on an average about £70. There was also the payment of fifths to the families of the ejected clergy,[9] and the expenses of removing some newly appointed ministers and their families ' to the country.'[10] The Glamorgan accounts contain charges for " bookes to the publique use,"[11] and in the same county 6/10 was paid in 1652 to the sheriff and bailiffs for

---

1 Cal. Comm. Comp. Vol. I, p. 493.
2   Ibid.   Vol. I, p. 367.
3 Rawl. c. 261,' p. 31.
4 *I.e., also approved* by the Commissioners.
5 Shaw : Hist. Eng. Church, Vol. II, p. 217.
6 *E.g., Steynton* in Pembrokeshire. Minister 'lately dead' says the report of the Commissioners of 1649 Act on 2 October, 1650. (Lamb. 915, ff. 97-98) ; it is let by the Pembroke Sequestrator in 1651 (Walk. c. 13, f. 9b).
7 Walk. c. 4, f. 67 ; used more especially with reference to Edmond Ellis of St. Fagans.
8 Alexander Griffith : Hue and Cry, p. 10.
9 Supra, pp. 135-137.
10 Supra, p. 145 ; this was also the case with two Glamorgan *schoolmasters,* Bright and Barcroft (Walk. c. 13, ff. 17b, 27).
11 Walk. c. 13, f. 17b.

the serving of precepts, probably upon refractory clergymen or parishioners who were unduly long in bringing their tithes.[1] Further, there were instructions in the Act for some solatium to the dependents of deceased ministers. £4 was paid to ' a poor minister's wife ' in Pembrokeshire,[2] and £30 to the relict of a godly teacher in Monmouthshire[3] ; Eleanor Roberts, the widow of Evan Roberts of Llanrhaiadr ym Mochnant gets £20 towards " the education of her children in godliness and learning,"[4] and the widow of the Llanbadarn Evan Roberts gets a similar sum for the same purpose[5] ; while the collector of Glamorgan is found paying £10 arrears in 1652 to Joseph Townesend as executor to his father, who had been one of the itinerants.[6] And it is practically certain that the " Mrs. Rose Powell, widdowe," who gets £70 from the Brecon treasury in 1650 was the relict of Robert Powell the approver, whose main sphere of interest lay in that county.[7]

There is no suggestion either in the minutes of the North Wales Commissioners or in the accounts of the South Wales counties of their duties as local Commissioners of Indemnity,[8] and the critics pass by this aspect of the Propagation Act almost unnoticed.[9] There is but *one* record, again, of the Commissioners following out the suggestions of the Maintenance Commissioners under the Act of 1649 to the effect that parishes might if conveniently situated,[10] *unite for public worship* : this was the order made at Roath on March 26th, 1652-3, when the Act was technically expired, that the parishes of Verwick, Llangoedmor and Aberporth " may conveniently meet together to hear the word and perform divine worship at the public place of meeting in the *town of Cardigan.*"[11] There is evidence of more diligence in conforming

1 Walk. c. 13, f. 31b.
2　Ibid.　f. 12.
3　Ibid.　f. 51.
4 Rawl. c. 261, p. 6.
5 Walk. c. 13, f. 47.
6　Ibid.　f. 22b.
7　Ibid.　f. 60. And it is not unnatural to infer that the " Mrs Barbara Matthews ' to whom £3 was paid out of the Glamorgan treasury in 1652 was the wife of Marmaduke Matthews, who had gone to New England in the days of the High Commission (f. 31b).
8 Supra, pp. 87-89. " Text of the Act."
9 The references in the ' Gemitus ' (p. 11) and the ' Seasonable Considerations ' (pp. 5-6) are only in general terms ; no specific cases of hardship are given. The former uses some strong terms, however ; ' entrapping articles,' ' profoundest subtilities,' ' this remediless Dilemma of Appeale,' describe both the text and working of the ' Indemnity ' clauses.
10 Firth and Rait : Acts and Ordinances, Vol. II, p. 147.
11 Lamb. 1006, f. 54.

R

to the spirit of the ordinance of 22nd March, 1646-7, for keeping churches in due repair.[1] While that ordinance placed this duty at the door of the churchwardens and the overseers of the poor who were to make assessments of the parishioners for the purpose, the collectors either made special grants from the funds in their hands or made abatement for reparation in the rents of the sequestered livings. Thus £14 14s. 4d. was spent in repairing St. Fagans Church in 1652,[2] £1 was abated in the rent of Panteg in Monmouth (1651),[3] £5 13s. 4d. was granted for the repair of the parish church of Michaelstone-y-Vedw in 1652,[4] £3 0s. 0d. likewise for the ' chappell ' of Llandegley in Radnor (1651),[5] and £33 13s. 0d. was ordered in the same county in 1652 " towards the reparacions of several [unnamed] churches and chappels."[6] £4 was specially allowed in the rent of Llanfrechfa for the repair of the *chancel*.[7] Nor were the parsonage houses wholly neglected. £5 was spent on each in the case of Llangwm and Cosheston in Pembroke[8] and £2 on that of Bryngwyn in Radnor,[9] all in 1650 ; £6 0s. 8d. divided between the parsonage houses of Rogiett and Llangattock-juxta-Usk in 1651[10]; £2 for that of Bishopston in Gower[11] in 1652 and £1 for ' reparacon ' of the Hay vicarage house in the same year.[12] Six shillings in the same year went for repairs to the ' tyth Barne ' of Llansantffread.[13] The disposessed rector of Robeston in Pembroke gives testimony of a very different kind ; he asserts that the farmer of the living " quite demolished the parsonage house and carried away all the stones thereof, *save seven or eight at most*."[14] Nor, according to Mansell, was there much regard paid to those external adjuncts of the church fabric which were offensive to extreme Puritans. Not only the bells of Merthyr,[15] but those of Gelligaer and Mynyddislwyn also,[16] were sold off, the monu-

1 Scobell : Acts and Ordinances, Vol. 1, p. 139.
2 Walk. c. 13, f. 31.
3   Ibid.   f. 50.
4   Ibid.   f. 57b.
5   Ibid.   f. 68b.
6   Ibid.   Ibid.
7   Ibid.   f. 44.
8 Walk. c. 13, f. 7.
9   Ibid.   f. 66.
10 Ibid.   f. 51b.
11 Ibid.   f. 23.
12 Ibid.   f. 63.
13 Ibid.   f. 63.
14 Lamb. 1027, f. 49.
15 Wilkins : Hist. of Merthyr—Nathan Jones's account p. 93.
16 Walk. c 4, ff. 65b 66.

ments of Llandaff Cathedral were effaced and the organ broken to pieces,[1] while the font at Bedwas was placed under a ' Ewe ' tree to water horses and cattle in.[1] Some expense was also incurred in making arrangements for the new *schools* ; there is an outlay of £2 18s. 0d. for repairs at Wrexham,[2] £5 at Bala,[3] £20 at Ruthin,[4] and close upon £60 at Swansea.[5] £50 rent per annum was paid at Bala for ' a house and garden now employed for a school house.'[6] There are orders for *new* schools to be erected at Dolgelly, Llangollen, Welshpool, Montgomery, and Llanidloes.[7]

Much correspondence[8] and some bad feeling[9] ensued when the administration of the sequestered livings was handed over at the expiry of the Act to the County Committees for Sequestrations who did such duty before it came into operation. The surplus revenue had to be transferred to the Trustees for Maintenance, established in England since 1650[10]; and Daniel Lloyd, the Treasurer for North Wales, made a special journey to London to give them a full account.[11] It is true that the Lord General's letter[12] of April 25th, 1653, to the late Welsh Commissioners in which he desired them ' to go on cheerfully in the work, protect good men, and execute things settled upon by former Acts ' practically gave another lease of life to the Propagation. Settled ministers, many itinerants, and all schoolmasters proceeded with their work as before, and thus continued until the ordinances of 1654, one appointing Commissioners for the Approbation of Public Preachers,[13] the other for ejecting scandalous ministers and schoolmasters.[14] But to the legal minds of the Commissioners' agents it was difficult to conceive of an Act being alive after its official death, and the Lambeth MSS. testify that the financial side of the Pro-

1 Walk. c. 4, f. 66.
2 Rawl. c. 261, p. 26.
3   Ibid.   p. 32.
4   Ibid.   p. 31.
5 Walk. c. 13, f. 23—£59 15s. 7d. ; a certain ' Ensigne Thomas Williams ' seems to have been responsible for the ' repayration.'
6 Rawl. c. 261, p. 32.
7 Rawl. c. 261, p. 21.   Orders given 19 Nov., 1650.
8 Cal. Comm. Comp., Vol. I, pp. 688, 689, 692, 697, 705, 710, 726.
9   Ibid.   p. 727.
10 Shaw : Hist. Eng. Church, II, p. 215.
11 Lamb. 1008, f. 279.
12 Cal. St. Papers, 1653-4, pp. 293-4.
13 Firth and Rait : Acts and Ordinances, Vol. , 855-8 : 20 March, 1653-4.
14   Ditto   ditto   Vo . II, 968-990 : 23 Arg., 1654.
   The jurisdiction of these ordinances extended over *England and Wales*, and powers were given to revise the appointments of all former authorities.

A History of the

pagation very soon fell into the hands of the two great London bodies,—the Committee for Compounding, soon to be replaced by a new body called Commissioners for Sequestrations[1] co-ordinating the activities of the County Committees of that name, and the Trustees for Maintenance already referred to. Inevitably some interests were sure to suffer in the transition, and some schoolmasters in North Wales fared worse. Notwithstanding an express order of the Trustees on June 14th, 1654, that the " Receivers of Wales " were to pay unto all schoolmasters within the 13 counties all arrears of yearly salaries and stipends settled upon them by the C.P.G.W. on the particular original orders being produced,[2] yet on December 4th of the same year they have to interfere in favour of Martinus Grundman of Welshpool, his usher Nathaniel Raven, and Thomas Quarrell of Montgomery to get their arrears under the Act paid.[3] A similar order in favour of Robert Edwards of Llansilin occurs on March 19th, 1654-5,[4] while as late as April, 1658, the Registrar of the Trustees was to search for the original papers " upon which the salary of Edward Wynne of Glynceiriog was granted."[5] Some light on the obstruction is afforded by State Paper Dom. Interr. G. 27. John Davies of Newtown could not get his arrears paid without a special order from the Commissioners of Sequestrations in London, as the Montgomeryshire ' agent ' under the Propagation Act said his powers to pay had ' determined ' with the expiry of the Act.[6] £27 10s. 0d. owing to Thomas Williams, his usher, who had a wife and four small children, were kept in the hands of the same agent " because he wanted an order to pay it."[7] A similar reason was given by the county official in the case of the £20 arrears due to David Evans of New Radnor.[8] The schoolmasters of Dolgelly and Bala—Griffith Jones and John Evans —took the unprecedented course of a direct petition to the Protector, alleging that with the ' ceasing ' of the Act their source of revenue was alienated and that the Trustees were

1 Calendar of the Committee for Compounding, Vol. I, p. 668 (Ordinance—Feb. 10th, 1653-4).
2 Lamb. 1008, f. 42.
3 Lamb. 972, ff. 67-68.
4 Lamb. 972, f. 127.
5 Lamb. 980, f. 218.
6 f. 123.   26 Sept., 1654.
7 f. 148.   31 Oct., 1654.
8 f. 165.   16 Nov., 1654.

unable to regain control over it.¹ The case of these two, however, is somewhat different. They claim no arrears under the Act, but for the two succeeding years ; the Council of State by a special order directed £80 arrear to be paid to Jones and £70 to Evans. Thus these ' good men ' were ultimately ' protected.'

NOTE : ALEXANDER GRIFFITH v. WILLIAM WATKINS.

One explicit charge of dishonesty is brought against a Propagation official. A. G.'s detective ingenuity discovered a letter written on 8th November, 1651, from William Watkins, clerk of the Commissioners in Brecon and Radnor, to the approver Jenkin Jones, intimating that £12, the rent of the prebend of Llanwrthwl, could be ' safely paid ' by the latter, wherever he pleased, ' because it is such an Arrere that the Treasurer knoweth not of, for it lieth not in charge before him' (True and Perfect Relation, pp. 34-36). The inference from this last statement is that it was money due from the time when the prebend was sequestered, but *before* the Propagation Act came into operation (p. 35, second letter). Again, A. G.'s animus against Watkins was palpable, and there is no evidence that Jones received the money. The rent for 1650 was duly accounted for to the Treasurer (Walk. c. 13, f. 59b), and if it be said that it was an old debt, the incident argues not only the culpability of the Propagation clerk, but also the laxity, if not collusion, of the old County Committee for Sequestrations, the personnel of which happened to be closely connected with the notorious Petition of 1652.

1 Cal. St. Papers, 1655-56, pp. 221-222. March 13th.

XVII.

THE SOUTH WALES PETITION OF 1652.

Thus far the criticism of the Act, both as regards its moving personalities and the nature of its administration, has proceeded either from Royalist pamphleteers or from the constables' reports made in 1662, and applied indiscriminately to how affairs developed in both North and South Wales. In 1652, when the Commissioners were in the heyday of their authority and the apparatus of the Act was in full working order, an attack in the form of a petition, emanating from South Wales and Monmouth, and currently reported to be signed by 15,000 hands, was made in the interests of ' well-affected ' but disillusioned Puritanism. Some light is thrown on the nature of the Petition in the Journals of the House of Commons, but its full history and real significance was revealed to the world two years later by the pen of the acutest defender of outraged Anglicanism. A situation so piquant, —with charges whose subject-matter were confined within a well-marked geographical entity, and constituting evidence so strictly contemporary both as regards attack and the rebutting evidence,—calls for separate and independent treatment.

(i) HISTORY.

On Wednesday, March 10th, 165$\frac{1}{2}$, the House of Commons was informed that divers petitioners from South Wales were at the door ; they were called in ; and Colonel Freeman presented at the bar a " humble petition of several of the Inhabitants of the Six Counties of South Wales and the County of Monmouth, well-affected to the Parliament and the present Government, on behalf of themselves and the rest of the Inhabitants there." It was at once referred to the C.P.M. to state the matter of fact and report their opinion therein to the House.[1] On the 16th March, the Committee found the Petition " ambiguously drawn and containing only things in general," with no person named,

1 C J. VII, p. 103.

and discovered also "some things therein represented as Crimes which if proved would not appear to be so." They refuse to grant the 'Commission to the country' which the solicitors for the Petition strongly demanded, 'conceiving it might be of dangerous consequence to do so without clear grounds'; rather do they demand from them particular charges, detailing the names of ministers unjustly ejected and of persons who had embezzled monies. The Solicitors, pointing out that they had no more yet in charge than the mere prosecution of the Petition, want a convenient time to send to the country for these details. A letter was to be sent from the Committee to the Commissioners in Wales enclosing a copy of the Petition, and desiring an account of their stewardship by the 18th May. On that day the agents of the Commissioners presented a *letter* to the Chairman having 'inclosed in it a full account touching all the particulars in the said Petition contained,' and 'a *Book*[1] also. . . . of about sixty sheets of paper containing all the proceedings of the said Commissioners in obedience to the Act.'[2] Both letter and book were read in the presence of both parties, gave much satisfaction to the Committee, and was allowed even by the Solicitors of the Petitioners to be 'ingeneous,' adding that 'they were glad to see the Commissioners could give so good account of their proceedings.' But the question was not closed; the Solicitors demanded a copy of the 'book,' and again pressed to have a Commission appointed to the country to examine witnesses upon the subject-matter of the Petition. The C.P.M. in answer gave them until the 21st May to exhibit their 'particulars,' but the Solicitors' only answer was to press once again for their 'Commission.' By this time, too, information had reached the Committee that the Petition had been contrived and printed in London by disaffected persons, and that copies had been sent down to malignants in the country with instructions for the

---

1 This 'book,' the most important document of the Propagation period next to Walk. c. 13, cannot be discovered. Vavasor Powell examined it before May, 1652 (Letter to "Perfect Diurnall" (May 3-10, 1652)); it was lodged with John Phelps, clerk to the C.P.M., and taken away on one occasion by Harrison (Relation, p. 9); John Walker saw it lying at Lambeth some time between 1704 and 1714 (supra, p. 107). The present Lambeth Librarian is certain that it cannot be found there now. Alexander Griffith is emphatic that the Petitioners never had a copy of it for leisured examination (Relation, pp. 11, 42).
2 According to the copy seen at Lambeth, this document was 'drawn up' on the 20*th April*, 1652 (Walk. Suff., Part I, p. 151, col. 1).

subscribing thereof; that the same was chiefly signed by
' Malignants their Servants and Tenants, and by Women
and school-boys in the counties of Brecknock and Radnor.'
The Committee refer also to ' a design therein of very dangerous
consequence to the peace of those counties whereof they
conceive themselves not impowered by Parliament to take
full Cognizance thereof.'[1] Letters were also sent from
J.P's. in those counties dwelling on the same danger, and
some time in June especially important information was
conveyed to the authorities. No Commission satisfying
the Petitioners was ever granted, but the latter succeeded
in bringing in a reply (in the form of ' particular charges ')
to the statements of the Welsh Commissioners by 16th
July, 1652, and another rejoinder to their ' general ' answer
of 18th May by 20th August of the same year.[2] The whole
matter was in continual agitation before the C.P.M. from
March, 1652 to the dissolution of the Rump in 1653,[3] when
the question was finally shelved as far as the Petition was
concerned. Feeling in the Committee ran so high, if the
historian of the Petition is to be believed, that Richard
Creed, the Commissioners' agent, was seen dictating the
words of an ' order ' to one of the clerks, that Major-General
Harrison snatched up the ' Book of sixty sheets ' and took
it away with him, and that meetings were adjourned to
certain dates which turned out to be ' fast days ' when no
business could be transacted.[4] One of the chief organisers
of the Petition was for some time committed to the custody
of the sergeant-at-arms for alleged malpractices in connection
with it,[5] and another was ordered by the Council of State
not to depart from town above 10 miles for one month, to
leave a note of his place of abode, and to enter into a bond
with good securities to appear for examination.[6] This
Petition itself, the story of its fortunes in the C.P.M.,· the
' general answer ' of the Commissioners and the rejoinder

1 C. J. VII, 271. Summary of a Report read in the House of Commons on
March 25th, 1653, by Col. Bennett on behalf of the C.P.M.
2 Relation, pp. 8-9.
3 With the qualification that on 8 Sept., 1652, the C.P.M. declared that ' they
would make no further proceedings in the said cause ' except to present to Parliament
a report on the same drafted by a sub-committee on June 29th, with the result that
the Petitioners ' did patiently waite in expectation of what the Lord would be pleased
to direct them to do therein.' (Relation, pp. 11-12).
4 True and Perfect Relation, pp. 9-11.
5 Cal. St. Papers, 1651-1652, p. 354 ; 1652-53, p. 143.
6 Cal. St. Papers, 1651-2, pp. 380, 381, 416, 420, 425, 432, 433, 447, 455, 456
(August-Octcber, 1652).

of the Petitioners, together with other matters of allied interest, were marshalled into what is now a very rare and important Commonwealth tract known as " The True and Perfect Relation of the Petition, etc."[1] Its author was Alexander Griffith, the ejected vicar of Glasbury ; it was published in 1654 and addressed to the Protector, in the pious hope that an omnipotent soldier would do what the decadent Rump and its Committee had failed to do, viz., send " a Commission to the country."

(ii) THE PLAINTIFFS' CHARACTER.

It is open to grave doubt whether a good deal of the information supplied to the C.P.M. concerning the Petitioners was not correct. The chief sponsors were William Thomas of Brecon, John Gunter of Tredomen in the same county, and Colonel Edward Freeman, Attorney-General for South Wales and M.P. for Hereford. The latter's professional duties had brought him into conflict with the masterful spirit of Col. Philip Jones, who was a member of the Committee for Compounding at Goldsmiths' Hall[2] ; in fact, he had boldly objected before this Committee against many names submitted to it as proper persons to hold sequestration appointments in South Wales, coupling with this an accusation that Col. Jones held ' sequestration monies ' in his own hands[3]. Only two months before the Petition was presented there was a proposal before the same Committee that Freeman should be named a Commissioner for sequestrations in every county in South Wales ' as his appearance would much countenance that service.'[4] It is possible that the other two were disappointed office-seekers under the Propagation Act, that they were among those nettled by the ' humble acknowledgment ' presented to Parliament by 19,000 South

1 A close collation of { The Petition (gereral) of March, 1652, [N.L.W. 275] and { The Petition as copied into the 'Relation,' and also of { Vavasor's letter in " Perfect Diurnall,", [B. Mus.] and A. G's copy in the ' Relation,' show that the virulent critic was quite an honest scribe. As the ' Relation ' is the only authority for the ' general reply' of the Commissioners (May 18th, 1652), this question of honesty is vested with not a little importance.

2 Appointed a member on December 18th, 1648. (Cal. Comm. Comp., Vol. I, p. 135.)

3 Cal. Comm. Comp., Vol. I, p. 517. December 12th, 1654

4 Ibid. p. 507, November 25th, 1651.

Wales supporters of ʿthe Act on June 20th, 1650[1], and felt
themselves included in the ' Offenders of a deeper stain '
alluded to in the ' declaration and remonstrance ' sent in
from the same quarter on June 28th.[2] In other directions
it is certain that they harboured distinct grievances. On
October 25th, 1651, they are described as County (Sequestration) Commissioners for Brecknock[3]; on November 25th,
there is an order reappointing them to the same office[4];
on December 2nd, they send in to headquarters a vigorous
diatribe against the working of the Propagation Act[5]; on
December 16th, the sequel came with their displacement
from office[6]; and naturally the Committee for Compounding
were not surprised to hear of difficulties arising when the
new officials took up their duties.[7] As a consequence of
the Petition and its reactions, Gunter suffered slight
imprisonment, and Freeman in June, 1653, was deprived
of his Attorneyship.[8] Then beyond some references to the
former in the Thurloe State Papers in which he is still hot
on the trail ōf some of the Propagators in the ostensible
interests of the Protectorate,[9] little is heard of either of the
three until the death of Oliver and the eve of the Restoration.
This ominous silence and the resuscitation of their fortunes
at this particular time throws a flood of chequered light
on their activities in 1652. A tract of 1659 accuses Philip
Jones of having Thomas and Gunter dismissed in 1651[10];
another advocated the recovery of the Attorneyship by
Freeman.[11] Early in the same year the latter is prominent
on a Committee appointed on February 5th, 165$\frac{8}{9}$,[12] and
introduces a bill on 9th March, 1659-1660,[13] both abortive,
and both designed to reopen the question settled by the
accounts given in by the Treasurers under the Propagation
Act in 1655. All three appear as Commissioners in important

1 The Humble Acknowledgement of the Inhabitants of South Wales and County
of Monmouth (N.L.W.).
  2 A Declaration and Remonstrance of the Inhabitants of South Wales (N.L.W.)
  3 Cal. Comm. for Compounding, Vol. I, p. 493.
  4   Ibid.   p. 506.
  5   Ibid.   p. 513.
  6   Ibid.   p. 517.
  7   Ibid.   p. 530.
  8 Cal. St. Papers, 1652, p. 423.
  9 Vol. II, pp. 93. 129. Letters received by him giving details of their movements.
  10 Articles of Impeachment of Transcendent Crimes . . . } Art. XIII,
committed by Philip Jones. Thomason Coll., B. Mus.   }   p 9.
  11 Twelve Queries Humbly Proposed to the Consideration of Parliament and
Army, Query VI, p. 4. Thomason Coll., B. Mus.
  12 C. J. VII, 600.
  13 Ibid., VII, 868, 880.

acts that ultimately led to the King's coming home. Thomas is Commissioner for Brecknock in the Militia Act of March, 1660[1]; Gunter appears as Commissioner of Assessments in January, 1660,[2] and for the Militia in March for the same county; and Freeman is named Commissioner in the same Acts for Hereford and for Glamorgan (Militia).[3] Gunter about the end of 1659 had information about South Wales to impart to the Army Commissioners,. and it was little probable that it would be to the advantage of his opponents in 1652. But in this latter year, though the watchwords of the Petitioners were loyalty and good affection, the 'particular charges' themselves contain evidence of their personal animus towards the officials of the Act and of their desire to make shipwreck of its fundamental proposals. They recount how they[4] had offered £95 for the tithes of Llantilio Crossenny and had been refused[5]; they even make an offer, and repeat it more than once, to farm the whole sequestered livings for £20,000, to which the Commissioners naturally made no reply. Finally, it is almost certain that if the agents of the Commissioners had followed the Petitioners' suggestion by accepting *capital* sums for the livings—fifths included as in the case of Glasbury,[6] fifths plus 'taxations' as in the case of Lawrenny and Nantcwnlle[7] —they would not only break the letter of the Act, but also involve themselves in actuarial difficulties. Their dealings would be described as being *too* 'ingeneous,' the accounts in 1655 would not be accepted, and correspondence longer and more bitter would ensue at the expiry of the Act between the Treasurers and the London commissioners and trustees. Some allowance must be made the Petitioners for the turbulent county from which the ruling spirits hailed. Brecknock was the favoured home of discontent in Wales during the Commonwealth. There was not only the personal vendetta over appointments and the information lodged with the C.P.M., but also the petition of the inhabitants of Brecon

---

1 Firth and Rait: Acts and Ordinances, Vol. II, p. 1447.
2   Ibid.   p. 1382.
3 Firth and Rait: Acts and Ordinances, Vol. II, pp. 1369, 1432.
4 It is difficult to say from the N.L.W. copy of the 'Relation' whether the word is Petitioner*e* or Petitioner*s*.
5 Relation, p. 28.
6   Ibid. p. 25.
7   Ibid. p. 28.

against Edmund Jones as Recorder,[1] the petition of the county against the M.P. elected for the First Protectorate Parliament on account of the menaces and terrors that secured his return,[2] the angry interchange of letters in the early months of 1654 between Jenkin Jones, the erstwhile Approver, and three ejected clergymen (all hailing from the county),[3] and the High Sheriff's return for 1658, on which Walker draws so copiously in proving his theory of an illiterate ministry during the interregnum.[4]

It was almost inevitable that the Puritanism of such ' well-affected ' Parliamentarians should be clouded with suspicion. The meticulous care taken to analyse the ejected clergy according to the University degrees[5] they held and to infer saintly devotion to duty and efficient preaching from the imprimatur of the Chancellors of the two Universities is more typical of David Lloyd, Anthony à Wood, and John Walker, than of the protagonists of ' godly and painful men.' It is possible, and even probable, that much of the Petitioners' information concerning rents and tenants was supplied by the ejected clergy,[6] and the absolute accuracy of the Glasbury report both as regards name of tenant and amount of rent suggests the collusion of Alexander Griffith himself. It has even been said that he was one of the chief promoters of the Petition[7]; and it must be admitted that the passages in it descanting on the failure of the itinerant system and the closing of churches on the Lord's Day are surprisingly similar to passages in other anti-Propagation literature of the same author[8]; further, the enthusiasm and ability he displayed in compiling the ' Relation ' in 1654, and the close parallel, both as regards date and substance, between his energies and those of John Gunter and his informants in 1654,[9] seem to point very strongly to more

1 Cal. St. Papers, 1651, p. 287.
2   Ibid.   1654, pp. 271-272; the Complaint of the County of Brecon (1654). N.L.W.
3 True and Perfect Relation, pp. 50-52.
    (a) Letter of Thos. Lewis, Thos. Powell and Griffith Hatley to Jones, (February 6th, 165¾).
    (b) Jones's rejoinder, (March 2nd, 165¾).
    (c) Clergymen's reply to (b), (March 6th. 165¾).
4 Sufferings (especially Part I, pp. 151, 160-161).
5 Relation, p. 19, ' Particular charges.'
6 For inaccuracy of much of this information, vide Chap. XVIII.
7 J. H. Davies : Gweithiau Morgan Llwyd, Vol. II., p. 295, Note (2).
8 Cp. Strena Vavasoriensis, p. 5; Merc.-Camb.-Britannicus, p. 6; Relation, pp. 30-31.
9 Thurloe State Papers, Vol. II., pp. 93, 124, 128, 129.

than accidental collaboration. It is natural in these circumstances to find the Petitioners lacking in enthusiasm towards
the extremer developments of Puritan thought in church-
essentials and church-government. "The Light of the
Gospel," asserts Colonel Freeman in supporting the March
Petition with delicate irony, "shines only in some few
corners of the country, where they are ingrossed into
particular distinct Congregations,"[1] implying but scant
sympathy with Baptists and Independents. Again, when
the lists of degreed clergy[2] and the accusation that the
Commissioners bestowed but small care on the reparation of
churches[3] are placed side by side with the sympathy for
' the few that still desire the publick worship of God[4] and
the remark that ' [Propagation] Pastors and their particular
Auditors take more delight in Teaching and Expounding
the Word of God in private houses and other places than
the publick worship of God in publique churches,'[4] there
is but one conclusion. The Petitioners had at heart as little
desire to desert the ancient fabrics of the Church, whatever
changes stern necessities of State might order for the nonce
in the *form* of worship, as to lose the learned but disestablished
incumbents. The same undercurrent of opposition to the
new Puritan fervour, finding expression in public debates
and disputes, appears in the interesting "contestations"
passage[5] where reference is made to ' rents and divisions '
at Swansea, Merthyr, at Bedwas on Low-Easter Sunday,
and at Mynyddislwyn on Easter Monday in 1652. And
it was the most obscure of the three organisers of the Petition
who in his ' alarum to corporations ' (1659) had the courage
to call the old Approver, Jenkin Jones, ' a giddy sort of
Heretick . . . a Leveller,' who was desirous of erecting
' a Righteous Government after the manner of John of
Leyden and Knipperdolling.'[6] When the ' well-affected '
kept such company and uttered words so strange to Puritan
ears, it was indeed essential, as John Jones of Maes-y-garnedd
in a letter from Ireland to Morgan Llwyd expressed it, " to
observe what hands promote it, who they be that subscribe

1 Relation,pp. 3-4.
2   Ibid.   p. 19.
3   Ibid.   p. 46.
4   Ibid.   p. 47.
5   Ibid.   p. 30.
   6 " An Alarum to Corporations," especially the ' Title Page ' and Advertisement
(p. 8).   N.L.W.

it, and to take exact notice what temper they are of, and what kind of ministry they are and would promote."[1] Nine years later Vavasor Powell cannot find a better term for such critics than ' Prejudicated persons,'[2] and in one of the Radnor Assizes of 1652 he could not forbear from " reviling and cursing Collonel Freeman in his person and in his place for preferring the said Petition."[3]

---

1 *August*, 1652. Gweithiau Morgan Llwyd, Vol. II., p. 295, Postscript.
2 Bird in the Cage Chirping . . . a brief Narrative of the former Propagation . . . p. 4. (1661).
3 The Petition of the Six Counties of South Wales, p. 22 (" For Mr. Valvasor Powell . . .). A. G. savs ' last Assises,' i.e., Spring.

XVIII.

THE SOUTH WALES PETITION OF 1652—contd

(iii) An Examination of the Charges.

(a) Unfair ' Letting ' of Sequestered Livings.

Thus for effective criticism of the working of the Act, the Petitioners laboured under serious disadvantages. They disliked the Act itself, and especially the officials who administered it; the leaders came from Brecknock; they were not genuine Puritans; and, like the majority of strong partisans, they eagerly snatched at pleasing information which might, or might not, be exact. Especially is this the case with the charges of favouritism and dishonesty in letting the sequestered livings. Cut off, as the Petitioners were, from the authentic sources of information by their hostility to the Sequestrators and Collectors, they had to rely on hearsay evidence, the gossip of disappointed applicants for livings, and the secret intelligence of the ejected clergy. Such evidence was quite overshadowed by the accounts sent in by the Treasurers under the Act of 1654, which had to be submitted to, among others, three Justices of Great Sessions, and to be subject to the possible review of a Parliament in which the constitutional party was in the ascendant, Harrison not a member, and his party a small and despised minority. Forty-five instances are given in the Petition— sixteen from Radnor, eleven from Pembroke, seven from Brecknock, four from Monmouth, three from Carmarthen, and two each from Glamorgan and Cardigan. Of these, taking the valuation of 1650 as a working basis, these being the rents usually reported to the Petitioners, thirteen cases tally with those given in Walker c.13, eighteen are set at a *higher* rate than described in the Petition, fourteen are actually set at a *lower*, which is an indirect proof of the credibility of the accounts given in by the Treasurers, drawn up as they were two years after the Petitioners had submitted their case. Naturally, the information was most approximately correct for Brecon and Radnor, very nearly so in Cardigan and Pembroke, but in the other three counties very serious mistakes were made. It was most essential that a very strong case should be made in Philip Jones's home-county of Glamorgan, but only two instances are adduced—Cheriton, where the Petitioners made a mistake of £10 on the wrong side,[1] and Bishopston, where it similarly amounted to £15.[2] In Monmouthshire, the living of Grosmont was said to be let at only £10, when in reality it was £40[3]; in the case of Llanfetherin, much was made of the fact that the farmer was Charles Goddard, "his wife being Mr. Cradock's *neer* kinswoman," not knowing that his rent of £50 in 1650 was raised to £80 10s. 0d. in 1651.[4] The tithes of Llangunnor in Carmarthen were not set, as alleged, to the ' own brother ' of John Hughes, the Sequestrator, but to David John Griffith in 1650 and 1651, to Nicholas Chappell in 1652.[5] But these are small digressions from truth compared with their information about the group of impropriate livings once held by Lord Henry Percy in the Llanelly district of Carmarthen, and another group sequestered from the Earl of Worcester in the Llanelly district of Brecon. The former, say the Petitioners, has been set and let at £60 a year and to Sir Henry Vaughan, a compounded delinquent ; really, they had been valued at £500 a year, and Sir Henry, though evidently a slow and reluctant payer, had sent in £200 in 1651 and £350 in 1652.[6] It is true that Crickhowell, Llangenny, Llangattock, and Llanelly in Brecon had all been set at £150, which is the Petitioners' total for the whole group, for it was evidently not within their knowledge that the living of Cwmdu had been set separately at the rate of £50 a year.[7] And it was surely lack of information that

Relation, p. 27.
1 Walk. c. 13. f. 15b.
2 Relation, p. 27.
Walk. c. 13. f. 16.
Relation, p. 28.
3 Walk. c. 13. f. 43b.'
Relation, p. 28.
4 Walk. c. 13, f. 43b (1650) ; f. 49 (1651).
Relation p. 26.
5 Walk. c. 13, f. 37 (1650) ; f. 38 (1651) ; f 40 (1652)
Relation, p. 26.
6 Walk. c. 13, ff. 21, 38b.
Relation p. 26.
7 Walk. c. 13, ff. 59, 61, 61b.

prevented the Petition referring to livings in the hands of Commissioners and their friends and relatives, which most probably lay at the root of Vavasor's remark that he 'objected against some of their proceedings' in South Wales.[1]

(b) HIGH ARREARS.

The Commissioners admitted the high state of arrears, £1,594 12s. 3d. in 1650[2] and £4,523 15s. 4d.[3] in 1651, but the detailed lists furnished by the officials of the parishes sequestered, the rent at which set, the name of the tenant, and the exact sum of arrear (if any) in each case, seem effectively to traverse the Petitioners' charge that the arrears were by collusion allowed 'to rest in the tenants' hands.' The men in arrear include yeomen like Robert Edwards of Coychurch and noblemen like the Earl of Carbery, and range from friends of the Commissioners like William Bassett of Cheriton to old delinquents like the Vaughans and Somersets. Still, the Commissioners are hard put to it to account for such large deficiencies, and in doing so adduce reasons that are not suggested in the Rawlinson MS., and only faintly so in the dry balance-sheets sent in by the Treasurers. First, comes the statement that 'most part of 1650[4] and in some places much of 1651 was spent and most of the profits raised by the scandalous pretended ministers before they were ejected'[5]; secondly, that livings were let to parishioners at somewhat a lower rate than to any 'particular farmour'; thirdly, that when an ejected minister was much in debt, or had a large family and with no 'other estate,' he was admitted tenant of his old living at somewhat of an under-value; next, that Easter-offerings 'received of the Papists' which 'heretofore made some vicarages considerable' had fallen off; and they wind up by touching upon the general

1 A Perfect Diurnall (May 3-10, 1652)—Letter.

		£	s.	d.	
2 1650.	Revenue of sequestered livings as set	9,518	5	8	⎫
	Disbursements to ministers, schoolmasters, etc.	7,923	13	5	⎬ Relation,
					p 41.
	Arrears in the tenants' hands	1,594	12	3	⎭
3 1651.	Revenue of sequestered livings as set	10,418	5	2	⎫
	Disbursements to ministers, schoolmasters, etc.	5,894	9	10	⎬ Relation,
					p. .
	Arrears in the tenants' hands	4,523	15	4	⎭

4 So in the original; read 'most part of the revenue of 1650, ...''
5 Entry in Walk. c. 13, f. 5b. (Pembrokeshire accounts):— "£3 6s. 8d. This the minister of *Spittle* [Spittal] received before he was ejected"; 'his Quarter stipend' according to f. 8b.

S

disgust against tithes, the disturbance put upon the country by malignants 'at the least invasion of the enemy,'[1] not forgetting to emphasise the discontent caused by the promoters of the Petition. On the question of letting livings to parishioners the Petitioners and the Treasurers are in direct conflict of opinion, as the former assert that this particular development became popular with the Commissioners *since* the 'exhibition' of their Petition.[2] The parishioners farmed the same number in Brecon during the year of the Petition as they did in 1651, and in a county of numerous parishes like Monmouth an increase of nine in 1652 over 1651[3] does not seem sufficient to establish the Petitioners' case conclusively. Again, a comparison of the lists of sequestered livings and rents respectively charged for them in 1651 and 1652 shows that in the latter, while in the counties generally they remain *stationary*, three anomalous cases stand out. The sixteen Radnor instances mentioned by the Petitioners as having been set at too low a rate are still further lowered[4]; Goddard's name does not appear as tenant of Llanfetherin, but the rent has been lowered by £15[5]; the Pembrokeshire sequestrator *raises* the rent in eleven cases.[6] If the Petition was the prime moving cause of these fluctuations, its arguments must have succeeded inversely with the ratio of distance from the Petitioners' headquarters.

(c) THE ITINERANT FAILURE.

The Petitioners stand on far firmer ground when they discuss the failure of the great Propagation experiment to supply the place of the ejected by itinerant ministers, and they press this point home with wearisome iteration. Arguments from diverse quarters lighten up this central theme. Fabrics are not 'upheld' because no ministers come to preach in them[7]; tithes are not paid because there are no services in return[8]; acts and edicts of Parliament

1 Reference to the invasion of the 'king of Scots' in 1651, culminating in the battle of Worcester.
2 This probably means its first mooting 'in the country,' and not its presentation to the House of Commons.
3 p. 238, supra.
4 Walk. c. 13, f. 67.
5   Ibid.   f. 53.
6   Ibid.,   f. 11.
7 Relation, p. 46.
8   Ibid.,   p. 45.

cannot be proclaimed 'for want of Teachers to publish the same '[1]; children are not catechised because the churches are closed[2]; the alleged dishonesty of the officials accounts both for the lack of settled ministers and the ' sad complaint ' of the itinerants that they are badly paid.[3] But of this last charge and of the startling statement that some of the ejected *were* paid for *not* preaching[4] not a single 'particular' is given, notwithstanding the C.P.M.'s reflection that these open statements were the besetting sin of the Petition as originally presented. The more trite accusation that the itinerants were mostly illiterate is supported by only one instance, that of *Walter Williams of Glamorgan.*[5] " When the act of Parliament for publick Thanksgiving for the victory obtained at Worcester against the late King of Scots was sent down to the County of Glamorgan to be publiquely read in all Churches and Chappells . . . [he] answered that he could not read the same." There is no evidence to disprove the statement.[6] But when the Petitioners definitely assert that " the town of *Brecon* had not been supplied with a constant able Teacher or Minister for two years last past "[7] they were disregarding the fact, or unaware of it, that a ' Mr. Lambe ' was being paid £40 7s. 0d. as ' lecturer ' at that town for 1651 and part of 1652.[8]

(d) DELINQUENT MINISTERS.

Accusations were levelled against the Commissioners of allowing persons—three in number—to preach and officiate who had borne ' actuall Armes against the Parliament.' One was *Hugh Rogers* the itinerant, who did so " whilst the late King had any visible strength or interest in the Nation to protect him " ; he was also said " to formerly revile and vilify the Parliament and Army and all the godly party and their proceedings."[9] Assuming this to be true, Rogers proved a true Puritan convert, for he lived to be

1 Relation, pp. 33, 47.
2   Ibid.   p. 32.
3   Ibid.   p. 2⁵.
4   Ibid.   pp. 44-45.
5 Relation, p. 33 ; Walk. c. 13, ff. 26b, 31b.
6 He is probably the ' Walter William' who kept a conventicle in 1669 at Llan-degveth in Monmouthshire. (Cod. Ten., Vol. 639, f. 188b.)
7 Relation, p. 31.
8 Walk. c. 13, f. 63.
9 Relation, p. 29. Rogers is also charged, in company with Richard Creed, of having attempted to ' disengage ' John Gunter from prosecuting the Petition (p. 12).

ejected from Newtown at the Restoration,[1] to be granted
two licences under the Declaration of Indulgence in 1672,[2]
and to deserve the good word of Philip Henry (Diaries,
p. 285). The second was *Robert Prichard*, 'parson '·
of Nevern in Pembrokeshire, who is said to have ' deserted
his habitation, joyned with the enemy, and acted with
Captaine Edward Lloyd his father-in-law in Kidwelley
Castle against the Parliament, and as is generally believed,
hath not yet subscribed the Ingagement."[3] The records
are silent on the first group of charges, and in the incomplete
lists of those who took the Engagement his name does not
appear. But the Commissioners[4] at Haverfordwest on
2nd October, 1650, describe him as a " preaching minister,"
and he must have been satisfactory to both C.P.G.W. and
C.A.P.P.,[5] as it was probably on his death that Oliver Thomas
in 1658 was presented to that living.[6] The third case
is " *one Hughes of the County of Carmarthen* " who is charged
with taking part in the Poyer rebellion of 1648 and yet is
' allowed to hold one or two benefices.'[7] Only three persons
of this surname figure in the religious records of Carmarthenshire at this period. William Hughes, vicar of Llanarthney,
was ejected ' under the Act,'[8] and another William Hughes,
vicar of Llangathen, instituted on 2nd July, 1618,[9] was
either dead before 1650 or was sequestered ' before the
Act,' as his living is farmed out in 1650, 1651, and 1652.[10]
The other is Stephen Hughes who, though inaccurately
described as holding the living of Mydrim in 1645,[11] might
have held the living of Merthyr after the ejection of its rector
William Evans in 1650.[12] But the whole tenor of this famous
Puritan's life traverses the possibility of his ever having
been either a tacit or avowed Royalist, and if his name

1 Calamy : Account, Vol. II, p. 712.
2 S.P. Dom., Car. II, 38A, pp. 246, 270.
3 Relation, p. 29.
4 Parochial Survey—Lamb., 915, f. 154.
5 C. P. G. W.= Commissioners for the Propagation of the Gospel in Wales.
  C. A. P. P. =   ,,   ,,   Approbation of Public Preachers.
                          [= 'Triers '].
6 Shankland : ' Diwygwyr Cymru '—Seren Gomer : Tach. 1901, p. 324.
7 Relation, p. 29.
8 Walk. e. 7, f. 212.
9 Lib. Inst., Meneven. p. 72.
10 Walk. c. 13, ff. 37, 38b, 40b.
11 Vide T. Shankland's article ' Stephen Hughes ' in ' Beirniad,' Hydref, 1912,
p. 176.
    12 The ' William Jones ' who was ejected from Merthyr in 1653 (Walk. e. 7. f.219b)
is surely a clerical mistake made either by the constable of 1662 or by Walker's aman-
uensis at Lambeth. As to the exact name of the ejected rector, Walk. e. 7, f. 212 is
the highest authority.

is to be equated with the ' one Hughes,' it is still mysterious how his close relationship to John Hughes, the official sequestrator in Carmarthenshire, did not receive a passing remark from the Petitioners. Still more mysterious is the next person that is incriminated. He is "one *Thomas Price of the County of Cardigan*, setled by the Bishop since. the reducing of that county to the obedience of Parliament ; and one that hath kept an Alehouse and a great frequenter of Alehouses."[1] There happened to be an abundance of Prices holding livings in Cardiganshire from 1620 to 1652, of whom one was approved by both C.P.M. and C.P.G.W., two were ejected ' under the Act,' while the others proved unexceptionable to the Puritan authorities. But there was no *Thomas* among them. Nor does the ' Liber ' contain the name of a single holder of a living in that county who was settled there[2] since the final pacification of Cardiganshire in the early months of 1646[3] ; and some time before that institution and induction in ancient form had become obsolete, and Chancellors, Vicars General, and Commissaries of Faculties were simply ordered by the Lords and Commons to observe as much of the old routine as was necessary to preserve some ecclesiastical order, until they were wholly superseded by the joint machinery of the C.P.M. and the Westminster Assembly. No person of the name was placed in Cardiganshire by the C.P.M.; the only surviving Propagation accounts contain no allusion to him. A ' Thomas Price ' held the living of Llandilo Graban in Radnor on 8th November, 1649,[4] and a ' Thomas Price ' was illegally inducted[5] by ' the late Bishop of St. Asaph ' (although the living was ' in his gift ') into Llansantffraid Glan Conwy on May 14th, 1646,[6] but on February 23rd of the next year David Jones is appointed by the C.P.M. to ' forthwith officiate the cure of the said church as Rector.'[7] However, as neither Radnor nor Denbigh is Cardigan, it is seen that the Petitioners' information about the personnel of Western Wales was singularly inexact. There is, indeed, no direct evidence

1 Relation, p. 30.
2 Lib. Inst., Meneven., pp. 23-35.
3 J. R. Phillips : History of the Civil War in Wales, Vol. I, pp. 355-6.
4 Lamb. 905, f. 33.
5 i.e., because the power of inducting and instituting had been sequestered from the Bishops by an ordinance of Parliament.
6 Lib. Inst., Assaphe, p. 147.
7 Lamb. 902, f. 12.

to rebut the charges of implied or actual delinquency in any of these cases, and it must be remembered that the Civil War and Commonwealth period was full of trimmers and apostates, from Edmund Jones, the Monmouth delinquent from Llansoy who afterwards "gave proof of deserting the King's interest,"[1] to political spies like Henshaw and Needham and military converts like George Monk. To the Welsh Commissioners even Robert Prichard was a ' preaching minister ' ; to the Petitioners he was a person ' especially befriended.'[2] But quasi-Puritans were not morally well-equipped to wage a campaign against so-called anti-Puritans, and men with the political outlook of the Petitioners could but ill afford to put fastidious patronage of the ' godly party ' side by side with accusations against other men of delinquency and malignancy.

(e) SCANDALOUS MINISTERS.

But they do not seem to be aware of their illogical position and proceed to out-Puritanise the Puritans. They state that several persons " now imployed and stipended to preach and officiate are deboyst and drunken persons, scandalous in their lives and conversations,"[3] and give examples. Of these, *Thomas Field* [*of Lawhadden*] *in Pembrokeshire* had been appróved by the C.P.M. on 5th May, 1649, and had received £42 increase of maintenance in addition to his former £24 out of the impropriate rectories of Lamphey and Warren belonging to ' the late Bishop of St. David's '[4] ; he is described by the [parochial] Pembrokeshire Commissioners as ' Clarke ' simply[5] without the epithet ' preaching minister.' Whether this implied a lapse from the highest Puritan standards is not at all certain ; however, there is no record of any later ejection by either the C.P.G.W. or the C.A.P.P. ' *John Phillips of Pembroke* ' comes next, but whether the vicar of Llandeloy[6] of that name or the rector of ·Morvil,[7] he had been already ejected, early in 1650,

1 Cal. Comm. Comp., Vol. II, p. 1524.
2 Relation, pp. 44-45.
3 Relation, p. 30.
4 Bodl. MS. 326, f. 252.
5 Lamb. 915, 1. 175.
6 Walk. e. 7. f. 212b.
7 Lib. Inst., Menev., p. 41.

if the former,[1] before October, 1650, if the latter.[2] So also
had ' *David Evans of Cardigan* '—vicar of Llandyfriog—for
scandal and simony,[3] early in 1650.[4] The other two both
boast the name of *William Jones*, one in Brecon and one in
Monmouth, the first being incumbent of Llanfihangel Cwmdu,[5]
the second of Goitre.[6]   Nothing is known to prove their
guilt or otherwise ; but the fact that they were beneficed
clergymen instituted by the ' late Bishops ' and had escaped
scatheless from the County Committees, the C.P.M. and
the C.P.G.W., indirectly prove that they were not notorious
evil-livers. The Commissioners, therefore, had in two cases
already given their answer ; and the other three, in the face
of the evidence, must receive the benefit of the doubt.

(*f*) THE CASE OF MATTHEW WILLIAMS.

The ' silencing ' of *Matthew Williams* stands in a category
of its own. Differing from all nine cases referred to above,
he is described as a ' godly able man,'[7] and he is placed
apart from a group of seven Episcopalians who are
likewise said to have been ejected without sufficient cause.[8]
Two men of this name appear in the records. One was
the vicar of St. Mary Hill in Glamorgan, ' ejected before the
Act,'[9] and therefore outside the ambit of the Petitioners'
case ; the other was vicar of Llangattock in Breconshire,
who was appointed to officiate that cure after the ejection
of Matthew Herbert, the rich rector pluralist who held
that living with that of Cefnllys in Radnor. But Williams's
added emoluments did not bring happiness in its wake
on account of the strained relations subsisting between him
and ' the sequestrators of the premises,' especially Thomas
Lewis, a member of the Brecon Committee for Sequestrations,
one of those who did *not* subscribe the hypocritical declaration
of loyalty to the Parliament from that county in 1645,[10]
member of most of the County Commissioners for Assessments

1 Living under sequestration (1650 accounts). Walk. c. 13, f. 6.
2 Lamb. 915, f. 166.
3 Walk. e. 7, f. 213.
4 Living under sequestration (1650 accounts). Walk. c. 13, f. 33.
5 Instituted 21 Nov., 1610. Lib. Inst., Meneven., p. 53.
6   ,,   14 Sept., 1622.   Ibid. Llandaff, p. 17.
7 Relation, pp. 38-39.
8   Ibid.   p. 29.
9 Walk. e. 7, f. 209.
  10 A Declaration of the Gentlemen and Inhabitants of the County of Brecknock,
Nov. 23rd, 1645. List on pp. 6-7 (N.L.W.).

and the Militia between 1645 and 1650, and farmer of the livings of Llanynys and Llanfihangel Talyllyn under the C.P.G.W. in 1650.[1] The cause is not so much as hinted at in the Bodl. MSS., but either personal antipathy towards the vicar or some natural reaction against the extending activities and peremptory orders of a Committee sitting in London probably accounted for an attitude that otherwise seemed unjustifiable. Williams seems to have been ' approved ' as early as August, 1646,[2] and between that date and February, 1647-8, arrears of salary amounting to £75 accumulated. The C.P.M. order these to be paid by an order of September 4th, 1649,[3] repeated on November 13th,[4] and when on March 7th, $16\frac{4 9}{5 0}$, the two parties appear before them, the arrears must be paid within ten days.[5] Then on March 10th, a special Committee, with Colonel Philip Jones as one of the members, is appointed to inquire into the case,[6] and the upshot is that on April 2nd, Lewis appears before the C.P.M. ' in safe custody.'[7] Finally, on April 24th, the £75 is deposited with the Clerk[8] ; on the next day the latter is ordered to pay the money to Williams ; and last of all, on May 3rd Anne Williams produced a letter of Attorney under the hand and seal of her father for her receipt of the £75 in question.[9] This latter fact, together with the express order of the C.P.M. on 27th April, 1649, that he was to have £50 out of the profits of the impropriate rectories of Llangattock and Llanelly in Brecon as increase of maintenance to his former salary of £30,[10] disposes of the Petitioners' statement that " he preached gratis for many years before . . . . not expecting any temporall reward."[11]   It is very probable that the Petitioners were correct in asserting that " there were no proofes of Delinquency or Scandall against him " ; it was sufficient that his protracted duel with Thomas Lewis led to the latter using his great influence with the South

1 Walk. c. 13, f. 59. The editor of " Old Wales " seems to suggest that Lewis was no true friend of the Parliament (Vol. I, No. 2, pp. 44-45) ; if this be really so, it is difficult to understand how he could become sequestrator of Church livings.
2 Bodl. 326, f. 18.
3   Ibid.
4   Ibid.   f. 18b.
5 Bodl. 327, f. 12.
6   Ibid.   f. 13.
7   Ibid.   f 13b.
8   Ibid.   f. 62.
9   Ibid.   f. 62b.
10 Bodl. 326, ff. 18, 18b.
11 Relation, pp. 38-39.

Wales Commissioners to procure his ejection. This is really the one strong case of the Petition, since it proved the possibility of ejection on other than orthodox Puritan standards, and because it would tend to ensure for their gravamina the sympathetic ear of the Committee who had originally approved Williams, and who afterwards persevered so tenaciously in seeing justice being done to him.

(g) Unworthy Schoolmasters.

The next charge is the failure of the education clause of the Act. According to the Petition only eighteen, or at most twenty-one,[1] "godly able Schoolmasters were stipended, qualified, allowed and approved of," while the records of the time put the number up to thirty-nine,[2] including the four described by the Petitioners as ' unfit for to undergoe so weighty a businesse.' The Hay, Crickhowell, Builth, and Carmarthen are particularly pointed out as market towns not supplied with schools.[3] John Williams had been a schoolmaster at Builth since 1650,[4] and most probably the Commissioners thought Carmarthen well supplied by the Grammar School founded there in 1576.[5] In the case of the other two, the Petitioners' information was correct, and the Trustees for Maintenance in July, 1656, pass indirect censure on the C.P.G.W. by stating that the Hay ' stood in greater need of a schoolmaster than Llangorse.'[6] The master and usher at Brecon are singled out for attack, the former, *Philip Williams*, ' having no competent learning for a schoolmaster,' and the latter, *Hugh Powell*, ' the only able man for learning . . . being a known Papist, if not a Jesuit.'[7] Nothing authentic is known of either, except that a ' Philip Williams ' and ' Hugh Powell ' subscribe the ' Word for God ' in 1655,[8] supporting Vavasor Powell

1 Relation, p. 40 (18) ; p. 22 (21).
2 Vide pp. 228-230, supra. This is the number of schoolmasters who were in receipt of payment for the earlier part of the legal year 1652, and of whom the Petitioners ought to have knowledge when they drafted their particular charges by 16 July.
3 Relation, p. 40.
4 Walk. c. 13, f. 62.
5 Schools Enquiry Commission Report, Vol. I, App. IV, p. 52 ; (quoted by T. Shankland : 'Seren Gomer,' Tach. 1901, p. 328) ; J. R. Phillips : History of the Civil War in Wales, Vol. I, p. 22.
6 Cal. St. Papers, 1656-7, p. 31. Later, there seems to have been some competition for the post of schoolmaster here, for Smith, late schoolmaster of Llangorse, is associated with it (Cal. St. Pap., 1656-7, p. 161) and Rice Powell, once schoolmaster at Talgarth (Lamb. 977, f. 45).
7 Relation, pp. 32, 40.
8 Names found on p. 11 of this tract.

in denouncing the assumption of the Protectorate by Cromwell. If they be the Brecon masters, it was certainly unique even in a time of religious chaos to find a devoted Papist joining the ranks of the most uncompromising Puritans, and signing his name next after a Commissioner of the Propagation Act.[1] It must be admitted that it is difficult to place persons named in a bare list with no semblance of description attached, and also it has been suggested that these two were among the North Wales followers of Morgan Llwyd.[2] But the close association of Williams and Powell in the ' Relation,' the close proximity of the same two names in the ' Word for God,' the fact that the name of John James, a Commissioner hailing from *Herefordshire*, comes only two places lower down, and the other fact that Vavasor had especially close connections with Brecknock about this time[3]—together they constitute as strong a case for the Brecon masters as for the Wrexham nonconformists. *David Evans of New Radnor* is referred to as a ' drunken deboyst man,'[4] but the Commissioners for Sequestrations had no hesitation in 1654 to order that certain arrears be paid him.[5] However, as the words of this State Paper suggest that he was not keeping school in 1654, and that the Lambeth MSS. do not record his name as having been approved by the ' Triers,' some proportion of truth may have rested in the accusation. Of the ' *Hugh Jones of the County of Glamorgan*,'[6] against whom a similar charge is brought, absolutely nothing has been discovered, and though his name might have been confused with the ' Henry Jones ' who figures vaguely in the Monmouth accounts,[7] the voice of historical evidence is equally silent.

(h) C.P.M. v. C.P.G.W.

Thus, taken generally, the Petition as a piece of serious destructive criticism must be said to have failed. The instances adduced are phenomenally few ; the information given is in some places inexact, in other places provably

1 ' John Nicholas,' presumably Capt. Nicholas, Governor of Chepstow.
2 J. H. Davies : Gweithiau Morgan Llwyd, Vol. II, App. VI, p. 323.
3 Thurloe State Papers, Vol. II, passim.
4 Relation, p. 32.
5 Vide supra, p. 244.
6 Relation, p. 32.
7 Walk. c. 13, f. 57.

untrue ; bold statements are made with no attempt to buttress them with evidence ; mere names are given with no determinate description ; and even certain aspects of the Commissioners' policy which were open to grave criticism are passed by unmentioned. But it contains a residue of information otherwise unaccessible in the surviving records of the time : the name of the usher at Brecon, and the reply drawn from the Commissioners that of all the clergy ejected under the Act in South Wales only one, an un-named parson from Monmouthshire, appealed to the C.P.M. under the provisions of the Act and had the judgment against him affirmed ' though he were in our opinion as meet for favour as any we proceeded against.'[1] This unwelcome revelation about the appeal told the Petitioners that they had little mercy to expect from the moderate and conservative Committee that sat in London, even though men appointed (and not merely ' approved ') by it had been summarily ejected by the Welsh Commissioners, and even though, according to the Petitioners, men recommended by it to their favour, in the manner of a ministerial ' exchange,' had also been rejected. Of these, two names are given, *Mr. Collier* and *Mr. Bywater.*[2] The former must be the minister of ' St. Saviour's in the London Tenth Classis ' in 1648,[3] and who therefore belonged to an advanced group of London Presbyterians, akin to Christopher Love, peculiarly distasteful to Cradock ever since his sojourn in the capital ; the latter is a more obscure man who in 1657 finds refuge in the town of Pembroke on the approval of the C.A.P.P.[4] And against these must be placed two men who were presumably recommended to the Approvers and accepted —the *Charles Nichollette* who was minister of Winston in the Third Suffolk Classis in 1645,[5] and the *Richard Hunt* who was member of the Third Essex Classis in 1648,[6] the one

1 Relation, p. 38. Mere conjecture would equate the ' unnamed ' either with John Cragge of Llantilio Pertholey, the opponent of John Tombes in the Abergavenny debate and the architect of long and learned sermons, or with Robert Brabourne of Monmouth. the subscriber of the Engagement (Bodl. D. 711. f. 9) who enjoyed the triple sanction of the Committees of Revenue, Compounding, and Plundered Ministers, and who in 1652 received a round sum of £50 in discharge of arrears of fifths. (Walk. c. 13. f. 57).
2 Relation, pp. 38-39.
3 W. A. Shaw : History of the English Church, Vol. II, App. IIIb, p. 403.
4 T. Shankland : ' Seren Gomer,' Tach. 1901, p. 324 ; Calamy states he was ejected from Pembroke in 1660 (II, 717).
5 W A Shaw : History of the English Church, Vol. II, App. IIIb, p. 424, 'Nikolets.'
6 Ibid. Ibid. p. 383.

receiving £10 in 1651 from the Glamorgan treasury 'for a journey to Wales '[1] and the other receiving £11 10s. 0d. in 1650 from the Monmouth officials on the order of Henry Walter, Walter Cradock, and Captain Nicholas.[2] Thus two were rejected, Hunt only received one payment and that a small one, while it is unlikely that Nichollette stayed in Wales at all. These facts point to the conclusion that the co-operation between the two bodies was far from being an auspicious success, and did but little to bring to a solution the crying need for more preachers on the hillsides of Wales. But the crafty reminders of men whom the C.P.M. on good information believed to be malignants could not destroy the affinity between old Puritans and new, a nexus curiously illustrated by the fact that William Young, rector of Pwlly-crochan in Pembroke, proved the only minister doubly approved by C.P.M. and C.P.G.W. who was rejected by the C.A.P.P.[3] That these considerations, however, do not preclude the absolutely independent outlook of the London committee, the cases of William Erbery and Richard Jewell abundantly prove   Though there is no evidence connecting the Propagators with the charges of heterodoxy levelled against the former in March, 1653, the acquittal[4] of this invincible Ishmaelite must have been much to the chagrin of the Welsh Puritans, moderate and millenarian alike. Jewell of Tenby was the first settled minister sanctioned for work in Wales[5] directly by the C.P.M., and only about five weeks before the Propagation Act came into force, he gets an order from them to the trustees for the sale of ' dean and chapter lands ' that £26 be paid to his use for the half-year ending July 25th, 1649.[6]   But on 2nd October, 1650, the Parochial Commissioners sitting at Haverfordwest refer to him as ' ejected.'[7]   It is not surprising that the Trustees for Maintenance of Ministers on 19th July, 1651,

---

1 Walk. c. 13, f. 26b.
2 Ibid. f. 45b. From neither payment is any relaxation of the anti-Presbyterian bias of the two Approvers to be inferred, as the ' Classical ' system (outside London and Lancashire) was a purely artificial product.
3 Cp. House of Lords' MSS., 1660 Petitions, Y. }
   Lamb. 977, lib. iii, f. 73.   }
          Appointment of *Samuel Edwards* to the living. (December 1654).
4 Testimony, p. 313. N.L.W.
5 Vide pp. 38, 69.
6 Bodl. 327, f. 185. February 13th, 1649-50. That it was actually paid to him is proved by Declared Accounts, Bundle 367, roll 3. (Record Office, Audit).
7 Lamb. 915. f. 104.

most probably on Jewell's appeal and supported by the
C.P.M., insist that the £26 arrears due to him on St. David's
Day, $16\frac{49}{50}$, be paid up in full.[1]

1 Lamb. 979, f. 316. His £52 a year derived from the impropriate rectory of Mydrim was ' to be payable at St. David's Day and St. James's Day in equal portions. This explains the apparent anomaly referred to on p. 239.

XIX.

THE END OF THE ACT.

John Jones of Maesygarnedd wrote to Morgan Llwyd that he was not sorry for the Petition since 'the more the Saints are tryed, the more their luster will appeare.'[1] But though this dictum contained a good deal of truth, though the Petitioners' arguments were inconclusive, and though the Committee stood firm in refusing a 'Commission to the country,' yet the stars in their courses fought for the discontinuance of the Act, the ultimate object that the 15,000 had in view. On account of the vicissitudes of a complex political situation the Rump as a body was forced into an attitude that its subsidiary Committee did not share in. The Army's clamorous demands for ' a new Representative,' Cromwell's disagreement with the Council of State over the Dutch War, the chicane and intrigue that delayed all proposals for a general Propagation of the Gospel, the sinister growth of the Fifth Monarchy party under the vigilant leadership of Harrison,[2] head of the Welsh Commissioners and the ' Ecclesiæ pestis ' of the Anglican tract-makers,[3] made the Rump to sacrifice what was dear to the hearts of all the forces that sought to undermine it. Signs of trouble were not wanting at the meeting of Parliament on March 25th, 1653, the date when the final unfavourable report of the C.P.M. on the Petitioners' materials and methods was presented,[4] the day also when the Propagation Act was timed to expire. On the same day the Petition of 1652, with the particulars of July and the rejoinder of August were ' presented ' to the Parliament.[5] The House ordered the report to be re-

---

1 Gweithiau Morgan Llwyd, Vol. II, App. I, pp. 294-295. Letter from Ireland, August, 1652.

2 Gardiner : History of the Commonwealth and Protectorate, Vol. II, chapters XVIII-XXV, where these issues are luminously treated.

3 ' Ecclesiæ pestis et fundi nostri calamitas.' (Gemitus Ecclesiæ Cambro-Britannicæ, p. 5). " Major-General Harrison " in margin.

4 According to the Relation, the report was originally submitted on the 23rd, but the debate on it was ' providentially put off ' until the 25th, (pp, 14-15).

5 Relation, p. 15. A new Solicitor, Charles Roberts, was in charge of it, vice Gunter.

committed, and the Committee was given power still further to examine the whole matter in order to bring in a new report ; they order the Act to be brought in and to be read as 'first business on the Friday next following, in order to the Reviving thereof *if the House shall see cause.*'[1] Three of the Welsh approvers, including no doubt 'the Approver who lived in London'[2] had appeared 'at the Parliament door to beg the renewing of the Act,'[3] and two days later Vavasor Powell was preaching at the Charter House. However, when the House met on the Friday following, rather than the Act being taken as the most urgent business, no reference whatsoever is made to it in the Journals of that day. The House resumed its deliberations upon the 'Proposals for the [general] Propagation of the Gospel,' and most ominous of all, Walter Cradock was excused from preaching to the Parliament at St. Margaret's, Westminster, on the 12th April, and an order was made that Obadiah Sedgwick and Philip Nye preach on that day.[4] From other sources than the Journals, especially the Newsletter of April $\frac{8}{18}$, 1653, preserved in the Clarendon MSS., there is good evidence that the Act was discussed and finally rejected.[5] " Signally they threw that businesse under foot, to the discountenancing of the honest people there, and to the countenancing of the malignant party of this Commonwealth."[6] But the 'Case of Wales,' as Cromwell refers to it, reacted very powerfully upon the political fortunes of the nation : it crowned the sins of the Rump in the mind of Harrison ; it drove Cromwell to distrust Vane and ally himself with the Fifth Monarchists ; and, as one of the most potent causes for the forcible dissolution of the Rump on 20th April, 1653, it gave to Powell, Llwyd, and the Major-General that 'rule of the Saints' which by many is looked upon as

1 C. J. VII, pp. 271-272.
2 Relation. p. 31. (Printed wrongly in original as 23). *Jenkin Lloyd* of Llangoedmor.
3 Certain Seasonable Considerations, (1654), p. 4 (N.L.W.).
4 C. J. VII, p. 274. Report of the proceedings in Parliament on April 1st, 1653.
5 Gardiner: Hist. of Comm. and Prot., Vol. II, p. 197. (Note (1)). The Newsletter refers to ' voting down the preaching propagators in *North* Wales,' which must be synonymous with ' *Wales.*' " At this period the Journals were irregularly kept." (Gardiner).
6 " The Lord General Cromwel's Speech delivered in the Council Chamber upon the 4th of July, 1653," p. 12 (N.L.W). [Opening of Saints' Parlt: discusses rejection of Propagation Act.] Cp. " A Declaration of the Lord General and his Council of Officers . ' . . reasons for the Dissolving the Parliament, Apr 20th, 1653." in ' A Brief Review of the most Materiall Parliamentary Transactions,' pp. 59-60.

the golden age of the Puritan movement in this country. And the Act, though officially dead, was very much alive in the minds of its opponents, who, notwithstanding the unmistakable sympathies of Oliver, thought the first year of the Protectorate a happy time to call for a critical review of its working. Anti-Propagation literature streamed from the Press, notably the ' Gemitus,' the ' Seasonable Considerations,' and the "True and Perfect Relation."[1] The atmosphere created by this continual controversy, the modicum of truth in the Petitioners' case, the abjuring by Harrison, Powell and Llwyd of the Protector's new ideal of government, the probable belief of Philip Jones and the other Commissioners that a thorough inquiry would only add more ' luster ' to their cause, the belief of the Protector that his government would not benefit by leaving real or affected grievances unremedied—co-operated in the issue of the ordinance of August, 1654, ordering a full analysis of the administration of the Act. Thirty-three men were named, who neither as Commissioners nor as officials had any former connection with it, given power to issue warrants, commit to gaol, surcharge accounts, examine and cross-examine witnesses on oath, and to issue ' discharges and exonerations.'[2] The upshot was that the South Wales[3] Treasurers' accounts were ' passed ' at Neath in August, 1655. But the animus, personal and religious, that had been engendered, died a hard death. About the beginning of 1659 a tract dwelt on ' the distressed oppressed condition ' of South Wales ' for divers years last past '[4] with special reference to the Propagation ; about the same time came the efforts of the Freeman-Gunter faction[5]; and on 23rd May, 1659, Colonel Philip Jones ' stood up in his place and cleered himself ' of the ' particulars ' exhibited against him in Parliament on the 18th by Bledry Morgan of Carmarthenshire.[6] In June, 1660, Sir Thomas Middleton and ' other gentlemen of Quality '

---

1 Alexander Griffith, in introducing the story of the Petition of 1652, suggests that " the Lord (who had hid these things from such as were formerly in Authority) hath reserved the same for your Highnesse care." (Relation : Ep. Ded. to the Protector).

2 Firth and Rait : Acts and Ordinances, Vol. II, especially pp. 992-993.

3 No record exists of the proceedings of the *North* Wales section of the Commissioners ; the *South* Wales accounts are embodied in Walk. c. 13.

4 The N.L.W. Catalogue (p. 65) half-suggests 1654 as the date of this tract, but there is definite internal evidence that it was written *after* the death of the Protector.

5 Supra, p. 250.

6 Weekly Post, May 24-31, 1659.

are found subscribing a loyal petition to Charles II. and referring to 'the conversion of Church endowments to their own use under the pretence of propagating the Gospel' by people who also 'sowed seeds of false doctrine among us.'[1] With that and the still-born reports of the constables of 1662 the Act passed under the somewhat scurvy protection of the Muse of History. Dr. John Walker devoted about 46 long columns[2] of his ' Sufferings' to criticise it, but admitted that he had 'never seen the Act,'[3] with the result that he refers to Vavasor Powell as *Commissioner*[4] as well as Approver ; Carlyle points no portentous moral over that ' case of Wales ' in Cromwell's speech of 4th July, 1653, and his explanation of the wolfish ' men '[5] in the context is open to serious doubt ; and the great historian of the Commonwealth, though admitting the importance of the Act in the politico-religious issues of the time, only devotes a little over two pages to it ; judging from the references in the foot-notes, his acquaintance with Propagation evidences does not pass beyond the shorter diatribes of Alexander Griffith.[6]

1 Mercurius Publicus, June 28-July 5, 1660.
2 pp. 147-170.
3 p. 149, col. 2.
4 p. 150, col. 2, and passim. It is certainly a matter of some surprise that the latest historian of the period has repeated this two hundred years' old mistake. (Morrice : Wales in the Seventeenth Century (1918), p. 44).
5 Letters and Speeches of Cromwell, (Ward, Lock, Edition, p. 494, Note 2); of Vavasor he knows nothing : "*with a Colleague, seemingly Welsh, named Powel,*" p. 518.
6 Gardiner : Hist. Comm. and Prot., II, pp. 196-197.

XX.

NON-MS. SOURCES.[1]

(i) *Acts and Ordinances.*
  (a) Henry Scobell : Collection of Acts and Ordinances. Vols. I and II. 1657, 1658.
  (b) Firth and Rait : Acts and Ordinances of the Interregnum. (1642-1660). Two Volumes. 1911.

(ii) *Journals of Parliament.*
  (a) House of Lords' Journals. Vols. IV-X. L.J.
  (b) House of Commons' Journals. Vols. IV-VII. C.J.

(iii) *Calendars.*
  (a) Calendars of State Papers Domestic. 1649-1660.
  (b) Calendars of the Committee for Compounding. 1643-1660. Vols. I-V.
  (c) Calendars of the Committee for the Advance of Money. Vols. I-III.

(iv) *Contemporary Works.*
  (a) Civil War and Commonwealth Tracts : National Library of Wales, Aberystwyth. N.L.W.
  (b) Thomason Tracts : British Museum. B.M.
  (c) Tracts in the Cardiff Free Library Collection. C.F.L.

The following have been examined at one or the other of the above :—

  (1) John Penry : Treatise (1587) ; Exhortation (1588).
  (2) Llyfr Gweddi Cyffredin (1630).
  (3) Robert Lloyd : Llwybr Hyffordd (1630).
  (4) Oliver Thomas : Carwr y Cymru (1630).
  (5) Trysor i'r Cymru (1677) containing " Drych o dri math o bobl " (by Oliver Thomas, and published originally about 1647).
  (6) Sail y Grefydd Gristnogawl (1649) by E. R.

---

1 Except (a) printed matter that has only been *casually* referred to ; (b) book s specially mentioned in the Appendices to Chapters III and XIII.

(7)   Walter Cradock: Saints Fulnesse (1647); Glad Tydings (1649); Divine Drops (1650); Gospel Libertie (1650).

(8)   Vavasor Powell: God the Father Glorified (1650); Christ and Moses Excellency (1650); Saving Faith (1650); Bird in the Cage Chirping (1661-1662) containing A Brief Narrative, A Word in Season, Spirituall Experiences.

(9)   Cristopher Love: A Cleare and Necessary Vindication (1651; Speech at his Death (1651).

(10) William Erbery: Call to the Churches (1652) including Letters to the Pastors and the Dispute at Cowbridge; General Epistle to the Hebrews (1652); The Welsh Curate (1652); Apocrypha (1652); The Sword Doubled (1652); A Scourge for the Assyrian (1652); The Idol Pastor (1652); The Wretched People (1652); The Bishop of London (1652); The North Star (1652), including correspondence with Morgan Llwyd; The Mad Man's Plea (1653); The Babe of Glory (1653); The Honest Heretique (1653); An Olive Leaf (1653); The Testimony (1658).

(11) Henry Nicholls: The Shield Single against the Sword Doubled (1653).

(12) Dr. George Griffith: A Bold Challenge (1652); Animadversions (1652).

(13) Alexander Griffith : The Petition of the Six Counties of South Wales (1652); Mercurius Cambo-Britannicus (1652); Strena Vavasoriensis (1653-4); Hue and Cry (1653); A True and Perfect Relation of the Petition of the Six Counties et seq., (1654).

(14) Edward Allen, John Griffith, James Quarrell, Charles Lloyd: Examen at Purgamen Vavasoris (1654).

(15) Rowland Vaughan: Pregeth yn erbyn Schism (1658); also quotations from other works in Ashton: Hanes Llenyddiaeth Gymreig [1650-1850].

(16) John Cragge: Light of God's Countenance (1654).

(17) Stephen Hughes: Introduction to 1659 Edition of ' Vicar Llan-ddyfri.'

(18) Jenkin Lloyd : Valedictions (1658).

(19) ? Authors : Seasonable Considerations (1654); Gemitus Ecclesiæ (1654) ; The Distressed Oppressed Condition (1658 or 9).

(20) Newspapers : Perfect Diurnall ; Weekly Post ; Mercurius Publicus.

(v) *Contemporary Works—Reprints.*

(a) Gweithiau Morgan Llwyd : Vol. I, ed. T. E. Ellis, 1899 ; Vol. II, ed. J. H. Davies, 1908.

(b) The Parliament Explained to Wales (John Lewis) 1646. [Cymdeithas Llên Cymru, 1907.]

(c) " Some Part of the Works of Mr. Rees Prichard " (1659) *Second* Issue ; Canwyll y Cymry (Rees Prichard). Ed. Rice Rees, 1867. Third Edition.

(d) Eos Ceiriog : o Gynnulliad a Diwygiad W. D. (Gwallter Mechain), 1823. 2 Vols.

(e) " Cerdd y Fanaticiaid " by ' Edward Dafydd o Fargam.' (*a*) Cymru, Nov., 1901, pp. 218-219. (*b*) Seren Gomer, July, 1902, pp. 169-172.

(f) John Miles : An Antidote against the Infection of the Times (1656). Ed. by T. Shankland for Welsh Bapt. Hist. Soc. I. (1904).

(g) Hen Gerddi Gwleidyddol (1588-1660) from Phillipps MSS. 12453 ; B. Mus. Addit. MSS. 14974, 14938, pub. by Cymdeithas Llên Cymru, 1901.

(vi) *Church History and Religious Movements Generally.*

(1) Allen, G. W. : Art. on ' Boehme ' in Encyc. of Religion and Ethics.

(2) Ballinger, John : The Bible in Wales (1906).

(3) Besse, Joseph : Coll. of the Sufferings of the Quakers. Vol. I (1753).

(4) Brown, L. F., : The Political Activities of the Baptists and Fifth Monarchy Men (1912).

(5) Burrage, Champlin : The Early English Dissenters (1912). Vol. I, Hist. and Criticism ; II, Illustrative Documents.

(6) Calamy, Edward : An Account . . . of the Ministers Ejected, II (1713).

(7) Crosby : History of the English Baptists. Vol. I (1738).

(8) Culross, James : Hanserd Knollys. Bapt. Manuals. Vol. II (1895).

(9) Dale, R. W., : History of English Congregationalism. Ed. A. W. W. Dale (no date).

(10) Edwards, Charles : Hanes y Ffydd (1677 Edition).

(11) Fox, George : Journal. Ed. Norman Penny (1911).

(12) Fuller : The Church History of Great Britain. (1655). Ed. Brewer. Vol. V (1845).

(13) Henry, Philip : Diaries and Letters of Ed. M. H. Lee, (1882).

(14) Henry, Philip : Life (1698).

(15) Hetherington, W. M. : Hist. of the Westminster Assembly (1843).

(16) Hobley, William : Articles in ' Traethodydd ' on ' Jacob Boehme ' (1900-1902).

(17) Jessey, Henry : Life and Death of (1671).

(18) McGlothlin : Baptist Confessions of Faith (1910).

(19) Nightingale, B. ; The Ejected of 1662 in Cumberland and Westmoreland. (1911).

(20) Palmer, A. W. : The History of the Parish Church of Wrexham.

(21) Palmer, A. N. : The History of the Nonconformity of Wrexham and its Neighbourhood (1889).

(22) Palmer, Samuel : The Nonconformists' Memorial. Vol. I, Second Ed. (1777).

(23) Powell, Vavasor : Life and Death of (1671).

(24) Rees, Thomas : Hist. of Prot. Nonconformity in Wales. Sec. Ed. (1883).

(25) Reliquiæ Liturgicæ (" The Directory "). Vol. III.

(26) Records, Broadmead : (*a*) Ed. E. B. Underhill (1847). (*b*) Ed. N. Haycroft (1865).

(27) Society : Chetham—Publications—New Series., Vols. 20, 23, 24.

(28) Society, Friends' Historical, Suppt. No. 6 by W. Gregory Norris.

(29) Shaw, W. A. : Hist. of the English Church during the Civil War and the Commonwealth. Vols. I and II (1900). [Especially authoritative and useful].

(30) St. Asaph, Bishop of : Landmarks in the History of the Welsh Church (1912).

(31) Taylor, Adam : Hist. of the General Baptists (1818).

(32) Thomas, Archdeacon D. R. : Hist. of the Diocese of St. Asaph. (1874). Collated in material points with the New Edition.

(33) Urwick, Wm. : Historical Sketches of Noncon formity in the County Palatine of Chester. (1864).

(34) Walker, John : An Attempt . . . Sufferings of the Clergy. (1714.)

(35) Whyte, Alexander : An Appreciation of Jacob Behmen. (1896.)

(63) Wilkins, David : Concilia Magnae Britanniæ et Hiberniae. Vol. IV. (1737.)

(37) Wilkins, Charles : History of Merthyr Tydvil , Chap. IX., pp. 93-96. [Nathan Jones's account[1] "found in an old chest in the Parish Church."]

Two contributions to the Welsh religious history of the time have proved especially helpful :—

(i) Davies, J. H. : Introduction to Vol. II of Gweithiau Morgan Llwyd. Pp. ix—lxxx.

(ii) Shankland, Thos. : Articles in ' Seren Gomer ' (1900-1901). (Particularly that of Nov. 1901 in review of " Diwygwyr Cymru " (Beriah Evans)).

(vii) *Political Developments.*

(1) Civil War and Commonwealth Tracts. Vide IV (a).

(2) Carlyle, Thos. : Cromwell's Letters and Speeches. (1845).

(3) Gooch, G. P. ; English Democratic Ideas in the Seventeenth Century. (1898.)

(4) Gardiner, S. R. : Hist. of the Commonwealth and Protectorate. Vols. I and II. (1897).

(5) Lloyd, David : Memoires. (1662.)

(6) Morrice, J. C. : Wales in the Seventeenth Century. (1918).

(7) Nalson, John : An Impartial Collection of the Great Affairs of State. (1682.)

---

[1] Mansell, writing to John Walker in 1709, refers to this account as a ' Manuscript extant under his own hand ' (Walk. c. 4, f, 65).

(8) Phillips, J. R.: History of the Civil War in England and the Marches. (1874.) Vol. I, History; II, Documents.

(9) Simpkinson, C. H.: Thomas Harrison. (1905.)

(10) Thurloe, John: A Collection of State Papers. Ed. Birch. Vols. I-IV. (1742).

(11) Williams, W. R.: Parliamentary Representation of the Principality of Wales. (1541-1895).

(12) Williams, W. R.: " Old Wales," Vol. I, Nos. 2 and 3. (1905.)

(viii) *Miscellaneous.*

(1) Joseph Foster: Alumni Oxonienses. (1500-1714). Vols. I-IV. (1892.)

(2) Registers of the University of Oxford. Ed. Andrew Clark, M.A. Vols. 10, 11, 12, 13. Oxford Hist. Soc. Publications.

(3) Register of Exeter College, Oxford. Ed. C. W. Boase. Ox. Hist. Soc. Vol. 27.

(4) Register of Brasenose Coll., Oxford. Ed. Dr. Heberden. -Ox. Hist. Soc. Vol. 55.

(5) Anthony à Wood: Athenae Oxonienses, Old Ed. and Ed. Bliss. (1820.)

(6) The Diary of Walter Powell of Llantilio Crossenny. Ed. J. A. Bradney (1907.)

(7) The Cardiff Records. Vols. I-V. Ed. J. Hobson Matthews.

(8) G. G. Francis: Swansea Charters; App. VIII. (1867.)

(9) G. T. Clark: Limbus Patrum Morganiæ et Glamorganiæ. (1886.)

(10) Dictionary of National Biography. D.N.B.

(11) Lloyd Records and Pedigrees. Ed. Lloyd Theakston and John Davies. (1912.)

(12) Charles Ashton: Hanes Llenyddiaeth Gymreig o 1650 i 1850. (No date.)

(13) Montgomeryshire Collections. (1883.)

(14) Pioneers of Modern Education. (J. W. Adamson.) 1905.

(15) The English Grammar Schools to 1660: their Curriculum and Practice. (Foster Watson.) 1908.

(16) The House of Lords MSS. Commission Report. Appendix I.

(17) 46th Annual Report of the Deputy Keeper of the Public Records. (Appointments of Bishops and Clergy in the Reign of Charles II in *Appendix*.)

SUPPLEMENT : ANALYSIS OF TWO COMMONWEALTH TRACTS.

Two compilations of Alexander Griffith, now in the National Library of Wales (Cwrtmawr Collection), are so rare and important, and their titles so little indicative of their full content, that a short analysis of each seems expedient.

(A) *The Petition of the Six Counties of South Wales et seq.* (1652).

 (a) Pp. 1-3. The Heads of the Petition of March 10th, 165½.

 (b) Pp. 4-6. Letter of ' Valvasor ' Powell against the Petition. (Quoted from ' A Perfect Diurnall ' of May 3rd-10th 1652).

 (c) Pp. 6-17. Answer of [A.G.] to Powell's letter and " dated from my house near Hereford, the 26 of May, in the Third year of the Abrogation of the Gospel in Wales."

 (d) Pp. 17-24. A Challenge to a public debate addressed to ' Mr. Valvasor Powell, one of the Itineraries of Wales." Dated from Glasbury, 9th May, 1652, and signed " Alex. Griffith."

 (e) Pp. 25-28. Speech of Col. Freeman in support of the Petition of March 10th, 165½.

 (f) Pp. 29-30. " Two Resolves " of Parliament upon the Petition. [The pagination from p. 6 is incorrect ; the above are the corrected numbers.]

(B) *A True and Perfect Relation of the Whole Transaction concerning the Petition of the Six Counties of South Wales et seq.* Published by A. G. 1654.

 (a) Epistle Dedicatory to the Lord Protector, dated March 23rd, 165¾.

(b) Pp. 1-3. The Heads of the Petition of March 10th, 165½.

(c) Pp. 3-4. Speech of Col. Freeman in support, March 10th, 165½.

(d) Pp. 4-18. Detailed account of the Petition's fortunes (and those of its sponsors) before the C.P.M. and Parliament up to the dissolution of the Rump.

(e) Pp. 19-34. A Copy of the 'particular charges' submitted to the C.P.M. by the Petitioners on 16th July, 1652.

(f) Pp. 34-36. The case against William Watkins and Jenkin Jones over the prebend rent of Llanwrthwl.

(g) Pp. 37-50. The 'general Answer' of the C.P.G.W to the Petition of March (submitted to the C.P.M. on 18th May, 1652) plus a rejoinder of the Petitioners to the aforesaid 'Answer' (submitted to the C.P.M. on 20th August, 1652). The Answer and rejoinder are for the most part printed in parallel columns.

(h) Pp. 50-52. Correspondence during February-March, 165¾, between three ejected Brecknock clergymen and Jenkin Jones, sometime Approver.

ADDENDA.

(A) 'Ejected before the Act' (p. 53). There are good grounds for adding three names to this list : Onacre of St. Florence (p. 131), Robins of Carnarvon (p. 139), and William Thomas of Penbryn (p. 124), who Ƀecame Bishop of St. David's in 1677. As to Robins, it is certain that he was not ejected before 1647, since the Surveyors of Bishops' Lands describe him as 'present vicar' of Llanbeblig in that year (Lamb. 904, f. 142).

(B). St. Juliets (p. 58). Though a Glamorgan church and parish were known under this name as early as the Taxatio of 1254 and as late as a will of 1690 (Clark : Limbus Patrum, p. 393), there is no doubt that on philological and other grounds it must be equated with the more familiar Llanilid. This latter form occurs in a parish list (circa 1566) found in Peniarth MS. 147. [Vide Gould and Fisher : Lives of the British Saints, sub Ilid.] The form 'St. Inlitts' occurs in the Stafford records of the religious census ordered by Archbishop Sheldon in 1676 (Salt MSS., f. 423).

(C). In the list of approved Puritan clergymen (pp. 63-70) at work before the Act must be included Nathaniel Cradock of Eglwys Cymun in Carmarthen. He was instituted rector there on November 20, 1622 (Lib. Inst., Men., f. 66), and in 1648 a serious charge against Poyer was that he had beaten two orthodox ministers, Evan Roberts and Nathaniel Cradock, and of the latter it is added that he 'lay afterward sick of the brusies and beatings he received about halfe a yeare in the City of London.' (A Declaration of Divers gentlemen of Wales concerning Collonell Poyer, p. 5. Printed April 19, 1648, with the official imprimatur of Mabbott. N.L.W.).

(D). 'Ejected under the Act' (pp. 115-133). These lists undoubtedly out-Walker Dr. John Walker. The direct evidence for the great majority is overwhelming ; in some cases it is frankly circumstantial ; in four instances must it be deemed somewhat unsatisfactory on account of the difficulty of arriving at the name of the actual incumbent at the exact date when the living was sequestered. Of these, two are in Radnor—Rea of Bleddfa and Winston of Newchurch, and two in Glamorgan—Bridges of Eglwys Brewys and Meyrick of St. Lythans.

(E). The Necessity and Practice of Elections (Rawl. c. 261). The testimony of the Rawl. MS. to this aspect of the Propagation Act deserves a more extended notice than n. 2 on p. 118. The Act definitely declared that when a clergyman held two or more livings, even should one of them be over the Border, he was to elect one, and surrender the others within forty days after notice (p. 85). Fourteen such elections are chronicled in the MS.

CLERGYMAN.	LIVING RELINQUISHED.	LIVING ELECTED.	PAGE OF RAWL. MS. REPRINT
Carter, Thomas ..	[unspecified] ..	Abergele ..	18
Fogg, Robert ..	Overton ..	Bangor-on-Dee ..	18
Griffith, Dr. George	Llandrinio ..	Llanymynech ..	18
Hughes, John ..	[unspecified] ..	Llanaber ..	19
Jones, David ..	Llansantffraid G.C.	Bettws (Denb.) ..	19
Langford, William	Welshpool ..	Llanfor ..	18
Lloyd, Evan ..	Holywell ..	Ysceifiog ..	19
Lloyd, Evan ..	Rhoscolyn ..	Llanbeulan ..	20
Lloyd, William ..	Llanfair P.G. ..	Llandisilio ..	20
Morgan, Robert ..	Trefdraeth ..	Llanddyfnan ..	20
Robinson, Hugh ..	Trefriw ..	Llanbedr-y-Cenin	19
Thelwall, Edward	Llanynys ..	[Ruthin Free School]	19
Thomas, Henry ..	Maentwrog ..	Festiniog ..	19
Thomas, Oliver ..	[Oswestry] ..	Llanrhaiadr ..	18

These compulsory elections show the Commissioners on their severe side. At least five pluralities connived at by the pre-1650 Puritan authorities were dissolved ; Thomas Carter, a Presbyterian member of the Assembly of Divines, minister of St. Olave's in Hart Street, a " Tryer ' in the Ninth London Classis of 1645 (Shaw II, 402), possessed also of an interest in the living of Saltwood in Kent (L. J., x, 115), came naturally under the same ban ; and in Oliver Thomas we have the surprising fact of an Approver who was also a pluralist for seven weeks (March-May, 1650). Incidentally, the latter entry proves two things : that Thomas held the living of Llanrhaiadr before the Act came into force ; and that Evan Roberts cannot have held that vicarage but for a very short time before his death (p. 63). They were not all severity, however. A future Bishop of St. Asaph (Dr. George Griffith), and next to Alexander Griffith the most vigorous critic of the whole Propagation system, was allowed to elect Llanymynech ; and, notwithstanding his pronounced Cavalier sympathies (p. 32), Robert Morgan was not only allowed to keep Llanddyfnan, but also, two months after his ejection, to exercise a vague supervision over his old living of Trefdraeth (Lamb. 902, f. 52). He survived to become Bishop of Bangor in 1666. A close consideration of these last cases, coupled with the fact that Robinson, only 14 days afterwards (Rawl., p. 20), and William Lloyd of Anglesey (Lamb. 902, f. 39 ; Exch. Ret., 1652) were later ejected even from their elected livings, demand that they be eliminated from the genuine Puritan accessions during the Propagation era ; and in including them in his list of 28, one of the most expert students of the period has involved himself in a double fallacy : a mis-apprehension of the active force of the term ' elected,' and of the passive pseudo-Puritanism of some of the electors (J. H. Davies : Gweithiau Morgan Llwyd, II, Introd., xlii).

INDEX (PERSONS, INSTITUTIONS, ETC.).

[n. = footnote.]

A.

B.

C.

Collyer, Edward, 130.
Commissioners for the Approbation of Public Preachers, records of, 110; 158, 220, 243, 267, 268.
—— for the Army, 251.
—— for the Ejection of Scandalous Ministers, 243.
—— for the Militia, 239.
—— Parochial (1650), 62, 166, 241, 260, 262, 268; records of (Anglesey and Pembroke), 109.
—— under the Propagation Act, list of, 82; duties, 82-89; previous (military) records, 90-91; extraneous duties, 91, 94-98; general outlook, 94.98; varying Puritan attitude, 94.96; records for North Wales, 107; for South Wales, 108; miscellaneous reports, 110; ejections, 115-133, 282; stringency, 134-135; contrast with Protectorate regime, 141-142; appointments of new ministers, 144-145; answer to Petitioners of 1652 lodged before C.P.M., 247 (and n. 1); detailed account of the Commissioners' defence, 255-269; relations with C.P.M., 267-268.
Committee for Compounding, 15; understanding with C.P.M., 37, 38, 49; buys in impropriations, 49-50; records of, 55-56; 240, 244, 249, 250.
—— at Derby House, 91.
—— at Goldsmith's Hall. Vide Committee for Compounding.
—— of Parliament (various counties), 36, 42, 46, 47, 48, 52, 71,216; records of, 56.
—— for Plundered Ministers, inception, 35; procedure, 36-37; arrangements for Puritan nominees, 37; orders to treasurers of Bishops' and Chapter Lands, 38-39; thoroughness, 41; desire for complete information, 42-43; solicitude for Welsh interests, 43; hampered by unexpired leases, 44; revision of County Committees' orders, 47; conflict of jurisdiction, 47-49; co-operation with C.G.H., 49; records of proceedings, 54-55; trial of Erbery, 179, 182, 268; injunctions regarding Brecon and Wrexham, 223; jurisdiction over schoolmasters, 223; inquires into charges of 1652, 246-248; relations with C.P.G.W., 267-268; final report to Parliament concerning Petition of 1652, 270; examines Petition of 1653, 271;

some of nominees forced to 'elect' by C.P.G.W., 283-284.
—— for Reformation of the Universities, 39; records of, 111.
—— of Religion, 34-35.
—— for Scandalous Ministers, 5, 223.
Committees (County) for Sequestrations, 47, 48 (n. 1), 239, 243, 245, 263; records of, 56.
Confession(s) of Faith, Particular Baptists (1644), 151 (n. 11), 207; (1646, 1651, 1652), 162, 207; General Baptists, 209 (and nn. 1-4); Westminster, 16, 177.
Congregation, Lords of the, 177.
Congregationalism, 194. (Vide Independents).
Consett, William, 202.
Constables (1662), reports of, 62, 235, 273; records of, 110-111.
Convocation (1640), 18, 30, 31.
Coote, Dr., 42.
Corbett, Mr., 148.
Cotton, John, 28, 195.
Coulton, Francis, 69.
—— James, 130.
Courtney, Hugh, 82, 91, 92, 95, 97, 99, 144 (n. 19), 190 (and n. 6).
Covenant, Solemn League and, 76 (and n. 6), 77, 198, 200, 201.
Coventry and Lichfield, Bishop of, 3.
Covy, Robert, 152.
Crachley, Ralph, 82.
—— Thomas, 47.
Cradock, Nathaniel, 282.
Cradock, Walter, 8, 12, 16, 25, 26, 27, 35, 46, 60-62, 70, 74, 75, 77, 78, 85, 146; defends itinerants, 156; settles at Usk, 159; attitude towards tithes and State pay, 163; towards prayers, 170; 171, 173; generosity, 175; advanced Calvinist, 177-178; opposes Millenarians, 185; distinction concerning Lord's Supper, 195; on 'delivery unto Satan,' 196; on religious toleration, 197, 198; opposes Presbyterianism, 199, 267; alluded to in Llanover MSS., 211; secular investments, 216; post-Propagation honours, 219, 220; influence on Propagation appointments, 236, 256, 268, 271.
Cragge, John, 14, 126, 141, 215, 267 (n. 1).
Creed, Richard, 236, 248, 259 (n. 9).
Crisp, Dr., 177.
Cromwell, Oliver, 79, 157, 185, 186, 197, 213, 220, 243, 249, 270, 271 (n.6), 272.
Crumpe, George, 127.

D.

Dafydd, Edward, 155, 165, 211.
Dancy, John, 82 (and n. 3), 97, 195 (n. 12).
Daniel, John, 82, 235.
Dare, Steven, 225 (n. 2), 229 (and n. 5).
Darony, Peter, 229 (and n. 6).

Dashfield, John, 53.
Dauncer, Garnons, 67, 127.
David's, St., Bishop of, 3, 4, 58 (Field), 19; (Mainwaring), 17, 19.
Davies, Mr., 145.
Davies, David (Gelligaer), 67, 148, 152,

E.

U

M.

N.

O.

P.

T.

Y

INDEX (PLACES).

[No consistent system of spelling the following place-names has been found feasible; they range from English corruptions like *Llandevally* to practically obsolete Welsh forms like *Llanddewi Efelfre*.]

A.

B.

▲

L.

M.

N.

O.

P.

R.

S.

T.

Printed by Western Mail Limited, Cardiff and London.

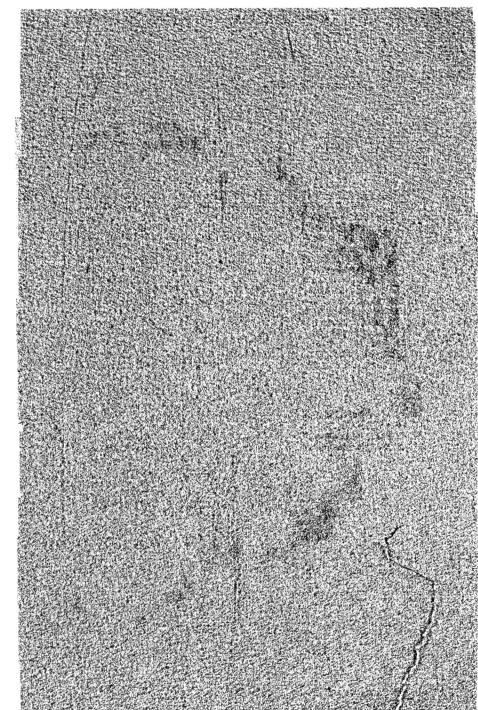

Lightning Source UK Ltd.
Milton Keynes UK
UKHW02f2314170818

327340UK00002B/13/P